The
Mother's Almanac

The Mother's Almanac

by Marguerite Kelly and Elia Parsons

Illustrated by Rebecca Hirsh

Doubleday & Company, Inc.
Garden City, New York

Designed by Clare Wilson

Library of Congress Cataloging in Publication Data

Kelly, Marguerite

   The Mother's Almanac

   1. Children—Management.
      I. Parsons, Elia, joint author. II. Title

HQ769.K367   649'.12'3
ISBN 0-385-01806-1

Library of Congress Catalog Card Number 73-9166

Printed in the United States of America

20 19 18 17

To Tom
and Kate and Mike and
Meg and Nell

To Dick
and Ramon and Nadia
and Amalia

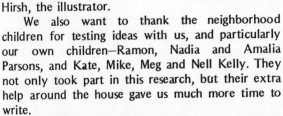

We are indebted to our Doubleday editors
Evelyn Metzger and her successor, Karen Van
Westering, who felt that mothers could write about
motherhood quite as well as doctors, and to the
team of women who carried our manuscript to
camera-ready mechanicals: Crista Borras and Sharon
Kirby, the typesetters; Beverly Baumgart, the
proofreader; Clare Wilson, the designer, and Rebecca
Hirsh, the illustrator.

We also want to thank the neighborhood
children for testing ideas with us, and particularly
our own children—Ramon, Nadia and Amalia
Parsons, and Kate, Mike, Meg and Nell Kelly. They
not only took part in this research, but their extra
help around the house gave us much more time to
write.

In addition, we thank our husbands for their
compliments and kindnesses, but mostly for trusting
our abilities enough to be patient. Finally, our
unreserved appreciation to Tom Kelly, whose
skillful editing taught us to regard the craft of
writing almost as fondly as the art of motherhood.

Preface

Today we can plan our families so well that babies are a sign of love, a sign that parents are ready to swaddle them in all the affection and respect they need.

Now we can wait for the right job, the right home, the right income, and then we find—no matter how ideal the conditions—that it's as hard to rear the first child as it always was.

Motherhood brings as much joy as ever, but it still brings boredom, exhaustion and sorrow too. Nothing else ever will make you as happy or as sad, as proud or as tired, for nothing is quite as hard as helping a person develop his own individuality— especially while you struggle to keep your own. In motherhood, there's so much to learn, so much to give, and although the learning gets less with each succeeding child, the giving never does.

If only to make ourselves feel better, we assume that new mothers today, like new mothers yesterday, have a lot to learn about child care (and cooking and gardening and making love too). Enthusiasm is not enough. Somehow techniques must be found, but today you can't look for much help from grandmothers—since they've got their jobs downtown—and you can't learn about babies from the big family next door, since there isn't any big family next door. Still, you don't want to muddle along. The quicker you solve the problems of motherhood, the more satisfied you'll be and the less you'll sound like the young and old biddies who go about wishing they had·had "the second child first."

As immodest as it sounds, we think we've found ways to help you nurture your child in the critical years before first grade. These answers, gathered from our errors and our successes, our friends and our research, all ripened in the years of introspection and deliberation that it took us to write this book.

We have divided it into three parts, but the first is perhaps the most important because it covers the realities of family life—not just the routine, the problems and the crises, but how you teach your child to become independent and self-disciplined. This will be his strength for life and this is your strength too, for a child who can take care of himself will be a happy child, hungry for all the enrichment and creativity you can offer.

In the second section we consider the influences that give this enrichment. The memory of picking apples on a country ramble or taking part in a family celebration can never be erased. We talk about these adventures here, as well as the values you instill and how you can do it (through pets and gifts and chores) and the enrichment of books and schools and theater and records. The influences you give your child in the early years will be as much a part of his structure as the bones in his body.

Finally, there are the avenues of expression you offer your child which we cover in our last section.

Here we tell you about the traditional arts and drama and crafts; the experiments your child can make in science and reading and the proficiencies he can learn. The skills of the kitchen and the workshop and the garden will give your child a lifetime of self-confidence. We hope you will find the recipes fine enough to use them yourself, long after he has grown.

There is no way you can expose your child to every enrichment, nor do we think you should. You're not creating a genius in the arts and sciences, nor a renaissance child who excels in every discipline, but instead you're rearing a quality child who is eager to draw the best out of life and glad to return just as much.

Since everything you do—or don't do—affects your child, we wrote not just a how-to, when-to book, but a why-to book. We speak to the mother, since she usually has much of the day-to-day responsibility, but most of our advice applies of course to fathers and grandmothers and sitters too.

The ages we give for particular achievements or games or recipes are arbitrary and based on our children and their friends. They certainly aren't precise or scientific (for neither are children) and will vary from child to child by many months. You also may think these ages are too optimistic. Perhaps they are, but we've found a child learns much quicker if you teach him the ground rules and have faith in his ability (and we have a lot of faith). Certainly we've come a long way since Dorothy Canfield Fisher, an avant-garde thinker for 1915, said, "The actions of a human being, even of 15 months of age, may not be without significance to a sympathetic eye."

Throughout our book we refer to your child as "he," "his" or "him." This is only for tidy grammar and not because we prefer boys. With five girls among our seven children, we wouldn't dare. Naturally our suggestions apply to both sexes. We think any boy should be able to play with dolls or cook or take modern dance without anyone's doubting his masculinity, just as any girl should feel comfortable with hammers and worms and trees to climb. The sexual role your child adopts will depend on your response to his activities, and not on the activities themselves.

Motherhood, we find, is more than a craft; it is an art. Like any other, the more inventive you are and the harder you work at it, the better the pay, for nothing is as rewarding as the love of a happy child.

Marguerite Lelong Kelly
Elia Esther Sanchez Parsons

Contents

Realities

Influences   95

Realities

Realities

There are many times in parenthood when happiness thrusts your spirits higher than the stars and the pleasure of loving makes living a throbbing delight. This is normal, but like sex, much too brief.

There are other, fortunately fewer times in parenthood when tension leaves no room for joy and self-pity can rend your soul. This is normal too.

As probably typical mothers we have known much more happiness than sorrow, but also, typically, we muddled through a dreary routine of confusion with our first children, through days and weeks that should have been better and disasters that need never have happened.

Somehow with our good husbands we have helped seven children finish their first six years during which we discovered, through the same painfully original research all mothers gather and forget, a number of ideas that worked and a great many others that did not. We have watched our babies grow to that rewarding stage between potty and pot, the years when all mothers' methods look their best. There were times past—we can admit it now—when we despaired of our children and particularly of ourselves. Motherhood was not for us.

One night one of us walked in tears and in the rain to the neighborhood bookshop, looking for some guide to cope with a two-and-a-half-year-old terror. Only Gesell was there to say that this too shall pass, but it wasn't clear how it happened and

why or what we could do to make it pass any faster.

Once one of us knew the lonely agony of waiting out the weeks for a stillborn son and learned to treasure the fullness of life in the midst of its emptiness.

Parenthood, we found, was much harder and less predictable than we thought it would be, and even now, as our children require less physical care each year, we find they need continually more emotional attention from us. This is typical too and another surprise.

We made mistakes more often that we expected, of every sort, and many more of them, but with love they were corrected more easily than we expected too.

We found there were many options in child care, each reflecting a parent's attitude toward his child and himself. This made it clear to us that parents must evaluate their own viewpoints together, honestly and often, so that their child may grow up with clear and consistent direction.

By the time we thought we had some of the answers, we found that Maria Francis Child, a forgotten pioneer of women's lib, had found them before us—childless though she was.

In 1831, she published *The Mother's Book*, which we think remains unique in the field of child care. She not only loved children, she enjoyed them.

In later books, American children have been ignored, denied, idolized, pampered and despaired of, but seldom enjoyed. Today, though we have a grand number of books to teach the techniques of a happy sex life, there are very few to teach us how to grow happy children. Both accomplishments are fun to learn, but since it takes such a little while to start a baby and so long to nurture a child, we pass on to you what we wish we had learned in the beginning, without a family trial for every error.

Like Maria Child, we think we have found techniques to make child care much happier and much less trouble. We feel we have learned, through research and through experience, which toys and games and crafts are necessary, not for play, but for work. These are the tools of childhood, as much as skillets and typewriters and hammers are ours.

We believe every activity in which a child invests his time will teach him something in return—either positive or negative—and, therefore, a parent must consider what he wants his child to learn, both in skills and in values.

This is a learning time for parents too.

When Freud taught the world that children had psyches, it disturbed the balance of family relationships—as it should have, for the balance, if not unworkable, was unjust. The heavy autocracy of Calvin and Victoria had stifled generations of children. No total credo has replaced it, however, and parents have been groping for new rules ever since. Children often drift uneasily in search of a niche while parents, in fear of mashing an id or an ego, pass the scepter of authority back and forth like a baton in a relay race.

We feel there is another position.

Although we consider parents the king and queen of a family, we think they must respect their subjects now, if only to avoid the guillotine later.

Respect is inherent in the fairness with which a child must be treated, and respect is the one commodity every parent has the duty to demand.

We hope this compilation will help parents give this respect and receive it, so that a child may inherit the legacy of stability he deserves.

We believe a child's respect for himself is increased in ratio to his competence. This is his key to self-love, the basis of a confident, complete adult. It will give him the bedrock to enjoy and withstand the pressures of our society.

Mothers, as well as children, feel these pressures, but perhaps they feel them less in other, single-ethnic countries.

Women in America, where all the qualities are stirred in one big melting pot of mores, don't have one national standard, they have them all. In addition, the pride of a new mother forces her to compete with her own mother (and *his* mother), not as they were once, young and inept, but as she knows them now—older and very ept indeed.

American women, urged by the ladies' magazines, spend the first ten years of their marriage trying to keep their sanity—or if they are college graduates, trying to find their "identity"—while pushing to be first the ideal wife, and then that other mythical creature, the ideal mother.

There is of course no such perfection, but you will go through an entire pregnancy before you find out.

Fortunately, the glory of birth transcends such anxieties, for you are overcome by its blessing.

Time and effort have made the most extraordinary things in the world—like canyons and temples and concertos—but the most remarkable of all creations must be: new people.

To you and your husband, the first baby is a miracle. For forty weeks you have known he would have everything you loved best about each other in a perfect marriage of the genes. By the time he arrives, with his father's big ears and a pointed head, you are much too pleased to care.

With each pregnancy you will expect that magically right combination of genes again. It starts love going for the new baby before there is anything to see or even feel.

The firstborn, however, will continue to grasp your emotions in an unexpected way. No pregnancy and no baby are as exciting as the first. Only he can make you feel so foolish, so confused, so frightened—or so exhilarated. Every action, every day are novel to you and to him. Every reaction, every emotion, every expectation, yours and his, are more intense, all of your lives.

You won't love this miracle child best, but you always will love him differently. It works out well enough. You also will have special feelings for the baby of the family or the only girl or the retarded child or the family clown (every family with more than two children has a clown). Each child has one extra line to your heart, which no other child can replace. You can tell your children about this when they are older, and you should, because a child should know his own special place in the family.

With your later children you will be less experimental and more relaxed. You will enjoy them much more, be bored a little more and find them much less miraculous. But no matter how many children you've had, you will be overwhelmed each time by your power to make life and to shape it.

When you are pregnant for the first time you feel superior to every frazzled mother chasing children in the supermarket and you know you'll never be that way. Savor that confidence. This faith in your own maternal wisdom won't reach that peak again until you are a grandmother.

Despite the current mythology, life with babies does not mean an occasional bad day when your Four spills his paints on the top-grade kitchen tile and the dishwasher breaks down. This is a normal day, even a good one. When motherhood is in full flower and you have two or three babies under six, you not only won't have money for a dishwasher, you're overdrawn at the bank.

As a new mother, it's more normal to be tired for weeks at a time, to be quick to cry, to be sure your husband is a devil with the girls at the office. You will look back wistfully to the career you left with the same distorted vision you once had looked forward to marriage. In those days you believed what you read in the magazines—that every good wife "whipped up" silky skirts (long, for evening), refinished furniture (with a French polish), and if she dieted, it was gourmet style. You thought you'd have drinks before dinner every night (with homemade paté on the side), screw to the beat of blue grass and keep the house clean without help—and easily with it.

After three or even two babies, you realize that wives don't live this way and husbands don't lead glamorous, proposition-filled lives at the office. The calamities you contend with at home are about as frustrating as those your husband meets from nine to five, and though your schedule is longer, you are at least the boss. In shaking down the realities of marriage you will find, as one wise young wife said, "Happiness is getting there."

The honest reason for having children is your own fulfillment and to rear them well can raise your marriage to glorious heights.

These years, when your children are under six and underfoot, are your years of apprenticeship. As the mother, you will learn simplified routines, safety precautions, an acceptance of the inevitable miseries most of the time and a plan of escape for the rest.

You will give more time to others—and have less time to give—and you will learn more about organization than a management trainee at General Motors. You will learn to give sit-down dinners for twelve—the height of logistics—to paint walls, mend sheets and collect for charity, and you will do these things even if you have a job, although you won't do them so often. The extent of your investment now will determine the richness of your growth. You will have more years without children than with them and they will be your years of harvest.

Every child is born with hope alone and then spends his next year gaining faith and the rest of his life hanging onto it.

Your child learns this faith because you instinctively go to him when he cries, giving food when he is hungry, warmth when he is cold, entertainment when he is bored.

The child whose needs are attended with reasonable speed will learn, as he should, that the world is a dependable place. This trust in others gives him the base he needs to develop trust in the most important person in the world—not you, but himself.

We believe if parents love each child and respect him, he will love the whole world and be kind to it; if his curiosity is nourished as a child, he will become an imaginative, creative adult; if he is self-sufficient when he is small, he will learn the tough joys of independence, and if he has wide, firm boundaries when ne's young, he will reach for freedom when he's grown.

We could pretend your child will be a joy if you just give him paints, books, action, adventure and attention. This is not so, for your child must be civilized too.

No matter how deep your love, you won't enjoy his company much if he depends on you for everything—and then doesn't bother to say thanks. A child is precious little fun unless both of you operate within a framework—loose as it may be—of discipline, of safety and of decent manners. These boundaries, which you lay before first grade, will channel his bold spirit. This lets you trust him enough to loosen your reins, helping him conquer his world even as you fence it.

A skill, like talking, is worth helping a child achieve early for the happiness it brings, but other skills bring great satisfaction too. This is why we think a One should try to feed himself, a Two should begin to dress himself and a Three should make his bed. Each small job a child masters gives him new psychic strength.

In this way he will become independent, for a child builds his self-confidence not on what you can do for him, but what he can do for himself.

This independence is the prelude to the sense of responsibility he needs to care for pets, to do his chores—even to make simple gifts, for charity is not indigenous to children and indeed it must begin at home.

Although a child's make-up is set genetically, his values, his stability and, to an unknown extent, his intellect are determined by you. Malnutrition of the mind or the body will suppress both mental and physical growth.

If you accept the premise that you can help your child raise his intelligence—and what mother doesn't?—you must realize that you can limit it too.

We think parents have no right to withhold knowledge on the highly questionable theory that intelligence is fixed. No one has ever reached his full mental capacity, nor has anyone ever fulfilled his potential for goodness or love or happiness either, but it does not mean we stop trying. It is difficult enough to be a mother; let us forgo the role of God.

According to nutritional studies, a proper diet can change an I.Q. as much as twenty-two points and, conversely, an improper one can cause retardation. Other studies show sweeping differences between babies whose environment has been either creative or sterile. If findings on rats are applicable to people, the more stimulation a baby receives, and the earlier he receives it, the more his brain grows in size and in weight, and therefore in intelligence.

The brain has been compared to a giant computer, more sophisticated than any ever manufactured. The cortex, where knowledge is banked, can store ten million facts in its circuits in a lifetime, but only if the circuits have been programmed for use. The methods of measuring intelligence are still inexact, but authorities believe the brain reaches half capacity by the time a child is four, three fourths of capacity by the time he is eight and total growth around the age of seventeen. If a child has enough of the right stimuli, you can stretch his horizons for life.

We believe a child is quick to learn instinc-tively, but with help he learns quicker and likes it better. His furious chase for knowledge is basic—a joyful, endless quest. A child, of course, should not be pushed into learning, but parents have the obligation to offer it. Any activity, however, that makes either of you nervous, tired or cross should be dropped, for as we all remember from our childhood, a bored or boring teacher is the quickest way to curb curiosity.

Whatever you teach your child should be in an easy, comfortable atmosphere where he may dare to reach any of a number of goals—or even dare not to try. A happy child certainly will not feel he must excel in all areas, but he should be able to investigate them, through enrichment, through work and through creativity. Education comes in many packages.

Your children will be at home for eighteen years at least, but you will be bound to them, for better or worse, for the rest of your life. Your children and, heaven help you, their children will be home for holiday dinners and for occasional loans. Since you only can stand such intimacy from your best friends, you may as well rear children who will be your best friends as well as suitable companions for all mankind.

It takes hard work and hard thinking to rear good people. The job is interesting, although the hours are bad, starting from the first day.

Fundamentals

Deliverance

The thought you put into any project decides how well it goes. This is especially true when you have a baby.

Your psyche and your body have nine months, a dozen books and a trusty obstetrician to help you prepare, but after seven babies we can tell you: You need more than that.

Before

From the rabbit test to the first contraction, you will need to follow your doctor's diet to control your weight. Take your vitamins, smoke as little as possible (for smoke affects the baby's growth), walk briskly to keep your body in tone, hold in your stomach as much as possible, so the muscles stay taut, and rub your belly with cocoa butter to prevent some of the stretch marks. Perhaps everything would go just as well if you didn't follow this daily regimen, but they are such time-tested rules, we don't think you should trifle with them.

All the well-followed orders won't prepare you for the doldrums of pregnancy, when doubts crowd you, for it is a long time between that decision in June and the delivery in March. You may have expected them, but you probably never knew about the unsung, inglorious complaints that caused them.

No one ever told you there would be such tedium and listlessness, such queer aches and fancies. You were prepared for the queasiness, which is common, and the craving for odd food, like pickles, which is not, but no one ever told you how much you would want to make love, and how silly you would look when you did.

You had no idea how the knowledge of this pregnancy would consume you, intruding itself into every thought you had, popping awkwardly into conversation, and then how much you would resent your considerate if casual friends who ask you your due date, again.

Motherhood can be as bleak as the worst pregnancy or as joyous as no pregnancy ever was. This will depend almost entirely on your competence.

You will need the easiest possible equipment to care for your baby, the simplest clothes, the most serene environment, but, basically, you will need to know what you are doing. You will need experience.

In child care, as in sex, practice doesn't make it perfect every time, but it sure does make it better—for both parents. With any encouragement, your husband will be as capable as you in each phase of child care except breast feeding.

Mid-pregnancy is a good time to learn about babies.

We think you and your husband would profit by childbirth classes, to understand the whole birth process better and to learn the exercises and breathing techniques that make labor easier. You will find that natural childbirth courses prepare your body best, whether you deliver with anesthesia or not. Many doctors think natural childbirth itself is a nuisance, but almost every husband and wife who try it become adherents. We wish we had delivered this way, if only because the father is allowed in the delivery room. Since your husband helped start this production he may as well be there for opening night.

As important as it is to prepare for childbirth, it's more important to learn how to care for your baby. There are many ways to learn, but we don't think a Red Cross course is best. To us, there's not much point in learning how to diaper and burp a doll, since you are, after all, expecting a baby. Instead, we think you should baby-sit for your friends or join a baby-sitting cooperative, where you can accumulate credit in advance. It takes a practical situation for you to find the best way to feed a baby and what to do when he cries. Other expectant parents have worked as volunteers in an orphanage or the children's ward of a hospital, changing babies, rocking them, singing to them. Basically, you are giving love, a commodity that expands with use. It also will help you show affection to your own baby, for most of us are very shy with our firstborn. At any rate, don't delay this apprenticeship until the last. Begin as soon as you're sure you are pregnant and continue until about the seventh month. By then you should be too busy to baby-sit since you will be making the many arrangements that will make your life easier after the baby comes.

You will be buying a layette, preparing a nursery area and painting a new bureau (with lead-free paint), but the baby isn't the only person who needs attention. Since the laundry situation dissolves with a newborn, we found husbands need a double supply of shirts, shorts and socks to keep afloat.

Between now and delivery you will pack The Suitcase. You also should build a grocery bank, gradually buying extra staples and enough convenience dinners to take care of the first two or even three weeks after the baby is born.

Most hospitals have tours for expectant parents, but if yours does not, we think you should ask for one anyway. This will make the delivery less formidable and you can choose the kind of room you want, too.

By the eighth month you are, we hope, experienced enough with small babies to have an opinion on the type of pediatrician you'd like. Ask your obstetrician for some names of baby doctors who are "board certified"—the best are likely to be—and they should, if possible, have offices near you.

The pediatrician you choose, like the house you will buy, will affect your life for years. Both are longterm contracts and hard to leave, so both should suit your style.

Although your obstetrician will recommend several pediatricians, you may want to rely more on the recommendations of your friends, for they know which ones have confidence in the capabilities of a mother. To us, this is a major prerequisite.

We think you can select your baby doctor better if you talk with him or his nurse first, at least by phone. You need to know the office hours, the cost—not just for each visit but for the immunization program—his views on breast feeding and his methods for seeing a sick child.

While you are arranging care for your baby, arrange some help for yourself. Having a baby is hard work and it drains your energy. You will need a mother's helper to attend to the housework and cooking and, to some extent, to the baby, for at least the first week at home. Ask new mothers for recommendations or apply to a reliable, bonded maid service.

The Layette

You will want to buy a basic wardrobe for your baby before he's born. This is all you need for the first three months, if you are willing to wash every other day.

6 terrycloth jumpsuits	1 bunting
4 kimonos	1 heavy carriage blanket
6 undershirts	6 bassinet sheets OR
2 bibs	pillowcases
4 doz. diapers	3 crib sheets
6 diaper pins	6 cotton pads
2 sweaters	6 flannel pads
1 hat	

The bunting should not be slippery and the diapers should be prefolded. You will need only 1-2 dozen diapers if you use disposable ones or have a diaper service. You also will need:

rectal thermometer	cotton balls
petroleum jelly	2 pint jars
baby lotion	

The jars will hold the cotton and the water you need to change your baby.

The Suitcase

The packing of your suitcase is recommended by the end of the seventh month, for babies are notoriously poor in arithmetic.

Although by the fourth child our bag looked like it was packed by twins who were each expecting triplets, we found that a bottle of champagne is quite as essential as a nursing bra.

This is what you need:
3 nightgowns/robe/bed jacket/slippers
6 pairs underpants
sanitary belt
1-2 nursing bras
toothpaste/toothbrush
talcum/deodorant/fancy soap
make-up/perfume/manicure supplies
curlers/hairbrush/shampoo
announcements/stationery/stamps
address book with phone numbers
mystery book
loaded flash camera
sherry/champagne/sodas and plastic stemware
cookies/crackers
skirt/blouse
baby's outfit/2 diapers

The bra is necessary if you plan to nurse your baby, because you need this extra support when lactation begins, to prevent stretch marks. It's worn with your nightgown and so are underpants, for the flow is heavy at first. The hospital provides the napkins.

The make-up and perfume—as much as you'd wear to your fanciest party—will make you feel glamorous and the thank-you notes and announcements will make you feel efficient. You also need some phone numbers with you, for many hospitals have no phone books in their rooms.

The flash camera (no, it won't hurt your baby's eyes) will give you much better, quicker and cheaper pictures than the hospital photographer, and they are especially nice to send home to an older child or to all those new grandparents.

Finally, though we may sound frivolous, the sodas, cookies and sherry will give your visitors something to talk about besides the baby. It's surprising how little your guests will find to say about him, when you can say so much. The sherry also is dandy to offer the nurses at the end of the day. They like to feel human too and nothing seems to make them feel more human than a little bit of grape. It also guarantees a good back rub.

The champagne is to chill in an extra pitcher of ice and share with your husband. You can't be too sentimental when you've just had a baby.

During

When contractions start in your lower back and lock your body like a chastity belt, it's time to record their length, from start to finish, and their regularity. No two women follow the same pattern and no woman has the same sort of delivery each time, but your obstetrician probably will want you to come to the hospital when the contractions are fifteen minutes apart.

Check your suitcase, add your address book, take a mystery to read in labor and get a thick towel. You need the towel folded under you on the ride to the hospital, even if the waters haven't broken yet. Labor makes you feel self-conscious enough without sitting in a big, warm puddle.

You will be surprised that your arrival hardly ripples the businesslike air of the hospital, just as if you weren't carrying the once and future king. A nurse will take you straight to the labor room, possibly in an ominous-looking wheelchair. After a check by the doctor, you will be asked if you want to breast-feed your baby (and we hope you will). Then there's the remarkable "prep," with an enema to facilitate delivery, the shaving of pubic hair for hygiene, and the constant presence of clocks, everywhere you look.

Generally you're wheeled into the hall to visit with your husband, but after a while, it's back to the labor room where one woman moans, "Oh, my God," again and again, and you're so afraid you may sound like that. Since we never knew anyone who admitted she did, we prefer to think it's a tape recording hospitals play to keep their ladies in line.

Any fear you have of delivery is based almost entirely on a fear of the unknown, and particularly a fear of making a damn fool of yourself, for there is pain in labor and you don't know how you will react to it until it happens. Fortunately, the pains are so instinctive and constructive (and interesting) that you will behave quite properly.

When the exciting "push" pains of the third stage begin, your wagon will be wheeled into the delivery room, into a scene that looks like science fiction. A huge mirror hangs over you, so you can watch the production. Tools, tubes and dials litter the room, oxygen is at the ready if you feel queasy and glucose if you feel faint.

The doctor will be very attentive to your bottom, but have few words for you. If you have the luck to deliver in a teaching hospital—the best kind—you may be surprised to find him lecturing a group of students who stand just below your navel. Your work is so hard and requires such intense concentration, however, you won't even care.

Finally, you'll see your baby, all covered with a waxy-white substance, his head perhaps misshapen from the birth canal, and genitals that are huge compared to the body itself. When we first saw our son we pointed in disbelief and said, "What's that sticking out?"

The baffled nurse said, "You mean his nose?" and we only could say, "If that's his nose, send him back."

With great satisfaction, wooziness and perhaps some nausea, you will be rolled to the recovery room, staying there until the effects of any anesthesia you might have had are gone and you don't feel sick any more. Here women groan, attention seems almost nil, and you have nothing to watch but the clock and the other ladies, who still look pregnant too.

After

Following a hallway visit with your husband, too poignant ever to forget, you are rolled to your room and into bed, cleaned up and, amazingly, you even may make a few celebratory phone calls to your family before you fall asleep.

We found rooming-in the best arrangement, probably because it wasn't really rooming-in. It varies from hospital to hospital and ours was close to ideal for we could get help from a nurse any time. The babies were kept with us for five to eight hours of the twenty-four. Every morning at ten, they were brought to us in our semiprivate rooms for their feeding, bathed and with a bow in their hair, but they were taken out during visiting hours, our mealtimes and when we wanted a nap.

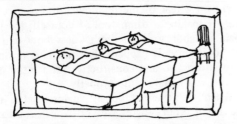

The rest of the time the babies lived in a nursery, where each newborn could be seen but scarcely heard through the windows that faced each mother's bed. The nurses fed the bottle babies at night.

Mothers in private rooms had their babies with them much more and were expected to assume more of the care somehow, which can be exhausting. Besides, we found the company of a roommate was pleasant, but since too much was not, we avoided the wards and felt the splurge quite worth it.

Your stay in the maternity wing may seem unreal, for it is still hard to think of yourself as a mother.

By the ninth month of pregnancy, you thought about only two things: making babies and making love. The idea of sex, in good old missionary style, became almost an obsession.

After delivery, your focus changes. Now you only think about your baby and your bottom.

Almost as soon as you are comfortable, a nurse slides a cold bedpan under you, runs the water and tells you, honey, to perform. Then there is the miserable afterbirth, which hurts as much as early labor, except no one holds your hand and says, "You're marvelous!" The stitches start to heal, which hurts too, because they shrink as they absorb, and you realize you are constipated and confer regularly with the nurses about it. Between getting an enema in the morning and shining a heat lamp on your stitches in the afternoon, it's mighty hard to feel maternal and impossible to feel sexy. Your breasts swell painfully, even if you are a bottle mother and have had a shot to stop the milk. Finally, you weigh—and still you've only lost ten pounds. You take a good look at yourself, see a few stretch marks, a bulging belly and a ridiculous stubble of pubic hair, which takes weeks to grow back. Even the wrap-around skirt you packed to wear home won't wrap very much.

And doctors wonder why mothers have post-partum blues. It's like two days after Christmas when the presents fall apart.

Although the nurses are very helpful, they may make you feel worse. As nice as they generally are on the maternity floor, their deftness in handling your baby makes you feel as awkward as you did on the first day of your first job. Even your husband looks like an intruder when he visits, for if some jewel of a nurse should treat you like an Earth Mother, no one ever treated a man like an Earth Father, more's the pity. Champagne was invented for days like this.

You can prevent some of the blues if you put yourself together as quickly as possible after the delivery. Shower soon (for giving birth is a sweaty process) and before twenty-four hours have passed, wear a ribbon in your hair, put on make-up and, by all means, wear your own nightgown instead of the hospital special. You also should send out your announcements when you are in the hospital. We don't know why, but from now on you, like every mother, will need a daily diet of small accomplishments to satisfy your sense of worth.

The pediatrician visits you the day after delivery to tell you your baby is grand, and returns at least once before you go home. Here you will get instructions, in fifteen minutes or less, about the care and feeding of your baby. It seems so simple.

Breast Feeding

Today more and more doctors recommend nursing for its ease, its nutrition and possibly the prevention of an obesity problem in the child's life. We've tried both breast and bottle feeding and we do think mother's milk is best and worth making a strong effort to give. Unfortunately, breast feeding has become almost a cult with many women, which is regrettable. Your milk may disagree with your baby's digestion (though not as often as many doctors would have you believe) and there is absolutely no sense in feeling guilty about giving a formula. We think the love and nestling you give with a feeding is at least as nutritious as the milk, and you can give it with a bottle as well as a breast.

The mother who breast-feeds her baby has a special joy, but there is a risk, too, for a failure can be devastating. Before you nurse, you must understand that it isn't a test of your maternal ability, but the completion of a natural cycle, which we think may fulfill the mother more. It also is mighty convenient.

Unless your doctor advises against nursing for health reasons, we think you will be glad you tried it, even if you're going back to work soon. No matter what size your breasts, you probably can produce good milk and enough of it if you relax, take a daily nap and eat well. Avoid any foods the doctor says may cause rashes, constipation or gas in the baby.

When you breast-feed, you will need to wear a nursing bra day and night, so the extra weight doesn't make you sag. Put cotton pads in the bras to absorb any leakage.

The breasts just make colostrum for the first few days, similar to the dextrose and water given brand-new bottle babies, but nature allows a time for adjustment. Your baby won't starve. Your milk will begin to flow about the third day, with your breast becoming swollen and hard but tender to the touch. This discomfort ends in about five days and can be relieved with an ice pack.

The nurse will show you how to wash your nipples every time you breast-feed and how to stimulate your baby's instinct for sucking. You will be clumsy at first, but so will he: furious at his hunger one moment, losing the nipple the next, then dropping to sleep in the middle of his meal. You both have a lot to learn.

Tap his cheeks if he falls asleep, but if he finds your breasts are too full and hard to suck, gently squeeze some of the milk into his mouth. If the nipple is too small for his lips to grasp, press the areola with your free hand and slip the teat in his mouth.

When your baby does begin to suck well, you will feel your uterus contract. It hurts, but the pain is sweet.

When you get home, become a clock watcher, limiting yourself to five minutes on each side so the nipples can toughen gradually as you increase to a total of thirty minutes by the end of the month. Until then, you also should rub a nonprescription medicine on them after each feeding, or they may become cracked and sore.

When your baby sleeps through a feeding your breasts may hurt, but this disappears soon. Use the ice pack but never a breast pump—that queer device that looks like a horn for a Model T but must have been invented by the same fellow who patented the rack. Although a pump does draw milk and relieve an oversupplied bosom, a baby elephant would be more gentle.

Just when you think you've adjusted to nursing, the help leaves, the confusion overwhelms you and your milk may diminish quickly. For this we recommend briefer, more frequent feedings, a lot of patience, some extra humor and a yeasty, low-carbonated European beer in the late afternoon. We liked to think it improved our milk supply, but we know it improved our disposition.

We also would recommend your calling an organization for nursing mothers, like La Leche League, which will assign a member to telephone and visit you regularly with encouragement and the kind of advice that only comes from personal experience.

After your milk supply is stable, give your baby an occasional supplementary bottle of formula, so he can learn to accept the taste of a rubber nipple and you can have more freedom.

Some mothers nurse only for a few weeks, others for more than a year, but we never could return to our normal weight until we stopped. At least you will have an excuse.

Burping the Baby

Whether you feed your baby with a breast or a bottle, be sure to burp him at least once during the feeding as well as afterward. No two babies burp alike, but until you know his style, bring up the bubbles by rubbing up and down along his spine, especially between the shoulder blades, while he falls over your hand or your shoulder. This pressure forces more gas from the solar plexus area where it often collects. If you lay your baby on his stomach afterward, the last bubbles usually come up in about fifteen minutes.

The Pediatrician

A good pediatrician will take the time to talk to each mother and to check the baby himself, with the nurse handling the preparations but not the instructions. He will give you enough facts and philosophy to make some judgments, at least, on your own.

This kind of doctor is hard to find. Most seem

to come in two varieties. One is so casual he not only will forget your name but your child's name too, and in the next few weeks he'll tell you blithely and consistently to "trust your own instincts," until you won't dare admit how desperate you feel in those bleating hours between midnight and dawn.

The other type of pediatrician is concerned about your instincts too. He (but frequently she) wonders if you have any. To this doctor, your child is his property, which he lets you watch because he is simply too busy.

The obstetrician, who once was so important, now means little more to you than a friendly plumber, while the good opinion of the baby doctor will matter very much. If the doctor thinks you're a dunce you soon will fit the role.

There is an art to dealing with a pediatrician, and if you don't master it early, you will feel so unsure of yourself you may have to change doctors to feel comfortable.

This is preventable if you act reasonably self-sufficient, without hand-wringing, but with enough curiosity to ask the reasons for his directions. Even the most curt doctor will give them. You can't make the many intelligent little decisions of motherhood unless your doctor teaches you a smattering of basic medicine as you go along.

He'll understand you're serious about it if you take notes every time you meet with him, but particularly at the hospital, for the first impression counts in this relationship too. Even if you never look at these notes again, which you will, the doctor will see you as a capable person.

When you get home, keep a rough chart for the doctor and for yourself, recording everything your baby does around the clock, and when he does it—when he cries and eats and sleeps and has a bowel movement. Use the chart to order your thoughts whenever you call the doctor. Write down questions and if you suspect an illness, take the baby's temperature. There's enough guess work to a diagnosis without adding to the problem.

This efficiency will help you see patterns as they develop so you can plan your own time around your child. Without this chart, your hurry, your concern and your fatigue will block out this pattern and you will get lost in the maze of motherhood.

Going Home

By the time you have been in the hospital five days, you know you can conquer the world. Then you go home. It takes such energy to dress yourself

and the baby, to gather the flowers and say good-by to your roommate and the nurses (who are now your best friends) that you are tottering by the time you climb the few steps to your front door. That's why you should ask your husband to tidy the place before you get home. It isn't that you wouldn't want to do it yourself, but it's over-whelming to realize that you can't.

During pregnancy you prepared yourself well for the problems of fitting three people together in one household—and then you find there are four. The presence of a mother's helper, as essential as she is, can shatter this fragile situation.

Your helper, whether a relative, a neighbor or, if you should be so lucky, a nursemaid, won't do everything the way you think it should be done—and it doesn't matter at all. It won't hurt you to let your mother-in-law have her way; you will have your way for years. Your helper is there to worry about the baby. You worry about yourself.

It is much harder on you to have company at home than it is in the hospital, so your husband should ask friends to stay away on your first day at home and to keep their visits short for the first week. Have a note put on the door when you want to sleep (just blame it on the helper) and muffle the phone with a pillow. We knew one dear lady who traveled across town by bus to see us, feathered hat, white gloves and silver baby spoon, and then only stayed ten minutes.

"It's not proper to stay longer with the sick, my dear," she informed us, for which we blessed her seventy-five-year-old sense of etiquette.

You will loll about the first week, avoiding stairs to prevent strain on the uterus. The flow probably will stop about two weeks after you deliver. To prevent infection, change pads fre-quently, take showers often (but not baths or douches), and when you start to make love, use condoms, both for contraception and hygiene.

On Your Own

When your help has left and you're in charge again, you should dress every day, as soon as you get up, unless you're ill.

There are at least two times a day when a wife should look good and smell good: at night when she goes to bed and in the morning before her husband leaves for work. This isn't some kind of obsequiousness to the breadwinner. Your own ego is at stake, not his. When you have a baby you leave the mainstream of society, and it's very easy to look as pitiful as you sometimes feel, which doesn't score points with anyone. That's why we think you should wear as much perfume and lipstick and even jewelry as you did at the office, and stockings in winter, too. Motherhood, like any other job, should be respected and, first of all, it should be respected by you.

Part of this respect is expressed in the speed with which you get a good figure again. There are those of us who have babies and then spend the rest of our lives waiting for the Rubens woman to come back in style. This, we have found, is unlikely.

In Greece, mothers still get their bodies into shape by binding their hips tightly and immediately for six weeks, using a length of linen, six feet long by a foot wide, which is supposed to push the organs back into place. In this country we do exercises, like the knee-chest, but be warned. Your figure won't return to normal without some help from you—certainly if you have had more than one baby. Neither, in fact, will your vagina, for which we give exercises too. You'll like these more.

Although you've begun the most creative phase of your life, you often will feel overcome by its problems. The vibrancy of your job will sustain you, however, as long as you count your blessings at least as often as you count your burdens.

Abdominal Exercises

You might be able to bring your weight to normal within six weeks, but your muscles won't be the same as they were before unless you do postnatal exercises. Start them after the bright red bleeding stops—and quit for a few days if it should start again.

Begin each exercise by lying flat on your back on the floor, but preferably on a rug, adding new exercises on the specified days.

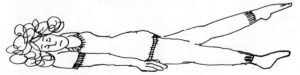

On the first day, with your hands at your sides, take five deep, slow breaths, right from the abdomen. That's all.

On the second day, spread your arms horizontal to your body, with elbows straight. Raise them, bringing them directly over your chest until the hands touch, doing this five times. And that's all to that too, but even this gentle exercise is tiring when you just have had a baby.

On the third and fourth days, raise your head slowly until your chin touches your chest; do this ten times.

On the fifth day, raise one leg as high as possible, toes pointed, keeping the knee straight and your hands at your sides. Keep the other leg flat on the floor. Alternate legs, raising each one five times, a little higher on the sixth and seventh days.

On the eighth day, raise your right knee to your belly, so your foot is pulled back to touch your bottom. Straighten the leg and lower it, alternating each leg five times.

On the tenth day, spread your legs slightly and pull your feet toward you enough so that your knees almost bend at a right angle. Lift your bottom so your weight rests only on your shoulders and your feet. Contract your anus at the same time.

On the twelfth day, cross your arms on your chest and raise your head and shoulders slightly five times. When you're stronger, clasp your hands behind your head, cross your ankles (or tuck them under a chair to hold your feet down) and raise yourself slowly until you're sitting, keeping your knees straight all the while.

Knee-chest Exercise

Finally, your doctor probably will recommend this exercise, which helps the organs fall back into place, but it generally is not started until several weeks after delivery.

Do it twice a day after urinating. Begin with two minutes each time and gradually increase to five.

Lying on the floor, face down, raise your bottom up in the air with your head resting on your crossed arms and the rest of your weight on your knees. They should be about eighteen inches apart, the thighs should be perpendicular to the floor and the back should be straight.

Vaginal Exercise

Birthing naturally enlarges the vagina, even with stitches to tidy it again. Tighten it by repeatedly firming the muscles between your thighs, as if you were restraining your bladder. At first these muscles will seem so flabby you can't believe you're constricting at all, but if you do this every day for about three minutes you can rebuild them easily. It's a pleasant pastime and can be done anywhere, except maybe standing on your head, and if done often enough it will add an extra dimension to love-making.

The Child

A child goes through many stages and the most dramatic occur between birth and first grade. Each brings pleasure, each brings pain and every one of them will make you react. If you know what to expect, we think your reactions will be wiser and the joy of these years will be multiplied, for both of you.

Infancy
When your child is born you will need to undergo a rebirth yourself to meet the many emotional and physical demands of motherhood. It doesn't take long to realize, no matter how much you deny it, that you can't handle every situation and your resolutions are about as flabby as your figure.

You probably will cope well with the anticipated, positive pains of labor and then be dismayed by the unexpected, negative aches of afterbirth, stitches and the brief, if poignant postpartum blues, when you discover you are nearly as fat as you were a month before and a sexpot you clearly are not.

Your adjustment to motherhood is quicker if you go out with your husband when your baby is about ten days old. Choose some place where you can sit when your knees start to quake and stand when your bottom starts to hurt.

Although most O.B.s ban intercourse until the six weeks' check, most new mothers do not. Three weeks is much more like it. They just don't tell, figuring it's better to have loved and hurt than wait another month. The quicker you return to the good life, the quicker your new family gets settled. Sex is a lovely tranquilizer, but remember to have your husband use a condom, to prevent infection—and pregnancy.

The extent of your husband's inclusion or exclusion in the routine of family living is just as important to the father as to the child. It will decide whether he will be a valid husband and father every day or merely a weekend warrior.

If you steal every bit of sleep you can you should be fairly rested in about six weeks. It takes most mothers at least that long to recover from the impact of birth. If you are too energetic it may take months longer. Exhaustion creates a real postpartum depression and you will be too tired even to recognize it. Fatigue diminishes the milk supply too, if you are a nursing mother.

With a new baby you find that life is lived in fifteen-minute snatches. Motherhood seldom goes smoothly, particularly if you have more than one child. If by some fluke one day is serene, you can bet the next one will be a pip. The bad days will teach you the short cuts, but it takes a long time to learn that solutions have to be changed almost as often as diapers.

For your own ego, you need to feel successful at the end of each day. If you make lists of your intentions at breakfast you only will have a record of your failures at dinner. Instead, keep your time fluid and your goals general. Caring for a baby all day is as intense as the toughest job you ever had and your time should be spent like an office worker, with the hard jobs done in the morning. After lunch is for taking walks, cooking dinner—the simplest routine. Eventually this will be such a respected pattern you can keep it for the rest of your life.

Because some drudge said, "Women's work is never done," you don't have to drag around from 6 A.M. to midnight to prove it. If you do you will be a very tired bedfellow, which is not the same at all as a good bedfellow.

During infancy your baby learns at a faster rate than he ever will again in his life. In the first four weeks he will learn to breathe regularly, lift his head, and return a smile and sometimes a laugh.

It is for you to stretch his five lively senses from the day he is born. He needs to hear your voice in everything you do—singing, humming, talking. He should be exposed to as much variety of sights, sounds and smells as possible, which will make him happier and brighter too. A baby who is treated to different environments will meet more germs, but gradual exposure will help him tolerate them better. The more he's kept in a sterile situation, whether restricted in activities, noise or people, the less stimulated he'll be.

Most of an infant's waking hours should not, of course, be spent in a bassinet or a crib. He won't last for more than a half hour in any one position if he is awake and neither would you.

A playpen is best now, not as a cage, as it is

sometimes used later—and shouldn't be—but as a cozy place where he can watch the world go by and with greater protection from drafts than he would get lying on a blanket on the floor.

A walk is excellent too. A leaf shaking in the breeze or a moving skyline will enliven your baby's mind the way a Picasso feeds your soul.

Your child needs mobiles or stabiles in every area where he is stationary for a long time, such as a crib or an infant seat. They should be homemade or so inexpensive you won't mind changing pictures even every few days if you have the time. A baby thrives on bright colors, geometric shapes, patterns, glittering foil, tassels. Leave the pallid colors and static designs for the pale in spirit. A picture on the television set is no substitute for growing plants, a music box, bells, a fish tank and mirrors.

Three Months

Everyone, even a small baby, tries to express himself, and he can if you don't anticipate his wants. Let him give the first yell before you feed him and let him try to turn over by himself. He likes to scoot around his crib, grunting and puffing, to reach a rattle, for he learns by doing by himself. Your help should be given at the end of that increasingly wide period between his first attempt at achievement and his first scream of frustration.

If necessity is the mother of invention, frustration is the grandmother. Every child needs a little of this frustration, but the smaller the child, the smaller the dose. This is not only to establish his place in the pecking order, which it does, but to force him to figure other ways to accomplish a job. In this way you show respect for his ability. You will manifest this respect in a thousand ways and the only way you can do better is to find a thousand more.

He coos by four months and will talk early if you encourage him. Compared to other animals, however, a baby is a very slow learner, for he has choice as well as instinct, and many more jobs to learn. His concentration is intense and he may forget his last skill temporarily while learning the next one.

Six Months

When your baby is six months old, you may be tempted to get pregnant again. Obviously, you are a Perfect Mother. Your baby is a babbling delight. Your household practically runs itself, even if you work. Regretfully, we must tell you that your schedule is as light and your child as undemanding as either will be until he leaves for college.

This is an idyllic stage now. All he needs for happiness is good health and a revolving set of small activities to sparkle the day. If you supplement this with about five minutes of playtime out of every half hour he is awake—unless he's being fed or bathed—he will love you. And if you don't do this, he will love you just as much, but he may not be as jolly or as quick. Besides, if you play with your child you will have a fine time youself.

Soon your baby will start to sleep less and move about more. When he can crawl, you will give him enough freedom to feel important and enough protection to keep him safe. He will pull himself to his feet, but he needs your help to sit down and then learn to push a chair around a room, like an old lady with a walker.

One

The changes in a child's behavior come not around the first birthday but when he learns to walk. Your whole attitude must adjust to his new skill. Although your baby is harder to handle now—awake more, demanding more—he will compensate for it by becoming an independent person, more striking every day. Each new angle of his personality will tighten the binding of love. When you share his achievements with your husband you draw your family closer together and even the weariest day ends positively.

Fifteen Months

Now your child is "into everything," but you can say it with pride, for he is happy and tractable (a glowing reflection on you).

You even may be self-confident enough to give wise, park-bench advice to the mothers of those rowdy mid-Twos, just alas as we did, for this is the age of the Expert Mom. Your baby is seldom dirty, his nose never runs green, and if he talks, he actually says "yes" as often as "no." More to the point, he sleeps two hours each afternoon.

You are, we're sorry to say, as unfeeling as the svelte young bride who tells her middle-aged neighbor how easy it is to diet. You just haven't gotten there yet.

Mid-One

Now you will keep more of your opinions to yourself and you certainly should. Not only is your child no genius, he can't even remember simple obedience. In another year, brand-new mothers will be telling you where he went wrong. Your only comfort will be the rightness of these "wrongs."

When your child becomes rambunctious, congratulations. This is your compliment for helping him grow into a curious, climbing, inventive child, with a new command of his own body and mind. Don't take it away now.

A child makes his major moves toward independence between mid-One and Three. He must reach out of his limited environment of cleanliness and acceptable behavior. Now he will sink to what may seem a disastrous ebb, with stitches, bruises and minor concussions in the next eighteen months, before turning into an angelic Three.

Eighteen months is a pivotal time, when many mothers simply give up, for the novelty of child care wears fine. Earaches and high fevers complicate life even more and every day you are more tired than the day before. Your child follows you everywhere and when he doesn't, you know he's getting into trouble. Your temper frays as your fatigue increases, just trying to keep up with your toddling child. It's your job to draw his physical boundaries very carefully, child-proofing every part of your house.

It may seem easier to keep him dependent on you through your restrictions and your coddling, but this curbs both self-confidence and curiosity.

It is curiosity that makes a mid-One seem so defiant, until by the end of the day, you only can pity yourself and ask, "If I'm such a good mother, how come Susie's such a brat?"

Your child's behavior makes more sense when you realize that he can understand a process only if he undoes it first and repeats it often.

When he does flood the floor—by flushing the john and the diaper too—you will look angry or sad and he will be less likely to do it again (even though he knows you are wrong), because he loves you. He doesn't want to make you unhappy. A child who knows the warmth of love, its frequent hugs and kisses and the sweet silence of affection, will return love with full generosity. Everything he does is geared to love and acceptance, first by himself and then by his parents. He'll be surprised to find that the capers that amused you as a One are considered naughty now and will be even worse later. He must understand that you sometimes dislike his actions, but you never dislike him. You just learn to say over and over to yourself, "What will it matter in a hundred years?"

Now your pattern of living will change almost every day, generally about a day too late. All of your intentions—of toilet training and table training and even (although you didn't tell anyone) of teaching him to read—will be postponed one to five years. Although there will be difficulties in the next eighteen months, they are more than offset by the joy of watching your child's individuality unfold. The overwhelming, awed love you felt when your child was born is nothing compared to the love you feel now. Your involvement with this child makes him more precious every day. It is absolutely essential to keep sharing all the good experiences (and a few of the bad) with your husband at the end of each day. These exchanges are the cement of marriage.

Probably the smoothest way for three or more people to live together is to merge some interests, and this is done most naturally through work. By now your child has eaten some of your burned dinners and seen you break a few dishes. He knows you need help. He just isn't sure you know it.

When you or your husband do a job, your child should be asked, when possible, to help. Let him hold the wood to be sawed and load the washer or scrub the window sills with you. He will enjoy most those chores which you prefer, since pleasure is contagious.

For play, spend about ten minutes an hour diverting him with some new activity. These interludes should be given at your convenience and when you're both content. If you wait until your child is cross before you play with him, you will have to play twice as long to make him happy again.

Probably no more than half of the playtimes are spent with toys, for there are so many and often better things to use. He enjoys planting seeds, wearing odd hats, having a tea party with you and feeding the goldfish—often too much.

Twenty-one Months

If your child didn't hear the starting gun of rebellion at mid-One he certainly will now. While this highly necessary period of achievement will give him the security no blanket ever can, it's quite likely to put a temporary crimp in your own self-confidence.

You probably are experiencing the first throes of desperation since your child had colic.

Motherhood is real.

It is forever.

It is not a game.

You cannot divorce your child.

There is no way out.

These reactions are normal. They call for balm, never shame. There isn't a mother alive who hasn't felt this despair, this resentment and guilt, and it is particularly strong with the first one or two children.

You have put his environment in order, rearranged his schedule, bought him new toys, and still he gets bolder every day.

Now it's time to take care of you. You will need more time alone and whatever special treats you can afford so you won't feel so sorry for yourself. This need cannot be overestimated, and it will last for another eighteen months.

Two

We know a doctor who said, in a back-of-the-hand consolation to a weeping mother, "Well, if there's anything worse than Terrible Two, it's Terrible Two-and-a-half."

Actually, we think Two is a dandy age, all year long, but it's almost as exhausting as it is exciting. This is the age you will consider before you plan another child. You may be healthy enough for another pregnancy and efficient enough to handle an infant on demand, but whether you have the stamina to cope with another Two again is the question.

He is as much fun as a present: You never know what to expect but usually you like what you get. No matter how bad he is (and he will be quite

bad), he is a delight. The moods of a Two swing like a pendulum. Your child will be funny, kind, destructive, ebullient, flirty, furious, curious, but always imperious, for a Two knows what he wants, at least until he gets it.

At this age, he won't give you much chance to do anything but keep track of him. Accept it. This is his year.

You need your husband's strength to keep in perspective the rebellion of your Two and you also need your husband's companionship to share the silly things he says. The joy that is shared is twice as great, but there is only one other person in the world who will be as amused and pleased by your child as you are, and that is his father.

You will watch your child take apart block towers and when you're not watching him, he takes apart the sewing machine and the radio and anything else he can find. He bites the dog and bathes the cat; smashes ants and chases pigeons. He mixes salt with sugar, milk with juice and then shrieks if his peas touch the meat on his plate. He climbs out of his crib and, given half a chance, will climb right up to the roof, and every time he knows he shouldn't. Even so, he doesn't want to make a damn fool of himself, or of you.

His curiosity runs in every direction. By now every little girl knows that her tush is more fun than her toes and little boys are practically born with an erection. However, we're a long way from Tahiti and a Two already knows enough to masturbate under the covers, no matter how enlightened the parents. Even a Two has a life of his own.

His personality develops rapidly and his control over his body and his speech makes his growth rate seem phenomenal. He will get angry when he works, often furiously so, and sometimes when he plays his exhilaration almost smothers him. These are times when he is out of control—his control and yours. This is a trademark of Two.

While his inabilities infuriate him, his accomplishments make him so proud his vanity is huge and he abuses his power as blatantly as a young teenager. The treatment is the same. You are sensitive and understanding, but you don't take him as seriously as he takes himself or as seriously as you took him last year or as you will take him again next year. If you do, each problem of the moment will become more important than either of you want it to be, for with your cooperation, he will dramatize every trifle to its ultimate crisis.

Instead, use strong safety precautions and watch carefully to prevent trouble, but unless it's major, you should look the other way when it comes. This is the time to use a low voice, a kiss and even more praise for his goodness. If you never learned tolerance you will now.

To control a Two, remember he has feelings. To control yourself, remember these feelings in the morning and maybe ten more times a day.

Although you will get angry, consider the damage before you scream. Some things may not merit as much fuss as you think at first. When you overreact you will be embarrassed afterward, even though only one other person will know how silly you were. Unfortunately, that other person will be your child.

We think you will find child care easier if you analyze your anger. Your bad temper today really may be caused by fatigue or low blood sugar or maybe the milkman reminds you of your creepy cousin or maybe you haven't made love in four days.

If you help your Two begin to be self-sufficient you will give him the present of a lifetime: independence. He needs to achieve this attitude now, and if he does he will look like a winner to everyone, particularly to the person most important to him—himself. He can learn to dress himself if the clothes are simple, if you're not too particular and, like anything else, if he gets the practice.

A child also needs to make some simple choices for himself as a part of his independence. If he has no choices he will be rebellious, but if he has too many he will be indecisive. It is difficult to begin to hold a Four accountable for his actions if he has had little chance to exercise his will at Two. Offer an either/or choice at this age—between apple juice and orange, for instance—whenever his decision is only of consequence to himself.

With the help of his parents, a Two talks in sentences, but speech is just one way to communicate. Give a child clay and he will sculpt as loud as he can shout. He needs to try every avenue of self-expression you can think of—in art, in the kitchen, in simple crafts, in the workshop, in the garden. He can do a little bit of everything but never very well. He needs more and more books and records to encourage quiet times and will find a morning spent with friends in a play group is better than in a department store with you.

With your good example a Two learns to give, not just through making presents but by helping others. He is able now to hold an electric hand mixer for you, to vacuum and to hang his pajamas on a low peg. He even can strip shellac with you when you refinish, as long as you watch him carefully. Compliment him often and give him no job that takes longer than his ten-minute attention span or he will associate boredom with work. Don't expect perfection and, in fact, feel lucky if you don't have to do the work again. When you must, do it when he's not looking, so he won't feel ridiculed. This undercuts his self-confidence badly.

Although the pediatrician may say mid-Two is the most difficult age, all the children we know reached it about twenty-six months. For all the solutions and techniques you use, living with a Two is like living with dynamite. Just when you think everything will blow apart like a plot from the Hardy boys, the fuse begins to sputter.

He gets saucier every day until, by twenty-six months, you are drained. Nothing surprises you any more. You may even be too numb to notice that his self-control, and therefore yours, increases steadily every day between twenty-six and thirty months, with just enough backsliding to keep you in your place. It's amazing you love him as much as you do.

As our favorite Irishman used to tell us, "If you hang long enough, they say you get used to hanging."

Mid-Two

As your child settles into mid-Two, he is less mischievious now but so rigid you're sure that if you fall down the steps at noon on Wednesday he would have you repeat it every noon, or at least every Wednesday.

Your demanding mid-Two needs to be reminded that parents run the show. Do this by changing the routine a little each day—a different plate for breakfast, a different story at bedtime—so he won't get so set in his ways.

He enjoys order in others and regularly returns the cat to his bed, but seldom his toys to their shelf. Nevertheless, a child needs a place for everything and the responsibility of putting away a few of his own treasures. He develops a sense of order through his own efforts, not yours.

This need for order is a paradox, for a Two dismantles everything he touches. Don't think of it as destructive, but "unbuilding." It is the taking apart, over and over, that teaches construction.

For your own peace, expect much less of your

child, laugh a lot and insist that he nap or at least rest an hour or two a day. It doesn't matter whether he needs it or not. You need it. If you keep the custom your Three will nap again, if only to oblige.

Three

A Three is almost too good. Even when he's bad he has the wit to understand reason, for now he begins to see what fairness is all about. He can share better and take turns, for he revels in people, whether they are the realistic friends from storybooks, or from the games he invents or from the neighborhood. He likes to visit and enjoys overnighting with a friend, partly to pack a suitcase, and even may want to visit relatives for a few days.

He cooks, gardens, paints, makes his bed and spends a lot of time feeling proud. He yearns to start school now and we think he should, although he catches many more colds and you find the "hurry, hurry" syndrome inevitable. You also find that it isn't possible to rush a Three.

He has much energy and uses it fairly well, which makes him more settled, especially if he gets daily exercise outdoors, like tricycling and walking, and some work on indoor play equipment. Early talkers are curious about words and letters and may recognize at least some of them in the newspaper, but the more active child will talk less and may need your help to speak in complicated sentences. Your child also may need help with puzzles, for the longer he takes to coordinate the small muscles, the more restless he'll be. This makes concentration difficult.

At Three, there still will be a few accidents with the pot, unless reminded to use it, and a few tantrums too. He will give up his bottle in public, suck his thumb when tired and want to be cuddled, any time.

Although your husband's job may require frequent absences, arrange your child's schedule to give them time alone together at least once a week. Sons and daughters—particularly daughters—must learn to develop deep relationships with a man now.

There are some lessons that are almost too hard to learn twenty years later, and this is one of them.

Mid-Three

A child changes now, as he does every half year. Behavior improves about the middle of an even year, but gets worse, as now, in the middle of an odd one. At least the turf is familiar.

This is the age for exploring new worlds. Our Mali did it by running away from home (around the corner to the neighbor lady), but Ramon by announcing that he wished to lunch by himself. As we watched, he marched to the corner stop sign, sat down, ate his sandwich and marched home again. That's how babies grow up.

A mid-Three not only begins to flex his independence, he also wonders about your omnipotence, testing it more each day. He doesn't need to be near you when he plays and can restrict certain toys to certain areas. For the first time, your house isn't one big playroom any more.

He is curiouser and curiouser now, and "Why?" is the watchword. Schedules may need changes, with a later bedtime so a child can see his father for more than a good-night kiss. Plan a longer rest for your child so he won't fall apart every evening when his father walks in.

Four

A Four is to childhood what a circus is to show business—a lot of laughs but enough uncomfortable moments to keep you off-balance. A Four tries everything, as he should, but his initiative is often your despair. Alone in a room he will nail your rickety antique chair together and if you still haven't missed him he will paint it for you too.

A Four is suddenly much bigger and more energetic, but inevitably clumsy. We found that classes in modern dance or tumbling are a dandy way to help a child control his body, and have even seen them give enough basic coordination to bypass the awkwardness in puberty.

You will find your Four needs your respect even more now, for he feels on top of the world one time and surrounded by giants the next. We remember our generally amiable Nell who put every child's anger into words when she stamped her foot and cried, "Even though I'm only three feet tall, I still have my rights!"

Every measure of respect you give a child, from knocking on his door before you enter to keeping the secret he shares, will be returned tenfold as he grows up.

Self-dramatization is another way for your Four to figure out his place in the world. He regrets that babyhood is over, but he's too interested in the rest of the world to dwell on it much. Some grown-ups, other than his parents, assume great importance and he has long talks with friends about God, whether you go to church or not.

You will want to write down everything he says now for a Four is so free, poetry springs spontaneously from his lips.

Your child will be very serious one moment, ridiculously silly the next. Boys and girls kiss each other, show bottoms and use scatological language, all of which they think is hilarious. To some children, dirty words become so commonplace that adults only can blink in disbelief, as we did when our Meg, in a sudden hush at a family reunion, said, "Pardon me, please. I farted." Or another day, when she spilled her milk at dinner and said, "Oh shit!"

When chided, she cunningly lied (for Fours do lie).

"I was speaking Spanish," she said, and added that she had learned it from a neighbor of great Latin propriety.

"She said to me, 'Meg, don't put your foot in the shit.'"

May you follow that old Spanish proverb—especially if you have a Four.

Five

A Five is a giver, passing peanuts to company and making presents as if every day were Christmas. Like many of us, he is at his best in the morning and his teacher may appreciate him more than you do. He is unself-conscious: singing, performing, playing roles and chatting with all the garrulity of a Fifteen. At this age, he is in harmony with himself.

Your Five, as nice as he is, does wish everyone

else were as fine as himself. This sanctimony often leads him into situations he can't handle. He becomes quick to tease now, but whines just as quickly if teased in return. He also is likely to be cross or even have tantrums again, for your Five is so sociable and so adult you may forget he is still a young child. He needs ten hours of sleep at night, an hour of afternoon quiet and much more fruit and fresh vegetables and milk than potato chips, cookies and sodas.

He wants to read his own books now, to make sense out of the numbers on the yardstick and to find the answers to concrete and even abstract phenomena, like rain and gravity.

By Five, your child's personality and talents become sharper every day. Already you can see the general field he probably will enter as an adult (although you won't try to guide him at all). The child who likes to collect and sort rocks and seashells now is apt to be scientifically curious all his life and the child who wants to paint every day will keep a strong interest in art. His weaknesses are balanced by his strength. He won't excel in everything, but it won't bother him for another year.

Six

Your Six is a conformist, needing to do whatever anyone else can do, but not too differently. Even his pictures are increasingly rigid.

He can dress himself completely, but not tie his shoes, and will wash his hair every week and badly, but seldom comb it. He still won't wash his face or pick up most of his toys unless told and often helped.

Now he makes his own breakfast when necessary, cares well for special toys, can play soccer, but not baseball, and carries a lunch box on any possible occasion. He needs many adventures and much hard exercise, but he shouldn't start any new lessons, like music or dancing. First grade is quite enough, even for the most self-confident Six.

When he does begin school, he will adore his teacher, whether he loves reading, writing and arithmetic or not. A Six cares what his classmates think of him, but is quick to sock someone who disagrees with him—and quick to cry if he's punched back. Now your child expects more of himself but so does everyone else. Once he turns Six, the teachers, the neighbor ladies and even the other Sixes will treat him with more justice than mercy, for accountability begins in earnest now. This is one of the harshest realities a child must face, but each bit of respect and kindness, of toughness and competence you've given your child will form the backbone he needs to stand tall for

the next few years. This is the time, like the young teen-age years, when it will be hard for your child to feel he's master of his own fate. With your continuing encouragement to be independent, however, the transition will be easier.

Every mother has real goals for her child, as well as fantastic ones.

"My daughter will be President one day *or* find a cure for cancer." (You know she'll actually do both.) It is the real qualities—of kindness and integrity, curiosity and imagination—that count, for you are no longer rearing just a lovable child but shaping a likable adult. Now you begin to accept your child for what he is and realize that followship is just as important as leadership.

By Six, he has been given enough trust by you to go through life expecting candy and just enough doubt to keep him from taking it from strangers.

The Family

Sometimes we think a *ménage à trois* would be easier than an old marriage and a new baby. Many parents feel resentment, most feel ineptness and all undergo unexpected changes. The carefree husband may become the overprotective papa; the shy man suddenly blooms; the complete woman falls apart and girlish wives grow up.

No matter how young or old your marriage, your first baby greatly affects the essence of it. The style of your life is interrupted. Nothing is impromptu but little can be planned. You can't even make love without worrying about the next feeding. Because of so many nursemaid jobs, the baby becomes the catalyst for dozens of small frictions.

Like most new mothers, we succumbed to that awful joy of giving our husbands small commands— and many—just to prove there was someone in this world we could manage. Fortunately, we couldn't get away with this petty tyranny for long, for they knew they were as capable as we were, if not as

practiced. If you never ordered your husband around before this is no time for him to start playing Step and Fetch It. Instead, his jobs should include primary ones—diapering, feeding, bathing the baby.

It has been natural for a woman, kept in her place by the mores of a millennium, to make motherhood appear full of inscrutable nuances that no man could master. This was nonsense, of course, but she had to gather her laurels where they grew: Only women were gentle, sensitive and soft enough to attend to a little baby; only mothers were patient enough and natural enough and interested enough to keep up with a Two. This strange mystique developed until sooner or later only the mother could communicate with a teenager except it turned out that she couldn't, and neither could the father. He never had.

Today's father, between his work and his commuting, often is away from home twelve vital hours a day. Not only does he have little energy left for his baby, but if his father was a commuter too, he's had a slim model of fatherhood to follow.

You and your husband will have to work together to emphasize his role and to arrange your baby's schedule to suit your husband's free time. In this way you'll encourage intimacy between father and child, which comes only with his direct involvement. To care and be cared for bind two people as tightly as a newborn's grasp.

Whatever your husband does for his child, however, should be done with little advice from you. If you let him follow his instincts, no matter how they differ from yours, you are showing respect. This is the keystone of good parenthood.

Respect yourself as well as your husband. For all the initial joy and sense of importance your baby brings, you're entering a time that will test your sense of self-worth and decide the shape of the rest of your life.

The Hamleting you felt as a teenager will be nothing compared to the irresolution which can hit you now as your personality submerges under the deluge of work as wife and mother. You've tried so hard to get to the "happily ever after" and now you're wondering—after what? Although you can accomplish many things now, none are done as well as you'd like and it's been a long time since anyone asked what you thought about foreign policy or much else either.

The less money you have the more impossible your situation will look, for a lack of money can gnaw at your happiness and the simplest solutions are overshadowed by the problems. It's particularly galling to see other couples your age, who seem to have the same income as you, do so much with it (even though they complain twice as much about all the things they can't afford to do). Take heart. As we always discovered, they have Parent$. Somehow that knowledge helps.

To make the pressure-cooker atmosphere worse, you probably are lonelier now than you ever have been. Old friends move away but others don't fit as well into your new life any more than you fit into theirs. Now you'll have to start a serious search for new friends, rather than wait for your husband to bring them home from the office. You're the person who needs the help and you set the style, so it's up to you to do the looking.

Once when our constant companions were a One and a Two, we marched through a stranger's gate, uninvited, and introduced ourselves to a young mother and daughter—the start of a long friendship. We continued this brazen pattern for years, for that day we learned a truism: All young mothers are lonely.

As the months go by, however, no number of good friends will solve your problems. The complaints of early motherhood, listed singly, may seem silly, but taken cumulatively they can become monumental, rotting the whole fabric of marriage.

First decide exactly what bothers you most about motherhood. Is it its inherent disorder? its debts? its loneliness? its lack of privacy? its sameness? its hard work?

The important part of any problem is its admission, for only then can you reach a solution. You may need time alone every day, to play the guitar or read. You may need a maid a few hours a week—who doesn't?—or someone to help with the heavy work once a month. Some mothers feel reincarnated by a visit to the hairdresser and others are happy with a few hours a week to window shop or go to church without a crying baby. Others like a drive-in movie or a late, sexy dinner at home with wine and candlelight. You need to find two or even three solutions to get reasonable serenity. Since the problems often change, so should the cures.

Even if you can't afford the beauty shop, you still need the luxury of at least one perfumed bath a week and time to set your hair and manicure your nails. Send your child to a neighbor (a favor you'll return), take the phone from the hook and enjoy. It won't be the best, but it beats nothing.

This attention to your *toilette*, as the French say, is necessary and is equal to the shaves you ask of your husband on the weekends.

The way you let yourself look is almost as important as the way you spend your time. One is generally reflective of the other.

It becomes strangely easy to get out of the habit of bathing regularly unless you keep to a fixed time, no matter how brief it is or how busy you are. Otherwise you'll find yourself putting it off in the morning, because the baby is hungry, or at noon, because you've used all the hot water to wash baby clothes, or until naptime, except the baby is hungry again, or finally until night, but by then you're just too tired.

Of course, a bath without interruption will be rare for years. By the time your child is Three you'll bathe with an audience of not only your child, but a few neighborhood ringers and every animal you have but the goldfish.

Your main problem may be the enormity of your housework. If you feel overwhelmed by it, ask a friend to help you once a week and you of course will help her just as often while your children play together. Even mending with a friend will make you feel less like a drudge. Unless you have a job, too, you can't expect your husband to help regularly with the housework, since you don't help at the office.

Basically, all solutions must come from your own attitude. You'll decide whether to watch soap operas or read a book; fill crossword puzzles or

learn to be a better cook. Unless you're prepared to work at it, motherhood can become very depressing. You need to accomplish a little bit every day—something that can't be undone by another wash, another meal, another day of dust. A day in which nothing new is learned or nothing permanent is done is a day wasted as far as your psyche is concerned, for none of us ever stops growing.

The solutions you develop will help you deal with motherhood, but your marriage itself needs regular reinforcement.

We think every couple should get away together maybe once a season—just a day (and especially a night) will do, but be prepared. Your pre-Three will scarcely speak to you when you return.

As you and your husband and your baby work out an easy relationship, you'll decide again whether, or when, to have another child.

Whether you're adopting babies or having them by the bagful, you should remember that each parent should give twenty minutes of undivided attention to each pre-Six each day. The size of your family should depend on the time you think you can give, not only now but during those vital years when your children are between Seven and Twelve. This is the time when parents and children seal their bond tightly enough to carry them through the adolescent years.

It's an effort for two to live happily, but it requires much more effort for three (or four or five or six).

Sitters

An evening a week without your child is an investment in marriage. New parents need to reinstate themselves often, as a couple, whether they go to a fancy restaurant—or just couple again in the back seat of the car. The best mothers aren't mothers all the time.

Unfortunately, sitters are hardest to get when you need them most—when there's so little money between paydays and not much then.

We overcame these problems best through a baby-sitting cooperative. It brought new friends to us and to our children—and it was free. Our sitters were our fellow members—generally wives at their homes by day and husbands at our house by night. The pay was not money but printed tickets which we had earned by sitting ourselves.

The co-op we joined, in transient Washington, D.C., had only the necessary ten families when it started, but four years later it had ninety more.

If your neighborhood has no co-op, it's simple to start one. The rules, which follow, may seem complicated, but every one of them is needed to keep it running smoothly.

If you join a co-op you'll probably use some paid sitters too. Your choice will vary as your child gets older. An infant, we feel, receives the best care from someone who has been a mother, but an active boy of fourteen is dandy for a rambunctious Four. A responsible pre-teen girl is ideal to watch the baby during your nap or while you spend time with an older child for it's her last chance to play with dolls and her first chance to play grown-up. When all else fails, bonded agency sitters are reliable, but exorbitant.

A good sitter, like a good mother, pays attention to the child first—not the telephone or the television. Even a teenager will accept this rule if you emphasize it enough. If you have doubts about a sitter's ability consider how you think a crisis would be handled—a burglary, a fire, a convulsion. Obviously, a scatterbrain won't do. You need a sitter who sleeps lightly or not at all, who can diaper and burp a baby and who can cook simple meals. Above all, a sitter should be kind.

We remember how blessed we felt, returning home to check on an address, when we saw our three pajamaed pre-Fives lined in a row on the sofa. They were spellbound as their dumpling of a gray-haired sitter smiled benignly as she explained a picture book to them. We were blocks away when the soft, sweet words finally registered: "And in this picture the little children are boiling their parents in the big pot."

Charles Addams, the cartoonist who brought vampires to Main Street, remained a favorite with the children for years, and so did the sitter. She was a very kind lady.

Sitter Rules

Maggie and Susan, two pretty girls who have sat with more children than any mother ever will, believe these two dozen rules will guarantee you good sitters. We agree.

☐ Ask for references.
☐ Establish your rates when you hire the sitter, not when the job is finished.

33

- Allow no company; baby-sitting is work, not play.
- Tell your child in advance if you're going out, who will sit and when you'll be back, since it's your return, not your leaving, which worries him.
- Post the emergency numbers for police, fire and poison control and the phone numbers of the doctor and a nearby friend. Add the number where you can be reached each time you go out and call if there is any change.
- Ask the sitter to come fifteen minutes early so she and your child can adjust to each other—a time for which you'll pay.
- Provide after-dark transportation.
- Supply all sitters with coffee, tea or sodas, something to eat, a lamp to read by and if you'll be out late, a pillow and blanket.
- Ask your sitter to take phone messages.
- Explain the care a pet might need, but put it in another room if the sitter objects to it.
- Show the location of lights, thermostat, flashlight, thermometer, television and phone.
- Leave a key for any double lock and explain all locks or alarm systems.
- Tell your sitter if any part of the house or any food is off-limits.
- Leave a fairly specific menu if you can't feed your child before leaving.
- Tell the sitter if your child has any allergies.
- Give precise, written instructions if your child needs medicine.
- Leave at least one book to be shown or read to a child of six months or older.
- Specify which television programs your child may watch.
- Show the sitter which clothes your child should wear and where to find the diaper pail.
- Leave a pacifier, magic blanket or other consolation.
- Explain the rituals of naps or bedtime.
- Name the bedtime if you can't tuck him in before you leave.
- Tell the sitter the discipline you allow—but it should never be as stringent as your own, for it's not given with your love.
- Expect a sitter to tidy up after herself and your child, but never after you.

Baby Sitting Cooperative

The following set of rules, which may seem foolishly complicated to the new parent, has allowed our large, diverse cooperative to exist for fifteen years despite the combined eccentricities of its members.

To us a baby-sitting cooperative is the ultimate in a credit economy: It takes a steady flow of play money between buyers and sellers and a lot of mutual respect. For viability, a co-op seems to work best with a president, a treasurer and a monthly secretary; a minimum of ten families and a maximum of eighty (although we've seen it work with more) and an initial printing of three thousand half-hour tickets the size of those "Get Out of Jail Free" cards.

½ hour
Capitol Hill
Baby-sitting
Co-operative

The Operation of a Co-op
1. Full-time members sit and use sitters in the night and the day, while part-time members use them only in the day.
2. Every new member must be sponsored by another member and every old member must get a replacement if her sponsor leaves.
3. Each member may sponsor only three members at the same time.
4. A member should give a coffee to introduce anyone she sponsors.
5. A new member receives a loan from the administration of 30 hours of scrip, in 60 half-hour tickets, for immediate use, to be returned when she leaves.
6. A member must pay the loan of anyone she sponsors who leaves the co-op with an outstanding debt.
7. Every member pays annual mailing costs as well as scrip dues of 14 hours a year for full-time membership, 7 hours for part-time, payable in advance in April and October and prorated for new members.
8. A member, if out of town for three months or more, may become inactive and pay no dues.
9. Members may buy scrip from others at a rate set by the administration.
10. A member may repay two-thirds of her loan at any time.
11. Members must either sell scrip or give it away if they accumulate more than 20 hours above their loan—even if the loan has been partially repaid—to keep the economy viable.
12. A member who loses scrip will not be reimbursed.

Duties of the Administration

1. The president shepherds the flock, processes new members and every six months makes and distributes new membership lists with the name of the husband and wife, the name and year of birth of each child, the address and the telephone numbers of home and office.
2. The treasurer keeps a separate reserve of scrip in the co-op bank to loan to new members, prints scrip as needed and balances the intake and outgo of tickets and money each month.
3. The president and treasurer serve for six months without pay, unless the membership exceeds 80 families; then these officers each receive three hours compensatory time every month.
4. The administration adds a vice-president after 80 families have joined; this officer serves for six months, earning three hours a month, and helps the president and treasurer with their work.
5. The administration chooses monthly secretaries from a pool of volunteers, in order of their turn on the waiting list.
6. The monthly secretary fills every sitting request as soon as possible, first calling those who are lowest in scrip but calling every member, if necessary, to fill the sit.
7. The monthly secretary is paid a half hour for each part-time member, one hour for each full-time member and an extra half hour from all members in December since it's such a busy month.
8. The administration adds another monthly secretary when the membership exceeds 40 families, and the two secretaries divide the membership and the pay.
9. The administration meets in executive session each month with new and old secretaries.
10. The members meet twice a year and whenever 20 per cent of the membership request it.
11. The cooperative may make by-law changes if 30 per cent of the membership attend a meeting.
12. The administration may drop the name of any member from the list who doesn't use the co-op for six months.
13. The administration may ask a member to withdraw, but only after receiving a written complaint and conducting a closed hearing with both members involved.

Two mimeographed forms make a secretary's job much easier. The first will be a record of sitting requests for the month, with columns for the name, the date and the time of the sit and—when the sit is filled—with the name of the sitter.

The second form is provided by the outgoing secretary to help the next one remember which members are short of scrip and also who are busy and when. It simply has spaces on the left for a list of active members, with their scrip balance, and on the right, a graph of 31 spaces to serve as a calendar. This lets the secretary mark the busy evenings—from sitting dates to night school classes—as the members mention them, so she only needs to call those who might be free.

name	date	time	sitter

Duties of a Member

1. Arrange all daytime sits yourself, whether you're a full-time or part-time member.
2. Sit at your home by day, the child's home by night.
3. Accept your fair share of sitting jobs.
4. Ask the monthly secretary for night-time sitters 24 hours in advance, but you'll have to arrange your own on shorter notice.
5. Make calls to the secretary before 10 P.M. and almost never on Sunday.

name	phone	scrip	1	2	3	4	5	6	7	8	9	10	11	12	13	14	15	16	17	18	19	20	21	22	23	24	25	26	27	28	29	30	31

6. Give a 24-hour notice to the sitter and the secretary if you cancel your plans to go out, so the sitter can take a job somewhere else.
7. Arrange a co-op replacement or pay for a sitter if you cancel your promise to sit without a 24-hour notice.

Payment
1. Pay only in scrip.
2. Figure time to the nearest half hour (2 hours and 12 minutes earns 2 hours in scrip, but 2 hours and 16 minutes earns 2½) but don't pay the time difference if the sitter comes earlier than you asked.
3. Pay immediately after a sit to avoid controversy later.
4. Pay a minimum of two hours for any evening sit.
5. Pay an extra hour for Saturday night.
6. Pay double after 1 A.M. and for Arsenic Hour—5-7 P.M.
7. Pay double for children from two families, triple for children from three families, whether the families are in or out of the co-op.
8. Pay only one extra hour for communes and for long-term house guests, both of which count as single families.
9. Pay a flat eight hours for your child to spend the night at the sitter's home, beginning no earlier than 7 P.M. and ending no later than 9 A.M.
10. Figure your own pay scale for a full weekend.
11. Pay a 2-hour penalty to your sitter if you cancel within 24 hours of a Saturday night sit and a 1-hour penalty for any other same-day cancellation.

Working Mother

Every mother—about one thousand times—agonizes over the most basic choice in motherhood: to work or not to work.

The choice is completely personal and never simple. You have your own style to discover and you're the only person who can find it. The decision is yours, and while your husband has the right to help you reach it, only you have the right to choose.

Your chief consideration will be your child. No two babies are alike, but we do feel that any child will prosper more if his mother can stay home for his first three years. They are the most critical in his life.

However, some outside work—part-time, temporary or voluntary—is essential for even the most dedicated mother of a pre-One. You can't shut the world out of your life, just because you've had a baby. If you do you'll feel your mind shrink to the size of a prune and the restrictions of motherhood will make you feel claustrophobic. It takes so little to lift you, but without some reassurance from the outside world, you can sink so low.

Realistically, motherhood lasts forever, but its duties have a comparatively short term. You must fight to keep your independence so you can allow your child to be independent too.

The longer you wait to get out of the house regularly, the harder it will be to believe you can ever leave such a dear baby. Every day he pulls the lines to your heart a little tighter.

If these bonds are too tight, however, the effect will be as stifling for your child as it is for you, for he also needs outside influences. The more people he sees, the less rigid he'll be.

When your baby is six months, it not only is feasible for you to go out at least once a week during the day, it's necessary. You may want to be alone—to play tennis or read in the quiet of the library—but we think these are such productive years, you should spend some time in the sort of accomplishments that feed your soul. A baby leaves little creative energy for you to paint pictures, but there are other ways to produce.

To us, an unpaid job brought enormous rewards. After years of work with schools, settlement houses and political precincts, we found that no other work ever demanded so much as volunteer work and nothing taught us so much either. When you work with people you learn, not just about how they live and think, but how to organize, how to run meetings, to hire and fire, to unwrap red tape and tie loose ends. Unlike a paid job, you can assume as much responsibility as you want, for your job description, like your hours, are very loose when an employer pays with a smile and a thank-you.

Although you may contribute only two hours a week outside your home, you can multiply this in the kitchen with the telephone and the typewriter—a happy combination that keeps your mind stimulated even while you bake cookies with your Two.

There are more tangible rewards too, for volunteer work, by its diversity, lets you keep in touch with your field and investigate new ones.

Today the United States Government equates volunteer work with job experience, if it's comparable to the skills you need in civil service. It takes, they've found, as much expertise to supervise forty workers for a mailing for eight hours as it does to supervise one worker for eight weeks in an office. You may have to negotiate when you take the federal exam, but the higher rating it brings translates to a comparable salary in private industry.

We remember how frightening it was to ask for an interview for a paid job, even after years of volunteer work, but without those years, it might not have been possible at all.

Part Time

After your baby's first year you may give in to the lure of a paid part-time job—perhaps as much as twenty hours a week. The money hardly compensates, for you're using your peak energy hours and scampering to keep ahead at home. You probably won't net much once you've paid the sitter, but, nevertheless, it's not a bad idea.

The psychic rewards are great, for unless you're one of those rare wives who are given some small percentage of your husband's paycheck for your very own, you're going to feel more and more resentful. A part-time job erases this friction.

If, however, you clear more than you truly need, it should go into the family till, just like your husband's paycheck. To keep the money you earn for yourself while your husband shoulders the family expenses would cause justifiable resentment on his part. There is nothing sacred about a woman's salary—something to remember when you take a full-time job.

Full Time

Some women have such an urgent money need that they must work full time and that's that, but we think leaving a pre-Three for forty hours a week is very debatable.

There is a huge effort involved, on everyone's part, for no matter how much help your husband gives, you will feel the constant burden of two jobs. You still must go to work after answering your restless child half the night, and then you find that child care and housework can consume your strength until there's none left to play with your child. If you think it would be hard to decide that a family walk at night is more important than folding laundry, you're probably not ready for a full-time job. A child takes precedence.

If you stay home you probably will reconsider your decision again and again. After the baby's first year, for instance, you may find yourself becoming possessive or domineering and are afraid you may overwhelm your child. Conversely your child may overwhelm you, and in both cases outside work may be the answer. Or you may have such a fine job offer or such an interesting career that it is irresistible.

Once you do decide to work, regardless of the age of your child, you mustn't feel guilty about it. This is one more adventure to be enjoyed, and you will if you have a relaxed attitude. To make success more likely, from everyone's viewpoint, you need enough sleep and enough good food for a steady supply of energy; a job either so interesting it keeps you lively or so simple you can forget it the minute you leave; a husband who's willing to share the housework, the car pools and the marketing; and, finally, you need the best, most reliable sitting arrangements you can find, which applies of course to part-time work too.

There are several kinds of child care to consider.

Child Care

For the first year the best and most expensive arrangement is a mother's helper. She cares for both the home and the baby, but when the choice must be made, she knows that loving a fussy baby all morning is more important than cleaning a house.

The person in charge of your child should welcome his playmates, take him on outings and, we hope, be someone like you—affectionate, easygoing and responsive. A sitter who treats a child's sobs with silence or who warns of bogeymen or spankings can create serious fears in a child.

Sometimes a relative will watch your baby, which is cheap but may be fraught with friction. A member of the family often feels a right to interfere with your methods the way no sitter would dare to do.

Because a sitter's dependability is essential for a working mother, we think the person you hire should be paid a little more than the customary salary or should be given a monthly "reliability bonus" for regular attendance, which we found works well. The few extra dollars are worth it.

Day-care centers are good for a Three. You can judge the quality of any center as you would judge a school—by the eagerness of the children to get there every morning (page 112). These centers unfortunately are rare for pre-Threes, but it isn't impossible to start one.

No matter what sitting arrangement you make when you work, your child must be prepared for it.

Any child will need some special comfort, like one of your perfumed scarves and—for the child who can talk—full, matter-of-fact information: You're going to work, just like Daddy, and you'll be home every night, just like Daddy.

Begin the sitting arrangement at least a week before you begin work, because your child will need you around for at least part of the time the first few days, whether he'll be at home, at the sitter's or at the day-care center. If he's in unfamiliar surroundings bring him home after lunch, since a nap in a strange place can be the last straw for a child.

When you do leave him full time, he should know just what he'll be doing all day and at what point you'll be back, and you should never, or almost never, be late. If the arrangements are good your child can adjust to them.

Infant Day Care

When some professional women in our neighborhood couldn't find day-care centers for their pre-Threes, they simply started their own.

The venture, unbelievably called Wee Care, Inc., is legally incorporated to care for children between One and Three. It hires "caregivers," each one to mother no more than five children a day, either in her home or in rented quarters. This approach creates an individualized style of day care, for each caregiver can treat the children in her own way. The homes are provided with toys, cribs and potty chairs and each child has extra clothes and diapers; a bottle and a pacifier; a bib, a blanket, a towel and a special toy.

The program operates 8:30 A.M.-5 P.M., Monday-Friday, but not on legal holidays. Each child is enrolled for a certain, regular number of full days a week—as many as five, as few as one. Tuition, based on income, is paid in advance on a biweekly, nonrefundable basis.

The group was easy to start, some trouble to run (even with a paid administrator), and requires occasional fund-raising parties to pay for the toys and scholarships.

There are some negative aspects to any day-care operation, for despite elaborate health rules, children from One to Three seem particularly susceptible to illness, for they share their germs better than they share anything else.

If infant day care is good enough, however, most mothers find the freedom it gives them and the joy it gives their children more than balances an extra cold or two in winter.

Day-care Centers

Much of the criteria for judging a preschool applies to a day-care center. However, since your child will be there all day, every day, the center must try to meet his social, intellectual, emotional and physical needs as completely as you do.

A day-care center should have spacious classrooms and a playground with several pieces of climbing equipment and room to run, but it should never be so perfect that it's self-contained. A child needs a variety of adventures—short walks, other playgrounds, fancy field trips—that make each day different from the next. These often are woven into creativity, as they are at our favorite center, where the children market for yellow foods on "Y" day and then, with great importance, cook their yellow lunch.

Food and sleep are most important to day-care children, for the constant company and continuing activity seem to make them hungrier and sleepier than they would be at home. Each child should have his own cot or blanket for the regular daily nap (and for an irregular morning one if he'd like), and should have a hot lunch with snacks in the midmorning and midafternoon. There also should be breakfast for the children who come early and an extra snack for those who stay late.

If you work the good health of your child is more important than ever. That's why a day-care center should have strict rules, forbidding any child to attend if he has a fever or to come back to day care until his temperature has been normal for one full day.

To run a good program, the center must have a director with a teacher and one or two aides—men and women—for every eighteen children in each age group. Since the staff members take care of the total child, they need to offer a lot of hugging, lapsitting and cuddling. For this they must not only be affectionate, but articulate, smart, patient, creative and so secure a child can dare to feel safe enough to show his sadness and his anger as well as his joy. This is what helps a child keep his individuality, which is tarnished easily when he spends most of his waking hours as part of a group.

Because teachers and aides must give so much of themselves, none should work for longer than seven hours—and this includes an hour for lunch. Although the teaching staff works on staggered shifts, aides often will substitute at lunch or when a teacher is sick, so they must be well qualified through schooling or experience. Warmth is not enough.

The staff should involve the parents with a few hours of volunteer work a month and should hold regular meetings with them as a group. The teacher also should give a progress report to each set of parents regularly, to let everybody exchange information about the child. This makes child care smoother at school and at home.

Even if your child is in the best of all day-care centers, he'll need an extra amount of privacy at home to compensate for the lack of it at school, and he'll need an extra amount of undivided attention from you and your husband. Day care is a supplement to parents, never a replacement.

Mechanics

Child care can get so complicated that you can spend most of your prime time on the mechanics of motherhood instead of the pleasures.

Whether you have a job or not, you need to learn the tricks of this trade too, so you can take a half hour to bathe and dress your baby if you want—or do the job in seven minutes flat if you must.

Diapering

Sixty thousand diapers later, we find that the mother who can change her baby quickly has one less job to resent. We think it should be a production only the first time.

Change even the tiniest baby at a waist-high table, so you won't get a backache. Lay the diaper over him, for an infant often wets during a change and a boy is liable to catch you foursquare. Slip the diaper he'll wear under his fanny and if it's a cloth one, twist it at the crotch, in a figure 8, for double thickness and a tighter fit. If you pin the back over the front, it stays on better.

Wash the baby's bottom each time you change him, either at the table or over the bathroom sink. Use a soapy cloth to wash, a wet one to rinse and pat the skin dry with a towel. Washing the skin removes bacteria—the main cause of a rash—which is one of the baby's most common and least necessary problems. It is also cyclical, since the saltiness of the urine burns any chafed skin, making the rash worse and the fussing more. Waterproof pants intensify it for they hold heat and help bacteria breed faster. Use them when you must or the wonderfully convenient, wickedly expensive disposable diapers.

Another way to prevent a rash is to smear the clean area with cornstarch or petroleum jelly (the cheapest, best but least attractive coating you can use). A rash is also less likely if your child goes without diapers for a half hour each day. Summer sunshine is especially good for the skin. Sexy too.

When you use cloth diapers (your own or from a diaper service), rinse a dirty one immediately, for no one likes to find one soaking in the toilet. Wring it and put it in a plastic bag with the wet ones. If you wash diapers every day or two, they need no soaking and neither the job nor the smell will overwhelm you. For a young baby, diapers should go through the washer twice—the second time without soap—as this residue often is too caustic for a baby's skin and can cause a rash. We've found that both the rays of the sun and the high heat of the dryer will kill any remaining bacteria.

To prevent most of the squirming while you change a young baby, fix a mobile above the changing table, strap him into place and give him two special toys, one for each hand, for balance. At nine months you can change him standing on a straight chair in the middle of the room. His newly developed depth perception won't let him fall (at least not more than once), and it keeps him in place without force.

Expect to diaper your baby for nearly three years, although a Two should be encouraged to get his own diaper when he needs it and to put the wet one in the hamper for you. This is an early step in toilet training.

Bathing

A baby is only sponged until he loses his umbilical cord—about ten days—and then he has the treat of a real bath. This is such a nice job, it's almost always a husband's favorite part of child care. The bath needn't be daily, but it probably will be because it's such a pleasure to see your baby have a good time.

Wash an infant in a sink or a basin, never a bath table, for it's unstable and a nuisance. Cushion the bottom of the sink with a towel, the way you would wash crystal, and add several inches of water, no warmer than spit. Soap him all over, even his head, and hold him like a football, for he's slippery. Because a bath is at first a stressful situation, talk and sing to him all the while, the way you always should when you think he might become fearful. Rinse, dry and rub him with lotion, for water removes skin oils. Some babies have such dry skin they should only be bathed a few times a week.

His bath is his joy for the next few months and soon he'll sit up and splash so much you'll graduate him to the tub. Before putting him in it, make sure the spigot is not too hot because he'll be sure to touch it. The tub bath probably will give you a backache, since you'll be leaning over, and maybe a few other aches. Once you've been goosed by a plastic duck when taking a bath of your own, you'll want to keep his toys somewhere else. We put them in a bag made by sewing one end of a face towel on a hanger, doubling it and sewing the side seams together.

A One will adore his bath, because he thinks it's such a happy, sexy thing to do, and will hate his shampoo, because the soap stings, but he needs both. The more he feeds himself, the more food he rubs everywhere, including his hair.

Shampoo his hair by rubbing a soapy washcloth on his head, but when he's older he may forget his fears if he can watch in a hand mirror as you sculpt fancy hairdos out of suds.

Soon he may be afraid of the bath itself and you may be like an harassed mother we met, whose pediatrician told her to ignore the fear; it would pass in three weeks. Actually, it lasted much longer, she said, but by the time three weeks had passed, she couldn't remember when the baby hadn't been afraid of his bath, so it wasn't a worry any more.

For practical solutions to this fear, your child will get almost as clean if you let him play naked outdoors with the hose or with a bucket of water, or you can bathe him in a small, plastic tub that sits in the bathtub. A child also can be enticed into the tub with an addition of bluing or bubble bath with mineral oil, or for that matter, of you. Always remove him before you pull the plug, for he has no concept of size and may be afraid of going down the drain. If he's still scared, take comfort. By the time you have another child, a bath won't seem so important. We think our Mali may still have some of her original belly button lint.

Dressing

We found dressing our first babies a complicated job, for which we went up and down stairs like yo-yos, and though we never ironed very much, the laundry seemed ominous. Babies later, we learned to carry a day's supply of clothes and diapers downstairs in one arm in the morning and a child in the other, like a football. We even found it only took four minutes to iron four little organdy dresses (a day's supply). Like us, you also may find the joy of looking at a fancy-dancy baby is worth the effort.

A baby is dressed in the same way he is diapered: strapped on the changing table in the early months or standing on a straight chair later.

It is the buying of the clothes that makes dressing either easy or hard. To simplify your life, choose simple clothes, with few buttons and easy neckholes. Since bootees are kicked away so quickly, buy pajamas with feet and dress babies by day in tights or white socks (so they'll always have mates).

A child needs no shoes until he walks, except to placate clucking grandmas in the park, but when you do get them they should have enough space at the toe to fit the width of your thumb. Put a strip of adhesive tape across the bottom of the leather sole, to prevent a slip, and another inside the back of the heel, to stop sock eating.

Study the labels of all clothes you buy. Miracle materials and fluffy packing can mean almost anything. A snowsuit should never be made of slippery nylon, for a baby wiggles so much he can slide through your arms. The hat should be connected to the collar of the suit, to avoid drafts on the neck. To prevent the loss of mittens, pin them to the cuffs of the snowsuit or run a length of yarn through the sleeves and pin a mitten on each end.

Carry a sweater for your child in the summer, for most supermarkets are overcooled, and at the beach protect his tender skin by dressing him in a shirt and hat.

For safety, buy bright colors for any outerwear or bathing suit, which helps you find your child quickly, and for your budget, buy only in two colors—like navy and scarlet, yellow and orange or green and brown, so coordination is easy. You not only will need fewer clothes, but you'll feel organized. It also helps your child put himself together, which we talk about in La Toilette (page 71). You can expect a Two to begin to dress

himself, a Four to put on his shoes, a Five to lace them and somewhere, somehow he'll learn to tie them between kindergarten and college.

Fireproofing

For safety, you may want to fireproof your child's much-washed pajamas and bedding, for its original protection only lasts through about twenty launderings. The boric acid solution is sold at the drugstore. To make this recipe

Combine   9 oz. borax
               4 oz. boric acid solution
               1 gal. warm water

Soak the clean clothes in the solution until it impregnates them completely; then dry as usual.

Eating

The same nutrition chart your fifth-grade teacher pointed to in Health and Safety still applies today. However, there is a lot of new information on which you need to keep current, since the quality of our foods has changed so much in the last generation.

The chart still calls for at least three servings of milk or cheese, four of fruit and vegetables, four of bread and cereals and two servings of meat or fish a day. A good diet not only keeps a family healthy, but helps to keep everyone content from one meal to the next, for food affects dispositions so much.

This is why the classic breakfast of juice, egg, milk and buttered toast still starts the day best. The juice provides the sugar for energy; the egg, milk and bread give the protein to harness the energy and release it as needed, and, finally, the starch in the bread and the fat in the milk and butter satisfy the appetite. When the ratio of the sugar to the protein to the fats is in balance, the body is in balance too.

Protein is so important that a major shortage of it in the first year of life can cause brain damage. Cells are made, repaired and destroyed every day and it is protein that builds and repairs them.

All foods contain some of it, but like a pound of cotton and a pound of lead, the quality is much higher in some food than in others. Eggs, fish, dairy products, nuts and chicken have the most, but you can multiply the quality by combining the right foods, like red beans and rice or macaroni and cheese—to get a protein almost as complete as an egg.

Since the heat process destroys so many nutrients, it's best to use cold-pressed oils and unheated honey, which are sold with health foods. For more vitamins, use natural cheeses, brown rice, iodized salt, dark flours, steamed and raw vegetables (the more colorful the better), pure semolina pasta, raw fruits and rare beef, lamb or veal. These have a much higher content of vitamins and minerals.

The fresher the fruits and vegetables you serve, the more natural sugar they contain. Older ones convert the sugar to carbohydrates, which doesn't satisfy the body's basic need for sugar. Neither, unfortunately, do refined brown and white sugars and syrups, which are added to everything from cornbread mix to canned peas. Some nutritionists blame these sugars for all the ills of the world and we're afraid they may be right about some of them—like the killing of B vitamins. Until scientists know for sure, we think mothers should use any sweetener sparingly, substituting honey for sugar and serving fresh fruits and vegetables as much as possible. Certainly you'll let your child splurge with sweets sometimes, but a well-nourished child has little craving for candy.

If your child eats a fifth of his food when he snacks, then it must provide a fifth of his daily nutrition. Aside from fruit, the best snacks are nuts, raisins or cheese, and bread or cookies enriched with soy flour and wheat germ.

All snacks should be served with pure fruit juice or milk or water, rather than a sugared drink. Your child also should be encouraged to drink water frequently, especially during hot weather.

Infancy

Although you'll decide whether to breast-feed or bottlefeed your baby before he's born, the subject can get emotional at the hospital. Nursing mothers traditionally agonize so much over their milk supply, which is slow to start and erratic besides, that pediatricians and nurses often find it easier to order a formula at the first sign of trouble.

Of course your baby needs a formula if you work or if you want a looser schedule, but if you do bottlefeed, be careful to hold your baby as closely and as gently as you would if you were nursing, ignoring the temptation to prop a bottle. This is seldom necessary and even twins can be held at alternate feedings. Your tranquillity is an added dividend, for feeding times give you the chance to gather your thoughts, read a book or visit with an older child.

A bottle baby requires a well-organized mother, for it takes a knack to make formula, but at least your husband can take the 2 A.M. feeding, which continues until your baby is about twelve pounds. A good stretch of sleep at night will give you back your energy quicker than anything else.

No matter what method you choose, you will burp the baby the same way (page 21) and want to follow the rules of self-demand. Your baby will cry when he's hungry, and you will feed him, of course, but if he has finished a feeding within the last two and one-half hours, he almost surely has a stomachache. Fresh milk on top of partly digested milk may make it worse, but it won't make it better. Instead, give your baby warm water to drink, hold him and try to forget your other jobs.

However, if some night you're very tired and ready for bed and the baby hasn't had anything to eat for maybe four hours, wake him up for his feeding. Sometimes it's your turn to demand.

Three Months

Some pediatricians start solids in the first few weeks of life, but most introduce them between three and six months. Manufacturers now stretch baby foods with so many extra ingredients that you may decide to make Baby Dinners (page 45) or mash a banana or a poached pear or a baked apple. Before you season though, remember that what is bland to you is tasty to a baby, for his palate is more sensitive.

Any new food, including each type of cereal, must be served daily for five days to test for allergic reaction—perhaps a milk rash or the heaves or possibly even extreme dislike, which may signify a potential allergy. An allergy generally disappears if the problem food is stopped and then introduced again at One, but if you continue it without stopping, it usually gets worse. It takes nearly a year for a child to sample all the permitted food, but it's impossible to isolate a problem food if it's served in a jumble. Children are most sensitive to milk, grains, eggs, citrus, spinach, starches and seafood, which is why doctors have you test them so carefully.

A pre-Two never is given raisins, nuts, melon, corn, cherries, berries or chocolate, for they're too hard on the digestive system and some of them can choke a young child.

Six Months

A child sucks much less now, wanting to chew instead, and begins to surrender his thumb or his pacifier. He enjoys gumming a bagel—better for him than a teething biscuit, which is sweet—or a steak bone, and is ready for a few finger foods, like a banana. Everything will taste better to the child who can feed himself.

You don't, of course, give him books or any toy when you're feeding him, because this is telling a child to work and play at the same time. Six months is not too early for a child to learn that eating should be an efficient job, completed in about twenty minutes in a calm, pleasant atmosphere and without being coaxed to eat one more bite for Mom. When a child is cajoled to eat he discovers an unholy power. We think food is neither a plaything nor a weapon. Instead use positive discipline, congratulating him with cheers of "All gone!" When he starts to fiddle with his meal, it's time to take it away.

He enjoys a yogurt and fruit dessert now, which you can make yourself. You're lucky if he likes it, for yogurt helps the body make its own chain of B vitamins. However, it works so hard in the small intestine it can keep a baby wide-eyed, but not fretful, the first night he eats it.

Your child's plate should be heavy, with suction cups on the bottom so he can't throw it on the floor too easily. He can sip from a cup you hold, but he can't manage a spoon for another six months. Since he puts not only food but everything else into his mouth now you can expect frequent bouts of diarrhea.

One

Now he can hold his own cup if you wrap a rubber band around it so it won't slip through his hands. The cup also should be too heavy to tip easily—one more way to help your baby feel adept.

Sugar has been a favorite since birth, when he had his first belt of sweetened water, but his appetite drops so fast now, you can't afford to give cookies to satisfy what little hunger he has. Although a child triples his birth weight in his first year, he only gains three to five pounds in his second.

Even so, he still continues to need five small meals a day: a full breakfast; a midmorning snack; lunch; an after-nap snack and dinner. This same schedule lasts until first grade.

For snacks give your child juice or raw vegetables and any protein, like cheese. No fruit should be given less than an hour before the next meal; it would be like a dessert before soup. In any case, avoid snacks without vitamins, such as dry cereal or potato chips, for carbohydrates only guarantee fussy behavior.

Mid-One

As mothers, we must have made most of the mistakes you can make in child care, especially in eating, and we've been astonished to find that the bad patterns were so much easier to set than the good ones.

In no time our toddlers learned they could skip lunch and get sweeter, bigger, earlier snacks from their anxious mothers, just because they were hungry. This was folly, of course, for a heavy snack in midafternoon simply makes a child too full for dinner and then too hungry to wait patiently for breakfast the next morning.

We watched other mothers offer simple snacks and then hardly notice themselves allowing a steady flow of dry cereal, cookies, fruit and milk until the next meal was barely touched. Either way will encourage a finicky eater and a whiny one too. He'll be a terrible pain until you decide that a meal isn't a nonstop production.

Two

Although you won't demand that your child clean his plate, you won't give second helpings or desserts until he has. Obviously, if he has some food left on his plate he isn't hungry and your refusals should be explained like that.

Considering that his taste buds are so much more intense than yours, you shouldn't expect him to like everything you like, and he particularly may not like the texture of some foods. They may be too gritty, like roe, or spongy, like liver, or slimy, like oysters. Other dishes, like stew, have their flavors combined, which bothers some children. Still, you should put a bit of everything you cook on his plate and expect him to taste it, on the grounds that this may be the day he is old enough to like something he didn't like when he was younger (such as a week before). Unless your child has an allergy, an illness or a birthday, you should never cook a special meal for him in exchange for peace at the dinner table. If you do your child will restrict his diet more and more until you're ready to divorce him if you ever smell hot dogs, tuna fish or peanut butter again. Having worked ourselves into that box, we found only one sure, if painful, exit. This method is a lot of trouble, but if you're desperate enough it's worth trying.

Begin when you're willing to stay indoors for several miserable days, without company, without any treats in the house and, to be kind, when your husband is on a trip. First, tell your child he no longer can have snacks or desserts until he will eat what he is served at meals. Then cook every outlandish dish you can think of until, after a certain amount of fasting, he'll find that even lamb curry or crab imperial tastes good. You can expect some backsliding afterward and when that happens, you simply quit desserts and snacks again.

Mid-Two

When your child outgrows the high chair, his company at the dinner table is less and less charming. Somehow he's expected to act as grown-up as everyone else and instead he'll talk while you're talking (the way he plays next to his friends but not with them). He will feed the cat, spit out his meat, hide his peas in his bib and spill his cup at least once. (We remember one ghastly night when two children spilled a total of eight glasses of milk.) These are the same things your child does when he eats lunch with you in the kitchen, but it's much more annoying at dinner, when you've tried so much harder. Regrettably, a pre-Five can't be much better than this and you'll spend the next few years finding ways to escape, none of which will be too satisfactory or permanent. Realistically, you should know that in eating, as in everything else, the solutions that work one week will collapse the next, for your child isn't static, thank goodness.

If you think your child would profit by having family meals, and we do, you need to decide how frequently you can stand it. It should be no less than once a week, however, and probably couldn't be more than four, although we know one organized mother who had her three pre-Fives eat with their parents nightly—but only for 10 minutes. First she gave them an early dinner alone, without dessert, followed by a communal bath, and then invited them downstairs in their sleepers for salad, which one of the children usually made. It was served as a splendid first course for the parents and a last course for the children and worked very well, although the youngest child, at Nine, still thinks a good dessert is green and oily.

The rest of us endure, but less grandly. If you can tolerate four family meals a week, you might plan on a pick-up supper of sandwiches another night, an adult meal at a restaurant or with friends at your house or theirs on still another night and a late and fancy dinner for the two of you at home—a corny routine but it improves your cooking and helps you feel civilized.

The other basic solution is to feed your child early six nights a week and for this you can 1) cook your own meal in advance to give him some of it; 2) save a plate from the night before; 3) freeze TV dinners from your leftovers; or 4) feed him dinner at noon and a sandwich for supper.

A child's separate dinner shouldn't be a production and it doesn't deserve all the resentment it generates, but, somehow, cooking two balanced meals every night can make you feel like Milly the Martyr. That's why we settled for family meals. They should be served with style, for food should pique a child's sense of sight as much as his sense of taste. You'll find candlelight makes everyone's behavior better, for a child is awed into near goodness and you can't see enough of the badness to correct him so often. Wine will improve your behavior and we recommend that too.

You can help your child act his best by sitting him on pillows or phone books high enough to handle silverware well. Strap him to the chair so he can't leave when he feels like it, but don't expect him to last longer than twenty minutes. This means that even a soup must be served alongside the dinner plate, for to a Two, dessert is the only course worth waiting for.

Three

Your Three almost seems grown-up to you now—and to himself. Here is a child who's old enough to have sampled a few soda pops in some Garden of Delight with Grandpa and wants more, any time. You may succumb, giving sodas to your child as often as water, which starts a bad pattern.

Besides the high sugar content in sodas, a twelve-ounce can contains about half as much caffeine as a cup of coffee. Since your child weighs so much less than you, forty to seventy milligrams of caffeine will affect him much more, causing him to be jumpy, wakeful and cross. Your Three will do much better with water, milk or juice, none of which are addictive.

Four

"You take what you eat and you eat what you take" is the motto of the Amish *smörgasbord* restaurants in Pennsylvania and their way suits our independent Four very well. A picky eater can serve himself from your own simple buffet, taking as much as he wants (but including a vegetable) and finishing it all.

A Four will drink all of his cup if he pours for

himself. For this he needs his own small unbreakable cup (but not a paper cup, for it tips too easily), and a small unbreakable pitcher.

A Four also is big enough to have a proper lunch with you at a department store and little enough to enjoy it.

Five

If your Five doesn't have extra sweets every day, his eating habits will be normal in first grade and he'll be satisfied with a few cookies, rather than join the lunchbox contest, where each child jockeys for more sweets and treats than all the other children. A lunchbox needs milk or juice, a sandwich, some fruit or raw vegetables, two cookies and perhaps some nuts. Sodas and candy bars give a child nothing.

Snacks are heartier now with nuts or raw or dried fruits as well as cookies and milk. Your child usually will eat a whole sandwich for lunch and enjoys pared carrots, celery and seeded cucumbers from a jar of water in the refrigerator.

Six

Finally, it happens. A Six can have dinner with you almost nightly, eating nearly everything that is cooked for the adults and with manners that aren't too offensive, even to visitors. However, you probably have at least one other child by now and while you and your husband will want to eat alone at least once a week and your Six will join you for one more quiet evening, the rest of the time is a one-ring circus. Lower your standards and enjoy the show.

These are some of the best, easiest and healthiest foods you can make.

Yogurt

The best yogurt has no preservatives and since it should be a part of the daily diet, you may enjoy making it yourself. It's cheap and easy and an older child will like to help you, if only to watch it bubble. The milk must be scalded first to kill the bacteria, and containers and utensils must be very clean. Use either fresh or reconstituted milk, with extra milk crystals for more thickness.

Scald   1 qt. milk
Add   ½ c. milk crystals

Cool for 10 minutes. Meanwhile place 5 wide-mouthed 8-oz. glass jars in a pan with warm water up to their necks. When the milk feels warm on your wrist (about 110°)

Add   3 tbsp. commercial yogurt OR
                     1 pkg. yogurt culture

Stir with a metal spoon. Pour into the jars, cap them and cover the pan. The cover and the bath help distribute the heat evenly. Keep the pan on a heating tray, over a pilot light or in any place warm enough to stay about 110° for 3-10 hours. For a mild flavor, heat 3-4 hours, refrigerating just when the yogurt stops bubbling and has turned to custard. For a sharper taste and thicker consistency, heat overnight, or for 10 hours, before refrigerating. These amounts should yield about 37 ounces of yogurt.

Serve yogurt with a spoon of honey or fresh fruit and if the taste is too sharp, a little cream. Never add sugar or chocolate, since either may kill B vitamins. Save 3 tablespoons to start a new batch within 5 days.

Baby Dinner

In a covered pot, and using no salt or spices
Combine   1 c. water
                     1 chicken breast
                     ¼ c. rice
Simmer 15 minutes.
Add   3 whole carrots
                     ¼ lb. green beans
Simmer 15 minutes longer.

Grind or blend the meat and rice with enough broth to make it moist. Mash the carrots and then the beans. Store separately in individual servings in the freezer in plastic sandwich bags, tied tightly, or in a plastic ice-cube tray, which must be bagged and tied. Defrost a meal at breakfast, so the servings will be at room temperature by lunch. As your child gets a few months older and can chew better, you can grate your leftovers instead of blending them.

Sprouts

A Two likes to eat sprouts and especially to grow them. Serve raw, either by the handful or in salads or combine with cooked vegetables. Their chemistry undergoes an almost magical change from seeds to sprouts, creating a very high value in protein and vitamin C. Any seeds you grow need constant dampness and, of course, no soil. They mature in 3-5 days, according to their size. Buy them from supermarkets or health food stores, but don't buy gardening packets, for these seeds may be chemically treated. In a bowl overnight
Soak   ½ c. wheat berries OR
                     mung beans OR alfalfa seeds
Line a big tea strainer or colander with cheesecloth

or a paper towel to contain moisture. Pour the seeds into it and run cold water over them twice a day. Don't cover them (or they may mildew) and keep them out of sunshine.

Sleeping

A newborn sleeps best on his tummy, for the pressure brings up bubbles better. He likes to nestle his head in the corner of the crib, cushioned as it was in the womb. He'll sleep most of the time, heaven and colic willing, and can sleep for an eight-hour span when he's about twelve pounds.

Three Months
Now he plays in his crib for as long as an hour before breakfast, if he has a mobile, a crib gym, a cloth book and a soft tinkling toy to amuse him. He'll nap every afternoon, but his morning naps grow shorter. In the next few months you may find he can tell which of his many blankets has the magic to put him right to sleep—and it's never the one you knitted.

Six Months
This is the time when you begin to adjust the baby's sleeping schedule to yours. We put our Kate to bed at 10 P.M. to fit her father's late shift, for there's no rule that says a baby must sleep from six to six. Besides, 10 A.M. is a civilized time for a baby and a mother to wake up.

Nine Months
When Ramon was this age, a nursemaid would have been heaven—not for the days, but for bedtime. Fortunately, his father enjoyed the ritual of putting him to bed and it was their special time for years.

One
Gradually the morning naps disappear until your baby settles into a two-to-three hour sleep after lunch. One day, if he's a climber, he'll surprise you by crawling out of the crib. Since it's safer for a child to climb out of a low bed than to scramble over a high one, it's best to lower the rails and admit he no longer can be contained.

Mid-One
The vivid dreams start now, and with them, some fears. We recommend a night light or a hall light before these fears ever start and certainly a soft doll or a stuffed animal in the bed. All of us need the reassurance of an old friend, and bed is certainly the best place for an old friend.

Two
You'll find your Two needs positive discipline for he'll have invented a dozen ways to postpone bedtime. Set bedtime four hours after he wakes from his nap, so he'll be sleepy, and precede it by restful activities—a bath, a soft song, warm milk or a story read in a sleepy voice. Give him lots of kisses, lay him down firmly and don't be in a hurry to answer his calls or you'll start a new tradition. The more rituals you have, the harder it is to enforce the bedtime.

If your child wants you at night, soothe him in his bed but every reward you offer—water, a cracker or a toy—will give him another reason to call you again. Only let your child sleep with you if he's very sick, so you can care for him and catnap too.

Mid-Two
This child is ready to quit his nap now, just when you need the respite the most. We've found that every mother of a mid-Two is adamant about her child doing one of three things: He must eat everything on his plate, be toilet trained, or take a nap. To us there's no choice. A child's nap is the glue that holds a mother together. He'll fight against it, stay awake and probably scream at you, but keep the practice just the same and call it a rest.

Three-Six
A Three, with more pedal toys, more playmates and maybe a nursery school, will be tired enough to sleep, but he won't return to the nap unless you've continued the pretense. We think a child is much easier to live with if he has enough sleep at night—about ten hours—and you'll be much easier to live with if he sleeps one more hour in the afternoon. Some children can adjust to less sleep, but others scarcely cope.

A Four will go to his room for quiet play or to look at books, and to please you, he may pretend to nap. Sometimes he will. If he does, he must get extra exercise afterward unless you don't mind a very late bedtime.

If your child still has trouble going to sleep, the bedtime you set may be unrealistically early. We think the hour can be flexible until nursery school begins, but be more relaxed about it on weekends. A little whoopee time is good for the soul.

One of the nicest habits a child can begin, from his viewpoint, is a visit with you in the night, a pattern that sets nicely in less than a week.

If he needs you, go to him, stay in his room, even get in his bed if it's big enough. If you think that's a poor solution ask the tired, resentful parents who share their bed with a wiggly, leaky child from 3 to 5 A.M.—every 3 to 5 A.M.

When our Kate had that miserable habit, we introduced

Jake

One day when we were feeling in charge, we said we saw Jake galumphing around the neighborhood the night before and wasn't he a sight. Just that, nothing more.

Kate, without trying to resist, asked about Jake and immediately she was greeted with great surprise.

"You mean you don't know? You mean I never told you?"

Incredulous, we told her about Jake, who had made himself at the city dump out of bits and dabs that were there. He used drain pipes for arms and legs (we went to look at our drain pipe) and ice trays for shoes and applesauce cans for his kneecaps and elbows. He made the middle of himself out of venetian blind slats, vertical, so he could be cooler in summertime. His head was a gallon paint can, the same color that was in her bedroom in fact, and he had light bulbs for eyes. Jake wore a saucepan for a hat, but mainly so he could bow to the ladies and show off his fine curls of 0000 steel wool, his only vanity.

Jake was nine feet tall and carried a plumber's friend.

When he walked he went ka-plink, ka-plunk, but only the grown-ups could hear him, and not even all of them. Every night he made his rounds, visiting little children to make sure they were sound asleep and tucked in their own little beds, where else. If they were the front door opened magically and he came in, very pleased with himself, and went up the steps, ka-plink, ka-plunk and with many, many squeaks, he bent himself enough to go through the bedroom doorway. He straightened up his nine feet in time to bend down again to kiss the nose good night. It is the nose, Jake said, that was responsible for good and happy dreams and it certainly seemed to work for Kate.

The first time she slept the whole night in her own bed, she found a little gift from Jake. This wasn't a bribe, because it wasn't promised, but a thank-you present, for letting him come in out of the dew. If there's one thing Jake hated it was wet weather (the rust, you know). The other thing he couldn't abide was sand, because it got in his joints, but since Kate was so special, Jake always trudged to the seashore to insure her good dreams.

Jake never promised gifts, but very occasionally left one or a funny note or a picture if the child had stayed where he belonged.

There must be 1,024 variations of the sandman routine and you probably will be more comfortable making up a Jake of your own. It's fun for you, it stretches your child's imagination—and it works.

Behavior

Discipline—the most misunderstood word in the language of motherhood—is just another way to say love.

A child's behavior varies from age to age, from good to bad and then when you think you can't stand it any more, to good again. To help you anticipate this behavior we've written a chronological account of what you can expect and what you can do about it. Basically, all solutions revolve around the boundaries you set. They are the essence of discipline, and every child at every age needs them to feel comfortable in his society and to feel the security that comes from knowing someone cares enough to bother.

There are, we found, two sides of discipline—the positive, which makes a child want to be in these boundaries, and the negative, which keeps him there. However, it will be the physical limits, like the rim of a coin, that hold these sides together and the good manners you'll insist upon that will add the luster.

The ratio of positive to negative discipline determines his behavior. Your attitudes are fed into your child's make-up as surely as chromosomes at conception and can be almost as hard to change. His character is like a fallow field. Something is going to grow there and whether it will bloom with dandelions or daisies depends on the seeds you sow.

Having tried more methods of discipline than we care to remember, and a few we'd rather forget, one secret became clear. The more positive we were, the less rebellious the child. Each successive child was easier to handle, not because the child was more disciplined, but because we were. We finally learned that since a young child's capabilities couldn't be raised, our standards had to be lowered.

You can be as relaxed with your first child as your last if you remember that the best discipline, like the best medicine, is preventive. It begins at birth, when you help your child get good food and enough sleep and exercise and activities—and especially praise—that make all of us happy.

Because respect is the heart of any relationship, all discipline must include it. When a child's rights are accepted, he'll begin to accept the rights of others. This is why you knock on your baby's door before you enter, correct your naughty Two in private, ask permission of your Three to see his latest drawings and only tell your child to hurry when you must.

A child learns well from a person who respects him, who lets him enjoy some time alone and who takes a few minutes a day to explain concepts or to listen singlemindedly to his ideas. The respect you give now—or don't give—is returned in kind ten years from now.

Part of this respect hinges on the amount of safety and freedom you're willing to give your child, especially during his first years.

Personally we found it much less fatiguing for ourselves and less provocative for our children if we let physical boundaries say no, instead of us. This extra freedom buoys a child's ego, keeps you calm and, most importantly, prevents at least some of the accidents that beset families. The more active and inquisitive your child, the more precautions will be necessary.

If you let your baby stand on the front seat of the car, you'll drive more nervously than the mother who uses a car seat and if you keep your ornaments on low tables, you'll sweep away a lot of memories. When you remove a temptation, you remove a rule and the fewer rules there are, the easier your child can live in dignity with the ones that are left.

Even if you follow the philosophy of preventive discipline your child will need some corrections. For this we have the techniques of positive discipline (The Light Side) and negative discipline (The Dark Side).

48

The kind of discipline you give will depend on his behavior and on his age, but your child will be Three before he can begin to be accountable for his actions. Until then, he needs you to praise the good (even as there is less and less to praise), ignore most of the bad and postpone the spankings until he reaches that magic age. After Three, he won't need many, for reason usually works better.

Even if your child stays within every boundary you set—which he won't—we still must urge good manners too, from the table to the telephone.

We hope you won't think us as old-fashioned as our mentor, Maria Child, but we think every member in a family must have enough self-discipline to be kind to each other. This is the trick of a contented household.

Infancy

There are few flat statements we would dare make about motherhood except this: Love never spoiled anyone, especially an infant. The cries of a helpless baby must be answered, even if neither of you know what's the matter. If a child learns he can depend on you in his first year he'll obey you in his later ones, for he listens best to people who listen to him.

In the early months you give milk, kisses and a steady change of diapers and scenery to keep him comfortable and interested, assuaging most tears before they fall. The baby should learn early that a crib is for sleeping, a playpen is for playing and a high chair is for eating, or you'll pluck toys from the applesauce and scrub dried bagels from the crib rails. When you simplify life your baby learns to do his jobs, like eating and sleeping, with dispatch. This is the way he begins to discipline himself.

Six Months

This is the easiest age of all, but you still will need to second-guess him more every day. He will squirm when you dress him, which is why you strap him in place on the changing table, and he will throw toys

from the jumpseat for you to return. In this game, according to some experts, a child is sorting out the relationship between the movement of his fingers and the bang on the floor, but we suspect he's simply sorting out the relationship between baby in his jumpseat and mama going off her rocker. If you hang a few toys from the tray on lengths of elastic, he can reel them in for himself and the game will pall. For every problem there is at least a partial solution, if you think about it long enough: a comforting idea two years from now.

Nine Months

When he crawls, you'll have to forget how he was going to respect property. It's too much to ask of a pre-Three and certainly of his friends. He needs an increasingly child-proofed environment to protect him from himself and make life easier for you.

One

Now you become a master of diversion, swapping the hammer he found for the pull toy that rattles, and when that doesn't work, using a cross, no-nonsense look to carry your message. Since you mean so much to him, this often is punishment enough.

Fifteen Months

Suddenly, your child will get bolder every day—and he should. He needs to learn enough daring at this stage to last the rest of his life.

Although he doesn't want to damage anything, not all of his experiments will be successful. That's the way it is with scientists. One thing is certain: He'll be much sadder when he breaks one of his toys than when he breaks one of yours—just the way you are. It's as hard for him to understand the value you place on a teacup as it is for you to see the importance of his little plastic plane.

Your reaction to his experiments should be measured. A certain amount of cat catching is all right, too much is cruelty and must be stopped. Every child must feel his food a little bit, and at every meal, but you must decide, at every meal, when he has gone from eating to playing. Now you'll correct him with body English—physically removing him from the scene of mischief—but don't fuss or even mention the transgression or he'll have to cry about it to keep his dignity.

Fifteen months is the first watershed in motherhood, when you're likely to let your child's bewildering quest for independence sink child care to a service level. Though you still confer with the pediatrician, there is that universal inclination to exaggerate, depending on how the last week went. Frankly, we found it very hard to be objective in those brief sessions and think a husband probably gives the best day-to-day advice now. He not only has a greater stake, he makes home visits.

To keep a light heart, you also will need to evaluate your child together regularly, as unemotionally as if you were talking about someone who didn't belong to you. A child lucky enough to have two parents should have the guidance of both.

Mid-One

You will be giving some rules, but not too many, for motherhood is an easy power to abuse. Without any rules at all a child would be the tyrant of the first grade, or at least, a most unpopular person.

When you make a rule, your child will need at least a week to absorb it, and still it must be repeated. Speak clearly, directly, eyeball to eyeball, holding his hands and using the same words each time. He'll concentrate on the new rule so hard you can expect him to forget most of the old ones temporarily.

Your child will have a much better chance to be good if you give a direction he can obey and if you're willing to see that he does. When you don't care enough to follow through, he certainly won't.

Everyone is addicted to praise. The more we get, the more we want, which is mighty helpful to remember when dealing with children.

You always can find something to praise in a child's behavior, which guarantees more of the same. However, you mustn't praise everything with the same intensity, or he'll value none of it, nor must you praise everything good that he does, or he'll feel oppressed by such constant attention.

The indirect compliment often is best, beginning with a mid-One. No matter how preoccupied your child may appear, he hears every word you say about him to others. We found there was no finer way to say "I love you" to a child than for him to eavesdrop on a compliment, particularly if you're talking to his father. Conversely, an overheard criticism is so powerful that it's almost an intolerable method of rebuke and shouldn't be used.

When your child disobeys, which will be often, your criticism must ring with kindness. If your standards are too exacting your pre-Three will become either very anxious or very naughty. He knows he can't win.

You surely have gone through the agony of a correction from a favorite boss—who wasn't even twice your size—so you can appreciate the power you carry. Just multiply it by 10. Your love and acceptance are more important to your child than anything else in the world.

He can understand being put in a corner for scrubbing the toilet bowl with your toothbrush, but the enormity of a spanking horrifies him. This should be the extreme punishment reserved for extreme behavior, like running in the street or playing with fire.

Twenty-One Months

Sometimes you can see what's making your child behave so poorly and other times not even the best pediatrician can figure out why. That's what is called a stage. If we remember that we all need more love in the bratty periods of our lives, it's a little more acceptable. Guide him with matter-of-fact praise for his goodness—for sharing a toy or coming when called—as if you expected this behavior all along and give more and more physical exercise to work off tensions. When he doesn't obey, there are many reasonable methods of correction, most of which center around his isolation to a corner, or for a tantrum, to his room. The respite will be even better for you.

Two

A Two, like a young teenager, is building a lifetime of self-confidence and like a young teenager, he needs his boundaries as loose as you dare to make them. This lets him think he is making his own decisions.

To do this, give few commands, always prefaced with an advance notice, and then give enough time for a child to obey. Also be sure to say your pleases and thank-yous, as you would to anyone else.

Although you may phrase an order politely, your child should know he has limited options. You don't ask, "Shall we go walking now?" but, with no doubt in your voice, "What will you take on your walk? Your magnet or your magnifying glass?" (Please remember he may take the plumber's friend instead or anything else to show you that he's master of his own destiny.) By giving him lesser choices, his independence is preserved and so is yours.

A change in a basic rule should be an event and if it's less than that you're breaking too many rules.

Your child should be like a special free-wheeling Twelve we know who explained happily to her mother that her good friend Babs was reared with great strictness.

"Just like me," she said, to her liberal mother's astonishment, explaining, "She can do anything she wants—only she better not try."

You'll set slightly different boundaries than any other mother, for each of us has a different threshhold of tolerance which no one can know but you—not your sister, not your neighbor, not even your doctor. You may draw the boundary very tightly in one area, very broadly in another, but to be comfortable, you must draw it yourself.

Any correction for breaking these boundaries must be quick, private, without humiliation or roughness and always followed by a kiss within about ten minutes. It also must be directed to the action and not the child. There's a great difference between telling a child he is bad for throwing a ball in the house and telling him that it's bad to throw a ball indoors.

The closer your child gets to twenty-six months the lower your spirits will sink, for this is the nadir. You may rant hysterically and have tantrums too bizarre even to tell your husband, like the mother who sprayed the instant whipped cream all over her little child's head—after he had done the same thing to her sofa. This behavior is normal for both of you, for to be charitable, a Two is as trying as he is funny—and he is very, very funny.

He is also a rather uncivilized person. Now he slowly learns that his family won't condone fighting, sauciness or physical or verbal attacks. It's not only uncivilized behavior, it's a pain to live with. In fact, we even think it's a poor idea for a child to name a doll or a punching bag after his baby sister and hit it when he's mad, for you're trying to teach him to live by his wits and not his fists. A child can learn to work off most of his aggressions with a good dig in the garden, a workout with some bread dough or a hammer and nails.

Mid-Two

You can teach a mid-Two a little about giving but it isn't easy, for getting is more his style. Now he's beginning to learn right from wrong and like one of our favorites may say, "No, no, no" while emptying a bottle of Chanel No. 5 on her overalls.

There may be stages now, yours and his, when you're just getting through the days as best you can, like a reformed alcoholic, one hour at a time, one day at a time. This is when you need a sitter for an hour every afternoon, or a job on the lunchtime shift of the neighborhood restaurant or some volunteer work, so you won't take your child so seriously. You need a rest every day, a Mother's

Pickup (page 75) and to play a game to see how many times you can say "yes" instead of "no."

As always when you have a problem, you need to keep a daily chart. Record what time he fell apart and when you did, what you both ate, how many nos you gave in a day (and how many you needn't have given). Sometime you can see patterns and therefore solutions, but since it takes so long to chart and figure you may see his behavior improve anyway. That's because he's nearly Three.

Three

No one wants to be as good as a Three. This child becomes an accessory before the fact, instead of after it, and therefore so angelic you can see what a fine mother you are. He'll be even better if you tell him exactly what you expect of him and why, before he asks.

A Three is not unlike one of our teenagers who was outraged at a certain job required of her, until we explained the need to do it.

"You know, Mother," she flounced, "even a teenager will do something if she has a reason."

At Three, a child can connect kindness with courtliness and likes to practice good manners. Help your child get along well with company by having frequent visitors and telling them your house rules before they start a game. Above all, teach your child now how to share. It's a hard lesson to learn, but it's the basis of generosity and fundamental to love.

There are some pitfalls in discipline now, for your child may act so adult you forget he's just a baby. This is when you can overreact to his misbehavior and catch yourself using the same angry words your parents used with you when you were young.

The methods you use to discipline your Three will affect his values for years.

If, for instance, dessert is a reward for a clean plate then he'll think he should be bribed to eat.

If you say a shot won't hurt when it will or you'll be home soon when you won't, he'll doubt your word.

If you promise money for a job he'll put a price tag on family cooperation.

If you put property rights ahead of personal rights, you'll rear a materialistic child.

If you take the blame for his mistakes he won't learn accountability, and

If you don't make a big fuss over him sometime, he won't feel he's worth the trouble.

Four

The Four (known as the out-of-bounds Four) is as funny as the Two, but he's more rational, because he talks so well and because he often lets his conscience be his guide. Now he needs to be the big shot: faking bravado, telling outrageous lies and playing grown-up. When our son asked, "May I call you by your first name?" we answered, "If you want to, but you're the only boy in the world who can call me Mother." So Mother it was.

Your child needs more special duties now, more independence and wider boundaries every few months to reward his reliability.

He changes so quickly that what you think is clever handling one month, or even one week, will be a witless bore the next. Never continue any job or reward or routine to the point of boredom, either his or yours. Today you might draw a fine Goodness Chart on which to paste gold stars; next week you might start a Job Jar (page 146) and days. later you may change his nap and bath schedule.

He'll be stubborn quite often now and insist on doing things his way. It helps to remember that you are bigger than he is and if not smarter, at least you know more. You're still Big Mama and what you say goes.

Five

A Five can meet his own high standards as long as you let him get enough sleep, good food, plenty of praise for good behavior and plenty of love all the time. Serious arguments start now and you must remember: it takes two to make a stubborn child, and the other one is you. Try not to make a big issue of something that doesn't matter.

Parents and policemen have a similar technique. Both operate best when one of their team is the "good detective." Although you and your husband need to be consistent in your policy, your approach will be different. If both of you are tough at the same time, your child will feel abandoned, and if both of you are soft, he'll have trouble handling criticisms later from other people.

The positive side of discipline is the anchor for you both and the basis for the discipline you give in puberty, when the whole cycle is repeated and reinforced. Both of you will have some bad times—always will. We can remember once shrieking at our Five, "Damn It! Quit That or I Will Hang You by Your Thumbs in the Doorway Until Tuesday!" Whereupon her blond-haired visitor rolled her big blue eyes and said thoughtfully, "My mother always boils us in oil."

Six

A Six is an interested, interesting, reasonably obedient child and, like the Texas politician, he knows you go along to get along. This is the age of conformity and he needs to please his buddies, his teacher and the neighbor lady, most of whom seem to have your standards, thank goodness. This is the time to appeal to your child's courtliness by having him open the door for you. To do this, always stand in front of it without saying anything until he opens it out of impatience and then slip through first. Thank him profusely as you do for all good manners and he'll think it was his idea.

When school begins, you'll forget most of his poor behavior and feel a certain amount of confusion and shame over the discipline you gave at one time or another.

At least mothers have improved since our pal Maria Francis Child said, "Call me modern if you will," for her opposition to spanking and advised other punishment.

"Do not shut the child in the closet, but simply tie him in an armchair when he has been naughty."

Now we use whipped cream.

Boundaries

Motherhood can be fairly easy or it can be quite anxious, depending on the limits you set. We set quite a few.

Childproofing the Child

A newborn can be very strong and can flip over without a warning, as we remember to our amazement when our hungry Mali rolled over to her back in a rage at only five days old. As a practice, strap your child in place on the changing table or in the infant seat and later in the high chair, the car seat and the stroller.

As for harnessing a toddler, what begins as a safety measure becomes no more than a leash. We would oppose it totally (perhaps because it looks so demeaning) if it weren't for that horrendous trip alone with two pre-Twos, when one disappeared at the airport. Ordinarily, a mother should set aside more time for her errands and carry fewer packages. A child's hand is much nicer to hold.

Just as you teach your child that "hot" can be dangerous long before he tries to cook, you also should teach him that streets are not playgrounds—especially if you live in the city. You'll watch your child carefully, but by mid-Two, he can understand the concept of danger. Let him help you fill a paper bag with some impersonal objects—twigs, a plastic teacup, an inflated balloon—and leave it in the street for a few minutes at rush hour. A bag of breakage for him to examine is a graphic lesson in caution.

When your child is Three, you can trust him on the sidewalk if you draw his boundaries in chalk on the cement or on the ground with a stick. These barriers will be as difficult for him to cross as a chasm. Expand these boundaries every few months, according to his own expanding sense of responsibility.

We don't think any pre-Six should cross streets alone. Any streets. If the traffic is very light he'll forget to watch for cars, and if it's heavy he'll have trouble noticing everything at once. A young child, no matter how bright, has trouble gauging distance in relation to speed.

The House

Block the top and the bottom of any stairs or you'll be running up and down all day to keep track of your child.

Use a gate in any doorway you don't want him to cross. You also can slip a sock on the knob, fastened with a rubber band, which a child can't open (and possibly you can't either).

At the start of each day, put your wastebaskets above his head, which is much easier than picking up the trash, and check the floor for small items which could choke a child.

Have no matches or cigarette lighters within reach, plug empty electric sockets with blanks and band the head-splitting edges of low tables with foam tape, especially if they have marble or glass tops. Lay rugs over skidproof pads and jam books into their shelves so tightly a child can't remove them.

Realistically, a child can respect no more than one treasure in a room. The rest of your breakables can be handled two ways. Either stay in the same room as your child and say "No" to him and his friends every time an ornament is touched or put your treasures out of reach. In either case a child will learn not to touch them when he's Three—and not before. Naturally for us the easy way won every time, but occasionally we think you should take an ornament from its shelf, talk to your child about it, let him look at it, smell it and caress it to see why in the world you like it so much. Then put it on a higher shelf so he won't investigate it on his own. In this way your pre-Three can be trusted as long as twenty minutes awake and alone in one room.

The Kitchen

The kitchen is a pre-Two's favorite playroom. To keep it safe, turn the pot handles inward on the stove and boil and fry foods on the back burners and simmer on the front ones. Pick up broken glass with a wet paper towel. It works like glue, if not like magic.

Use and immediately discard those household cleaners you don't need regularly. Store the rest in a high cupboard, locked if your child is a climber. Babies taste new foods regularly and drink juice from odd-shaped bottles, so sampling a little lemon-flavored furniture polish isn't as peculiar to a child as it would be to you. Three tablespoons of it can kill a One and a fingerful of dishwasher compound is nearly fatal at that age. There are a quarter-million lethal household products available, most of which aren't labeled poison.

A young child is especially intrigued by some of your favorites—whiskey, cigarettes and vitamins—all of which can be toxic and also should be kept out of reach.

The Bathroom

A bathroom requires special precautions for no place has so many lures in so small an area. Your child will turn on the shower (and frighten himself witless), so, if it's possible, reduce the hot-water thermostat to medium.

Keep any razor out of reach and all medicines in a locked cupboard. Throw away obsolete drugs and store the rest in childproof safety bottles. Your child, as smart as he is, can't understand why sweet cough syrup is all right one day and *verboten* the next.

Because a pre-Three is sure to lock himself in the bathroom one day, or flush a diaper down the toilet or squiggle pictures from the toothpaste tube, we think it unwise to let him go there alone. When you have time to join him, let him flush and brush as long as he wants. This curbs a little of his curiosity.

The Car

The most careful, sensible parents often forget about limits the minute they step into an automobile. We can't think of any place you need them more.

With more than one thousand young children killed in automobile accidents every year, you don't have the right to relax these boundaries. Your child is irreplaceable.

Strap an infant in a car bed that is wedged lengthwise between the front and back seats. A baby held in a passenger's arms is much less safe in an impact. The lighter a person weighs, the farther he'll be thrown forward in a sudden stop.

As your child gets older, he graduates to a car seat, then a safety harness and when he's forty pounds or Four, a seat belt, but every one of them should be government certified. Safety is the prime advantage of all these restraints, but not the only one. They also keep your child from blocking the rear-view mirror or yelling in your ear.

If you have more family (or car-pool children) than you have seat belts you must install more belts, but if your child won't wear his seat belt,

refuse to start the motor. Tell him why, but only once, and don't say another word until he surrenders. After a few of these silent scenes, which never last more than ten minutes, he'll cooperate out of boredom. If he unbuckles when you're driving the treatment is the same. Pull over to the side of the road and wait. That's the way we learned to wear seat belts ourselves.

The Light Side

Every child tries to rule the house, but you'll never meet the child who really wants to, and you'll pity the one who does, for he is never happy.

Although parents are in charge, we do think you should respect your child enough to listen to his ideas, especially on family projects. Even if his suggestions are bad, he'll like to examine the options too and learn that he's the very important, very junior member and not the focus of the group.

Some families hold structured weekly meetings but for us informality works best, in a setting where everyone has a full chance to speak. We never put a question to a vote however, unless we don't care what happens (or like a Chicago alderman, we know what the outcome is going to be).

We think you'll find this positive approach to discipline will let your child make a few decisions, so it will be easier for him to accept the many you make.

Still, every mother should shrink herself in half and imagine what it feels like to be ordered around all day. The more a person is told what to do, the more recalcitrant he grows. Dignity becomes so precious that your child will stall every request and say no to every order, even as he complies.

Your orders will range from the simple request to the urgent command and not one should be given unless you're willing to enforce it immediately.

A child learns quickly how many times you're willing to repeat the order before you mean what you say. It may be once or it may be seven times. If you shorten your fuse he'll believe you the first time. Otherwise you'll be a nag.

Quiet Responses

A child is often blamed for a noisy household, but it's the mother who decides how noisy it will be. A lively family is a joy, but senseless clamor eventually shatters everyone's nerves. There are ways to avoid it, all hinging on respect. If you whisper when he shouts, the loudest child will lower his voice the way you do when your boss has laryngitis. If he doesn't, tell him you can't hear for all the noise. Eventually, you may shout less yourself.

Goodness Chart

Goodness deserves recognition. A chart full of gold stars on the bulletin board guarantees compliments. Use any accomplishments you want, but not too many.

Easy Obedience

Discipline is easiest if you take a positive point of view. It's never "Time for your bath," but "It's time for your duck to have a swim," and it isn't "Bedtime," but "Let's hurry to bed so we can read a long story instead of a short one."

Although your maneuvers get more sophisticated, the positive technique still works—even, we were surprised to find, for a Seventeen.

Advance Notice

A Two especially needs a ten-minute warning before bed or a bath, a meal or a walk, so that he can adjust to the idea. After that, you should have a "Let's go/no-nonsense" attitude he can respect, although he may try you out with a game of procrastination. At this point, resort to body English. Pick him up, give him a smile and get on your way.

Warning

Every child finds obedience hard sometimes, but there are a couple of techniques to make it easier.

We found it best to give our children a stern "To the count of six" or whatever, but the punishment was never specified, which made it more dicey.

Choose whatever number you think will give your child time to finish the job, counting slower or faster so he can obey. Or using the same principle our Creole aunt would threaten, "I'm going to *claquer* you!"

We quickly did as we were told, since we didn't know what would happen and now our children do the same. And we still don't know what it means.

Indoor Summons

Unless you think your child is in danger, don't go to him when he yells. If you hear "Come see how many doodlebugs I caught for you," just call to say where you are and say absolutely nothing more. He'll come to you.

If you want to talk with your child and it's not an emergency, call his name and say where you are and if he answers, "What?" or "Why?," don't answer back. Sooner or later he'll learn to call, "Coming, Mom" (in ten to twelve years), and in the meantime you still will have a little more peace than most mothers, and probably more doodlebugs.

Outdoor Summons

No mother can call loud enough to be heard by her child a half block away. You either will sound like a shrew, or the other children will mimic you and embarrass your child. Use a whistle or a bell instead.

Instant Obedience

Every mother has a special tone to warn her child of danger, which requires instant obedience. This is the sharp, serious voice that keeps him on the curb or away from the hot spigot and if it doesn't, you should give a single swat on the backside to emphasize what you say. If you use the same tone to tell your child to put down a vase or pick up his toys you'll dilute your control when you need it.

Allowance

We include this subject in discipline, not because we think it should be there, but because so many other people do.

To us, an allowance is just another way to give a little love—not essential for a pre-Six but nice for him to have. We think you should remember that the gift of an allowance, like any gift, has no strings attached and should never be given as a reward nor withheld as a punishment.

A child shouldn't be paid for communal work any more than you should be paid for driving the car pool or your husband for cutting the grass. This is the difference between a family and a business.

The allowance your child receives is his own, to be used as he likes. Whether he wants to spend it on candy or sock it away in a sock or throw it in the gutter is his business. Although you will encourage some thrift, he needs to experiment for himself. However, since a preschool child is so likely to lose his money and because we don't believe in giving children much in the first place, we keep our stipends very low.

A Four will enjoy perhaps a nickel a week, graduating to a dime by Six, when he finally can begin to appreciate money. After that, we follow the advice of a pediatrician who gives her nine children annual increments of five cents a week at every birthday, so that a Seven receives fifteen cents, an Eight gets twenty cents. This regulated schedule, of whatever sum you set, eliminates any whining about who deserves raises and when.

Making Up

Most quarrels with your child are over in minutes, but some arguments are so angry they can fester for hours.

Whether you're right—or wrong, as mothers often are—you surely said more than you meant, for which you should apologize quickly and, since you're the adult, you should apologize first. After that comes the big make-up.

A Three will welcome a quiet visit at bedtime and a chance to mend the ties. We found darkness sheds a special light on lovers and small children, unlocking words too tender to say by day and softening any tough ones. Now he can understand why you got so mad and forgive you for getting as mad as you did. Somehow what was inexplicable to him by day becomes quite sensible by night and a problem that was hopeless to you in the morning has a fresh solution.

The Dark Side

No matter how well you handle your child, neither of you will be perfect, even some of the time. There will be enough weeping and punishments to make you appreciate the good days.

If you think there isn't enough sunshine you may be saying "No" too many times. To give you less to fuss about, simplify the rules of the house and remember: Your child's sense of injustice is more acute now than it ever will be again in his life. It takes great wisdom to fit the punishment to the crime.

Fussiness

If an infant is fussy, he may be bored, for not even a baby enjoys staying in one place for longer than a half hour. Move him often, from tummy to back/ to the bathtub/ the carriage/ the *very* gently sloped infant seat/ the carryall/ the blanket on the floor or a rest in your arms, with or without a feeding.

When a Two won't eat, won't take a bottle, won't play—and won't stop fussing, take his temperature, for he may be sick. If he's simply out of sorts, put him quickly to bed so he may glue himself together in privacy and without any special treats. If a child is given a lollipop when he's cross he'll think poor behavior is rewarded.

A Four to Six gets sent outdoors to run back and forth a dozen times, then is retired to his room to rest with books or records.

The Corner

By mid-One the bloom of rosy motherhood gets paler every day, and it's time for some negative discipline. Corners must have been invented for this.

When your child disobeys, escort him to The Corner or simply put him on a chair, holding his shoulders in place the first few times until he'll go there when he's told. Expect a mid-One to last no more than two minutes, a Six no more than ten.

Whining, Foul Language, Back Chat

Some of us can stand a child who whines or who talks back and some of us can stand one who uses nasty language, but no mother should tolerate all of these by the time he is Four. In the manner of our foremothers and after fair warning, we think you should march him to the sink, rub a bar of wet soap in his mouth, rinse it quickly and give a kiss when he stops crying.

Bickering and Wrangling

Every household has its fractiousness, but you can make some of it less likely most of the time and refuse to put up with the rest.

We finally have learned it's easier to prevent a fight than to settle one. That's why it's best for Fours—visitors or brothers and sisters—to be interrupted every half hour with a small adventure, a story or something to eat. Sixes can last almost an hour without wrangling.

Fist Fights

Children must learn to resolve their differences for themselves—up to a point. A fist fight is that point, we think, particularly if one child is bigger than the other.

Separate your fighters, putting them in different rooms, for it's hard to fight an absent enemy.

A Three begins to understand that words start fights—and stop them. When all of you are calm (in about ten minutes), talk over the quarrel to show each child the other's point of view—but never talk so long that you have a rematch.

The discussion can be such a bore a Six may find a fist fight rarely worth the bother.

Neighborhood Squabbles

If your child is in a neighborhood quarrel, listen to both sides as the arbiter, not the champion. The mother who automatically believes her child is right is as unfair as the one who always takes the word of an outsider. Each situation is different. If you must punish do it with dispatch, discretion and, of course, in private.

Biting

Even at six months, a child discovers he can bite you, pull your hair and kick while you change him. It won't be funny at all at eighteen months and then he must be corrected. We remember a sweet and simpering Two who would admonish her squalling baby brother with "Temper, temper," even as her teeth marks flared red on his arm. She never did it again after we put her own arm in her own mouth and pushed her own chin up until she bit it. This same technique works for hair pullers and pinchers too, but kickers go to the corner.

Tantrums

A child has a tantrum when he's tired and wherever he can get the most attention: on the escalator at the department store or crossing the street while you're holding two packages and an infant. Haul him to the quietest area you can find and let him alone. Even if he holds his breath until he turns blue he'll stop if you're not looking.

Strangers aren't worth such dramatics. When he has contained himself, give your affection freely. There will be many fewer scenes if you run your errands in the morning, when he isn't tired, and also if you are careful to give him twenty minutes of single-minded attention every day—before he cries for it.

Lying

A child who lies is either afraid of you—or he's Four. For a Four, just roll your eyes and listen to the brags, but other ages will stay honest easier if you ask the right questions. After the curtain is pulled to the floor (again), ask, "How did that happen?," not "Who did it?" or "Why," since you know who did it and who cares why. When a child is given a yes/no choice he may try to lie his way out. For a serious lie, wash his mouth with soap, but if he tells the truth, congratulate him, for this is how he learns that misdemeanors are less important than lying, which can become habitual with the crafty Five.

Jealousy

We remember holding three bottles every afternoon—one for the new baby, another for the two-year-old sister and with a stretch of our fingers, a tiny bottle for the doll, who, her mistress said, was very, very jealous.

If your child is mad because there's a baby in the house help him to talk about it and keep him busy with more diversion and exercise. Show lots of love and show it before he falls apart. If your children nap at different times—though tough on you—you can give them each individual attention. You should know though that no matter how much attention you give your firstborn, he'll never quite forgive you for having another baby, no matter how close the children become. The emotional demands of your first child are much greater, so you must learn to give more, and give most of it when the younger one isn't around to get jealous too. On the days when jealousy almost consumes your child, he may be tired or coming down with another cold.

Grievous Behavior

Anger, like all intimate emotions, should be a part of a child's life and he shouldn't be protected from it. A spanking is a mother's automatic reaction to anger and a child can accept it, for it is a sign of love.

Only spank a pre-Three if he runs in the street or plays with the stove or matches or. touches the power tools. A Three to Six may need to be spanked occasionally, with a "pantsdowner" given for extremely naughty behavior. Use your bare hand, not a hairbrush or a wooden spoon, so you can gauge your force, but don't ever spank your child if you think you're at the point of absolute rage. It's so easy to hurt a child and the guilt you feel certainly will hurt you. If you're that angry your punishment should be later, tough and verbal.

Finally, never postpone a spanking until your temper is completely calm or until you get your husband to do the job for you. A spanking given in cold deliberation will frighten and confuse a child for he sees no love in it.

Stealing

There is a little larceny in anyone's heart, but you can expect a Four, Five or Six to put it into practice at least once. Whether he does it the second time depends on how you treat it the first time.

If you act as if it were a joke he'll steal again, and if you cover up for him he won't learn to be responsible for himself.

We think any child who steals from someone's home must apologize to the owner privately, but in person, and return the loot. If he steals from a store, however, we think he should pay for it with his own money—and by mail, since only the most hardhearted manager can resist a weepy little child and that would undo the lesson before it's learned.

It was our Kate who, at Five, coveted a fifteen-cent art gum eraser from the stationers the way we might yearn for French perfume. When begging didn't get her the eraser, she simply carried it home in her underpants and surprisingly forgot all about it until it bounced out of her dirty clothes that night.

Through tears she had to dictate a letter of apology for us to write, copy the words on her ruled paper, tape fifteen of her nineteen pennies onto the paper and mail the letter herself. The store manager was so pleased at her display of "honesty" that he gave the story to a newspaper and wanted to give Kate a dozen erasers too.

We hid the newspaper, declined the reward and witnessed the overnight reformation of a little girl who learned that a shoplifter's career is not a happy one.

This may sound like tough treatment, but honesty is a tough lesson to learn.

Playing with Fire

Fire stirs such primitive emotions you can expect your child to be fascinated by it and the more it's forbidden, the more fascinated he'll be.

When our first Five played with matches one Sunday morning (to the delight of his little sister), each was spanked by both parents and marched to the closest fire station for a tour and a tough lecture by the fireman.

Afterward we let Ramon help build fires in the barbecue and said he could strike matches in our presence if the itch ever got too bad. It never did again.

With trepidation we let our later girls light fires at Five, under supervision, and for them the fascination bordered on disinterest.

Manners

There are days and weeks, as we all have learned, when only sex and good manners hold a marriage together. With a child there is only good manners.

The *Babees' Book*, a collection of medieval etiquette for children, advises them to stand until told to sit and "Do not claw your flesh or lean against a post."

"Keep from picking your nose, your teeth or your nails at meal time," it said, and advised them not to eat their food with a knife.

Mothers still are giving the same rules today, with about the same effect.

A Three likes to learn the reason for every rule of etiquette, although some seem pretty silly. When a child sets the table, for instance, tell him the knife blade faces inward so it won't hurt the person at the next place. And that's the essence of good manners. Nothing should be done or said that could possibly hurt someone else, especially someone's feelings. This is why a child shares his toys, tiptoes when someone is sleeping and stands to show a visitor how welcome he is.

Don't let us mislead you. Your child won't have truly good manners by first grade, but if he's been exposed to them early they will be natural to him later.

Sharing

If you want your child to have friends he must

have good manners, which is the reason he must learn to take turns and share toys.

To a child, a toy is an extension of himself, the way money is to some adults. Unlike an adult, however, he has no finesse at all when he grabs his playmate's wagon and this brings grief every time.

A child finds it equally hard to share power or status, which is why he resents a new baby or a sitter or a visitor. Chickens and children know you can shift up or down in the pecking order but never sideways.

Teach your child to share just as you teach him anything else—slowly, by example and with a few tricks. Start as early as mid-One, just for practice, but expect little success for at least another year. If a rocking horse is in dispute between mid-Ones, only distraction will work, but mid-Twos may regulate their turns begrudgingly with a timer—a device that will work for years.

By Three, you'll find a cupcake teaches sharing quicker than anything else. Give one child the knife to divide it—and the other child first choice. It will be cut exactly at midpoint, without complaints from either party.

Conversation

Good conversation is like city traffic, one of us discovered as a child. Words are slipped in when the path is clear, but each interruption is like a little crash.

Drive safely.

Since your child will start interrupting as soon as he starts talking, he needs to be taught the stop-and-go of conversation, learning when to speak and when to listen.

It's easier for him to take turns when he's having a conversation with just one person, especially someone his own age, but it will be years (would you believe, a decade?) before he can take part in a conversation easily with two or three adults. He should start learning this fine art early,

since it doesn't come naturally.

You begin to teach it when the two of you are visiting alone, by using clear diction and a pleasant voice, looking him in the eye when you speak and letting him talk as much as you. Slowly he'll understand that you pause when you finish a thought and that's when he has his say.

When you have company you'll want to include your child in some of the conversation before you send him out to play, but treat him as a participant, not as a performer. This is basic courtesy. If you were in a room with two other people who wouldn't talk to you, you'd feel excluded and if they talked to no one but you (or only talked about you), you'd be embarrassed. A child is no different.

Whether you're talking to your child alone or when you have company, you can't permit him to interrupt constantly. If you do you'll catch that most common disease of motherhood: prattle. It creeps up on you slowly until sometime after 6,413 interruptions you realize that you can't finish a sentence, let alone a thought, even when there's no child around to interrupt. Having had virulent cases of prattle ourselves, we think you'll find it easier to stop interruptions before they become a habit. To do it, touch your finger to his lips when he interrupts and keep talking until you've finished your thought. He has to learn that anything short of a disaster will keep a few minutes.

Telephone conversations are a special problem. The phone is every mother's salvation, but your child will find it hard to believe you're having a conversation when you're not opening your mouth. If you have a running conversation with him while you're on the phone he'll think that phone calls are meant to be interrupted and this will irritate your friends. Avoid some of the problem by using the telephone when your child is asleep or outside, and let him color the morning comics during any others.

Tea-party Manners

A mid-One learns his table manners best at tea parties. We used a tiny, cheap and very proper china tea set, the kind that pleases a mother as much as her child, and greeted our first daughter after her nap with a proper "How do you do, Mrs. Jones." She shook the paws of Mr. Bear and Mrs. Giraffe and sat down at the low table which had a napkin, a plate and a cup and saucer at each place.

The cookies were in the middle, the sponge was out of sight, the juice was in the cups and Kate poured from the teapot as needed. She also graciously ate the cookies for Mr. Bear and Mrs. Giraffe to spare them the embarrassment of leaving their food untouched.

Mealtime Manners

We once heard a father of four ask a Chinese restauranteur how his children ever learned to feed themselves with chopsticks, to which Dr. Chang replied, "You've seen the way American children eat spaghetti with a fork? It's the same way. Not very well."

A Three is ready to have some meals with his parents. Conversation and good table manners are hard to choreograph and harder to perform. Whenever your child joins you for a Sunday dinner, or any special occasion, he'll behave better if he uses the same kind of plate and silverware you do. If you use candlelight and ask him questions (as you would of any company), he'll behave with some gentility. A Five should eat with parents as often as possible, for manners, like tennis, only can improve with practice. He certainly won't learn them magically on the day the grand duchess of the family arrives for dinner.

Company Manners

Your Three learns to make his manners quicker if you let him spend the first half hour in the living room when you have company, because example always teaches best.

Here he'll learn to shake hands, take coats and pass the cheese and crackers. Eventually your child begins to see that party manners are so natural and nice, they're good enough for every day.

By Six he should be able to talk with your guests almost as comfortably as he does with his own, but hopefully with more decorum.

Car Manners

Just as your child needs to learn the art of conversation, so must he learn the art of silence. It can become essential when you and your husband are driving on a freeway. For us, hand signals worked best.

When you bring your thumb and forefinger almost together: quiet.

When you squeeze them or clap your hands: absolute quiet.

And when your child claps his hands for you, it's time to do a little listening yourself. With your good example, he probably won't overuse this privilege.

These same signals work when you're on the telephone.

Telephone Manners

It takes a Four to talk well on the telephone, but he only should answer it when he knows how. Your friends deserve that courtesy.

Begin teaching him at mid-Three by ringing his toy telephone for him to say something like "Hello, the Johnson residence, Billy speaking."

He can answer your phone when he gets this adept, and by Six he should be able to chat a minute and be careful enough to remember most messages.

Too Many Whys

A child asks "Why" for two reasons. Either he asks once, because he wants an answer, or he asks over and over again, because he wants attention. To break the cycle, give an answer as detailed as you think he can understand, then have your child explain it back to you. This turns a whiny why into a conversation.

Independence

There is nothing instant about learning.

Your baby masters a skill by repeating it over and over, the same way he one day will learn to compute numbers or drive a car. Learning is layered and each new skill is built upon the last. The more you teach a child, the easier he is to handle, the less he whines and the less he says "no."

You can't force your child to learn, but if you put him in a situation where it's easy, where he is regarded as a capable person, his abilities will soar.

He learns not by watching, but by doing. He does need encouragement but more than that, he needs simple, step-by-step, eye-level demonstrations, slow of movement and of speech.

Even after he learns a skill, he'll need at least twice as much time as you to do the job. Try not to hurry him, for the child who is rushed regularly, like the child who is often corrected or ridiculed, will perform only under stress—never very well and with little joy.

Any adult has learned a skill, like cooking, and then has burned the pot. A child needs the right to err too, without making a production out of every mistake. Regressions are common in all areas and ages, but they are more obvious in children. Praise the new skills and ignore the lapses. A positive parent seldom produces a negative child.

Remember—the time you spend shaping an independent child will result in a teenager self-reliant and self-confident enough to be a giver, not a taker.

Coordination

No child under Six is as proud of his mental skills as he is of his physical ones. He measures himself by the way he handles his body.

Your baby's play is work to him, from the day he is born. He builds every move on his gradual understanding of distance, size, shape and quantity.

It takes this accumulation of knowledge for your child to turn over or stand, but when he finally triumphs he will look more exultant than an Olympic winner. Nothing is as exciting to a child as making the difficult possible.

One of our best friends, small and slight at Ten, is completely in tune with his body. This isn't, we're sure, because his parents are athletic, which they're not, but because they refused to let his delicate build hamper him. Instead they gave him an environment that let him have a thousand small victories a day.

Even at Two he was encouraged to throw pebbles at a brick wall, hammer nails into soft wood and climb up and down a stepladder, not as a show-off, but as a worker. He operated alone, although a parent was near to keep him in bounds and they praised some of his efforts, but never all, so he could believe their sincerity.

Today his coordination is so sure that he plays goalie on the neighborhood teenage soccer team and his self-confidence is so solid he thinks it only fitting.

Since every person has a different ability to run, swim, climb, aim and catch, your child may need more practice and more help than another, but don't work with him if you grow irritated at his ineptitude. His skills are a measure of his ability, not yours.

A child should be encouraged to work in his own fashion, as baffling as his approach may be to you, for he seldom tries anything by himself that he can't accomplish fairly soon. He does need you to show him a new skill, like jumping, as soon as he has learned an old one, like walking.

When you can help your child be dextrous, you are giving him self-confidence and self-reliance.

Infancy
The more a baby squirms, the easier it will be for him to inch about, but he needs help with his coordination. Give him a daily workout (page 64) and place him on a hard, safe surface, like a playpen floor, so he can roll over easier. A slightly sloped infant seat, while making no physical demands, stimulates his curiosity, which propels a child to move more than anything else.

Grasping is a baby's first skill. He instinctively will clutch your finger at birth but he'll do it on purpose at about two months. Give toys that are easy to hold. A small doughnut shape is precisely what he needs to hook his finger and thumb, rather than a large, stuffed animal.

Three Months
You can develop his arms and legs better by increasingly strenuous daily exercises. Hold out your forefingers and let him pull himself to a standing

position on your lap—an easier place than his crib—for as long as he likes. This exercise strengthens his body, but he's the only one who knows when his back is ready to feel the strain of sitting and standing and you shouldn't hurry him.

He'll learn to use his body better if you put some toys just slightly out of his reach. If they're colorful he'll try harder to grab them. By four months, he clasps his arms like pincers to clutch the bigger toys. As he develops better coordination between the things he sees and the way he handles them, he is learning the same hand-to-eye skill he'll one day need to read and write.

Six Months
At this age you should offer anything to your child squarely to his middle, so he can decide for himself whether he's right-handed, left-handed or ambidextrous.

When your baby learns to sit, he'll topple over often, since he doesn't know how to lie down again. Once he feels comfortable sitting, he's ready to play So Big. "How big is Jamie? Soooo big," you say, stretching your arms until pretty soon he'll hold up his arms too.

In the next few months you will teach him to crawl by getting down on the floor with him, giving him plenty of room and letting him go in any direction he wants. He'll use the furniture to pull himself upright, but we've never seen a baby who could sit back down the first few times without help. If you clip the back of his knees with one hand while you catch his back with the other he'll learn to fall squarely on his bottom.

Until a baby is about nine months, everything looks flat from above, which causes him to crawl from sofa to floor as if they were both on the same level.

If your child is a climber before he has learned depth perception—our sympathy. You'll be his constant companion. A doorway swing, a walker and a playpen help contain a vertical child.

Nine Months
If you don't believe your baby uses a lot of fuel now follow him around the house for a half hour,

doing whatever he does: sitting up, falling down, crawling, lifting. Even discounting the size of the objects he deals with in relation to his size, you will be exhausted by the work—and he won't be fazed.

We think that teaching a nine-month-old to climb up and down stairs is a smart use of time. It's helpful to you and safer for him and makes him feel proud and brave. You will, of course, lock the gate when you can't go with him, for you have to be ready for anything with this age.

You also have to be careful with his boundaries even if you live in an apartment, as one wacky caper taught us. Ramon, who practically lived in his walker, got a good-by kiss from his father and then noticed that the door was left slightly ajar. In a flash he scooted down the hall, straight to his friend's door, where he pounded, was admitted and was eating his friend's breakfast bacon before we could put on some clothes. Time: two minutes. A lesser known reason for mothers to dress before breakfast.

One
If a One isn't walking, he'll be a most adept crawler and the more adept he is, the less reason he has to walk. When he does start, you'll be rightfully wary, for his propensity for trouble will skyrocket, and you'll be weary too, from listing to starboard on those shuffling walks, stretching your forefinger low enough for him to reach.

Fifteen Months
Once a baby can walk, he wants to do more and more with his upright body: run, walk backward, jump. Between his first and second year he'll master these after a thousand falls, a few goose eggs and maybe some stitches.

When his legs are steady, take him in a stroller to different terrains—grass, cement or sand—for short walks there. A child has so much to discover.

Now he loves the push-and-pull toys, because they give a sense of mastery. When our Meg was this age she found a small, twenty-five cent wheelbarrow in a junk store which she wheeled everywhere, precariously, carrying all her goods with her. It was a pastime that lasted for at least a year and taught coordination better than any toy we ever saw.

Mid-One
This child is ready for a wheel toy he can push with his feet, for he is peripatetic now. He likes to splash in calm water—a lake or a pool—but often won't lift his face if he falls in it. For this reason, you must watch him very, very carefully and empty the wading pool immediately after use—a practice to continue for at least two years or whenever a younger child visits.

Two
Whether your Two is a swashbuckler or a dreamer, he needs every chance to climb, both in and out of the house. Climbing equipment develops such coordination of the arms and legs and such self-confidence that it's worth a long walk to a playground if you have none. In any case, your child needs to walk every day, as much for the exercise as the enrichment.

Mid-Two
A mid-Two is a whiz with his wheel toy but he probably isn't ready for a real tricycle for another six months, unless he can alternate feet when he climbs stairs. This is the skill he needs to pedal a trike.

Nothing makes a mid-Two feel more like a daredevil than a chance to balance along a low brick wall—a compulsion to play Harold Lloyd that some of us have to this day.

He loves a rocking horse, for it's so sexy to bounce on it, and the bigger the bounce the sexier the horse.

Three

By Three, your child should be able to go on twenty-to-thirty minute round-trip walks, and will like to play outdoors: climbing, running, triking, rolling a hoop and wrestling. He can toss, bounce and kick a ball (but not catch it). In the bathtub he may try to blow bubbles with his face barely in the water.

Four

A Four has mastered the tricycle and can move on to a scooter—a short-lived love. He likes a rope ladder and tries to slide down the biggest slide in the playground—the one with the three bumps. Despite the equalization of the sexes, boys are more likely to use wrestling as a proof of their strength, and for them an old mattress is ideal. So is a punching bag, but boxing gloves are silly for a pre-Six. As for walking, a Four can go as fast as you but only in short spurts.

A Four needs to feel capable for he compares himself constantly to his friends and needs to be as adept as they.

Five

A Five finally is able to pump a swing, if you teach him. It takes an amazing combination of physical skills. He likes to show how far he can jump, how high he can climb a tree (not very), how fast he can run, how long he can skip. He can't, however, compete in games, no matter how big and self-confident he feels.

Six

A Six isn't ready for competitive sports either, but he can take part in a game as complicated as baseball, if he plays with kind folks, like his parents. He's ready now for pitch and catch and likes to bat a ball, roll an automobile tire and float and swim under water and perhaps can pass a beginner's swim test.

A Six may be ready for a small, twenty-inch bicycle, if he can ride it on a sidewalk, in a park or any place completely free of people or cars. He can't be responsible for balance and safety simultaneously.

Having put training wheels on the first bikes—and removed them almost immediately—we're sure of this: A Six is too old for a four-wheel bike. He'll have a few more spills without the trainers, but he'll learn quicker and feel much braver.

Exercises and Games

Infant's Daily Workout

Changing time is best to exercise your baby. Hold his feet as you pedal his legs gently, and eventually he'll return the pressure against your hands.

Catch Finger

Your baby—from three months to three years—will like this game.

Hold your forefinger so he can try to catch it before you snap it down. He'll laugh greatly when you let him win, which should be at least half the time.

Crawling

The quickest way for a child to crawl is for you to teach him. Get alongside him on the floor and simply show him how, first by crawling yourself. Next lift his left hand and right foot together, then the other hand and foot, locomotive style.

You probably would have learned to dance by yourself, but it was quicker and easier when you had a partner.

Climbing Stairs

At nine months, a mountain is for climbing.

When your firstborn begins to crawl and has decent depth perception, teach him to climb up and down stairs, even if you have to go to someone else's house to do it. He'll be one less package for you to carry and he'll feel very important too.

This skill is taught best by crawling upstairs yourself, which your child will imitate, even as he laughs. Any child loves this scramble, with never a thought to getting back. At the top he may cry (or fall backward), until he learns to slither down on his tummy. This is taught gradually, a few steps at a time, by literally moving his arms and legs backward, then carrying him the rest of the way, for he'll just want to go upstairs again. With some practice, your child will climb to the top and come slithering down at a terrific speed, controlled by catching onto the balustrades.

Even when he starts toddling, he still may scramble up and down the stairs on his belly for months before he dares to walk up a step at a time. When your child is a little bolder—usually by Two—you'll see him teeter at the top, then cautiously walk down—a great sign of derring-do. We almost negated the adventure by saying each time, as our child swayed from tread to tread, "Don't fall down the steps, Katy!"

This was silly, since she didn't want to fall and a warning couldn't have stopped her. As we learned, if you're going to broaden your boundaries you'll have to broaden your faith.

Walking

You'll want your baby to walk early because he wants this wonderful new view of the world. He can get it sooner if you don't carry him everywhere and if you bicycle his legs daily. A baby also walks quicker if he has a walker, for he feels protected enough to be daring. After that he'll push a chair in front of him or walk in front of you, clutching your forefinger.

Finally he takes a few ecstatic steps alone, usually clutching a toy in each hand. As he gains stability he'll depend on the walls for balance instead. This quaint native custom, with its trail of fingerprints, continues until he's about Twelve (yes, years, dear).

Balance

The earth is a wobbly place to a child. He needs practice to feel steady.

For a Two, drag thick yarn on the floor in a simple pattern, so he can walk on the twisty string. An older child will make his own complicated patterns.

You also can place a wide plank, 4'-6' long, on bricks or blocks of wood, 6" above the floor for a young child, higher for an older one. A child automatically walks this plank a dozen times a day, without even wondering why it's there. If you want to make a permanent balancing board, see page 106.

Swimming

The sooner you give your child the chance to swim, the quicker he'll take to the water. Even an infant will like to splash with you, but because a pool can have so many germs and chemicals and a river so much pollution, you'll want to send a sample to the city government for a test if you have any doubts about its purity.

If you're lucky enough to have a pool that offers swimming lessons for babies, take advantage of it. A baby can learn to paddle above water in his first year and loves every minute of it.

Whether you can give him lessons early or not, you can prepare him for swimming by letting him feel the buoyancy of the water, bouncing up and down in it with him. Later pull him along, but with his face out of water or he'll be scared. A Two may jump into your arms from the side of the pool and a Three may hold tight to your hands while you stand sideways to buck the ocean. Once a child learns to bubble, he may be ready for more advanced lessons, but be careful to find an instructor who can teach the rudiments of swimming and particularly of breathing, in an understandable way.

We think life jackets are essential in any water but a swimming pool. Here they can prevent a healthy fear of the water which every child should have. If you do get one for the pool, be sure it's certified for safety and can support his weight, because a child in any kind of support—even the simplest plastic tube—will depend on it to stay afloat.

Even when your pre-Six can swim, you must watch him very carefully. Lifeguard or not, the buck stops with you.

Bubbling

Most children are afraid to go completely under water, even at Four, because they don't know how to bubble. We helped Mali, first by demonstrating this silly game, then by doing it with her.

We shouted, "One, two, three," dropped to the floor of the pool and bounced straight up again. After a few times and enough laughter, we grabbed Mali's hands, counted again and went down together, over and over, until she learned to blow bubbles as she came up. It worked, but we don't recommend it until your child is comfortable in water to his waist.

Posture

Good posture is essential for physical dexterity. But you won't teach it by saying, "Sit up straight."

Your ribald Four likes to know that flesh is

laid on bones, which he can understand better if he dangles a cardboard Halloween skeleton, bending its arms and legs and finding the same bones in himself.

Once he's familiar with his skeleton, sit on the floor together and both of you reach back and each touch your own spine with your fingers. Bend over, wiggle your backbones and feel the vertebrae move. Twist your bodies into all kinds of shapes, freeze and breathe deeply. You both can feel it's easiest to breathe when the vertebrae sit one on top of the other. Have him stand sideways in front of a mirror. His ears should be in line with the shoulders, not in front or behind them. Any child will accept occasional, simple corrections of posture later if he first learns why.

Pitch and Catch

Nothing teaches coordination better than a ball.

An infant should have several balls which he can follow with his eyes and later can throw and chase. One ball should be large and colorful, one should be bumpy enough for a good grip and one should be made of foam rubber, because it's so light and it's good for years of indoor play. When your child learns to sit, spread his legs apart and roll a ball between them, the first game of catch.

The child who walks steadily will lift the ball, throw it—and be amazed to see it land behind him.

A Two can kick the large ball, throw the indoor one into a laundry basket and can hold his arms tightly together to catch any ball his father carefully throws. A Four is ready for a rubber ball bigger than a tennis ball but small enough to fit in his hands. He'll throw it overhead and underhand on his own, but he'll do it better if you show him how and let him shoot into a low basketball hoop. A Five kicks a soccer ball and learns this very basic game, and a Six will try to bat a softball with his friends, none of whom will succeed either.

We don't think a child can kick and throw and chase a ball too much, for nothing will make him more nimble.

Beanbaggery

A Two likes a beanbag better than a ball because it stops right where it lands. A handful of dried beans sewn in an odd glove makes a fine bag—an easy job for a Four.

On a dawdly day, suggest your child throw the bag high and catch it on the move or hold it between his feet and hop with it. He should alternate his tossings with the right and left hands.

Let him pitch the bag into a chalk circle, a game made harder if he shuts his eyes first or flings it over his shoulder.

Bat and Ball

We found our son could hit a ball by the end of his fifth summer, after his father had made a target for him by tying a plastic ball—the kind with holes—to a string and hanging it from a clothesline. It dangled just above Ramon's waist, so he could swing at it again and again, aiming either for a moving ball or a still one. Though it flipped around and over the clothesline, it always returned to the same level—a splendid game to play all alone and every hit brought immediate pleasure.

Talking

The articulate child is blessed for life.

We believe in early talking, not because your child (and thereby you) will seem brilliant, but because the sooner he talks the happier you both will be. Language is one of the best ways a child can feel in control of himself. It lets him tell you his stomach hurts or he's lonely or he's afraid of things that go squish on his plate. When a person can't express himself, he's frustrated and angry.

At birth a baby gasps his first breath and cries out to the tickling of his feet. His furious screams will never be so welcome again, but for weeks this is the only way he knows how to talk to you. Within his first year he'll babble every sound in every tongue on earth—most of which he'll forget when he learns your language. The average child is said to know perhaps three words when he is One and sixteen more when he is fifteen months old. We think a mother can extend this vocabulary considerably.

It's not how much you talk to your child but how well you talk to him that counts, for a child understands many words before he can use them. You'll want to speak slowly, precisely, to tell him whatever you're doing, using the same words every time. You should tell him the name of anything he eats, wears and shops for and you should explain why you're going someplace or doing some particular thing, the way you would to any friend.

Infancy to Six Months

By six weeks your baby will communicate with you through cries and smiles, but when he's about three months he will coo—the single most enchanting sound a child will make. It's important to follow your instincts, answering him coo for coo, your faces close together. This is his first conversation. He'll make new sounds every week—some because he's so happy; some because he's so tired and some because he's so mad. Frustration has its place. Although some of his sounds aren't as pretty as a coo, you'll want to repeat many of them. The more a child exercises his vocal chords, the faster his voice box develops. This lets him control the sounds he makes: the key to talking.

Talking is a game that's more fun to teach than any other and it delights a baby, if only because of the single-minded attention he gets. We learned our technique from a marvelous, toothless, eighty-year-old Irishman who stood over the carriage of his marvelous, toothless, four-month-old granddaughter for a half hour saying, "Hell—ooooooo," over and over. Finally, like a trumpet player watching a fellow suck a lemon at the bandstand, Kate was compelled to imitate him until she could sing it back—not very well, but enough to satisfy them both.

Since only grandfathers have the patience to try this game longer than ten minutes, you probably will give your lessons in three-minute snatches.

Nine Months

His attempts at talking will be almost impossible to understand, but give him the respect of listening to his language as well as he listens to yours. Otherwise, he'll grow discouraged and instead of speaking in two-word sentences by eighteen months, he might take an extra year to talk that well.

Keep repeating his sounds with delight when he says anything that might be a word. He'll be so pleased it will become a word, whether intended or not. As long as you each know what a particular sound means and he uses it consistently to describe the same thing—it's a word. If your neighbor doesn't know that "boom-boom" means vacuum cleaner or "putat" means pussycat, that's her problem. As long as you respond to your child's words with standard language, you aren't teaching baby talk.

Whenever you dress him, you'll put *socks* on *feet* and *hats* on *heads*, pointing to each as you do it. You'll touch his eyes and his knees and his forehead and elbows and say each word as you go. One day he'll surprise you and touch his eyes when you say the word and you'll know it's time to teach him about eyebrows and eyelashes too.

Fifteen Months

By fifteen months he can fetch familiar things for you, if you ask him in short, one-thought sentences—and if he isn't ornery that day.

Mid-One

Your child may stop talking while he masters a new skill, like walking. The more active he is, the less patience he'll have for talking, for children are as single-minded as anyone else. They can't grow taller and fatter at the same time.

Even the most nonverbal mid-One can understand everything that concerns him, whether you're talking to him or not.

As soon as he is familiar with one word, use a synonym to increase his precision and his scope. In this way, big becomes large, huge or tall. Be specific when you talk, pointing out not a "baby dog" but a "puppy," adding the color in another year and eventually the breed.

Two

By Two you should require your child to say "please" and "thank you"—just as you do—and help him enunciate clearly, without baby talk. Speak in complete sentences and expect the same of him, which helps him think more clearly.

Soon you can use more complex language games to teach adjectives and adverbs and reinforce his vocabulary even more by books and records and singing nursery rhymes. Your child may talk even quicker if you put your own silly words to music, like "Here comes the plumber/Looking like a drummer."

The plumber may think you're a little daft to introduce him that way, but he'll sure have something to tell his wife that night.

Three

Until a child can be understood clearly, he'll whine more, fuss more and have more temper tantrums to exorcise his frustration.

Some children are late talkers because no one talks to them or because the conversation is too fast to follow.

If a child screeches, "Ee, ee, ee," and points to

something he wants and his parents automatically give it to him, that child will have no reason to build a vocabulary. That's how our Nadia, the charmer of the preschool set, got along almost entirely in pantomime until she was Three.

Still other children are slow to talk when they're told "no" too often, for it takes nerve to make words.

Occasionally a child may have a physical problem. We remember a family with more children than money whose Four never talked until he had a tonsillectomy. A few days later he knocked hard at a neighbor's door and sang the full lyrics of "The Isle of Capri."

You can use our techniques to help a child of any age to talk, but the older the child, the swifter his progress.

Four

Every day, as your child needs less and less concentration to develop physical skills, he'll astonish you with his huge collection of words and the queer ways he puts them together.

Help him learn a few new words each day—not fancy, "look-at-me" words (or you'll have an aggravating little show-off) but words with enough variety for him to choose exactly the right word for the right moment. In fact, synonyms can be your social salvation. The experts would never agree with us, but we think sex organs should have nicknames unless you're talking to your child about sex. We remember too well when our Kate and Mike, Four and Three, plagued their crusty bachelor uncle at a party, asking if he had a ding-ding. He may have been annoyed (no doubt about it), but at least he could ignore it easier than if they had chanted, "Uncle Tom, do you have a penis?"

Five

By now your child should know his full name and address, but he should know home and office telephone numbers too—a matter of simple rote. Since a Five is so sure of himself, he will never get lost, although he'll be distressed how often you do.

Teach him to ask help from policemen, mailmen and mothers, no others, for he must learn not to talk to strangers. This is a lesson we completely skipped with our outgoing Meg who, at Seven, classically insisted she had never met a stranger. When we explained that a stranger was someone her parents had never met, she brought home a very large and inebriated fellow she found on the sidewalk.

"Jack," she said, "I want you to meet my mother. Mom, this is Jack. Now he's not a stranger any more. Can he have some coffee and then can I

go to his house to watch television?"

He did and she didn't—and we got a television.

Talking Games

We found talking games were the best way to make a child feel comfortable with words—their shadings and their tempo—and make him crystallize his ideas. Most of the games, which lasted for years, centered around the parts of speech.

Start with the Grandfather's Drill at four months and well before the first birthday graduate to Nouns, then Verbs, then Prepositions. Adjectives and Adverbs, which are not as necessary, come later. Your games will sound like Dick-and-Jane readers, which may explain why a Two likes these books so much and a Six does not.

The Grandfather's Drill

All sounds and words are taught the same way—starting as early as four months.

It may seem silly to try to teach words so soon, but it doesn't hurt if it's a way to show love and not a demand for performance. Babies, like all of us, revel in attention. This technique works for the next three years.

Practice first before a mirror, speaking slowly and enunciating each syllable, so you can see your mouth and lips and tongue synchronize to make a particular sound. Do the same with your child, talking at eye level and inches from his face, so he can see "bye-bye" and "Dad-dy," as well as hear it. Say a word over and over, slowly and distinctly, the way you would teach a foreign language. To a baby, it is a foreign language. Do this as many as twelve times at a stretch, and in a matter of weeks your child will try to imitate you.

Continue teaching each new word slowly and close to his face, even when he begins to speak fairly well.

In another year your child will wrestle with difficult sounds better if you use props—a candle flame or a feather to emphasize the breathy "wh" sound of "what," rather than the flat "w" sound of "water."

Nouns

Most of the first words you teach will be nouns, which you'll do by naming everything you touch and then by teaching the Guessing Game I before he talks and the second one when you think it's about time he did.

Guessing Game I
At nine months our amusing friend Suzannah enjoyed this ancient dialogue, carried on entirely by her mother.

"Where is Suzannah's shoe? In the refrigerator?"

"No!"

"Under the table?"

"Nooo."

"On the dog?"

"No, no."

"On Suzannah's foot?"

"Yes!"

Suzannah didn't learn how to say shoe that day, but she did learn what the word meant and her mother referred often to her daddy's shoes and the newsboy's shoes and the fact that the dog had no shoes. Everything on a foot was a shoe; there were no slippers, socks or sandals for another nine months.

Guessing Game II
Almost every child will point to what he wants, instead of trying to name it, which will annoy you more and more.

When he points to his juice next time, pick up the salt cellar, the pot holder, the tea strainer, saying, "Is this it?," "You mean this?"

And finally, when he is almost furious, "Oh, the bottle. Say BOT-TULL," and say the word face to face, several times, after you give it to him. He'll be too angry to say it then, but he'll try the next time or the next.

Verbs

Action verbs are taught more easily than any words, as you hop, skip, walk and run, saying the words as you go. He'll think it very funny. When your child says, "See," "Go," "Look," he's speaking in complete one-word sentences—a comfort.

Prepositions

The abstract concepts of prepositions are the hardest words for a child to understand and about the most important, for it's hard for a conversation to make sense without them.

Play a game of hide-and-seek with a small toy, placing it *on* the table or *in* it, *behind* it, *before* it, *under* it or *over* it. You'll do most of the hiding and most of the looking and all of the guessing, calling out each preposition until you find the toy.

A child can understand prepositions in a few weeks, even before he learns to talk.

Adjectives

When your child has mastered a word like "ball," roll one to him gently. Rub his fingers on it, saying, "Round ball." Go about the room, pointing out everything that is round. Try to roll a block so he can see the difference. Tell him it's square, then show other things that are square. This is the prelude to abstract concepts.

Your little girl's dress and her dolly and especially herself are pretty, an adjective to be used often and in front of the mirror.

Your child will learn "hot" and "cold," because you touch his fingertips to the spigots; "loud" and "quiet," because you yell and then whisper; "dirty" and "clean," because he looks at himself before his bath and after, and "sweet" and "sour," because you touch lemon juice and sugar to his tongue when you cook.

A Two begins to learn colors, and as soon as he does, you should define them more accurately—not blue, but navy; not red, but scarlet.

Every time a child learns a new adjective, he can describe his world more precisely than before. In this way a child can tell you, often with novel insight, how fog tastes or a kitten leaps or a sunbeam rests on his shoulder. These descriptions don't just spring from his mind, for the use of words, like skills, are built a layer at a time.

Adverbs

A Three can understand such adverbial concepts as here and there, if you physically put yourselves—here and there.

He'll like the Adverb game best though, for it's the beginning of charades and funny enough for the whole family.

To play it, each person walks/sits/looks: slowly,

sadly, loudly, softly, gaily, proudly, fearfully, bravely, happily, sillily and whatever other-*ly* you can invent.

Toilet Training

A child has little control over his bowels until Two, the bladder until mid-Two. A Three can stay dry through the night. If you start toilet training too early you'll have to wait months before your child can control himself, and you both will feel like failures. The older your child, the less you need to explain, for with his natural curiosity he has followed you to the pot, flushed it for you and asked many, many questions. Eventually he tries to mimic you and will tell you about every b.m. he makes—afterward.

When your child has stopped rebelling—between mid-Two and Three—you can have your turn. This is the end of pamperdom.

We found ourselves angry when we realized our daughter was old enough and smart enough to pull down her wet diaper and hand us a dry one. Clearly it was time she trained herself. We told her so emphatically and were businesslike about it. She was expected to be trained like the rest of us. We gave her one week to do it—a deadline she met.

There may be other ways to train a child but let us tell you. We've never met a mother whose exasperation didn't trigger the training.

You'll find it calls for single-mindedness on your part. Plan a full week to train your child, and this means you won't go out at all, unless he's asleep for the night, and invite no special company to distract you.

It's your job to make training easier for your child and each success he has will make success more likely the next time. Basically, toilet training is just one more step toward his independence.

If possible, train your child in summertime; you'll have less laundry. We recommend buying twenty pairs of dimestore underpants, better and cheaper than half as many training pants, which should be changed when they're wet anyway. Your child should wear pants or dresses that have no straps or other complications. Handicaps aren't needed during this training week.

He needs a potty on every floor, because his feet can't run quite fast enough. It either should be a chair or a special seat on the toilet with a step to reach it, since a toilet is gigantically high to a Two. Everyone wants his feet to touch the floor when sitting, especially if the chair has a hole in the middle. Children are as afraid of falling through a porcelain pot today as our foremothers were of falling through the privy a hundred years ago. It's the curse of the age.

One enterprising mother of a competitive little boy found a child's urinal with a target painted on it. In his striving for a high score he trained himself in two days.

When training begins, explain to your child that he should sit on the pot when you ask him, until he learns to sit without being told at all. Don't let him stay longer than ten minutes or not at all if he objects. You won't, of course, play games or read stories, for this teaches a child that pottime is playtime, but stay with him if he likes.

With your reminders, he'll go to his potty about eight times a day. Let him sit there as soon as he wakes up—not when you wake up. Leave a bell in his crib or bed if you usually don't hear him. He'll ring it, you can bet. He sits on the pot again right after breakfast, after juice time, again at lunch, then after a nap, after supper and before bed. And any other time he mentions it.

Your child will be very proud of his successes, which you'll praise. Let him empty the potty in the toilet, even though he spills a little, and let him flush it himself. You may flush too quickly and hurt his pride.

It is important not to overreact to a bowel movement—or the lack of one—or to thank him for doing one for you. It's really not the most important thing in the world and a great deal of emphasis is a distortion.

Ask him to tell you when he makes a mistake—and he will if you don't fuss—and to help you clean it.

Have him put his wet underpants in the diaper hamper, get fresh ones and put them on without any help, for you want him to learn how good it feels to stay dry. You'll not even use diapers at night and, yes, you will do a lot of wash, but there's a good chance you can put the diapers away after a week. We found the shock of a midnight deluge surprised our children so much that bedwetting never became a problem.

If your child hasn't trained himself in a week one of you isn't ready. Go back to diapers with as much good grace as you can pretend. Whoever wore them to college?

Postlude

Once a child is trained, he should learn to pee in an assortment of places—in other people's bathrooms, in a meadow, in the ocean, from a boat (always downwind), never in a pool. By Four, he'll insist on using every facility he can find. We know one little girl who, in the midst of the model rooms at Sears Roebuck's, insisted to her distracted mother that she had to go potty. She insisted and insisted and then she disappeared, returning in a few minutes and reporting that she had indeed found the pot.

"I picked that pretty blue one," she said loudly, pointing to the floor display nearby.

Bedwetting

All children occasionally wet the bed until they're Eight. A cold night, too much water before bedtime, a case of nerves or plain laziness may be the cause.

A Five who consistently wets the bed will be embarrassed about it and may feel unhappy about himself. For this reason, we feel a mother can't treat bedwetting lightly and must help the child overcome the problem, but never with threats or bribes. We wouldn't dare presume to offer a cure, for there are too many physical and psychological causes for it. It isn't the end of the world, but you do need a doctor's advice.

La Toilette

"Ah chèrie, make your toilette, if you please," our old tante would implore each morning, for to her, an unkempt child at breakfast was a sacrilege. Today we agree and insist our children wash, dress, brush their teeth and comb their hair before coming to the breakfast table, a routine they began learning by Two, mastered by Six, and sometimes practiced by Twelve.

Just as you had to learn the mechanics of caring for your child, so must your child learn to take care of himself. This is the essence of independence.

Cleanliness

Bathing

When your child is Two, your bathroom will be your cleanest room, because you have nothing to do for twenty minutes a day except scrub the tiles and wipe the medicine chest. This is how long it takes him to bathe himself—a soaking sort of job—which is one more sign of his independence.

A Three scrubs too, washing hair ribbons, underpants and the ring in the tub—not too well but with vigor—and by the middle of this year can be trusted alone in the bath and even with his two-year-old sister. By the time he's Five, any fear of the bath is gone and he can wash his hair, if you're not too particular.

Washing Up

A child, starting at Three, should wash his hands and face at all the normal times. If you keep his nails short they won't show dirt—for it takes an Eight to scrub them clean.

Any child likes to wash his hands, but never his face. He should splash it for himself and rub it reasonably clean on the towel. Which is why we buy black towels.

Brushing Teeth

Your mid-Three likes to watch his favorite person—himself—when he brushes his teeth. Hang a magnifying mirror from the bathroom towel rack, to dangle about two feet above the floor. He'll do a better job for such a splendid fellow. He won't brush his teeth well, but he'll learn the right technique and initiate the habit.

Let your child use two brushes—one for morning and one for night—so the bristles have a chance to dry and harden.

Bacteria from food forms a plaque on the teeth

when it's twenty-four hours old, and this can cause decay. Your child needs to brush the teeth on all three sides. On the cheek side and the tongue side, he should brush vertically, flicking the bristles outward. He simply scrubs the molars any way he can. If the gums bleed, don't worry. It's part of the gum toughening process and will stop in a few days.

An older child may like to use dental floss, which you'll cut. Teach him to slide it between his teeth to remove the food.

Combing Hair

We found our Nadia, like most young children, had such a sensitive scalp that by Six she preferred to brush her own hair, counting the strokes as a distraction.

When it was a little smoother, she used a comb with widely spaced teeth and we taught her to hold it at an angle, making quick little strokes downward, untangling first the ends and working slowly up to the scalp.

We combed—and occasionally cut—the snarls for her.

Dressing

Before a child learns how to do a job, he must learn how to undo it, the same technique you use when you carefully take apart a chair to learn how to upholster it.

In this way, a Two can put on his socks, but he would rather take them off. He'll spend a lot of time removing his shoe laces but he won't be able to replace them for at least a year, or tell his left shoe from his right for another. He'll put on his pants and shoes and shirts many times, over many months, before he always does it right. In the meantime, he'll be furious every time he puts both feet in the same pants leg.

He'll button some things, but seldom correctly, for he almost never starts at the bottom, and he'll pull on his shirt, backward. Still he considers this dressing himself, and so do we. If you keep your standards low, your praise high and his clothes simple, he'll be dressing himself completely, quickly and competently by Three. Until then you'll help

only before he reaches despair, and as casually as possible. This lets him pretend as if he could do it himself if he weren't in a hurry to do other, more important work.

A child not only needs help sometimes to dress himself, but he needs help to keep his clothes. Since he'll remove at least some of them when he visits, if just to be convivial, it will pay to order three-line labels that give your last name, your address and your phone number. Sew them in his clothes (but not on elastic waistbands or the thread will pop), and paste them inside belts, boots, shoes—and your umbrella. You'll be surprised at the rate of return.

To keep mittens, hammer grommets into them and into jacket cuffs, snapping them together. You also can attach one mitten at each end of an elastic string and run it through the sleeves.

Putting on a Coat

There are two laborious but self-sufficient ways a child can put on his coat. They almost always are used in good nursery schools and almost never used at home. They should be. The happiest children attend to themselves.

The first way is a test of your housekeeping. A Two can put on his coat by throwing it on the floor, spreading it to show the lining. Have him kneel just behind the hood and, looking like a pint-sized Houdini putting on a strait jacket, he slips each hand into an armhole, flips the jacket over his head and shoves his arms through the sleeves. Even the hood falls flop on his head.

Dust him and send him out to play.

An older child can lean his coat against the back of a low chair, sidle his back to it and slide his arms into the sleeves.

Buttoning

Your child will feel like a chowderhead when he struggles to button his clothes. Help him, not by doing it, but by teaching him to button from the bottom up. This way, the buttons and buttonholes have a better chance to come out even. A right-handed child should push the button halfway through with his right thumb and forefinger and grab it fast on the other side with the left thumb and forefinger, before it gets away. Particularly inept children will use their teeth, which is fine too. The success of the job is more important than the technique.

Zipping

There will be zippers in your child's life, so teach him how to outwit them, most of the time, and buy coats with toggles for the rest.

Like all dressing skills, your child first will learn to unzip his clothes before he can zip them. A Three can zip a placket, but it takes another year before he can zip his jacket.

When he learns that the tab has to be pulled all the way down to the bottom of the track to undo a zipper, he's ready to learn to zip. It requires such manual dexterity you have to explain each step graphically and congratulate him freely. Teach him to pull the tab to the bottom of the track until it touches the metal catch. He must keep it steady while he fits the other side of the zipper into it.

Be sure to tell him to hold the bottom of the zipper with one hand while he pulls the tab with the other, or the teeth won't mesh. Your child should learn to lock the zipper by pressing the tab flat after he zips—especially important for a little boy.

Booting

The fine art of booting is seldom taught at home and hardly learned until first grade. Here is a method we devised to make life less complicated for a mid-Three.

Keep an 8-inch square of waxed paper inside the back of the boot so the heel of the shoe can slide into it easily. This method works even if his new shoes have almost outgrown his old boots. He can use the same paper repeatedly.

Rights and Lefts

Most pre-Sixes don't know their lefts from their rights generally because they haven't been taught in a comprehensible way. Paint your child's right toenails with a felt-tipped pen that isn't water soluble. Match it with a big dot of the same color pasted to the inner sole of his right shoe. He'll know his lefts from his rights in a few days, but he may never be able to look at his right toe without thinking it should be green.

Lacing and Tying

You never should bother to show a child a skill unless he's interested, whether it's toilet training or tying shoes.

All children go through a period of unlacing any shoes they can find. When your child has passed this stage, teach him how to lace a shoe. This concept is tricky to master, unless you're willing to demonstrate the same techniques a half dozen days in a row. Don't use a cardboard toy shoe. It's the shoe on the foot that interests him.

Dip exactly half of a white lace in vegetable coloring so your child will see the colors crisscross. If he starts lacing at the top of the tongue, instead of at the bottom, it will be easier. This trick can be learned by a mid-Three, but it takes a dextrous Four or an average Six to tie his shoes.

Frankly, we were never able to teach any one of our children this skill. Instead, they learned to tie from a fellow Five. After tying the half knot, Claire had them make the standard loop with one end, another loop with the other and tied the two loops together in another half knot.

If you want your child to tie in the standard fashion, perhaps he can learn from the neighbor lady.

Probabilities & Possibilities

With parenthood comes a crowd of obligations, often unexpected, but most of them as inevitable as rain. Your child will get sick—and so will you—and sometimes he'll get bored and scared and surely get cross, which you can expect between 5 and 7 P.M.—every 5 and 7 P.M.

While the bother of routine living will nibble your soul, the bigger problems can swamp it.

When you have a second child, you'll have to shepherd your first through the pain of having a rival and when you move across country you'll have to deal with his adjustment while you deal with everything else.

You may have to struggle with a handicap, either in your child or yourself, and find the pity of strangers can be harder to take than the problem itself.

There will be those questions—of sex, of death, of divorce and many others too—and they always come when you least expect them. Not surprisingly, most important questions are hard to answer, but if you know what to expect, you can handle them more wisely.

Although there are few simple solutions in child care, there isn't a situation you'll meet that others haven't met first. For this, be grateful. Every mother who has ever lived has found some ways to make some things better. The problem is to discover which ones will work for you. The search is worth it, for the easier you find motherhood, the happier you'll be.

Miseries

Some miseries are inevitable. No matter how creative, enriched and self-sufficient your child, motherhood sometimes can be the most dismaying job in the world.

For us, it was the third child that brought calm to our house, but it could have happened sooner if we had figured out the right solutions to deal with the extraordinary bits of life, like fears and illnesses or the very ordinary chaos of car pools and the daily Arsenic Hour.

It turned out to be a matter of good preparation, lower standards and the knowledge that this too shall pass.

Arsenic Hour

Between the nap and the twilight
   When blood sugar is beginning to lower,
Comes a pause in the day's occupations.
   That is known as Arsenic Hour.

When you were pregnant there never was a moment you could forget it, even when you wanted to. Although you wouldn't ask the doctor, you worried when you drank too much and if it was safe to make love so often. You walked every day, slept eight hours at night and every nap you took was wrapped in virtue, but most of your attention went to the food you ate—the milk, the liver, the fruits.

Though you and your baby may continue this regimen the first year, the cracker box and the television create cyclical problems as your child gets older.

Actually there are three essentials for mothers and children—enough sleep, enough physical and mental exercise and enough of the right foots—just the same things, in fact, which you once took so seriously.

Without them there is bound to be a daily collapse, first of the child and then of the mother, which almost always strikes between five and seven. Experienced mothers jokingly call it Arsenic Hour and an astonishingly high number of other mothers begin to look forward to it as Sherry Hour, which is no joke at all.

The full quota of sleep at night is necessary and so is an afternoon nap, even if you have to pretend that your child is resting while he climbs in and out of bed.

You need a half hour of exercise, not to make you tired but to make your body alive. Vacuuming, cooking, dusting and driving do not constitute exercise. Walking, biking, playing hopscotch and touching toes do. Your child, like you, needs at least one special interlude a day to renew the soul, which seldom happens unless you make it happen.

However, it is the third essential—the quality of the food you both eat—that decides why five to seven is so much worse than any other time of day. This is the time when you pay for any imbalance accumulated from the day's diet. An overdose of carbohydrates and sugar—of cookies or alcohol or the caffeine in sodas, tea and chocolate, as well as in coffee—drop the blood sugar level. This causes fatigue and bad temper. We think safety comes in many guises, and good nutrition, as dreary as it sounds, is as sensible as a gate on the stairs or a lock on the poison cupboard.

Mother's Pickup

We've never known a mother of a Two who couldn't use a boost. This one will spark your metabolism in the morning or steady your nerves for Arsenic Hour.

Mix   6 oz. orange juice
           3 tbsp. brewer's yeast

The yeast is more palatable if it's grown on molasses instead of hops. The Pickup takes about twenty minutes to work.

Errands and Car Pools

Those outings to the pediatrician and the supermarket can be simply dreadful and at least some of them will be, no matter how efficient you are.

For any short trip, put your child in a safety-tested car seat, harness or a seat belt, and take a small special toy. Carry a package of crackers in the glove compartment of your car. They're a godsend in a traffic jam.

Keep paper and pencil and playing cards in your purse to fill any waiting time.

To the Pediatrician

For the first four years, trips to the doctor can't be avoided and are bound to involve a twenty-minute wait and some confusion. Minimize it, dressing your child in simple, everyday clothes (no pediatrician wants a fashion show) and bring a few toys and a sandwich or a bottle.

Still, a doctor can't jab a baby with a needle, poke a stick down his throat and a thermometer up his bottom without initiating an anxiety he'll remember next time.

You only can help a baby with sympathy but never tell a One that a shot won't hurt. The best thing you can do for a young child is to keep him entertained in the waiting room. For a mid-One draw a face on your palm, with one eye in the life line so it winks when you bend your hand.

A mid-Two will enjoy an envelope of geometric shapes cut out of cardboard. Your child can close his eyes and tell the shape by feeling it. And a bag of colored zippers appeals to a Three.

At mid-Three, the anxiety is over and your child should feel comfortable with the pediatrician—or you have the wrong pediatrician. A child is usually in awe of his doctor; but yours may be like the fresh little girl in our old tante's joke, whose doctor, knowing the child's aversion to skivvies, looked down her throat and said, "Aha, Sarah! You're wearing no underpants!"

To which she replied, "Why don't you turn me upside down and see if my hat's on straight?"

To the Supermarket

If you must market with your child establish early and very firm rules as soon as he thinks he's too old to sit in the cart.

A Two can face you, standing on the rod between the front wheels, as if the cart were a fireman's truck. We called our Mike a fireman and brought his hat to wear—the only thing that kept a child like that from plucking the bottom can of peas from the pyramid.

Let your child choose one family treat but tell him you won't buy anything else he asks for. If he starts begging for more, return the treat you've put in the cart. This is a very tangible way to show a child you mean business. Some people call this bribery and some people are right. It's all in the way you phrase it. Not, "If you'll be good, I'll buy you some treat," but, "If you won't be good, I won't buy you any."

We still wince when we see the corn chips. We never bought any because we never knew the children liked them, and we never knew they liked them because they couldn't ask. Poor little tykes.

Car Pools

Before your child is Five you and your husband will participate in car pools. For your child it means hilarity, noise and camaraderie, and for you it means a little more free time and, possibly, much chaos.

After a combined nineteen years of car pooling, we know that there can be benefits only if the car pools are limited to five to six children and each adult adheres to a few rules. On this we are ruthless.

You must have your child ready to go out the door when the driver beeps, and if your child is sick you must cancel in time for the driver to avoid the trip.

If you drive be punctual. Buckle children in place and allow no nonsense. If they get rowdy pull to the side of the road and wait, in silence, which calms them much quicker than commands. When you deliver, stay until each child has entered his house.

If you're going to be out of town on your duty day or if your child is sick or you are sick or your car is sick, you still must drive or get a replacement—or send a taxi.

To the Barber Shop

Trim your husband's hair, then your child's, each sitting on a high stool. Once you've played barbershop at home, the real adventure is less frightening.

To the Gift Shop

This is one time you should tell your child, "Hold your hands behind your back." You can expect almost absolute obedience, for a child doesn't want to break anything either, but he only can last about fifteen minutes.

Fears and Fancies

Fears may start in the first year and all children will have some by Six. They stem from dreams, shadows, stories, television and even overheard conversations, for a child is a literal creature who believes exactly what he hears. In fact, when you read "Amelia Bedelia" stories to your child, you'll find he also thinks it reasonable to "dress the chicken" in a sunsuit rather than fill it with cornbread. When you look at life from the underside too, your child's behavior makes more sense.

A baby as young as seven months may be afraid his parents won't return, even when they leave the room, for out of sight is out of life then. This fear of desertion peaks at mid-One, although later he deliberately uses his tears to pull on your heartstrings.

By Two a child has found some reason to fear loud noises, strange dogs, sharp needles and hot stoves. A little of this is good, for a child without fear is like a child without antibodies. He has no protection.

He needs to know that fears are normal, to be discussed as matter-of-factly as anything else. If you show too much concern he may think you're scared too, but if you can turn the fear into a fancy it usually disappears.

The vividness of a fevered dream may last for life, but the fears need not. Our Meg, at mid-One, was terrified to cross any bridge by car until, at Three, she mentioned how scared she was the time the car went over the bridge. When we explained that she must have dreamed it, the problem dissolved instantly—a surprise, for most fears are more tenacious.

Some dreams are so real, a child wants to climb in your bed for comfort—a poor idea—but you can let him rest in a sleeping bag on the floor near you or on a couch in your room for part of the night. If you're too rigid in dealing with his fears they'll just get worse.

Your child may become afraid of daydreams too, of sliding down the drain, like a sliver of soap, for he can't judge sizes yet, or he may develop a galloping fear of elevators.

If your child withdraws from most play or regularly acts out his fears, he needs professional help. Don't hesitate to seek it.

The Great Penis Scare

The penis is an extraordinary creation, but as strange as it looks to a child, the lack of it looks a lot stranger.

When a little boy first sees a little girl completely, he is appalled. Obviously, she lost it. And when a little girl sees a little boy for the first time, she's sure she did.

That anyone could be so careless or so forgetful can frighten a child, though temporarily. The fear will be much less, or not at all, we think, if he sees his parents and friends naked sometimes. Trust your Four to carry on further investigations—fearlessly.

Desertion

The most self-confident child may feel abandoned sometimes, as parents shuttle to work, to shop, to parties. Not all sitters will be good and none of them will be able to comfort your child as well as you or find the teddy bear as quickly. At some point, your baby will cry when you leave, but if you handle it positively, the fear of desertion should be under control by Three.

For a baby of six months, play Peek-a-boo first by hiding your eyes behind your hands, and then by hiding yourself behind the door. Your quick reappearances help a child have faith that you always will come back.

Of course, you won't stay home if your child sobs when the sitter comes, for that would reward the tears, but you will need sitters who give comfort more often than milk.

You also need to be very candid with your child. Tell him, even before he can talk, when you're going out and where, who will sit and when you'll be back, in the same conversational way you would talk with a Six. A child can accept the fantasy of the tooth fairy or Santa Claus, as games

of love, but never the pretense that you'll "be back in a few minutes" when you know you won't. Honesty is not a plaything.

The Dark

This particular fear is the most common and we think the most preventable, since there's no rule that says a child must spend ten of every twenty-four hours in the dark. Use a night light before the fear ever begins or open his door into a softly lit hall. A Three will like his very own flashlight. It turns a midnight trip to the bathroom into an adventure, but tape both ends shut or he'll take it apart by noon.

A light sleeper is more likely to develop a fear of the dark if he isn't tired enough, either mentally or physically. When this happened to us, we provided extra activity and, to our regret, no nap time.

Another child, who became suddenly fearful, slept better when her mother sprinkled a few drops of her cologne on her pillow.

Nightmares

A fear is scary and a fancy is fun, but both can spring from the same source. When that same imaginative Meg had a nightmare about a bear in her bed, her father immediately chased him out of the house, loudly and with a broom, and said he went to live down the street with Uncle Tom. For years we would drop over to visit Harry the Bear (for that was his name), who wore electric socks and slept in an empty bathtub. Unfortunately, he always was asleep or in a snit or out for a soda when we called, but by turning a nightmare into a charade, the fear had turned into fancy.

Health Hazards

Motherhood is one long internship in paramedics.

When your baby is born, the doctor will insist that he's as close as the telephone, ready to answer every question, day or night—and then he goes on a trip or you go on a trip or the questions just seem too silly to ask.

In the first year you'll vacillate between being too casual and too anxious, perhaps as extreme as one careful mother we know who panicked when she picked up her baby and found the impossible—a dry diaper. Obviously something was wrong with his plumbing.

First she kept a careful record of everything that dear child did for the next twenty-four hours (for she didn't want to sound frivolous), left a message with the doctor's office and waited, frozen, by the telephone. The minute it rang she gave a full, nonstop account of the cries, the naps, the amount of formula left in each bottle and a description of each bowel movement until—inevitably—the man on the phone interrupted to say that it sure was interesting, ma'am, but he was the piano tuner. It's foolishness like this that will make you slow to call the doctor until—inevitably—you treat the baby's cold yourself for days before seeing the pediatrician—and then he tells you that your child nearly has pneumonia.

It's important to call the doctor when you have a question, even if it makes you embarrassed, but you're the one who will have to learn to distinguish between a cry of hunger and a cry of fatigue, which takes a few months, and between fussiness and an earache, which takes at least a year. The healthiest child may have a fall or a fever and the most attentive doctor will go out of town. It will be your day-to-day experiences that teach you to handle the small crises alone.

By the time your baby is grown, you'll think you know enough to write your own prescriptions—which you won't—or enough to write a book—which you will.

Home Medicine

We don't dare pretend to prescribe medicine, but we can't pretend that you can get along without home remedies. You need popsicles and lollipops quite as much as you need a thermometer and a hot water bottle and you need to know how to handle a fever in a hurry when the doctor can't be reached. Common sense is the common denominator of motherhood, and a few rounds of sickness help you learn it in a hurry.

Infant Cries

The pediatrician, if he is that casual type, will tell you that you will recognize your baby's needs by the different sounds of his cry. This is seldom true. By the time you learn to interpret a baby's complaints you probably have stopped having babies. However, there are only a certain number of things that can be wrong and it doesn't take long to check them.

A baby cries for a reason, and sometimes you can find out why and correct it and sometimes you can't. Nevertheless, it's your job to comfort him and sympathize. You want sympathy too when you have a hangover or a crick in the neck or a bad case of the blues. Babies get miserable too and, although it may not register on the thermometer, there are times when they need to be rocked and loved and crooned over. This takes precedence over almost anything else, except possibly cooking dinner. This is when you learn to cook with a baby in a sling, or on your hip, tribal style. It can be done and it really is much less distracting than hearing your child sob in his crib.

A baby likes to be rocked—an easier job in an armless chair—and he should be held close, on your left side—the instinctive position for mothers—so he can be near the heartbeat he knew in the womb. This probably is the first imprinted stimuli a baby receives and it should be re-emphasized after birth. Even a muffled clock, although its beat is different from yours, can soothe a child in his crib the same way it soothes a newly weaned puppy. You will find, as many mothers and many studies have before you, that the more a baby is cuddled, the less he cries.

Colic

There is a difference between a stomachache, which is occasional and erratic, and colic, which most doctors agree is caused by an immature digestive system. When he draws up his knees, tenses his belly and cries at a regular time, that's colic. And when you put a warm bottle on his stomach and give him a warm water bottle to drink and rock him for hours and you both cry, that's colic.

Mothers in some European countries will soothe an unhappy baby by swaddling him tightly below the waist but without diapers, leaving the rest of his body unfettered by clothes. Any solution you try will make you feel better, and perhaps the baby too.

In other generations parents walked their colicky children back and forth, and now again doctors find it a good idea. Today they say the passing objects, as well as the comforting heartbeat, console the baby.

Pacification

Most first-time mothers don't want their baby to have a crutch, but second-time mothers will take any crutch they can get. We're with them.

Some babies need to suck more than others, and for them a sugar tit was invented. This is the old southern device of a clean rag dipped into sugar and water (and some say, occasionally bourbon) for a substitute nipple. Today we wouldn't try that without 1) checking with the pediatrician, 2) triple-rinsing the cloth to remove all traces of detergent and 3) sterilizing the water. With this amount of trouble, you may as well skip the sugar tit and decide whether to put up with some fussing in his early weeks until your baby finds his thumb, or give him a pacifier. A thumb is preferable to many parents because it will never fall out of the crib at midnight for you to find on the floor while he screams. In any case, babies seem to keep their need to suck for about the same length of time, no matter whether they assuage it with a sugar tit, a pacifier or a thumb.

If your baby has trouble settling down one night and snuggles in his crib the next it probably has nothing to do with his day. Instead, notice which bunny or blanket is in bed with him on the happy nights and see to it that it's always there. If he has chosen a magic blanket you may have to scramble to get it washed and dried between naps, but it's still better than a fussy baby.

Spitting Up

If your baby spits up to be sociable after every meal, sponge it from his clothes with a rag dipped in baking soda and water. This absorbs the odor. If you're going out, take a soda-soaked wet sponge. The smell of spit-up, which is so routine to you, can upset those who have no young children. Also your baby will smell sweeter.

Teething

Your baby will probably cut his first front teeth between four and nine months and his first molars at Two (and if there aren't any accidents, he'll start losing his front teeth around Six, growing his second set in exactly the same order as the first teeth appeared).

A baby chews a great deal to cut a new tooth, drooling steadily, but he doesn't need you to rub the gums. It's one job he can do himself, and he should, for he'll know when to stop. Too much rubbing may cause a bone infection. Instead, help him teethe with a stale bagel to bite or a hard rubber necklace. You also need to protect him from the dozens of small things he'll try to put in his mouth. Besides the risk of choking, they often carry germs, which is one reason why teething has such a bad name. Unless your child gets sick, teething generally causes little pain except possibly when the tooth actually is cutting through the gum.

When there is more pain, give a lot more love and kisses and help him sleep better by bicycling his legs and taking him on longer walks. Because sucking makes tender gums hurt more, let your child drink milk from a cup or enlarge the holes in his bottle.

When his molars come in, he will drool twice as much, have a runny nose, look pale and be a little cranky.

Crankiness

After a child is Two, you'd think he could explain his crankiness, but this is often hard even for a Six. He has no idea he's cross because he didn't sleep enough or eat a healthy snack. A child's frame of reference is so small, he doesn't know what he should complain about, as we found when the doctor took wheat from the diet of our brilliant, if fussy, young friend. Her disposition did improve quickly, but so did her headaches and this was a problem she never had mentioned. At Five, she thought her head was supposed to hurt. It always had.

Another child may be cranky because his jacket isn't warm enough or his shoes pinch his toes, but it takes an Eight to explain even these obvious problems.

Suspect pinworms if your child has a bad temper, the fidgets and an occasional tummy ache. You can see tiny white worms in the stools or by shining a flashlight on a bare bottom at midnight, when they come out to play. A prescription and some extra care get rid of them quickly, but these parasites are airborne, spread easily and a great number of urban children get them every year.

Diarrhea and Constipation

The most proper mother talks about her child's bowel movements at parties the way she used to talk about politics. After your baby has had diarrhea or constipation a few times you'll understand her concern. It's miserable for the whole family. Diarrhea particularly is almost inevitable between six months and two years, for the same germs that cause tonsillitis and stomachache often travel to the intestine. It even can develop if your child has a cold, unless you curb his diet, for the normal caloric intake is too much. This is why a doctor vetoes fats and carbohydrates.

Serve apple juice, grated raw apple, gelatin, banana, cottage cheese, skim milk and dry toast.

However, at only eighteen calories each, a lollipop is one of the few things his body does tolerate which he can enjoy.

For the constipated child, give whole wheat or dark bread and add two tablespoons of prune juice to any other juice that tastes better. A baby improves with a drop of corn syrup added to his bottle.

Both constipation and diarrhea are improved by yogurt, that ancient, extraordinary food that makes centenarians commonplace in Bulgaria. Experienced travelers take it before and during an overseas trip, for it has a special strain of bacteria that, taken regularly for a few weeks, is said to prevent dysentary.

Sore Throat

Almost any sore throat can be helped by gargling three times a day with this solution, which a Four can do.

The Gargle
Combine   3 oz. boiled water
              1 tbsp. hydrogen peroxide
              ¼ tsp. salt
The disadvantage is the taste, which lasts 3-4 hours, but the results are worth it. If his throat still hurts after the first day or if fever develops, call the doctor.

Stomachache

Any stomachache that lasts more than a few hours can be serious and you should call the doctor. However, with us it always seemed to happen when we were traveling far from home and every time we were sure it was appendicitis.

This is when we learned that appendicitis generally starts from the left side of the stomach, wanders to the middle and then settles on the right, usually causes a slight fever and reacts to poking differently than gas pains do.

As a friendly nurse once taught us, a child who can talk fairly well will cooperate when you examine him, so long as he doesn't know which symptoms are which, for then he may be too cooperative.

Have him lie on the bed, arms relaxed at his side, and poke his abdomen with stiff fingers, slowly and firmly. If it hurts more when you push them in it's probably gas, but if it hurts more when you pull them out it may be appendicitis, and you need a doctor and a blood count to test for an infection.

Fever

All children run fevers sometime. It's the body's way of fighting an illness.

Each pediatrician has his procedure for dealing with this symptom. Learn beforehand how he wants you to bring down a fever, because somehow children seldom get very sick during office hours. This way you can spare yourself the agony of standing helpless while your child's fever soars.

Take your child's temperature whenever he feels warm to the touch. It's wise to call the doctor when your pre-Two has any fever, but with an older child there is less urgency.

Any child under Five with a fever of 103° is a very sick child, for high fever is a danger, especially to a pre-Two. Intense, prolonged body heat can cause delirium, convulsions and, on very rare occasions, can fry brain cells, causing permanent damage. Not all high fevers can be prevented, but their effects can be minimized.

Thermometers
Even the youngest baby feels the indignity of being spread-eagled on his tummy for three-to-five minutes with a thermometer up his bottom. Let him listen to Weather or Dial a Prayer, or any other thing that will talk nonstop.

The Chart
Keep a list of each temperature reading and the time, and record all the symptoms. Pediatricians rightfully get very irritated at a mother's vagueness, for a record of the ups and downs of an illness can help him in a phone diagnosis.

Treatment
As soon as your child runs a fever, pump him with liquids. Give him anything he will drink or suck, including crushed ice, gelatin, lollipops and popsicles, but avoid milk, which is hard to digest. The higher the fever the more liquid the body needs to keep from drying out.

If your child has a high fever put him in a room away from hot or cold air vents and near the telephone, so you can make additional calls to the doctor. Turn off any lights that may shine directly in his eyes, remove any extra clothing, and cover him only with a double sheet.

Some doctors recommend dipping your hand in water and rubbing it on your child's forehead, wrist and abdomen. Others recommend wrapping up the naked child in a wet towel covered by a dry one and holding the child for a half hour. And, of course, there is aspirin in liquid, tablet and suppository form, which take at least twenty minutes to take effect, to be given as the doctor prescribes.

Your child will begin to sweat as his temperature goes down. Change him, give more water and check him every hour. None are more than temporary measures until the prescription can cure the illness or the illness has run out its course naturally.

Vomiting
If a child runs a fever and vomits, too, call the doctor again and sit right by him for a child in this condition can dehydrate quickly. Give him gum if he's old enough to chew it, water by the spoonful every few minutes or bits of ice to suck on. Too much liquid drunk at once will cause more vomiting.

Convulsions
A convulsion is brought on by a temporary dehydration of the brain, caused by high fever. It's the body's defense against the high fever of an infection or a virus and nothing is as dramatic. We have watched several and they have never lost their chilling effect.

In a convulsion the child's body goes rigid and shakes hard. The eyes roll back, the jaw snaps, the neck arches, the tongue flips back, and thick saliva forms around the mouth. Although panicked, you must do three things almost simultaneously. Turn your child on his side to let the saliva run out his mouth, place the bowl of a spoon in his mouth so he won't bite his tongue and dip him in tepid water in the bathtub to bring the fever down fast. Very cold water can cause pneumonia. It will seem like hours, but a convulsion lasts less than a minute. The child then goes limp as if in a faint, and falls into a calm sleep. Put him in a safe place, call the doctor immediately and prepare for a rapid trip to his office or the hospital.

And now you know why every mother tells her child to wear his galoshes when he goes out—for the next eighteen years.

Family Illness

Life is grim whenever you, the mother, succumb to an illness, but it's grimmer when you don't. If you just lie on the sofa dressed and looking green your family won't be sympathetic. Instead they will spill more things than ordinarily, make more noise and look as pathetic as possible each time you remind them, "Mommy's sick." You still will be expected to cook and diaper. And at this point you may as well hang a scarlet "M" around your neck for Martyr.

Instead, give up, call your husband, put on a nightgown and go to bed. Then your family will take you as seriously as you take yourself. In fact, your child will be so surprised he may tiptoe and whisper, off and on, for as long as two days. Your husband will be respectful and he may not give you breakfast until noon, but he will take charge.

However, when all of you get sick, you will take charge. After you call the doctor, lie on the sofa, dispensing medicine, diapering babies and, resentfully, muddling through. Soft-boiled eggs, dry toast, jello, cottage cheese, and tea with lemon will seem like a banquet to everyone. Give plenty of liquids to prevent dehydration. Pass out lollipops to assuage tears and use records and television to get you through.

This dismal togetherness may be eased somewhat if you have made friends with your neighbors. Tell them everyone is sick and ask for their help unashamedly. As our Atlanta friend would say, "We can all get through if we 'hep' each other."

Calamities

Living in the city, we soon learned to appreciate the solitude of country life and were lucky enough to have spent a few vacations on a secluded farm and some on a quiet beach. This happy isolation fed our souls but forced us to grapple with emergencies we never had handled before. Every vacation had its bee stings, infected bites, cuts, bruises, even bad scratches from an attacking peacock, fishhooks in the head and one near drowning.

We learned to pack salt, soda, vinegar, peroxide and cornstarch and in fact use these first-aid treatments successfully at home before the doctor can be reached.

To be wise, paste emergency numbers on the telephone—the handiest place in the house. Include numbers for Fire, Police, Poison Control Center, the pediatrician, two neighbors and any office number for you or your husband.

Burns and Sunburns

Apply ice or cold water immediately to a burn, both to keep the layers of skin from separating into blisters and to lessen the pain. It takes at least ten minutes to cool a minor, first-degree burn. If you are out of ice use a package of frozen food on the burn.

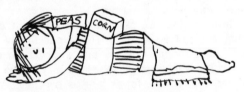

A sunburn almost vanishes if you first wash it with vinegar, then cover it with a cold wet towel until the skin feels cool.

For faster overall treatment in case of any large burn, no matter what its cause, wrap a wet towel around the child before going to the hospital. A child under Three can get dehydrated quickly from a large minor burn.

Bumps and Cuts

Ice stops bleeding in most cuts but it will intensify the pain for a few minutes until the skin is numb. Just rub the cut with an ice cube, and to keep your child quiet, give him another cube to suck.

For a goose egg, crush the ice. Put it in a plastic bag, then flop it on the bump like a pillow. The bits won't feel as heavy on a child's head. Call the doctor if he vomits, gets pale, sweaty or sleepy—all signs of a possible concussion.

Some mothers, more daring than we, use ice, a kiss and a butterfly bandage on a cut, but frankly we never hesitate to let the doctor or the hospital staff decide when stitches are necessary.

Although we are no food fadists, we have had spectacular luck using vitamin E. We simply smeared the contents of one 100 I.U. capsule on burns and abrasions three times a day for three days.

The results were always good, if curious, with the top layer of skin toughening and peeling, leaving a fresh pink skin beneath, to be coated one more day.

This helped prevent scars and though we may be superstitious we think it made stitches less noticeable too.

Splinters and Scratches

These can cause infections and the blood needs stimulation to flush them away. Soak the area with this solution.

All-purpose Solution
The water should be as hot as the child can stand it for ten minutes.
Combine   1 pt. boiled water
                  1 tsp. salt

Bites and Bee Stings

The itching caused by bites from gnats, mosquitoes, flies and spiders can make a child's vacation miserable. Vinegar, if used immediately, will lessen the itching and a hot poultice of the All-purpose Solution will ease the swelling.

If it's near the eyes, use half as much salt, applying first a hot compress for ten minutes, then a cold one in two hours and a hot one again two hours later.

For a bee sting, suck the poison and spit it out. Follow with ice or a lump of wet baking soda to prevent swelling.

Sprains and Strains

Apply ice for the first twenty-four hours, then soak the sprain in a hot All-purpose Solution or in epsom salts. A child can keep his foot or hand in a bucket more happily if you add marbles or pennies for him to handle (or footle, for that matter).

Broken Bones and Cracked Heads

Sooner or later, your child will break a bone and if he doesn't, he will roughhouse so much you may think he has.

Sometimes the most minor fall can injure a child, so you must watch him closely after he takes a tumble. Any sharp, localized pain, blacking out, double vision, paleness, cold sweat, chill or vomiting are signs that your child should be rushed to the hospital.

If it's a leg he probably won't be able to stand on it, and if it's an arm he might not be able to make a fist, or indeed bear to lift it to any other position than the one in which it was broken. It's much harder to tell about the skull, the ribs or the bones in the hands and feet. An X ray is the only way to be certain and the quicker the better. The doctor must set a broken arm or leg before there's any swelling, or else wait until it subsides—a painful twenty-four hours—and he must treat a concussion immediately.

If you suspect a fracture keep your child warm to offset the shock to his system and call your doctor. He'll either send an ambulance or have you take him to the hospital yourself. If you drive lay him next to you, buckled in place and covered with a blanket, with an ice bag on the tender area to minimize swelling. The doctor also may have you give him sips of cola on the way to settle his stomach, and if he suspects a concussion, will have you talk to him constantly to keep him awake.

Vomiting and drowsiness are the two main signs of a concussion—a small hairline crack in the skull. It requires bed rest and usually hospitalization.

Poison

If you think your child has had even a teaspoon of any nonfood, like liquid wax or a dishwasher compound, or if he's taken cigarettes, whiskey or vitamins, dilute the toxic with as much milk as possible, give Syrup of Ipecac (which should be in every medicine chest) and call the Poison Control Center. They'll check the ingredients so you can start treatment. You'll probably have to put your finger down your child's throat and tickle his tonsils to induce vomiting, unless he's swallowed a caustic, like lye, which will do as much damage coming up as it did going down. Unless you're taking an ambulance to the hospital, have a friend go with you to continue giving fluids and if he falls unconscious, to give mouth-to-mouth resuscitation.

Mouth-to-mouth Resuscitation

Have someone call the rescue squad for an oxygen inhaler while you lay the child on the ground, wipe anything out of the mouth with your thumb and tip the head backward, so the tongue can't clog the throat. Hook your thumb over the bottom teeth, to keep the jaw steady, and pinch the nose with your fingers, so the air can't escape—both necessities during the entire procedure. Cover his mouth with yours. To the mental count of 1, 2, 3, breathe out in a gentle puff, then turn your head aside to let the old air expel from his lungs while you draw a new breath for yourself. Keep an even rhythm, twenty breaths to the minute, and do this for at least fifteen minutes or until breathing is regular. Anyone who has had to have resuscitation should be hospitalized for forty-eight hours for general observaton—an essential in the case of a near drowning.

Hospitals — Emergency and Otherwise

There's little to calm the frenzy of an emergency, but you can handle it better if you know what to do in advance—and you should. There's bound to be at least one disaster in the first six years.

Learn the location of the nearest hospital, the hospital your doctor uses and any special procedures he recommends.

He surely will want you to call him even if you feel too frantic to spare the time. He can advise first aid, and decide whether your child needs hospital or office treatment. Home visits are almost impossible, since few doctors will leave a roomful of patients.

If your child does need hospital treatment the doctor will alert the emergency room and, if necessary, call an ambulance. If you call yourself the driver may go to the nearest hospital, no matter what you want. If you can't reach your doctor and you don't know whether you have an emergency or not, go to the hospital—the safe-not-sorry principle.

You'll be dashing out of the house, but do grab a special toy, your insurance identification and a blank check too (whether you have money in the bank or not). Officious nurses sometimes delay help until they are sure the hospital can be paid. The toy is to placate your child because the wait may be long—emergency rooms take the most serious cases first—and because he'll be cross, since he can't eat or drink anything until he has been treated.

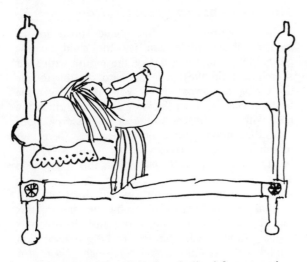

If your child will be hospitalized for more than a day you'll want to return with a few special toys and some snapshots of the family and maybe of the pussycat. Even if you're with your child he'll be lonely, for the friendliest hospital in the world is still remote and needs reminders from home. Good hospitals try to minimize the anxiety of a hospital stay by letting the mother wait with her child outside the operating room until he's sedated and letting her spend the night in his room.

When you know in advance that your child will be hospitalized, he should be told what will happen to him there. A pre-Four can't understand much besides tea and sympathy, but an older child will profit by a book about hospitals and a visit there beforehand.

He also needs to know about anesthesia and why doctors wear those silly-looking pajamas and caps. He'll want to know that the bed in his room will be stiff and narrow with crib rails, but if he's there for an operation he'll travel from surgery strapped onto an even taller, skinnier cot on wheels.

Of all the routine hospitalizations, we found a tonsillectomy was the scariest, not because of its slight danger, but because it was preceded by so many illnesses we wondered, "If this doesn't work—then what?"

A child has these same qualms too, we think, and needs special cheer. Our Kate, still groggy from

a tonsillectomy, was enchanted by the beautiful Spanish doll on her pillow but Nadia enjoyed her send-off most. On the night before the operation we turned a favorite family dinner into a party with a special dessert and with friends—at the doctor's suggestion. The food kept her adrenalin high and since she couldn't eat much for several days, she needed a full stomach.

If your child is having this operation he should know that it will hurt to swallow or even to talk at first, improving rapidly until, on the fifth day, he will have a brief few hours of real pain as the stitches draw tighter. On the other hand, he will have more ice cream, ginger ale, popsicles, gelatin (and soup) than he's ever had in his life—the silver-lining principle.

Convalescence

A convalescent child needs sympathy and many simple things to do. He also needs socks on his feet, since he only spends as much time in bed as his body needs and he'll seldom put on his slippers.

When health is low, impressions are deepest. Our girls still remember an occasional rose on a sick tray, with food served on doll dishes and a lollipop to stir their tea (the only spoon we could find, we said). It's nice to feel treasured when you're sick.

A convalescent child is frustrated easily. He can't even decide what to do without feeling weepy. To keep him a little happier, you can provide him with more records, more stories aloud, more loving and a few simple toys he can use to invent his own games, such as a flashlight, a magnifying glass, playing cards and some paperclips as "fish" for a magnet.

An older child finds a cookie sheet a good base for a puzzle or a coloring book, for its rim catches anything loose, but a bed table made from a cardboard box is good for the child who faces a long term in bed.

To make one, turn the box upside down, so the bottom becomes the table top. Remove the flaps and cut two semicircles on opposite sides of the box, to fit over the patient's legs. It will look like a two-way covered bridge.

Exceptions

Whenever your life gets complicated, you will have to spend extra time with your child to compensate for it, since any change, for better or worse, strains a family.

No matter how much you welcome another baby, a cross-country trip or a little renovation in the house, you can expect more tension. You may face a temporary situation, like moving across town, or it may be the grinding long-term problem of dealing with a handicap. Both sorrows and joys will exhaust you but the grit you develop will enrich you too.

The solutions you find must be peculiarly your own, for no circumstances are ever the same. However, since nothing in this world is unique, the answers which others have found can be the most helpful of all.

The Second Baby

Tell your child about your pregnancy when you tell your other friends. Some mothers can wait until the sixth month, although we only lasted about six weeks.

After the initial queries, your child will scarcely mention the subject. He hasn't forgotten.

You need to explain how life begins, develops and is brought forth, even if he doesn't ask. Let him listen to the heartbeat and feel the baby move.

Instinctively you will push your first child from the nest, encouraging independence much faster than you would have done. Don't be alarmed. This is good and healthy. Mothers don't have the stamina to handle more than one litter at a time, whether they are cat mothers or people mothers.

Even a One will react well to your expectations if you compensate with a special camaraderie—a relaxed trip to the pet store, a breakfast picnic in the park.

There are other specific ways to prepare your child for the new baby. He'll resent the baby using his crib, but he won't resent it so much if you provide a new bed and new bureau for him at least

six weeks before you expect to deliver. Prepare the baby's bassinet and changing table after you do this because at this time a first child comes first.

In the last months of pregnancy you'll want to tell your child what the maternity ward looks like, who will take care of him when you're away and how the new baby will eat. We should warn you: Your child will be more curious—and more jealous—when you feed the baby than at any other time, especially if you nurse. We think you'll be wise to ask a friend to show him how her own baby eats. It will help him get used to the idea later, but not very much.

As luck will have it, you'll go to the hospital in the middle of the night, but be sure to tell your child you're leaving. You'll also want to telephone him after you deliver. He'll accept your news—probably in silence, but he may be distraught unless the baby is a carbon copy of himself.

Our Mike sat in self-exile on the front steps all day, after hearing the news of a third sister. Only his father could lure him in again, but the next day he was consoled enough to announce it with lollipops to his friends.

We found snapshots were best to help a firstborn adjust to the tininess of the infant. Take pictures immediately of the baby alone, with Father, with Mother, and all three together. Use a flash camera and overnight-developing service—or, if possible, a camera with its built-in developing system—so your husband can hurry them home.

Your child can absorb the impact alone, then show the pictures to his friends, scribbling on them and probably flushing them down the toilet.

They're his pictures, and you probably will never see them again.

When you have a new baby, you may be ashamed of your love—not the rather prosaic love you feel for your newborn—but the overwhelming love you feel for your first child. This difference is completely natural. Each day you care for a child brings a new degree of love, no matter how bad either the day or the child. It will take months for your newborn to find his niche, and until he does, he won't know what he's missing.

On the day you come home, let your husband carry the baby into the house so you can hug the firstborn and make a great fuss over him. Give him a wrapped present from the baby, perhaps a rubber doll and bottle, so he may feed his baby while you feed yours, and maybe one superpresent, like a toy piano. He may like the oddities from the hospital, such as salt and pepper packets and flexible straws, but the real present you bring will be you.

Let your child show the new baby to any guests, and hope that they have the grace to bring a present to him rather than to the baby.

Your firstborn will want to touch him, smell him, tickle his toes, sing to him, hold him and later help you bathe and dress him. Everything you allow him to do shows your trust, but do stand by. He may never hurt the baby—at least not much—but there are bound to be times when he'd like to throw the baby out with the bath water. It won't be a patch on the jealousy he'll feel in three months when everyone koochy-coos the baby and nobody notices him.

The first few times your oldest sees you breast-feed, he may ask for a taste or pretend not to notice, or, as ours did, he may astonish you by yanking down your bra before company and commanding, "Feed her."

The more distracted you are by the new baby, the worse your firstborn will react. He'll realize almost immediately that you can't control him while you nurse the baby. That's why you should have morning and afternoon feedings wherever you think your older child will be most content.

One well-prepared Four we know, the paragon of his set, accepted the idea of a baby completely until his mother came home with a new sister and a colossal cold too. She didn't have quite enough energy to nurse both the cold and the baby and none at all to visit with Robbie. On that first day, when his father thought he was napping, he wrote on his toys with crayons and on his walls with felt-tipped pens, spread glue on the floor and ran his mother's clothes through the dishwasher. His mother could only stagger out of bed and say, "Why, Robbie, why?" Fortunately, his behavior was as temporary as it was disastrous.

Another favorite Four, picture-book pretty with brown eyes and yellow curls, climbed on a stool at

our house one day and pronounced, ex cathedra, his own rules to care for the new Suzannah:

"You DON'T Drop the Baby When You're Holding Her in the Air!"

"You DON'T Push Down on the Baby's Soft Spot!"

"And You DON'T Press on the Baby so Hard You See the Whites under Your Fingernails!"

Aside from these essentials, there probably aren't any other rules your firstborn needs to know.

Handicapped Child

We agree with a noted anthropologist—and a grandmother—who said that children "trash a marriage," even as they enrich it.

Indeed they do and the more problems a child has, the more a marriage can be hurt—and the more it can be enriched. Stress brings out the best and the worst in everyone.

If you have a child who is handicapped, either mentally or physically, he'll need much extra care and extra therapy. So will you. Some exceptional people can endure alone, but you won't know if you're one of them until it's too late. You and your husband will need more respect for each other than other couples and more respites together. You also will need the support and guidance from others, either through meetings of the local organization that deals with your problem or through group counseling—which often is about the same thing.

There's no need to invent the wheel—especially when the roads are so rocky.

Handicapped Parent

In one more marvel of nature, the handicapped mother learns to cope in a hundred ingenuous ways, as if the challenge of her role were a sport in itself. One dear friend, battling braces and crutches—and still a more dedicated mother than most of us—found it was a matter of adjusting the equipment and resolving the small, terrible tasks of motherhood so thoughtfully that she didn't feel overly tired or silly by her solutions.

If you have a back problem you'll be more self-sufficient, as our friend was, if you have the playpen raised by extending the legs or by mounting it on a platform.

The feeding table was better than a high chair, she felt, because lifting was less of a strain and the table was safer, because tipping was almost impossible.

Changing was done at waist level until the baby

was old enough to stand on a chair and a harness was used outside since the straps were easier to catch in an emergency than her child's hand—and since her child loved it so much her dollies wore it when she outgrew it.

Stooping is the biggest problem any mother has, but it's especially hard if you have a bone or muscle problem. We recommend the large plywood pincers to pick up the clothes and toys from the floor, but you can have fewer toys to fetch if you tie them to the playpen with elastic so he can reel them in for himself.

If he still makes trouble for himself and then cries about it he's been in the same place too long.

Three Sons

There must be a special place in heaven for mothers of three sons. You certainly can tell them on earth. They're those ladies with amused, bemused faces and an amazing tolerance for disaster—for they have learned that shouting doesn't help.

No other combination of children, not even twins, can create so much chaos or camaraderie. Even the most introspective child will join the team—them against you—and like all good players, they encourage each other to bigger feats of daring.

We recommend the advice of so many successful mothers of three boys. Give them as much outdoor playtime as possible, and indoors, set up two rooms: one for sleeping, with nothing but beds and bureaus, and the other for playing, with much climbing equipment. With three children, one is bound to be quieter than the others and he probably will need a corner somewhere else.

You will be frazzled in the early years but when your boys grow up, we think you'll find yourself perhaps more treasured than most other mothers.

Travel

Air Travel

An airplane ride of even two hours alone with a small child can cause anguish. We've seen the young mother in tears, struggling to walk those endless corridors to get from one gate to another to change planes. She carries her baby in one arm and her house in the other.

If you travel with a child you must plan the trip to the last minute. When making your reservation, ask for a stroller or a cart ready for you at the airport and one waiting for you at any connection and at your destination. Also ask for the seat on the plane with the most leg room—generally the front row of the coach section. This lets you lay your baby on a blanket on the floor and gives you more freedom, for a pre-Two is a nonpaying passenger who has no seat of his own and if the plane is full he travels in your lap.

Pack everything you need in a lightweight shoulder bag—petroleum jelly, disposable diapers, packaged pre-moistened towels, a large bib, a nonbulky blanket, a sweater, a few teething biscuits, two small toys, his magic blanket and such food as you may need.

Since you may have to carry this pack, the baby, your purse and perhaps a coat for at least a mile, you may want to hold all beforehand to see if you can do it. Nothing will force you to jettison the nonessentials quicker than this test.

Until your baby is about six months old, you will find it easier to carry him in a sling, but if he's a skittish toddler, consider getting a harness for his safety and your sanity. Use it a few times first, so he'll feel acquainted with it.

A Two to Six can walk—although the airport stroller can be helpful even for a Four—and at this age your child can carry a bag of his own precious possessions—books, crayons, paper, stick-on stars, coloring books.

Pack just enough formula and food to use on the plane and for one extra meal, for a pre-Two gets no meals at all. Take a light snack for an older child since he may not like what he's served. In any case, he'll get properly dirty which may surprise the people who meet you. They always seem to expect an immaculate mother and child.

To give the appearance of cleanliness, have your child wear a large bib or *tablier*, the sleeveless apron with pockets worn by boys and girls in French schools. Remove it just before alighting.

If you weren't able to reserve a seat and have to take what's available, sit next to the kindest, most tolerant-looking grandmother. And our best regards to you both.

Car Travel

Regardless of the tempo of your car trips, you'll need some basic tricks to keep your sanity, and keep your child reasonably happy.

For both your sanity and his safety, we suggest the same rules you follow in Car Pools (page 76) and in Car Manners (page 60). You also should observe his regular eat and sleep schedule, and take some old toys and some new ones, to be disbursed as needed. You'll need to sit with your child in the back seat occasionally, to hold him and play with him—before he starts to fuss. It's most important to run, stretch and pot every two hours—a schedule we found can be synchronized even in a large family if you limit the intake of fluid for the toilet-trained to four ounces of water or juice between stops.

We found a large breakfast in a restaurant was the one meal we could afford to order, because you get so much more for your money, but lunch and dinner were picnics, literally if not vernacularly. Fruit, crackers and cheese are good on-the-road snacks, but avoid candy and chips, for they cause thirst.

Infancy
This is the simplest age to travel.

Although you can carry more equipment in a car than you can in a plane, the list of supplies is just more of the same. Expect to change your baby in the car and wash his bottom at least once during the day, as well as morning and night, to avoid diaper rash or he'll be very fussy.

Six to Eighteen Months
We've had success with a portable crib if the car is big enough for it to fit on the right side of the car, out of the driver's vision. A child should wear the seat harness as soon as he's old enough to stand. Should you drive past his bedtime, change him into pajamas, so his life seems less disrupted.

Mid-One to Three
We find this is the most difficult time to travel with a child, as it is to do anything, for he lacks the flexibility to enjoy an adventure. His concentration time varies between five and fifteen minutes, at the most, and he's tremendously active. He needs to use his energy, so longer, more frequent stops are vital.

This child is old enough to accept strange beds but not strange foods. He'll need to stop in time to order your meals or prepare them so he can eat at his regular time. At this age continuity is essential.

Three to Six
Any child needs extra cuddling and coddling when he travels, but the Three to Six revels in a trip if it's treated as a Great Adventure, with much anticipation and map reading, and car games for a pastime. For some reason, children like to make the highway one big contest.

Counting Cars

Keep score on the number of station wagons vs. trucks, convertibles vs. sport cars, or red cars vs. blue ones. You'll soon be bored with this game—but not your Four.

Alphabet Game

A Five can find all the letters of the alphabet on signs (but not on license plates, which is too fast for him to read). Start with the letter "A," go on to "B" and follow the alphabet. The letter you're looking for doesn't need to start a word. The first to get to "Z" is the winner.

Carsickness

We thought car sickness went out of style with the pompadour until we had our Nell, who got carsick from the time she was a baby.

If you have a child like that avoid all rich foods while traveling and take a nonprescription drug for motion sickness with you. It will cause drowsiness too—a welcome side effect.

For mild queasiness, rely on chewing gum, pretzels, crackers and hard lemon candies, but for the pea-green stage, give sodas. A cola drink will settle the stomach best, but has so much more caffeine than the other flavors it may make your child jumpy.

Since car sickness embarrasses a child so much, you should treat it very matter-of-factly. Carry a few throw-away plastic bags, and sit him next to the open rear window. As our other children would tell Nell when we couldn't slow down on a freeway, "Aim for the Cadillacs, sweetie."

Moving

In the next few years you'll choose a pattern of living that probably will last for years and this pattern is directed by the place you live—a small town, a farm, a suburb, a city. It's a much more serious decision than it may seem at first, not just because the influence of a neighborhood is indelible but also because, to some children, a move can be drastic. However, you can soften the impact if you give your child a role to play. The emphasis should rest, not on the travails of moving or some awful reason for it, but on the joy of the adventure.

Before you begin to look for a house or an apartment, talk with your child about the important things it should have. Will there be a tree big enough to hold a tree house? a shady spot near a faucet for a sandbox? a little room just fit for a child his size?

Even a Two should be included in a little of the househunting, if only to feel his opinion counts (although you won't, of course, ever let him think it counts above the opinion of his parents).

Before you move you'll go through a nearly endless litany with your child, as early as mid-One: Yes, we'll take the sofa and the rug and your lamp, and no, we'll throw away the carrots and the broken vacuum cleaner and the trash can with the hole in it. By the time you've discussed everything in the house, from teaspoons to toilet paper, you're ready to pack.

If there's a box factory in your town call for a delivery of cartons. They arrive new, flattened—and without the bugs you'd get with the grocery store boxes. An older child can open them up for you as needed, but a Two can throw the spices in a paper bag, take the toys from the bathtub and carry the potty chair to the moving van.

When we moved half a block our Nell and Claire, a neighboring Six, amazed us first by tying three thousand books into bundles of four, and then by hauling them to the new house by dolly, by wagon and by doll carriage. It took a week, but it's hard to say who was more pleased—Nell or us.

Although you are busier than ever now, you must expect to give your child more attention during moving days. If you don't they can become a nightmare. You'll need neighbors to watch your child when you do the bulk of the moving, but the child who leaves his pleasant house to visit Grandma for two weeks, then returns to a new, albeit pleasant house, will be jarred by the impermanence of his life. A child adjusts, of course, but if he also is part of the move the adjustment will be easier.

Once you are in your new place, we think your child's room should be organized first, for as

disorderly as he may be, he needs order around him to feel at peace. The living room can wait.

Renovation

To live in a house during its renovation, as so many city families do, is a test of fortitude for everybody. Its confusion is tough on a marriage and tougher still on children, unless you make some basic decisions.

Your meals must be the simplest, your housekeeping almost nonexistent, and you must have some small area of sanity—if only a tidy, well-painted nook in a room, with comfortable chairs to sit in, lights to read by and a floor clean enough for crawling.

Your child needs to keep his regular routine somehow and some extra toys. Buy whatever seems special but cheap, for toys are damaged easily during a renovation and good ones may be a waste. Your child also will need extra loving, just like you, for the restoration of a house can be depressing and always takes longer than you thought.

Your child will need to play outdoors more often than usual, since he can't have company or run around the house so well, and he has many "nos" there anyway. You also will need sitters to take him out too so you can work more peacefully.

You must be careful to protect your child from an overdose of plaster dust—often the start of allergies—and the sanding of any old paint, for it can carry lead particles into his system. Your pediatrician can keep a running test on the lead levels in his blood, if you see signs of listlessness, but from the many children we know who have thrived in this crazy milieu the problem can be controlled.

You can expect other, more obvious physical dangers, but be surprised how your toddler will skitter to the edge of the big hole in the floor, as our intrepid Michael did every day for fifteen days until the new stairs finally were in place. Despite all the tools, wires and lumber that abounded, the only blood drawn was by his unhinged mother who nicked his ear while cutting his hair.

You should tell your child what the workmen are doing during each stage of the renovation, both for his own information and because if you don't he'll use your workmen's expensive time to ask them. Explain also the work you do yourself and the principles involved, showing him how the holes you punch in the lip of the paint can will drain the extra paint back into the can and how a wet sponge makes a plaster patch smooth.

If renovation does nothing else it imposes a remarkable sense of self-sufficiency on a child, for even a One realizes when you have tolerated as much chaos as you can and that day he'd better muddle through alone.

We found a Two makes a good apprentice or, as that Michael called himself so seriously, a "workin-ing man" (his only ambition in life for three more years). At this age a child will fetch tools for you, if he's taught their names, but you won't ask for the screwdriver for that's unsafe in a fall. A Three can tell brick nails from brads and what a ten-penny nail looks like too. This child lays the level on every horizontal he can find, but a Four is much more sensible. He measures instead, flipping out the six-foot rule like a master carpenter. A Four will be helpful one minute, gone the next, but a Five is a whiz and curious about everything. He'll be intrigued when his father shows him an old disconnected switchbox and with it can understand the principles of electricity, even if you can't.

A Five is also a pretty fine worker. Under a tough time pressure, we organized a crew of Fives to paint radiators and the work was quite good for a first coat. We found our Six, that diligent child, was eager to scrape paint from window panes and in fact was considerably better than her sister (a blasé Twelve) and could haul a prodigious amount of trash outdoors too.

A renovation, we found, brings out the best—and the worst—in all of us. You'll be amazed how fast the money goes, but how hard you work together. You'll be shocked how cross everyone becomes when the work drags along and how proud everyone feels at each bit of progress.

A child will never forget which balustrade he refinished, which tile he laid, which prisms he washed. For that sense of accomplishment alone, a renovation is worth it.

Questions

Some of the toughest moments you'll ever have—and the most memorable—will be the ones you spend explaining life well enough for your child to understand a little of it.

He's deeply curious about the world and who made it and wars and how they kill—all questions that deserve your thoughtful analyses, as simplified as they might be, for you'll find that any idea that intrigues you will intrigue your child too.

This is why a Two, as flummoxed by newscasts of the latest crimes as you are, needs explanations. Each year you can talk about the news a little more cogently, until your Five will be ready, as our Kate was, to grasp the sarcasm of most Herblock cartoons when we explained them and to realize, when she was Six, that if she could read her primer, she could read the big headlines too. When a child tries to understand the whole world, he has a slightly better idea of his place in it.

Although he may ask you about the nightly newscasts, the questions that could affect his own life fascinate him so much he may not be able to ask them at all. That's why he needs to know that parents might divorce each other, but they never can divorce their child, and he needs to know this even if you and your husband have never considered divorce. Since your child will know parents who do separate, you need to have these conversations or he may go through a fearful stage when every argument he overhears is one more sign of doom.

We also think you have to talk with your child about the bugs (and the bunnies and the people) that die and return to enrich the land and about the bugs (and bunnies and people) that procreate and why and how.

The abstract is confusing to a child but the more you translate it into simple terms, the less confusing it will be.

Sex

Once a precocious Five climbed on her grandmother's lap and said, "Tell me, *Grandmère*, tell me about sex."

The old lady—French, worldly and delighted—settled happily into a full, if delicate account.

"Now, *ma chère*, is there anything else you wish to know?"

"I just want to know how to spell it, *Grandmère*."

A child's questions about sex are generally like that.

Beyond a daughter's "How come I'm so plain and he's so fancy?," most children let the subject slide unless they're in a crowded elevator or in church. Bring up the discussion yourself, so you can explain it at your convenience. A child needs to know a little about everything, including sex, even if he hasn't asked.

He should know you think bodies are beautiful, which he will if he sees you and your husband walk around naked occasionally and if he can touch your bodies without your looking embarrassed. If you accept your child's natural curiosity about sex now he won't feel the shame it so often brings later.

When he is toilet trained, he (and, of course, she) begins to touch the genitals, obviously and regularly. You won't, of course, tell him that masturbation is bad, because it isn't, but you will tell him not to do it in public, because it bothers other people. However, it does reflect boredom or a need to urinate—or, more likely, a pleasant interlude.

We may be old-fashioned, but we think there's more to sex than human reproduction. The sex act is improbable enough without plucking people out of the regular pattern of nature. If you want your child to believe that intercourse and birth are normal, or even believe it at all, he needs to know that there are a lot of ways to make a baby.

A Two will be pleased to find that an insect is the yenta of the flower garden, matching pollen to seeds and collecting nectar as its reward. Although many insects pollinate the flowers, the bee, with its nectar-to-honey cycle, explains it best.

Show your child the flowers, colored to attract the bugs, and let him smell their different perfumes. This helps him understand that while bright flowers may need little scent, the white flowers often have much more to compensate.

Have your Two help you undress a flower, like an iris, big enough to hide no secrets. Let him jiggle the stamen and see the yellow pollen fall from its stalks to his finger, just the way it falls on the wings of a bee. He can track his finger down the bright yellow stripe of the petal—like a runway for a bee—right to the pistil, where the ovule of seeds swims in nectar. The pollen is bound to fall from his fingertip, just as it falls from the bee, fertilizing the seeds and giving us flowers next year.

And after you've explained all that, go inside and have a honey sandwich.

A Three can find the stamen, pistils and pollen in any flower without help. He likes to examine the blossom on an apple tree now and check the ovule as it swells to become the fruit itself, with its nest of seeds in the center.

A child should watch the birth of kittens or puppies—without touching them of course—and see an animal nurse its young.

Our two daughters, as foster parents to nearly one hundred gerbils, were distressed· one morning when Exter, the father of them all, cringed in a corner of his cage. Though he'd been up all night helping to deliver the tenth litter, the children were sure he was ill, but by afternoon Nadia ran in shouting, "Don't worry any more about Exter! He and Zester are mating again!"

By using so many natural examples, your child will understand cross-pollination of people more easily.

Since you'll be using biological names for the sex organs, don't be surprised when your child sidles up to a stranger—the stranger the better—and asks loudly and publicly if he has a penis? or better yet, if she has a penis?

This is not altogether accidental. Your child may look innocent, but he knows that something about babies, beds and bottoms is very exciting and that people wear clothes for more reasons than to keep away the chill.

Gradually between Three and Six you'll explain the hows, whys and wheres of human reproduction enhanced by a month-by-month picture book of fetal development—and of course you'll tell him that sex is an expression of love.

You can expect boys and girls of Four to kiss often and possibly play feelie more than teenagers at a drive-in movie. Truth to tell, we found an advanced Six with his fly unzipped on top of a dainty Five with her panties to her knees. They may have learned by looking through the keyhole, but we prefer to think they were simply inventive.

Keep a close eye now, but don't be too alarmed if your child experiments, for by Seven he'll be too modest to try and even too embarrassed to recall his youth.

No matter how much a child enjoys his experiments, he'll never believe the same of you. After perhaps dozens and dozens of small talks

about sex with our curious little girls, one suddenly asked, "But you only do it when you want to make a baby, right?"

Their question astonished us, but our answer astonished them more.

Death

Death is shocking and the acceptance of it comes almost as slowly for a child as for you. Be frank if you anticipate the death of someone dear to your child, so he can have the chance to say good-by too.

There are times when death is so sudden or inexplicable you only can attribute it to plain bad luck. Whether you're religious or not, don't pass the buck with phrases like "God needed her more" or euphemisms like "Aunt Harriet was called away," which will baffle him. What seems like harsh reality to you will be logical to him, if you treat it as a natural part of the life cycle. We think a child can make better sense of the ashes-to-ashes concept if he commemorates death with life, by planting a tree in the yard or even a bulb in a window box.

A Four, we think, is old enough to attend a funeral, but no child should have to see a beautified corpse. That can be eerie enough to make a child believe in ghosts.

We felt blessed, toward the end of a difficult fourth pregnancy, to have had the chance to tell our children that the baby couldn't live after birth. When they had absorbed this idea we explained the medical problems specifically to remove the mystery and any fear they could die the same way. Naturally there was grief when the infant died and we all wept and comforted each other. It was an event that enriched our lives even as it saddened us, and, in fact, was a catharsis for all the children in the neighborhood.

Today our children still talk about their dead

brother as if they had known him, occasionally assigning him the role of angel when they play pretend. This isn't because we told them he was an angel, but because this death added a new dimension to their games—and a certain status too. Children, like old Latin ladies, enjoy pathos. We remember our Tia Tata, at eighty-eight, weeping all day on the anniversary of her mother's death and our Tante Nini, who wore full mourning for various relations for eighty-four of her hundred and two years.

Many young children will never be faced with the death of someone they know, but the idea shouldn't be foreign. We found a casual procession of snakes, gerbils and goldfish explain life and death better than we ever could.

The first funerals were events as we remember when all the children in the car pool gathered at seven-thirty one morning to pledge allegiance, sing "God Bless America" and plant that first Peruvian guinea pig to die of the dread "wet bottom" disease. It took our animal lovers, Nadia and Meg, about seven funerals before the ritual was perfunctory. Death had become a way of life.

Divorce

Today, divorce is almost epidemic, striking one out of every three couples. Now you'll find yourself explaining it to your child frequently, either because you or your neighbors are taking this step.

Unfortunately, the death of a marriage is almost inexplicable to a child, for it seems so sudden to him. He's dumbfounded that two adults can't get along with each other well enough to live together—especially his parents. The thought that love can start—and stop—will haunt your child, for if his parents can stop loving each other, they just might stop loving him.

No matter how bad your marriage or how smooth your separation, the first year will be very hard on your child. He may behave as usual at home, although perhaps more quietly, then have

sudden tantrums or periods of confusion or inattention at someone's house or in his nursery school.

If he is in school have a conference with his teacher as soon as you and your husband have decided to separate, so she can give your child the extra support he needs. Above all, you'll need to have many little talks with your child about the divorce, for one big talk is never enough to assimilate such news. Even a nonverbal mid-One should be told—in twenty-five words or less—although he can barely comprehend the idea.

Of course you won't give a pre-Six any tangible reasons for the separation—for they're none of his business—but he's such an egocentric, he inevitably assumes some of the blame himself. Both you and your husband must cushion him with as much love and time now as possible, even though you're under a good deal of stress yourselves.

A pre-Six, that ultimate loyalist, can be fractured by a split, but it won't be so bad if neither parent snipes about the other—the same rule you follow in marriage. This lets him keep pretending that his parents, if not Superman and Supermom, are at least sort of super. This is a need all children have.

Assuming that you keep custody of your child, you should encourage frequent visits with his father. It is easy for a child to glamorize (or condemn) the parent he never sees. Even if your ex-husband should have a serious problem, like drinking, we think your child should spend some time around him. Slowly he'll learn to accept his father as he is—or not. The decision eventually belongs to your child. Of course, the same reasoning applies to the father, if he has custody.

Since young children have an oversupply of female company, a child in your custody—boy or girl—needs to be around older men, whether he has a weekly visit with his father or not. To a young child, a teen-age boy is man enough. If you pay a student to take your child out for an ice cream or a bike ride a few times a week it will help a good deal.

As a single parent, you'll be tempted to focus too intensely on your child, if only for the companionship. Although you probably will work, you will need to have some other outside activity to keep your relationship in perspective. It's especially important to go out at night, with or without a date, so your child doesn't think you only belong to him.

From a child's point of view, there's very little good you can say for divorce. Since you're doing what you think is best, you must ignore the guilt you feel (for some of it is part of every marriage, every death and every divorce) and treat your child with as much sensitivity as you would like to be treated yourself.

Influences

Influences

If you want your child to become an interesting, bright adult, you have to give him an interesting childhood.

Of course you want your baby to develop into a complete person—competent, respectful and independent—but without enrichment, his life will be like a room without windows. There won't be any sunshine or the chance for him to see the dazzling world outside.

From the moment your child is born, you and your husband will make a series of decisions, often unconsciously, which either will limit or stretch his world, depending on the influences you offer. They determine how far he can see and, ultimately, how much of the world he'll want to see. His values, his friendships, his adventures and his environment will shape him into a three-dimensional person—and you're the lady who'll do most of the shaping.

In 1831, our favorite arbiter of maternal behavior, Maria Francis Child of Philadelphia, quoted an educator who concluded that "the heaviness of the Dutch" and "the vivacity of the French" began in the nursery. She said, in those pre-Freud days, "The Dutch keep their children in a state of repose, always rocking or jogging them; the French are perpetually tossing them and showing them lively tricks."

Naturally a Dutch mother shouldn't try to act like a French one nor a French mother like a Dutch one. Some of us are quiet, some are loud; some shy, some not. Any way you treat your child is fine, as long as it's natural to you. You're rearing your baby in your own style, to share many of your interests and your own brand of humor.

You may be contained or you may be effusive, but you must be loving, for love and learning go together. Each is dependent on the other. Studies show such a strong relationship between the two that institutionalized babies can be markedly slower to learn and even can become irredeemably retarded when they lack not care, but caring. Your praise, freely given in words and kisses, invites his love in return, because love is a response, not an instinct. This mutual love will be his greatest preparation for life, particularly in his first year, when he needs you the most.

A well-loved baby is like a sponge, ready to absorb all the information in the world, if he has the surroundings, the excitement and the values that make it easy. Your baby, who at first seems to need nothing but diapers, milk, diapers, sleep and diapers, actually needs a great deal more. He has been coddled and nestled those weeks in the womb and has prospered by it; now he wants challenges and chances.

A child needs daily outings—from carriage rides to backpacking—and the stimulation of seeing people of all ages and in many situations. This is how he becomes a little more sensitized each day. Any equipment he uses—in his room, the back yard, the playground—will influence him. It needn't be expensive but it should both prod his imagination and improve his coordination.

Much that he learns will be drawn from books and from television programs, so both should be chosen with care. The violence—and the marvel—of a TV show seen only once may live just as long in a child's mind as a much-read storybook, since film has the extra impact of movement and sound.

Toys are invaluable too, if they're the right ones, and worse than useless if they're not. Select them judiciously, buying only half as many as you think he'll need—and then he only will have twice as much as he should. There are aids that will open his mind—a magnet, a padlock, a magnifying glass,

playing cards and, especially, a library card—for everyone of these makes a child ask questions. When a child learns to wonder about small things, he will learn to wonder about everything.

No matter how much you enrich your child, you still can't supply all the influences he needs (nor should you). His family background, his friends, his play group and his nursery school all will color his image of the world. The effect of these outside influences on your child will depend on the emphasis you give them.

Tempting as it may be however, don't agonize over everything he does and everyone he sees or your child will think he's more important than he is and he'll feel stifled too, because he'll have so few decisions left to make for himself. The child who is allowed to make his own choices (and his own mistakes) can find his own affinities, which is as it should be. He isn't cloned in your image.

Just as he develops his own interests, so must he develop an awareness of the intangibles, for they will govern his values. This awareness follows, we think, when you help a child be a responsible person, letting him care for pets and expecting him to do some chores too, as a contributor to the family. We also believe he should make presents as often as possible—the first of his many lessons in sweet charity. The strongest influences he'll ever know are the ones that will come from within.

It will be the total enrichment of the mind, the body and the spirit that turns him into an individual, as unique as his footprint.

Surroundings

The surroundings you give your child will never be perfect, but if they're chosen with care they'll help him progress naturally from hours of action to moments of solitude. When a child can mesh his activities with his environment he'll feel a little more confident at the end of the day than he did at the beginning.

Child's Room

You don't want your child's room to be like anyone else's room, because you don't want your child to be like anyone else—not even you. Still, like every mother, you're bound to superimpose yourself on your child in many ways, including the surroundings you give him, but gradually you should grow so attuned to him that his room will mirror his own personality. You'll need to make few changes in his first six years except in the bed, the toys, the paint and the pictures.

Infancy

Years ago, when cleanliness nearly won the race with godliness, a sanitary, superwhite nursery would have been a story book setting for a baby. Today it would look like a scene in Kafka, for as we've noted, an important part of a baby's growth depends on the stimulation he receives. A study of two groups of institutionalized babies, each given the same amount of cuddling and physical attention, showed that the babies with mobiles, patterned sheets and posters were much more attentive than those kept in a white, picture-free room. Once you've seen a small baby ogle the drawings on his crib sheet and try to trace their outlines with his fingers, you won't need a study to tell you that color and design give a child extra richness. This is why the walls in his room should have pictures and from the ceiling you should hang a kite or a piñata, a bird cage or a balloon.

A lighted lamp is another important stimulus in the nursery, for the shadows it casts will mesmerize a baby for minutes at a time. Also include a goldfish in a bowl and a green plant, for beauty is as necessary to a baby as it is to you, and as every mother knows, nothing is as beautiful as something that grows. If the light is too scant in the room for photosynthesis put the plant under the lamp and replace the bulb with one made especially for indoor gardening.

The basic necessities of his room should be assembled before you deliver. They won't be many but they should be colorful and functional. Besides a bed, you'll need a rocking chair, a soft light for night feedings and a shelf for his toys. You also must have a bureau to hold his clothes and a sturdy changing table to dress him. The best one we ever saw was a combination of the two—a converted Salvation Army dresser, circa 1920, without its spindly legs and mirror. It was big enough to hold all the baby's clothes, its drawers were soaped for smooth sliding (for a mother needs no added aggravations when she's changing the baby), and it was painted brightly, with wooden alphabet blocks for pulls. The bureau top had a tie nailed to its center to strap the baby in place and was covered by a long quilted pad, to keep him comfortable.

Unless you live in a one-room apartment, you'll

find it convenient to have at least one other changing area and some extra clothes in each part of the house to save steps, and another bassinet, to give your child a change of environment. You also may want to tack the ribbons from baby presents on the back of a door, with clothespins tied to the ends of them, to clip bootees, caps and mittens. If it's easy to take walks you'll take more of them.

Three Months
When you buy the crib, get the best you can afford, for it must be sturdy enough to last through several babies (if not yours, your friends').

At this age, your child should have a crib gym with rings to pull, a toy bolted to the slats and, if possible, transparent bumpers. A mirror is another good visual aid and a spellbinding one too, for it catches and refracts light in as many patterns as snowflakes under a microscope. Since your child will have neither the force nor the tools to break the glass, hang the mirror from the old bureau onto one end of the crib for the next few months. He'll be glad for such handsome company.

One
You can't believe how lively your child has become. He needs strong screens or guards on his or any low window or a screw in the sash to control the height it can be raised. Some babies now are able to rock a crib right across the room and for them you must sit the wheels of the crib on hard rubber casters. When your child begins to climb out of his crib, keep one side lowered so he can scamper out in safety.

Mid-One
By eighteen months a crib may be a cage to your child and escape is his only solution. For this climber we recommend a regular bed. Choose a sturdy one, low to the floor, with a firm mattress and a portable guard rail. He still may fall out of bed, but the falls are closer to the floor.

Whenever your child switches to a bed (unless it's the day before the baby takes his crib), his pride will be huge. We remember our Kate asking the postman, the druggist, the carpenter and every other fellow she met if they too slept "in a big girl's bed." She got many happy, if ribald replies, but she certainly could understand their pleasure.

Two
By Two, a child's room should encourage independence. There should be a tidy place for toys, low hooks for coats in the closet, more shelves for his growing library, a pajama bag to feed every morning and a laundry hamper to feed at night.

Your child can begin to learn where to find his clothes if you label the top edge of each drawer with a felt pen: "socks," "pants," "shirts," which he sees as he opens the drawer. A child quickly memorizes what the words look like (although he won't recognize them anywhere else) and can put away his own clothes in a couple of years.

Since a Two generally has more toys than at any other age, you'll need to make space. Dolls and stuffed animals are decorative but out of the way if you sew a curtain ring on the back of each one and hang them on cup hooks you've screwed to the back of the door.

Three
When your child has stopped dressing and undressing himself every day as a game, hang a rod in his closet low enough for him to reach. Let this rod—a broomstick will do nicely—rest in a pair of rope slings that hang from the pole above. The upper one will be for good clothes that he shouldn't wear without permission; the lower one for his everyday clothes.

Four
This child has a new project every day, each more involved than the next. Let him work with these projects on a folding card table so they won't be stepped on.

Five
A Five and a desk are meant for each other, perhaps now more than ever again. He wants to draw, to print, to play school quite as much as he wants to climb.

Six
When your child is Six you'll analyze his room and himself. Suddenly the low shelves are too low, the toys are outgrown, the pictures look silly. His personality must dominate, if it hasn't before. A precise little girl will want a place for her dollhouse and her collection of small boxes, as well as one

high shelf to hold the tiny glass animals, whereas another little girl, like our Nadia, may turn her room into a zoo of gerbils, snakes and fish. A Six doesn't want his room redecorated suddenly; he has enough changes at this age. When you interpret his interests as they evolve—even if this is stretched over a year or so—the room will suit him better. At least that's our excuse for taking so long.

Equipment

Your baby needs more equipment than you may have thought at first, because he'll be happier if he's moved from place to place.

The quality of his equipment depends on your income or your ingenuity in shopping at second-hand stores. You may have a better idea of how to spend your money when you realize that your infant will sleep at least fifteen hours a day—three of it during naptime—and take a total of three more hours to eat. On this basis, the crib and the infant seat, and later the high chair, are the most important expenditures. In addition, your baby probably will spend two hours a day in a sling, another hour in a carriage (which can be used indoors in place of a bassinet), an hour in a playpen or on a blanket on the floor, perhaps some time in a car bed and less than a half hour in his bathtub.

Bedding

A farmer's daughter once told us about the joys of the annual threshing season in Indiana, when she got her new straw tick. She would dive into it night after night until the mattress was hard and she had burrowed a niche all her own. This need for enclosure is primitive and shouldn't be denied to an infant. That's why we think for the first six weeks a baby should be kept in a cradle, a bassinet—which is easier to find—or a bureau drawer, for there he can nestle and feel secure. The mattress of this or any bed must be firm, for the sake of his back, and should fit tightly, to prevent suffocation.

Bassinet

Every woman has grown up with fantasies about motherhood and how she would care for her children. We saw one mother satisfy one of her whims by transforming the extra bassinet in the living room to a bed fit for her princess. You can do it too, if you had a fancy wedding, by gathering one end of your veil into a large embroidery hoop and suspending it from the ceiling, so it falls like a canopy over the bassinet: a proper way to honor royalty.

Crib

This piece of equipment should be the best of all, to be safe. The slats must be not more than 2 3/8'' apart, and the crib should be built as solidly as a piece of gym equipment—for that's what it becomes. Use bumpers to protect the baby's fontanel from hitting the slats.

Bed

When the crib becomes more of a gym set than a place to sleep, it's time to buy a bed. Then he'll have a trampoline. The simplest bed will do, as long as it has a firm mattress and good springs, but forget about a youth bed, which has to be replaced in a few years, and forget about a bunk bed too. It needs an acrobat to change the sheets. If you want more sleeping space for overnight guests, we find a trundle bed works well.

Carriage

Unless you can leave your carriage outside, get one that is so lightweight you won't mind pulling it up and down the steps. It should have a harness to hold the baby in place and as few plastic parts as possible for a summer baby, because plastic holds the heat. Some carriages can become car beds, which is handy, and all of them can be used as a bassinet for a nap, either indoors or out.

Infant Seat

This will give your baby a whole new slant on the world and give you a place to put him wherever you work in the house or while you shovel in the applesauce. Begin using it after the first month, propping it only a few inches at first, to protect his back. At any age be sure to strap him in place for safety.

You can expect a three-month-old baby to be happy in an infant seat for a total of an hour a day, at least, exclusive of feedings, but by four months, he probably will be too heavy or too lively to sit in it without tipping.

Sling

There are many types of totes on the market which let you carry your baby on your chest or your back or your hip while you shop or bike and especially when you must console him and cook dinner at the same time. The designs vary probably more than in any other piece of equipment, depending on the use you expect it to have and the size of your child. The best carryalls are made of fabric with enough support to cradle a very young infant and with tucks that can be removed during the first years as the baby grows—but these are never cheap. An older child needs a sling reinforced with an aluminum frame. Consider all varieties before buying, since you'll probably be using it every day and you'll want it to be comfortable for you and the baby.

Car Equipment

Car Bed

A car bed or a government-certified seat for infants is the only safe way to carry your baby when you travel by car, even if you only go five blocks. A bureau drawer is a good substitute, but any bed must have a firm, snug mattress laid over a strap, for a child must be belted for protection against sudden stops. Wedge the bed lengthwise, between the front and back seats, for more stability.

Car Seat

For years a car seat simply kept a child in place while raising him high enough to see. Fortunately, new government regulations are much more stringent now and children can ride with more safety. For a pre-Two, look for a government-certified car seat that's padded and molded and held in place with a seat belt; but a child from Two to Four may be happier in a harness (also certified) that's connected to the body of the car itself so he can move about. Your child should be forty pounds, or about Four, before he uses a seat belt, because the pelvic structure of a smaller body can't stand a sudden impact.

It's a certain amount of trouble to buckle a child in place, but it's impossible to replace a child.

Playpen

A playpen is almost a necessity for the first few months because an infant can see out of it much better than he can see out of a crib, and this is what he likes best. After he starts to crawl, however, he'll consider the playpen a jail, for nature intends for a crawling baby to explore. When this happens you'll have to depend on gates, locked doors and your own sharp eye to keep your child within your limits.

You can use the pen much longer as outdoor equipment, sitting him in it for at least a quarter hour at a time after a snowfall, if he's well bundled, or for as long as an hour in summer with blocks, a few plastic pots, a trickling hose and no clothes at all. Keep the pen out of the glare on a hot day and bind each of its legs with two-faced sticky tape to stop the ants from joining him and his teething biscuits.

The pen also may be used for an extra bed for a pre-One and a place to keep the Christmas tree when you have a Two.

High Chair

Because your child will spend more than an hour a day in a high chair, its construction will decide how convenient it is. Having tried every sort from the secondhand store—from a cane-bottomed antique to a five-way combination of bleached wood and plastic—we find the best is one that has very few places for spinach to hide. It also should be sturdy enough to be hosed down every month or two, have a strap to keep him seated and be steady enough to contain him even when you forget to tie him into it. A Two needs a tray big enough to use as a desk when he draws or sculpts, as well as when he eats. A feeding table may be easier at this age instead of a high chair, but we don't recommend it, unless you have a big kitchen. A child's equipment shouldn't take up a disproportionate amount of family space.

Stroller

Any stroller you buy should be easy to handle, for after your child is nine months, you'll use it more than any other piece of equipment except a crib. For years the most popular stroller had wheels that spun individually and in any direction, which made a mother wrestle every curb, but today many are more manageable, because they have an axle between each pair of wheels.

You might begin with the lightweight, umbrella sort for your baby—even before he can sit—but a big, active child probably will need a larger, heavier stroller later, with a tray in front to hold the things he brings and a basket in back to hold whatever you buy.

Gates

Gates are a necessity once your baby starts to crawl, for you don't want to be the sort of mother who always says, "No." A collapsible gate across a doorway and at the top and bottom of stairs will give both of you a feeling of freedom.

Back Yard

A preschool child needs a place to play outdoors if possible, but unless you have only a small patio it needn't consume your whole yard. A child isn't meant to dominate the outside any more than the inside. Rather, establish one or two pockets of space—one with climbing equipment and one for a Sandbox (page 106) and a wading pool (in which you'll never leave any water). With this layout, a pre-Three is happy in a 10' X 10' area and 15' X 15' will suit a Three to Six. A first grader, however, usually feels a back yard is too babyish, no matter how big it is.

The pocket you devote to climbing equipment should be covered with wood chips or four inches of smooth pea gravel, since grass won't grow there anyway. Also, some of the back yard should be shaded, because no one likes to play for hours in the hot sun. If you don't have a shady spot, plant a quick-growing tree, like a fig, to make it that way.

Any play equipment must be bought with great care, for the standard, relatively inexpensive gym sets often will rust, bolts will loosen and children will hurt themselves. We think it's better to buy one good piece of equipment—like a slide with a

rust-proof bedway—and make the rest.

Because your child likes to get in and out of places, over and over again, your lawn furniture will be his fort. That's part of motherhood. One parent we know succumbed enough to let the family's aluminum canoe rest on the grass for the children to play in, and we know a father who built a tree house without a tree, putting a small, A-frame house on stilts, with a knotted rope to reach it.

Co-op Playground

In many cities, particularly in older neighborhoods, an empty lot can stand vacant for years. This is a silly waste of land, for inevitably there are young families in nearby apartments whose children have little outdoor space to play. A cooperative playground can be the answer. We only suggest that if you do want one, don't wait for others to make it, for that might take a long time.

We found it took $500 (the proceeds of a neighborhood carnival), three weeks and a lot of hard labor for a dozen families to convert a big lot into a safe, scythed, fenced playground with equipment made of telephone poles, railroad ties, cement conduits, a load of dirt and some sod, all donated by businessmen. By renting the land with a token $1-a-year lease and by buying a $100,000 accident insurance policy for $40 a year, the owners of the lot and the parents who built the playground had legal protection, even though it was never needed. It did take some regular, community upkeep, but because dogs were banned and trash cans were supplied, the work was minimal.

Every playground has two main needs: a shady area for hot weather and a little hill, no more than 8' high. You may not be lucky enough to have a tree on the property, but you can have the hill, so Ones can scramble over it and the bigger children can play King of the Mountain. A hill in the middle of a lot also keeps grade school children from using it as a ball field, which, aside from the dogs, is the single biggest problem of a public park.

To build the hill, first have clean fill dirt dumped in one spot and then ask parents and children to run up and down it, again and again, to pack the earth. Water and cover with sod, then scatter grass seed occasionally before an expected rainfall so new grass constantly replaces the grass that is killed.

The equipment in any park must be very sturdy, which either means that you build it yourself or buy it from a school catalogue—a most expensive method. To make equipment, call the public relations department of major city offices, and especially of businesses, who can deduct their donations from their taxes. We were able to get 3' cement conduits to set on their sides in cement (so they couldn't roll). Once installed there was always a child or two inside, just sitting and thinking. Old telephone poles became fanciful horses, with goofy faces and rope tails. They also did nothing at all, but were so popular their backs were worn to satin in a few weeks. Other poles were cut into logs, notched at the ends and fitted together to make square forts, like Lincoln logs. Railroad ties edged the sandbox and others were erected, by the Herculean strength of a joint effort, to form a stanchion for swings. These were hung with ropes using leather seats for slings. One cautionary note: We recommend swings *only* if you can build a low barrier—perhaps out of something as simple as 2" X 2"s and chicken wire—far enough in front of the path of the arc to deflect a toddling child.

Climbing equipment can be made from lead pipes cut to any length and threaded to fit the joints. The rungs should be no more than 16" apart and the structure itself no taller than 5', with the uprights sunk into holes filled with concrete. An old tree trunk, either rooted in place where it grew or imbedded in cement, is a less complicated piece of climbing equipment for a pre-Three. Bind a heavy chain around it tightly several times and nail it into place, so the chain makes grips for a child's feet.

If you don't expect theft to be a problem, you can make a "Basic Board," with a stanchion (page 107) to provide a combination balancing board/seesaw/slide.

You will need to build a few benches too, so mothers have something better to do than hover over their children. A morning spent in a park of your own making can be quite as nice a social outing for you as it is for your child.

Homemade Equipment

Some of the best equipment your child can have will be the ones you make.

Since carpentry is hard for us, we recommend some short cuts, such as the new hot melt glue—a thermoplastic material—which shoots from an electric gun, bonds in sixty seconds under heavy hand pressure and withstands a two thousand-pound stress without any screws to reinforce it. Of course, the surfaces must be cleaned free of any old glue, roughed lightly with sandpaper and dusted before new glue can bind.

Any equipment will be stronger, however, if you use nails or screws in addition to the glue to hold it together. For this type of construction, paneling adhesive is easier than hot melt glue since it doesn't set as fast. To apply, squirt the adhesive from a caulking gun onto the clean, dry wood, pressing the pieces together for ten minutes until the parts are joined. This step leaves both hands free to screw the pieces together so you don't have to hold them in place like a contortionist.

Soap any screw for easier threading and pre-drill all holes except those that go into the studs, where you want the tightest fit possible. Roundhead wood screws are supposed to be best, because they leave no rough edges to scratch a child, or lag screws, which must be tightened with a wrench and have, as one adept father told us, "great authority."

Toy Bin

You wouldn't like to sew if you had to root through a big box to find the needle, the thread and the pieces of each pattern. A toy box has the same effect on a child. Instead, we suggest an open, wooden bin, 6' long, with slots about 6-10" apart to separate the beads and blocks, noisemakers and toy trucks, construction games and plastic letters. It will hang flush to the wall, as high as your child's waist and look like a long, skinny version of a washtub.

Assemble	one 4" X 8" sheet of ¾" plywood
	six 3" No. 12 roundhead wood
	screws with washers
	hot melt glue

Draw a pattern on the plywood before sawing it.

Cut	one 6' length, 15" wide
	one 6' length, 12" wide
	one 6' length, 4" wide
	two truncated right triangles
	(4" X 15" X 12" X 12")

The 12" length will be the back of the bin; the 15" length will be the sloping front; the 4" one will be the floor and the truncated right triangles will be the ends. You'll cut the dividers from the leftover plywood, but do it after the bin is glued together and you can make a pattern to fit. They'll be the same shape as the ends, but slightly smaller.

There are two preparatory steps to be done before the bin is assembled.

First, use a wood rasp to file down one long edge of the floor piece so there will be a broader surface for gluing. Next, measure the distance between the studs in the wall where the bin will be hung and then drill three holes across the top of the back piece and three across the bottom so they will align with these studs. Drilling the holes now makes it easier to hang the bin later.

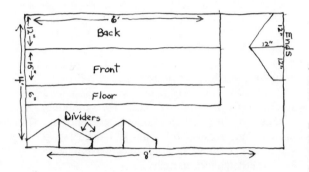

To assemble, fit the back perpendicular to the floor, to look like an "L," with the rasped side of the floor forward and facing the ceiling. In this way, the back piece can rest its weight on the floor of the bin—a necessity, since this equipment takes a lot of rough treatment.

If you haven't had help before, you'll need it now. Gluing is tricky, for this hot thermoplastic sets within sixty seconds. To make it bond, shoot only two feet of it at a time and quickly press the seams together for about two minutes. When tight, spring out the floor piece enough to feed another two feet of glue into the joint and then repeat once more.

Now you're ready to glue the ends in place. Outline the "L" of the back and floor with a quick drizzle of glue and press the end over it. Glue the other end in place the same way.

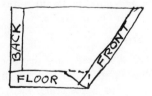

The front piece should be put in place now, resting on the rasped edge at about a 45° angle and fitting between the two ends. Shoot the glue from both top and bottom—any way you can—to hold the front in place.

For dividers, first make a pattern by fitting a piece of cardboard into the bin. With the help of a short prayer, it should be about 14¼" X 3½" X 11½" X 11¼". Draw the measurements on the plywood and cut them out. Shoot glue on the bottom, back and front edges of each divider and quickly ease it into place. File any rough edges and fill all crevices with the glue, so small toys don't get caught.

To hang the bin, slide a washer on each screw and screw through both the bin and the studs. Sand and paint it, and although it won't look beautiful (plywood never does), it is sturdy and it does work.

Work Table

When your child is mid-One, he'll like to paint and sculpt on the breakfast table or, ideally, on a low table and chair in the kitchen where he can have your company—and your supervision.

By Three, he needs a bigger work space with room enough for friends too. The kitchen is still the best place, but the size of the table is more important than its location. We recommend a long, smooth table made from an old or unfinished door and mounted on legs.

Indoor Ladders

A couple of straight wooden ladders with round rungs made the best investment we ever saw for active little boys. The ladders can be any length; the children, however, should be older than Two.

Horizontal Ladder

A horizontal ladder hung from the ceiling makes a spectacular apparatus for swinging hand over hand, as long as it clears 40" on either end, so a child won't bang into the wall.

Assemble   1 wooden ladder
               4 No. 0 hooks
               4 lengths 2/0 twist chain
               4 padlocks

Since the ladder should hang about a foot above your child's head, the length of the chains depends on the height of both your child and your ceiling.

Screw the hooks—the kind that hold the porch swing—into ceiling beams with one chain dropped from each hook. Loop a chain around each corner of the ladder, wrapping it under the side of the ladder, over the rung and then under the side again, to prevent slippage. Padlock the loops into place. Your child soon will realize that he must take a flying leap from a chair to catch the first rung, which is why you might want to keep an extra mattress on the floor. Raise the ladder as he grows taller.

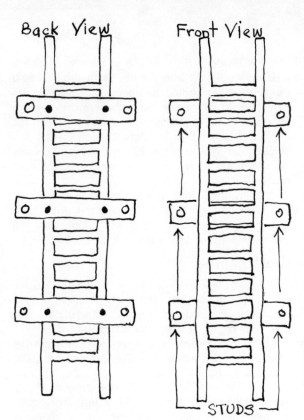

Back View Front View

STUDS

Vertical Ladder

This climber takes little space because it's bolted flat against the wall although far enough from it for a child to fit his feet on the rungs.

Assemble   one ladder
                 three 3' lengths of 2" X 4"s
                 six 2½" No. 10 flathead wood screws
                      with washers
                 nine 4¼" No. 16 roundhead wood
                      screws with washers

Because the ladder will receive heavy use, it must be attached to 2" X 4"s—the crosspieces—which then are attached to the studs in the wall. These usually are about 14" apart, but measure first to make sure. Drill three holes through the broadside of each crosspiece—as far apart as the studs—but don't attach them to the wall until they're screwed to the back of the ladder.

It's easier to attach them to the ladder if you first drill the holes you need. There should be a pair of them through each crosspiece—the same distance apart as the uprights of the ladder—and three more sets of holes into the back of these uprights. Drill them ½" deep—one near the top, one near the bottom and one in the middle.

To attach the crosspieces to the ladder, use the flathead screws (with their washers), threading them through the holes of the crosspieces and into the holes in the uprights.

To hang this Vertical Ladder—a heavy, two-people job—thread the roundhead screws, each cushioned by a washer, through each of the nine holes in the crosspieces and into their corresponding studs.

Sandbox

Our favorite kind of sandbox is filled with gravel—the smooth, small pea gravel that comes from a river bed. The stones are too small to hurt when swallowed, don't stick to clothes, don't attract cats and are cleaner than sand.

To make a sandbox, use a rigid plastic pool, about 4' in diameter. Dig a hole in the ground, almost as deep as the pool itself, and lay short lengths of 2" X 4"s around the edge. Drop the pool into the hole and adjust the wood so the rim of the pool is supported. Punch holes in the bottom of the pool for drainage and fill with pea gravel.

If you do use sand, we recommend the sterilized white sand packaged for sandboxes—not because we're fanatics about cleanliness, God knows, but because this kind is a little less sticky. Cover any sand with a screen when not in use, to keep the neighborhood cats away.

Basic Board

This equipment, which can be used either indoors or out, is simply a board with four strips of wood across its underside, letting it convert quickly from a Balancing Board to a Seesaw to a Slide.

Assemble   one 8' plank, 8" wide
                 four 7" lengths of 2" X 2"s
                 hot melt glue OR
                 eight 2" No. 12 roundhead wood
                      screws with washers
                 sandpaper
                 polyurethane

Place the lengths of 2" X 2" across one side of the plank with one strip at either end and the other two strips each 1" from the center. Glue the strips in place or slip a pair of screws through the washers and drill them from the topside of the plank into each strip of wood. Sand the rough edges of the wood and paint it with polyurethane.

Balancing Board

A narrow board, raised slightly above the ground, teaches coordination better than any other piece of equipment. For a teetering Two, lay the Basic Board over two bricks, but not under the

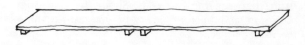

strips or it will be rocky. Graduate to cinderblocks at Three.

Beginner's Slide

To a true climber, everything vertical is his turf and he almost never misjudges his space. Unfortunately, he has a lot of poor imitators, which is why a child in the beginning needs instruction and a small slide.

We once watched Mike at mid-One, a Buster Keaton in rompers, when he saw his first slide—a tall playground wonder. He watched, eyes wide and feet apart, as three experienced children ran up and slipped down. In a moment, he went up the steps and down the slide, whirled around in exhilarated confusion and ran up the slide and slid down the steps—amazingly without injury.

To create a Beginner's Slide, simply hook one end of the Basic Board over the footrail of the bed, if you use it indoors, or lock it over a low wall or the seesaw stanchion. The strip on the end will hold it in place.

Seesaw

To use the Basic Board as a seesaw, you'll need to make a stanchion, with plumbing pipes cut to size and threaded at the hardware store. Once in the ground, it will look like a big, square croquet hoop.

Assemble   two 1½" pipes, 2' long
            one 1½" pipe, 1' long
            two 1½" elbows
            premixed concrete

The longer pieces are the uprights, the shorter one the crosspiece. Use the elbows to join them together. Dig two holes, 6" wide, 14" deep and about a foot apart. Fill with concrete and imbed the uprights to a depth of 12". Once set, a Four and a friend can drag the Basic Board to the stanchion and lock the two center strips astride the crosspiece: a seesaw.

Swings

Nothing is quite as sexy as a swing (except maybe sex). So let your child enjoy. Start with a doorway swing in infancy and work up to an old-fashioned four-seater lawn swing at Two, a rubber tire at Four, a traditional swing at Five and, finally, a heavy manila rope, knotted at intervals, which is rugged and tricky enough for a Six to climb and daring enough to sail through the air like Tarzan.

Basketball

Small boys like to imitate big boys, but it isn't possible in basketball unless you adjust the hoop. This gives a small child the same break as a Fourteen.

The hoop should be hung about 16" higher than your child's head and attached to a high fence, the side of your house or within the carport—anywhere that he can retrieve the ball over and over, without losing his dignity. Raise the hoop as he grows.

Because you'll be using the same hoop for years, we think the standardized, heavy-duty one is best. Let him use a soft, light ball at first, graduating to a basketball at Six.

Stilts

By the time your child is Six, he'll yearn to stand as tall as you. God bless stilts. These are sturdy, easy to make and safer than they look.

Assemble   two 5-6' lengths of 2" X 2"s
            two 6" lengths of 2" X 4"s
            two 4" lag screws, ¼" in diameter
            two 3½" lag screws, ¼" in diameter
            4 washers
            paneling adhesive
            sandpaper
            paste wax
            polyurethane OR paint

When a child stands on stilts they should be no higher than his head and no lower than his shoulders, with the steps 1' above the ground for a new stilter and as much as 2' for an advanced one.

The two 2" X 4"s form the steps of the stilts. To make them, cut off a triangle, 2" X 3" X 6", from each one, which removes at least one sharp corner that could scratch your child's leg. Smear the 6" side of each step with the adhesive and press it against one side of the 2" X 2" pole, at the height you want. The 4" side of the step should be on top to support the foot.

When the glue is dry, drill a hole, 4" deep, from the pole and into the step, 1½" below the footrest, and drill another hole, 3½" deep and 2" lower. Wax each screw before inserting it—so it will be easier to turn—and slide it through a washer, so the pole won't split under pressure. Tighten with a wrench. Sand the rough edges of the step and coat the stilts either with the polyurethane or the paint to avoid splintering, but neither sand nor paint the foothold itself, for this would make it too slippery.

To teach your child to stilt, have him stand on the porch step that's even with the footrests, and tuck the poles behind his shoulders, wrapping his hands around them from the back of the poles to the front. Then have him mount the stilts and march away, and, yes, it will take several days, and many spills, for him to learn.

Riches

There are a few necessities a child must have—like love and food and shelter—and then there are the riches, which are almost as important.

A child can get along, no doubt, without books and theater and music and television too. If he has no friends he'll invent some, and if he has no sense of his heritage he won't even know what's missed. Deprived of toys, he'll play with anything from a soap bubble to a firefly and if he isn't sent to preschool that's all right too. He'll still learn his lessons in first grade.

Just the same, childhood isn't the time to strip his world, but rather to embellish it. It's the trappings that give us the good life, that add the civilizing touch.

The riches you bring your child, and the quality of them, will be treasures he draws on for the rest of his life.

Heritage

You help your child's individuality grow in many ways, but an emphasis on his heritage is one of the best. When he can understand where he comes from, he will have a much better idea where he wants to go. Each time you continue a family custom or resurrect an ethnic recipe or use the language from generations past, you're giving him a stronger sense of himself. To keep this heritage alive, you and your husband will want to blend the customs of your families, even as you add a few of your own, like the way you let your Four use your great-aunt's favorite teaspoon for Sunday dinner.

If you live near your relatives your child will be that much richer, for each visit with them—even when you have little in common—introduces him to his culture. He's part of a family and the family should include his bizarre cousins as well as his stern old grandfather. There are such affairs as a family reunion—so much trouble for everyone and so tempting to postpone—but these memories fill the attic of his mind with such riches he'll still rummage through them fifty years from now.

Like the rest of us, however, you and your husband probably live so far from your hometowns that your child must rely on you to weave these memories for him, and the best way to do it is to tell him about his people—alive or dead. Your child wants to hear all the stories, whether they're silly or sad, but he especially wants to hear about his parents when they were small. The simplest account will charm him, as it does Nadia each time she hears about her daddy playing hookey in first grade, but like all children, she admittedly likes the odd stories best, and so did we.

We remember our Tía Tata's vivid apparitions of the devils and the lesser known virgins as if we'd seen them ourselves and we believed completely (as she did) her story of the Mexican revolution that made her cross-eyed and how she was cured by her nana who pasted orange peels on her temples. We also recall, in color and sound and smell, that glorious day our wild Tío Pepe brought a drunken turkey home for dinner—because drunken turkeys, he said with a flourish, were easier to pluck. To be sure, the turkey didn't agree and, made bold by tequila, zigzagged around the patio, gobbling wild turkey songs until the womenfolk finally cut off his antics. And then the plucking was just as hard as ever. In another age, a scene like that would have been the basis of a whole new feast day.

Every family has its wackiness, its excitement, its embarrassments and its gaiety. Your child should be a part of it all.

The Bulletin Board

This sense of heritage your child needs is fed early when he sees family pictures around the house. Our friend Sarah, at six months, had her own picture gallery, where snapshots of grandparents, uncles and cousins were pinned to a bulletin board in her room. Her parents pointed to the faces (whether she had ever known the people or not) and called them by name until she was as familiar with them as the pictures in her book. By One, Sarah could hold these pictures herself (in her more peaceful moments) and never destroyed any at all. We wish we had used Bulletin Boards too.

Friendships

We remember our old Tante Margot, a self-proclaimed *grande dame*, who would mutter at family reunions, "God gave me my relatives, thank God I can choose my friends."

A child is never too young to start trying, as we realized when we saw a snapshot of Meg and her two buddies on their bellies in a playpen—happy as pigs in clover and all only three months old. People are social animals, whatever their age. Although babies won't play cooperatively with each other until Three, they all answer each other's babble, touch each other's hair (and occasionally pull it too).

For the first two years, the size of a playmate is more important than the age. When a larger child plays with a smaller one, he almost always bumps him over, because the bigger child has more ballast.

You can expect a pair of Ones to play together for as long as a half hour before one of them cries. By fifteen months, your child will need to visit with friends and preferably with only one friend at a time. Because he may do very well with one playmate but be at his worst with another, he needs to know many children to select the ones he plays with best. This is true at every age.

Ideally you'll seek a few children you like and he likes and whose mothers you like too, even if it means introducing yourself to likely women in the grocery store. Every young mother is in the market for more friends.

When you have little children, a park often is the best place for them to play together, since they can share playground equipment much better than they can share their toys at home. Besides, in a park a child can make friends with those eccentrics he might never meet otherwise, like the dizzy old lady who feeds squirrels and the crusty fellow with his racing form. It's variety that makes life interesting to a child. Any cross section of perspectives gives texture to a child's personality for it helps him think about the world from many angles.

By mid-One your child wants the companionship of other children more and more, and a play group becomes important (page 110). It may be easier and cheaper to keep your child at home—no doubt about it—but he won't benefit as much. Although a play group is almost no different to a mother than a morning of small visitors, to a child it's much more special. The undivided attention from the duty mother and the regularity of the schedule give it some status and the rest comes from the formality of its name. Although this child barely can talk, he knows enough to call it "school."

A Two wants company all the time, more's the pity, and this means a constant eye. Every time you invite a young guest, you probably will invite his mother too. With both of you watching, you may be able to keep up with them.

When your child starts nursery school—usually at Three—you may think you can taper his social life, but soon he discovers that a peanut butter sandwich tastes much better when he eats it with a classmate.

A Four, you'll find, is a great planmaker and a friend is included in any plan. This child may learn his numbers and letters just to telephone invitations to a friend. By Five, he becomes so selective you won't make or accept any invitation without his approval, but you should continue to ask a variety of children to visit so he won't lose the daring he needs to make new friends when he begins first grade.

Friends are so important to a Six that he spends a lot of time wondering how much he means to them, then cavalierly drops them into slots—"best friends," "second-best friends," "sort-of friends" and "yuks"—their rank somewhat depending on their sex. At this age a boy prefers only boys for friends, while a girl wants to be with girls.

Any Six wants to roam more than a sailor on liberty. If he had his way, he'd travel up and down the block with a flock of other children all day, going from house to house for a snack here, a television hour there. You'll only want to allow this occasionally, for on a regular basis the group becomes more important than any other influence. No matter how nifty these children are, they can't offer him as much as his parents. Besides, the child who can visit with two or three children at a time, instead of many, will have a chance to make close friends. It's as important for a child to have quality friendships as it is for him to have quality care.

Schools

We once knew a lady with six children in school, grades one to six, and she said if she had it to do again, God forbid, she would say to each child the moment he awoke, from the very first day: "You're beautiful! You're marvelous! You're fantastic!"

"I would say that every day, a hundred times a day, for six years," she said, "and then maybe that child would be ready for first grade."

Although school seems unimaginable when you're holding your baby, this is the time you're preparing him for the great big world, first by giving him independence and later by sending him to a preschool where he can put it into practice. For toddlers we advocate a play group—or a "play school" as every Two insists on calling it—and for Threes a nursery school.

If you keep your child at home until kindergarten a miasma will settle over him, which makes even a good little child whine, pinch the baby and ask, "Why?" about everything when he plainly knows most of the answers. This good little child needs a lot more action, more friends and more ideas than you're able to give. He will profit as much by a few mornings away from you as you do by a few evenings away from him.

A father ironically often tends to be more protective than a mother and is sure preschool is silly, expensive and, although it may be all right for other children, it isn't necessary for any child of his. True, it almost always costs too much money and takes up too much of your time, but, personally, we've never met a child who didn't profit from a good preschool—nor a father who wasn't pleased with the results.

Once your child starts school he discovers new toys, new friends, new accomplishments and revels in field trips even though he's been there before with you. Although you might offer ideal surroundings at home—terraria and toys, canaries in cages and pizza every Tuesday—it will be the challenge of being a member of this first democracy that multiplies all of his enrichments. When your child

meets the same dozen children regularly he learns the pains and the pleasures of belonging to a group, where everyone else has just as many rights as he does. He also finds that while some children do some things better than he does, he excels in others.

In nursery school the shyest child learns to fend for himself, without a mother's intervention, and he learns that the bigger his vocabulary, the easier the fending.

While he learns new independence, he also meets a fresh measure of authority. A child in preschool truly believes that he can't cross streets, not because you've told him so often but because his teacher told him once.

Of all the schools our children attended—and they were as varied as snowflakes—there wasn't one that didn't benefit them in some way. However, if you think you must choose between a bad school and no school at all, then your child should stay at home—or you should start your own school. It is a lot of trouble, but we think the more familiar he is with the idea of school, and the earlier it begins, the more comfortable he'll be in first grade. This is how you teach your fledgling to fly.

Play Group

A play group seems to work best if it involves four congenial mid-Ones of relatively congenial mothers, who live within walking distance of each other. The children should be about the same size and no more than four months apart and the group should meet twice a week on a regular schedule, for no more than two hours. Rotate the sessions among the four houses, with each mother taking a turn. You'll need a push or pull toy for each child, two wheel toys for the group—for children now begin to learn about sharing—some big cardboard boxes, a few three-piece puzzles and toys, some clay and, of course, books and records.

A play group has no structure at all, but it does require organization. As we learned when we found a mid-One hanging out of a third-floor window, you can't take even five minutes away from the children while you prepare juice. Do this before the group arrives and also tidy the playspace, wash the breakfast dishes and lock any room you don't want a child to enter. Some days your presence hardly will be needed and other times you may have to do a song and dance in a funny hat to keep some jollies in the day.

The play group should graduate to a public facility—a church, a school or a settlement house—by Two, with mothers providing the toys and juice. You can double the number of children, use two duty mothers and split the cost of juice, cookies and equipment.

Preschool

Nursery schools are run in the morning only, from three to five times a week, accepting children no younger than mid-Two but generally between Three and Four. Admission depends on the child's readiness, which varies with each child. Certainly all children shouldn't start at the same age. Since it often takes a year to find the right school and get to the top of its waiting list, you should start looking far in advance.

Most kindergartens, public or private, are run for three hours, five days a week, in the same protective atmosphere found in a nursery school, but with considerably more emphasis placed on numbers and letters. Also, because the class size is often twice as big as a nursery school, the waiting list is much shorter in a private school and seldom encountered in a public school where there is a place for every child.

Finding the Right Preschool

There are aptitude tests to tell students whether to go to a school for engineers or one for architects, but there are, alas, no tests that tell parents what kind of nursery school their child needs. Where one child may need a place to expend tremendous physical energy, another needs an orderly, almost serene setting and a third may thrive in a highly creative school. Certain schools are better for some children than they are for others.

You and your husband need to analyze your child candidly, assessing the strong points and the weak ones and deciding which atmosphere makes him happiest so you can find the school that will provide it best. These evaluations should be made together, for this is another, albeit small, watershed in your marriage.

Most preschools are private and these generally have an arts-and-crafts direction. The rest are usually cooperatives (since they're cheaper), and in

these the parents develop the philosophy of the school and hire the teacher to carry it out. Because of this, there are many differences among the schools, and you must observe them carefully for they can be very good or rather awful. Whether your child goes to a public or private preschool, it will draw so much of your energy and your time that you'll want to study various established philosophies before you commit yourself. This will help you decide whether you like the work-oriented Montessori schools, the Waldorfs, where art and science are woven together, or the creative, freer Country Days.

No method is perfect, but the more you know, the better you can judge all of them. Ideally a school should be strong in all areas, but we've never found one like that and think you have to be realistic when you look. The best schools of any sort are elastic enough to handle children with a variety of personalities, backgrounds and abilities, enhancing their good days and helping them through the bad ones.

If you're the methodical sort you might find the schools in your area through the licensing department of your city government, but frankly we've never known anyone that methodical and think you can get the same help from neighbors, local churches and the mothers in the park.

You'll have to observe the schools, however, to see how good they are, for this information is too important to take secondhand. Do this without your child and stay a full morning at each school to see the complete picture.

Even a mediocre nursery school may be better than none, but it has to be good enough to keep him interested until Five, so you won't be tempted to put him in kindergarten too soon.

When you think you've found the right school, ask if your child can explore it, but only after the children have gone for the day. Since you may be looking for a school as much as a year ahead of time, your child will be too young to mesh with these older children. He's not ready to do this until the teacher thinks he's practically ready to start school, and then he needs to visit, so he'll feel comfortable when he does begin. His admission date should depend on his maturity, which never follows a calendar.

When he does start school you shouldn't plan to move or begin a new job until he's been enrolled for about two months. If you're going to have a baby you should start your child in preschool at least six weeks before delivery or six weeks after. One crisis at a time is enough for a child.

There will be some adjustment problems in the most stable situation, for it's a wrench to go into the big world. A good school expects it, however, and a good teacher can handle it.

Judging a Preschool

A well-run preschool, like a well-run any kind of school, is a happy place, where the children are happy to go in the morning, dawdle in their leaving and openly like their teacher and each other.

From a physical point of view, the room should be light and airy with running water, a record player, a pet and shelves low enough for children to reach all toys and supplies for themselves. There also should be an easel for every four children, a wheel toy for every two and at least one plant and one rhythmic instrument for each child.

The class needs a corner for housekeeping, one for blockbuilding and another for dress-ups, with a suitcase of costumes as well as a heap of hats, shoes, canes and even a crutch or two.

A nursery school particularly should have an area for quiet play with books, puzzles and small interlocking blocks which develop more dexterity with the fingers. Children also need a place indoors to jump, dance, tumble on a mat and climb gym equipment, all of which help them coordinate their arms and legs better (and give them a jolly time too). If there's no room for gym equipment outdoors there should at least be space for tricycles and trucks.

Although the most beautiful setting can't compensate for a bad teacher, a good one can make a dowdy place come alive if the program is exciting enough. This is easier if the school limits a class to fifteen children and gives the teacher an aide.

A good preschool chooses a teacher who recognizes that children are working when they play and respects each child for it. This respect should be the strongest underpinning in any school, flowing not only between the teacher and the children but among the children too. When there is this respect, children can be themselves, working at their own pace and in their own style, keeping their small eccentricities as long as they don't disrupt the class or offend anyone.

Each child should be able to go to the bathroom without waiting for the bell to ring (because heaven knows, that's his business), but there must be some rules in a school. A school will be a happy place as long as these rules are sensible and the children know the reasons for them—like returning a toy to its shelf so others may use it, but not so the room will look tidy. In fact, unless a school has signs of pleasant disarray, we would question its priorities.

Although there will be small personality clashes in any school, the children should be so absorbed in their work and play that there will be little time for quarrels and none for boredom.

Judging the Teacher

Sometimes a school can have an excellent facility, a strong philosophy—and a teacher who doesn't quite live up to either. To us, the quality of the school is more important than the quality of the teacher, because one is more permanent than the other, but if the school itself is weak, the teacher must be much more competent.

To run a classroom well, a teacher should have the day blocked into chunks of time, so children can complete their work and slip easily from passive to active play, without having to be herded.

When you observe, you should be able to see that the teacher obviously cares about each child and makes each one feel better about himself, but still stays in the background. This lets children develop easy friendships, so they will seek help from each other as well as the teacher.

We've found the best teachers have had several years of practical experience. They are imaginative and enthusiastic, have good speech patterns, clear ideas of discipline and are open with parents about the way they handle general problems, but discreet about the specific children involved.

We've also found that a man teacher may offer more to young children than a woman, since many children—especially boys—have so much female influence in their lives. Something as simple as hammers and nails aren't used in most nursery schools, not because of safety but because many women teachers don't handle them adeptly and therefore don't encourage their use.

A good teacher is a good disciplinarian, but like you, sets boundaries as wide as possible and uses praise and positive techniques to guide the children. This sort of person diverts the demon of the day before mischief is made, comforts a downcast child before he cries and uses carpentry, climbing and working with clay to channel energy constructively. Above all, this teacher only corrects a child when it's possible to follow through, and then only in private and never with a spanking.

In these ways a teacher treats all the children with equality and with respect—the only way they can learn to treat others the same.

The Cooperative

A cooperative, as the sociologists say, is a learning experience. You may have to hire teachers—and fire them—schedule mothers and keep them to it, interview applicants and agonizingly reject a few, which doesn't seem to faze a child and always hurts his mother very much.

You may have to supply the cookies and juice for a month or paint the bookcases, but the better the co-op, the less a parent will be expected to monitor the classroom. However, all cooperatives use parents to help on field trips and the best ones will take advantage of the special talents of parents, having them teach carpentry, modern dance or cooking. To help with the children is the most tiring—and stimulating—job you can have in a co-op, for children draw as much out of you as you're willing to give. We think it's the most rewarding job too, for you have the chance to see how your child gets along on his own turf.

We're particularly in favor of fathers helping this way, even if it means taking time from work.

Little children need men around them and the school often takes on a livelier air when they're there, since they haven't been preconditioned by those dreadful monthly co-op meetings. To us they are the most difficult and dizziest part of a cooperative.

Here, for some metaphysical reason, the most charming, intelligent women turn into somber ninnies when they talk about the health, safety and education of their children.

At least some of this is inevitable and we predict you'll natter like the rest of us over orange juice vs. orange drink and why cookies should be baked with brewer's yeast and honey. You even may endure, as we did in one of the drearier cooperatives, an hour-long discussion of the daily projects. There we remember the imposing teacher from Britain, much given to Freudian slips, who announced that the children would make styrofoam ornaments for the Christmas tree "which little boys particularly will like," she trilled, "and when they're done we'll let them roll their little balls in glittah."

It's silliness like this that puts the nursery school business in perspective.

First Grade

The first-grade teacher is often dandy, whether the school is public or private, but from then on, there will be that one excellent teacher, whose name your child will never forget; one penny dreadful, whose name he'll try to forget, and two mediocre ones, whose names he'll forget soon and their faces too.

There seems to be no way you can put a child in a building with at least a dozen classrooms and thirty children to a class, without scaring him a

little bit. It takes a strong, strong child to be ready for this.

It is self-confidence—not "reading readiness" or even reading—that makes a successful first grader. This child must be tough enough to be teased by older children, to say "I don't know" in front of a roomful of other children, to throw up in the hall without crying too much. A first grader must want to learn what everyone else is learning and at roughly the same time, and he can if he's a Six, for this child conforms to his surroundings as fast as a lizard to a lily pad.

A Five has a much harder time in the first grade, as we've learned through poignant experience, for he measures himself not against other Fives, but against other Sixes. This child may not be overwhelmed at first, but then be swamped as he advances until, in the pivotal sixth grade, the younger child is likely either to surrender or rebel with sloppy work, poor behavior or a shyness that will twist your heart.

You'll face an awful dilemma if your child has a birthday in the middle of the school year, but we think you'll be much wiser to let him wait a year before first grade. The best alternative we've found is a preprimary class—a fairly recent innovation by public schools and one of their best, for it fits between kindergarten and first grade and gives a child the dignity of going to a school, without the responsibility of keeping up with older children. Here he'll find it nice to be that big frog in a little pond. Next year he can be the big lizard.

Toys

A child needs his toys and play equipment the way you need your record player, tennis racquet and the morning paper. You can expect any toy or game that has lasted for generations—like blocks or a ball or a wheel toy—to be fun for all children, but a good toy, like a good teacher, makes learning a delight.

A mechanical bear does bring the laughs—which are important—but a toy also can be a tool. It may challenge the mind, like dominoes; build coordination, like a gym set; encourage creativity, like blocks, or it may quicken the imagination the way a rag doll permits more fantasy than a perfectly costumed bride doll. The more a toy puts a child in the role of participant, the better it is.

The best toys are geared to a child's size and age and require little instruction and supervision. If you don't have to hover over your child like a hen he can learn how much he can do for himself.

Not all children like the same toys. One child may be attracted primarily by paints, another by wheel toys and a third by balls he can kick and throw. Plastic nuts and bolts, which require mechanical ability, can enthrall one child and frustrate another, regardless of sex. Your child will have preferences as early as six months. Although you'll recognize some of them right away, others will take more time to surface.

When you see him get bored or angry with a toy, it's either too old for him or he finds it pointless, and in either case it should be put away. Other toys simply aren't good enough for a child to use. These are the ones that are made to be bought, broken and replaced within weeks. We find they make a child feel clumsy, guilty and eventually irresponsible, until he may learn to mistreat all toys.

That's why all of his toys should be safe and most should be sturdy and tough enough to last as long as the child is interested in them. We think some toys are put to such heavy use—the push-and-pull toys, the rocking horse, building sets, a wagon, stilts—that they should be top quality.

Care of Toys

You should know that all children mistreat some toys sometimes, but occasionally one energetic child will be hard on all of them, the same way he may be hard on his clothes. If your child uses a metal truck as a battering ram, a push toy to bang on the floor and a block to throw like a ball, he needs clearer boundaries. You still can have peace and he still can play with gusto if you let him ride his truck outdoors, use a real hammer to pound on wood scraps and only throw a foam ball in a particular part of the house.

You also can help your child take reasonably good care of his toys if they're not crowded; if he can reach them easily, and if he can keep all the pieces together.

When a toy does break, either put it aside until you can repair it or throw it away. If you let broken toys accumulate, they'll depress you so much you'll start to notice the cracks in the plaster instead of the daisies on the table.

When you buy new toys—hopefully not many more than are needed—you'll store some of the old ones, if only so your child won't look so pampered. This is a good instinct to follow. Too many toys can overwhelm a child. In self-defense he'll limit his choices anyway, playing with only a few of them. This is why you'll want to rotate all but the favorites, putting away a third of the toys every few weeks. When you take them out of storage they'll look to him like long-lost friends—a great deal better than they did when he saw them last.

Buying Toys

Buying toys takes some expertise, a sharp eye and much restraint, like shopping the sales. It's a trial-and-error process. Count yourself blessed if you succeed 75 percent of the time.

You'll find yourself shopping for them at least twice a year—Christmas and birthdays. These holidays always seem to arrive just when you realize that your child's toys are outgrown, lost, broken or boring. The dilemma of selecting the right toy for the right child at the right age is one that's never completely solved.

It's tempting to give the toys you once coveted—which is all right if you had the same tastes then as your child has now—or to buy them too soon, as if he were a prodigy—and that's never all right.

Most manufacturers suggest such a wide range of ages that a mother is encouraged to offer a toy too soon and by the time the child is old enough to use it, he's tired of the sight of it. In this area, at least, we feel it much better to go too slow than too fast. Besides, the waste of a good toy will make you feel as irritated as you do when you buy shoes that are too small or food that no one eats.

For safety, a toy should be nontoxic, non-flammable and not too noisy. A toy also should be washable, have smooth edges, no pins or buttons that can be removed and no springs that can catch the fingers, toes or hair. No toy should be made of glass, of course, nor of brittle plastic either, for this also breaks easily and can scratch a child.

If your child is still an infant his toys should be too large to be swallowed, should have no cord over 12" long that could wrap around his neck and certainly shouldn't have small, detachable parts that could lodge in the windpipe, ears or nose. A parent has to take special care in selecting toys for an older child when there's an inquisitive baby crawling around. Some toys, like marbles, are clearly dangerous for a baby and others, like a metal truck, depend on the driver. If you have any doubts about the safety of a toy don't buy it.

Although all good toys are educational, some require more guidance than others. If you buy a toy that needs a teacher, remember: You'll be the teacher. You may have to give frequent lessons with your child to make these toys come alive.

A first-time mother may assume, as we did, that her child will learn to count magically with an abacus. How foolish we were to think that a child in his innocence could decipher this inscrutable tool. Certainly we couldn't. Of course, the children obligingly pushed the colored beads from side to side and whirred them around the rods, but they never could learn to add and subtract with it—or learn Chinese either. If you want your child to enjoy an abacus or any other toy which requires specialized knowledge, you'll have to learn to use it yourself.

Even if you know how to choose a safe, sturdy, interesting toy, you might not know if it will be any fun, and that's the most important part of all. A few select toy stores may have clerks informed enough to advise you or they may let your child play with the samples. However, be wary of his impulsive judgment, for a pre-Six is dazzled easily by the biggest and the brightest. The way to find out which toys he likes is to watch the ones he chooses time after time, when he visits friends or goes to play school. The toys that enchant or challenge him the most will be the ones he'll treasure at home.

Infancy

The toys for a baby in his first six months are designed to awaken and then sharpen his sense of sight, sound and touch. A baby needs exciting surroundings everywhere—especially the ceilings. He'll look at them more in the next few months than he ever will again in his life. Kites are great, but mobiles are better. To make them, dangle anything that's vivid, shiny or amusing on ribbons, thread or nylon fishline, tying them to clothes hangers, embroidery hoops or simply straight sticks. The hoops can be hung from cup hooks in the ceiling, and the sticks or the hangers can be poked between books in a tall bookcase.

No matter how many gifts he has received,

you'll want to add a few simple stimuli for him each week, like magazine pictures hung on the kitchen wall. A ball of aluminum foil may not be beautiful to you, but he'll be so pleased. He also will like a silver rattle, because it's shiny and has such a clear, tinkly sound, and he needs a music box, soft toys, a hard rubber ring that looks like a doughnut and at least one activity toy fastened onto the playpen and the crib. Above all, you will want to give him some warm, cuddly stuffed animals—the same sort he will cherish for years and years.

Six Months

Once a baby can sit up and crawl he becomes interested in undoing everything he can. He tosses toys from his crib, pulls yarn out of a basket and empties your purse. As his crawling improves he empties shelves, boxes, drawers and anything he can open and reach. He should never think that this undoing is bad, but neither should you let him undo everything he sees for soon you'll resent it. He'll be content if you give him a plastic jar with a top to unscrew, a box of spoons to spill, an aluminum drip coffeepot to take apart—none of which he can put back together. It's very important for him to "undo" so he eventually can learn to "do": to nest blocks, to fill shelves, to put a puzzle together.

He has more and more waking hours now and small toys aren't enough. This is the time to buy or borrow a jump chair, a walker or a doorway swing where he can bounce happily for a half hour without fussing.

Nine Months

The best toys for this age are the artifacts of everyday life: hats, eggbeaters, pipes, keys, paintbrushes, pots and pans. Parents demonstrate their use over and over—much more often than they show their child how to stack blocks.

One

When your baby starts prowling around the house, you may decide he needs a playroom. He doesn't. He has one already and it's always the room you're in. In another year, when his curiosity sends him off on his own adventures, you'll worry every time

he leaves your side and you should. This year feel blessed that he follows you instead.

Since you want your child to explore life when he's an adult, now is the time to start. Provide a special basket or shelf, cupboard or drawer in every room to hold his toys and some of your discards too, choosing them according to the room. This is the way you continue to define his boundaries, for your home, like yourself, shouldn't be dominated by a child.

He needs scarves, a pocketbook without a catch, a tie and a big hat in your room, where you want more quiet. Hang a net sack in the bathroom for his rubber toys and in his room provide some low, open shelves for books and stuffed animals. He'll like to play with water in the kitchen, pouring from one container to another and he'll play with pots and pans, for if you use them daily, he has to figure they're fun. Encourage him to bang one with a wooden spoon, to fit the lid in place and eventually to nest a pot into a bigger one.

His own store-bought toys probably will be kept in the living room, where you at least can read the paper in comfort while he plays. Either a small rocking horse or the considerably more exciting horse on wheels is an excellent new toy and so are the simplest peg-pounding toys of beginning carpentry.

What looks like play to you is work to a child and he thrives on it. Everything he does has a purpose to him. As soon as a child walks he should have a push toy and a pull toy, the brighter the better, especially if they have their own special sounds as they move. These toys are his tests of skill as he maneuvers them through doorways, down the stairs, around corners.

A One needs a half-dozen books, an indoor sponge ball to toss and a large colorful ball to chase, a doll to cuddle, a few new bath toys and things that open and shut like a jack-in-the-box. Now he likes musical toys, like a bell, a harmonica, a maraca and, if he doesn't run with it, a wooden horn.

Mid-One

Your child's quest for independence takes on new dimensions at mid-One, and the tools he works with are more important than ever. He doesn't need a great many toys, and many of the best ones will be homemade, like Flour Clay for sculpting (page 208) or beanbags (or snowballs) for pitch and catch and for target tossing with you outside. Crayons, if he uses them in the high chair, are good now, and so is a small broom, a bubble pipe and a noisemaker.

His energy seems enormous now and it appears to increase every day as he is able to give less attention to the mechanics of moving and more attention to getting himself there. One child will run almost constantly and when he's not running he's pushing himself around on a little wheel toy. Another will become a climber of extraordinary skill. At this age you're likely to find him shimmying up the bookcase or sitting on top of the refrigerator with neither of you having any real idea of how he got there. No matter how much natural climbing instinct you think he might have, he still needs to be taught how to climb and slide and balance and you need to teach these skills before a calamity makes you sorry you didn't.

A mid-One uses a kitchen chair as the first two rungs of a ladder and pushes it before him everywhere he goes. This may be why he appreciates having his own stool so much. He'll use it with marvelous importance, backing his fanny onto it as if it were a throne, carrying it like a silver tray and climbing on it to reach even the lowest chair.

An indoor slide and, if you can stand it, an indoor sandbox on legs are used for the next few years, but your child also needs to play outside every day. Although you may have a well-equipped, well-protected back yard, you can expect him to go in and out of the house almost as if he were caught in a revolving door. Personally, we've never seen a mid-One happy to stay alone for more than fifteen minutes—if that long. Whether he plays outdoors or in, it's the plumber's friend, above all other toys, that all young children like best. It's a horse, a hat and a hundred other things. You don't have to show your child how to use it; he knows instinctively. And if he leaves it outside, someone else will gallop away with it immediately. So far we've lost seven.

Two

A child's life is either chaotic or organized, depending on instruction. Learning the use of toys, step by step, makes them more interesting and makes him feel more competent.

A puzzle teaches concentration, trains the eye to isolate shapes and helps coordination—if it's easy enough. If not, put it away for weeks or even months, for nothing is more frustrating than a too difficult puzzle. We speak from experience, for to us, nothing's harder than those three-piece wooden puzzles cut on the color lines: no hints at all. Wooden puzzles are the most durable, the most expensive and the best, and cardboard puzzles in a frame are the worst, for the thin pieces are hard for a child to handle. Whenever your child gets a new puzzle, scribble across the backs of all the pieces with a crayon, using a different color for each puzzle. When you have to separate a half-dozen puzzles, you'll find it a bit easier to sort them by the color of the scribbles on the back than by the color of the pictures on the front.

A Two still needs toys to pull and push, but now they should have a function: a doll carriage, a wagon, a wheelbarrow. Of the three, we think a wheelbarrow is best, for it's big enough to transport many treasures and it develops a child's sense of equilibrium because it's tricky to handle.

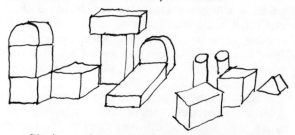

Blocks teach coordination too. Now he needs a dozen of those lovely big cardboard bricks that he can both stack and climb on and he also needs a bushelful of small wooden blocks in geometric shapes. They needn't be expensive—secondhand ones run through the cycle of soap and hot water in the washer will do fine—as long as they're smooth. Avoid the painted ones if you have a young baby or a puppy in the house who may chew them, since they're cut from soft wood. However, you should know that any child left in a room with the cheaper, brightly painted blocks and the unpainted varnished ones used by the best nursery schools will choose the brighter ones every time. So much for the experts.

Your Two won't be exuberantly building, jumping or climbing every moment of the day. It only seems that way. Some of the time he's relatively still—making music.

There are two types of musicmakers—those that make noise and those that make musical sounds. For noise, get a toy piano, a large whistle, a cheap, twangy guitar. For music, get a marimba, a tambourine and a durable bongo drum of wood and hide. A beautiful, marching drum from the toy store is a waste, because the skin is usually made of paper and when it breaks—almost immediately—it makes a child feel both incompetent and destructive. However, he'll enjoy a cylinder drum he's made from a grits box, because it's tougher and he expects much less from it.

Your child will like your old magazines, which you might mark with big, red Xs to identify them—and to protect your new ones. A stack of this X-rated literature will keep a toddler busy for a full ten minutes, so we recommend several stacks around the house.

Mid-Two

A child's play space at home, indoors and out, should be geared to much more demanding exercise now. Since he climbs constantly, he'll use your furniture less if you hang a Vertical Ladder bolted to the wall (page 106).

Toys should be more complicated for a mid-Two and some should be toys he can order around. He needs sturdy trucks he can ride and guide, snap-together blocks he can build so they don't fall apart every time he moves and a sexy rocking horse that will gallop when he bounces. Now he can toss his beanbag toward a basket and pound his hammer, again and again, at the head of a nail.

Many of the props he needs are compact and some are homemade. They're necessary to help him enact the dozens of different roles he fantasizes every day. Every time a child pretends he's the supermarket checker, carpenter or bus driver, he's trying to answer his own curiosity and forcing his imagination to stretch itself. It will stretch more if he has a basket with a handle to carry his possessions, a tunnel to crawl through, a cloth to hang over a card table for a house of his own and a variety of hats.

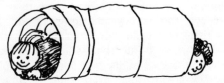

Wooden boxes are good to hold special sets of toys, but cardboard boxes—any shape, any size—are the joy of any child. A mid-Two will be as content with four or five of them as he would be with as many new toys (and your house will look tidy too).

The boxes should be big enough to sit in, to push, to pull, to stack. A child enjoys them even more when you refer to them by the proper names he gives them: a boat or a wagon, an island or a tower. Each time you encourage his imagination, it grows that much bigger.

Three

As a child approaches Three, his behavior becomes more predictable. He has a stronger preference for certain types of activities, boisterous or quiet. Any child should have some of both, for this opens his world much more. Even if your child is quiet, he still needs toys that make him run, chase, swing, swoop or jump, just as a rambunctious child needs books and records to enjoy his solitude more.

By Three he should have a small table or shelf for his records so he can choose which side of which record he wants to hear, reading the odd marks and scratches as quickly as you read the label.

A Three may want a gun. Children have pretend shoot-ups, whether they use their fingers or a stick or a plastic pistol, but the children who have homemade props seem to have less interest in war games and quit them much earlier. A gun we didn't mind was the water pistol. This has to be an outside toy and it's one that you'll want to replace as soon as it's lost or broken for the next seven years, for it brings a lot of laughs.

Your Three does need a sheltered place for his large, bulky toys, such as the tricycle, a rocking horse, or one of those big wooden "boats," in which one to four children can rock in tandem. This may be in a carport, the cellar, his own bedroom or, ideally, a playroom located next to the kitchen. For his smaller toys, he'll still need a shelf or a drawer in each room but most of the toys should be in one place now—preferably his own room.

Never expect to store toys in the boxes they came in, for they're not sturdy enough. Instead, keep them in strong cartons, baskets or cloth bags and on shelves. Toys, such as his interlocking plastic blocks or small cars, can be grouped together but never thrown into a toy chest. That only breeds disorder.

Since disorder confuses your child as much as it does you, help him sort his toys, but do this no more than once or twice a week. A child who gets too concerned in keeping his toys in order isn't going to enjoy playing with them and won't like his friends to play with them either.

Four

If he hasn't already, your child soon will have very sure opinions about what toys he wants for his birthday, Christmas or Saturday night. They are inspired by the toys his playmates have, the ones used in nursery school and those he sees advertised. Fortunately, he likes so many things it's easy to choose the ones that fit you both.

Children like to dress like cowboys, nurses,

sailors, farmers—any costume that creates a role. Your Four will like to play house with a stove you've made out of cardboard (page 223) and to throw a small rubber ball with one hand like a ball player. He also wants to use scissors on every piece of paper he can find and to work a jigsaw puzzle. He can work this puzzle best on a tray, so you can put it away when he's bored with it without disturbing the picture. Until he learns how, help him turn over all the pieces and separate the borders so he can make the frame first. He can assemble it faster that way, which makes him proud.

If your child is the sort who enjoys small toys, he'll like a farm with animals or some miniature cars. For more robust play, get a rope ladder, a tumbling mat or a mattress for indoors and hang an old tire from a strong limb of a tree in the back yard. He's ready to play "road safety" with his tricycle or scooter, which makes him feel grown-up, and it makes him aware of auto traffic long before he crosses streets.

By Four you can consider a swing, if you don't mind pushing, and if you put a low barrier in front so other children won't cross its path when it's moving.

Five

A Five, that great collector, has defined interests and saves rocks or toy cars or dolls. The most ardent doll collector also wants a bigger carriage and a dollhouse with all the paraphernalia.

A Five should have an assortment of brushes for artwork, a deck of cards to play the standard favorites—Old Maid and Fish—and stories read on records.

Now you can introduce a needle and embroidery thread, a small loom or a game like pick-up sticks, so your child can practice the same pincer movement he will use every time he holds a pencil at school. While these pastimes appeal to some children, others still can't get enough physical exercise and will like a soccer ball to kick and a knotted rope for climbing. He can learn to pump

his own swing now if you teach him.

A great amount of a child's playtime may be spent in elaborate "pretend" games, where the tricycle becomes the family car and the gym set is the house. Other games require no props at all and you may hear yourself saying that your child never plays with his toys any more.

Six

A Six wants to fly a kite (especially if he's helped to make it), to push a tire like a hoop and thinks there's nothing finer than having a clubhouse—in a tree, a cave or a garage—an obsession that reaches its peak in about two more years.

A pair of stilts will make a Six proud, although he must practice every day for many days before he can take more than a few steps on them. He's still too young for roller skates, because he can't coordinate his legs that well, and may not be ready for a bicycle either, for he probably won't go fast enough to keep steady. Even when a child is able to ride a bike, we don't recommend it, unless you have a cul-de-sac or a nearby park for him to ride it, for no Six is mature enough to ride in the street and no sidewalk is safe for a young biker and the neighborhood toddlers too.

We've found girls beg for the biggest, most complicated dolls, and then prefer the plain old baby doll that does nothing but drink from a bottle (for your Six to share secretly) and wet her diapers. Dolls are beloved now by most girls and most boys too, although they may be too embarrassed to say so. A Six feels pressured by society, if not by his parents, to accept the stereotype roles of boy and girl, until all boys think they must be rough and tough and all girls must be scared of worms. Of course this is silly, but it needn't happen if you encourage your child to choose the toys and books that let him follow his own interests. Just as a One may pick a puzzle over a beanbag, so should your daughter, at Six, fly model planes without feeling she must conform.

Enrichment

Books

You have more control over the books you offer your child than you have over almost any other influence in his young life. To our way of thinking, the only books that can harm a child are the ones so static and so boring that they destroy every child's natural love affair with literature.

You'll watch this sweet romance flower with each child and each time it will be as poignant as before, and perhaps you'll be lucky enough to see your Six, as we saw Nell, when she clutched her new library book and said, "I can't wait to get to the exciting part! Did you know, it always comes after the middle?"

Storytime, we've found, is one of the best ways to deepen a parent-child relationship and also to increase a child's attention span. To hold his interest, your voice should be light and expressive and your child should be able to comprehend most books so well he can save many of his questions until the story is finished.

We did find a child thrives on thirty minutes of storytelling a day, although it naturally will be broken into several short sessions for a mid-One and in one or two concentrated periods for a Six.

To a child, a story must be either real or preposterous, funny or informative. While Ramon, a serious Two, insisted on books full of content, the rest of the children wanted as much wackiness or, at the least, as much whimsey as we could find. It's for you to stretch a literal child to fantasy and a fanciful child to realism by offering some books that pull his natural inclinations in other directions.

The younger the child, the more familiar the setting should be (although this is a rule made for breaking), but any story must have a happy ending. Above all, it must be well written—no matter what style—so it pleases both of you every time you read it. If your child's books bore you, you've chosen the wrong ones. You'll know it when you catch yourself saying, "In a minute," whenever he asks for a story, and when you're finally cornered, you read the book, a yawn for every page. If you do this too often your child won't like books—any books—when he learns to read for himself.

Phoniness, in either text or illustration, also will be sensed immediately, for you can't trifle with the honesty of children. We believe the worst books are those abridged, assembly-line specials at the supermarket, and we found it much cheaper and wiser to buy high-quality books, either paperback or secondhand.

Since it's hard to find a wide selection of children's books, even in a good store, we think you'll want to follow the book fairs, where you can order them individually or through a cooperative purchase at your child's preschool, although you probably will rely on weekly trips to the library for most of the titles.

Just as all children's books shouldn't be read by children (nor by anyone else), neither should children read only children's books. Every young child should be exposed to poetry—good adult poetry—not only to learn to appreciate the rhythm of its sophisticated beat (as opposed to the amusing, political doggerel of *Mother Goose*) but because poetry has the scope and precision to conjure pictures that prose can seldom paint. The very brevity of poetry will give you time to read it again and again, so your child can draw a richer meaning every time.

We once baby-sat a Three named Cassandra who met us at the door with a book of poetry from her father's shelf, flipping straight to the page she wanted. She could and did match every thumping line of William Blake's

Tiger, tiger burning bright
In the forest of the night

and not as a rote performer, but as an involved participant, grasping heaven knows what marvelous images from it. She died a few years later, in one of those fluky accidents of illness that haunt every parent, but we can't help thinking that she had drawn more joy from one part of life, at least, than most people ever do.

Six Months

A baby should have his own cloth books in his crib, because he enjoys them, because he learns to feel comfortable with books—and because it gives you a little extra sleep in the morning. An adept mother masters the art of staying abed, and a well-practiced art it should be. We found little variety in the cloth books and the drawings were completely representational, but your child won't mind. His pleasure is in studying the pictures, tasting them, caressing each page.

Nine Months
Now he wants you to point out the pictures, naming the boy, the girl, the mama and papa, saying each word distinctly. He may try to say "moo" if you point to the cow (if you've said it enough times), but it will be much later before he'll try to say "cow." Soon he will transfer his love of cloth books to the small, stiff "Pat the Bunny," with its textured pages, and take it with him wherever he goes.

One
A One begins to turn the pages and will be content with a mail-order catalogue for a long time, pointing to all the toys, shoes and clocks he sees with "oohs" and "aahs" as he goes along.

Now his books can have more intricate drawings and he likes to find the ladybug or the butterfly in the background, which not only increases his vocabulary but makes him concentrate longer.

This is a good age to invest in some classics, like *The Real Mother Goose*, with its famous checkerboard jacket, or the charming alphabet book by Kate Greenaway or any of the R. Caldecott series. He is sure to like the illustrations by Ezra Jack Keats, a master of picture books, and those by that blessed fellow Maurice Sendak, for his work is a joy, starting now with *Chicken Soup and Rice*.

There are children who are restless before you've turned the third page and for them you need to be the most careful in choosing books, finding ones with almost no text but with dazzling colors, or books that involve some action. Also, when you can run like a deer or jump over a candlestick together, your child realizes that he is a part of a story or a rhyme, and will like storytime much more.

Two
A Two needs books that are so good you'll enjoy reading them almost as many times as he will enjoy hearing them. He should have fresh library books each week and at least ten books of his own, new or used, paperback or hard cover, poetry or prose, and another ten every year thereafter.

Your Two will take reasonably good care of books now and should be chastised if he doesn't. Generally, a child who likes the stories he hears seldom will destroy them.

A Two will recite nursery rhymes with you, for the cadence has much appeal and he likes to see their pictures decorate his room. He is happy with the artwork of both José Aruego, whose flowers fairly spring from a page, and Pat Hutchins, whose animals teach prepositions as they move through the books.

Mid-Two
A mid-Two is so rigid that the book which makes him happy one night is the book he'll want to hear every night, which we wish we'd known before we had impulsively bought Kate that book about a wretched child named Eukalalie. Although any Two gets caught on one particular book, you still will need a variety from the library to make reading more pleasant—especially for yourself.

Your mid-Two will want to hear about true situations, for he is the greatest fan of realism since Daguerre invented the photograph. He wants to know about letter carriers and firefighters and his parents at the office—most of which are told in quite dreary books—but he will be just as charmed, and so will you, with the realistic, if zany, *Let's Be Enemies*, or *A Flower Pot Is Not a Hat*.

Small books with small, detailed drawings are lovely but your child will be enchanted (and who isn't?) by Brian Wildsmith's orgy of color in any books he illustrates.

At this age your child will weep for "one more story"—especially from the sitter—for he has learned to manipulate an adult's love of books into a later bedtime. For this your only defense is to offer two stories and stick to that, or offer one story and ritualistically read "one more"—almost never exceeding your limit.

Three
Since a Three is good enough to know when he's naughty, he enjoys books with mischievous children, like *The Temper Tantrum Book*. Some books now should be informative, like *What's Inside: The Story of an Egg That Hatched*, and you'll do well with photographs of animals as they actually look—an adjunct to the many zoo trips now. Other books you offer may be a combination of reality and fantasy, as in the cozy Edith series, where photographs show a doll and her friends, the stuffed bears, who behave just like people.

Books in a series may be your salvation—or they may not. Personally, we found the ones about that Little Engine that Could, Dirty Harry, and

George, the obstreperous monkey, were dreadful, but the children did not: one of life's less sweet compromises. You need to take precautions, because a Three can tell some books by their covers.

Once he checks out one book from a series, he'll recognize the characters the next time in another book, and want to read about them again—and again. That's why we think you should spend some time going through many series with the librarian, skimming one of each set yourself, before introducing it to your child. When you find one you like, you can get others with confidence. We would recommend the series by Dr. Seuss and by Rosemary Wells now and also the books about the Happy Lion and about Frances, that nice, nice bear.

Four

At this age there are books for every interest and excellent ones in almost every category. If your child is impatient, you can choose pop-up books—which are fun but require little of a child's imagination—or those with scant text but with sophisticated drawings or story line. For most children, however, the art shouldn't overpower the story any more.

A Four needs to have the world explained to him. The George Zaffo books on trucks, trains and tools are among the better ones, although we suspect the best of these books haven't been written yet.

Besides learning the usual facts about a farm, a city, a small town and some of the skills and professions of the people who live there, he needs to begin to know why there are traffic laws, why there are wars, why there are jails, why men have governments and manners—and what happens if they don't. Books that take up these subjects force you to exchange ideas with your child and this is the grist for so much of the talking that lies ahead.

Your child is ripe to appreciate wit and likes *Stone Soup* and *Dinosaurs and All That Rubbish*. There is also *How Does the Czar Eat Potatoes* (the title alone makes it worth reading) and the Judith Viorst books, which show that some storybook families act real. He'll like the basic *Winnie the Pooh*, if you tell him first that it's about a little boy and his nursery full of stuffed animals, but without this explanation, he may be confused. We were.

Four is the time when a child likes to hear his language turned upside down, as it is in the Amelia Bedelia series. He enjoys daffy, contemporary poetry, like *Upside Down and Inside Out Poems for All Your Pockets*, but a Four also loves the old-fashioned *A Child's Garden of Verses*.

We also recommend the stories you make up yourself, for although the plot may be scrambled, it will be different from any story any child has ever heard.

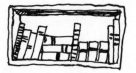

Five

Now his appetite for reading is bigger every day. Your child wants to hear that leaves turn red when the sap is drawn from the branch, that melanin makes animals black, that rain is just warm snow and that a baby grows in the womb. He wants Greek myths and legends now and stories and folk tales that tell about the culture and customs of other people, like *Princess of the Full Moon*. You also will find Augusta Baker's definitive list of black literature for children, which is available in most public libraries, will help you choose well-written ethnic books.

There is the sophistication of the Madeleine series, about elegant living in Paris, or for that matter, the charming Babar books, about elegant living among the elephants in Africa or the hilarious poetry in *Meet My Folks*. This is the age when your little girl is quite likely to think herself a princess who got swapped in the crib, and so the stories about kings and castles make her feel right at home.

Six

You may want to introduce resource books now, like the simplest supermarket set of Golden Press encyclopedias, or a book on gardening or one on cooking, such as Craig Claiborne's *Kitchen Primer*. There are few good history books for children, but we do recommend Leonard Weisgard's *The Plymouth Thanksgiving*.

When you read to your child from these books, they become such familiar friends he will turn to them naturally for information when he begins to read well.

There are many good, easy readers on the market, but some are imitative and often not quite that easy to read. The best of these books we feel are the science books of the "I Can Read" series by Harper and Row. We recommend a careful consideration of all of them, because a poor choice will bore a child after the first few readings and he may decide that reading to himself is a bore.

You'll want to continue to read to your child long after he has learned to read, because it will be years before his ability can catch up with his interests and because it's such a warm, friendly thing to do. Books about Dr. Dolittle are lovely and fairy tales become so enchanting now and your child's span of interest so long that you can expect absolute, knee-hugging silence when you read the Tasha Tudor stories.

There are also the warm *Lordy, Aunt Hattie* and *Sweet Pea*—the evocative, but far from patronizing stories set in the rural South; the nonsensical poetry by Edward Lear, and the many fine classical English stories by Milne and by Kenneth Grahame.

Perhaps it's our own proclivities, but we find any books that make us laugh are very good books. That's why we read to our Sixes from James Thurber's splendid book, *The Wonderful O,* about the fellow who hated the letter "O" ever since his mother got stuck in a porthole and they couldn't pull her in so they had to push her out. He left that letter out of his kingdom later, your child will be happy to know, and Ophelia Oliver became Phelia Liver.

That's very ribald to a Six.

Storytelling

Not all stories have to be written before they can be told.

When Mike was young, his father started the wacky Michael J. Smithfield stories, which proved that any story is good if 1) it is improbable; 2) specific numbers are used, like 17 or 1,224; 3) treasure is discovered; 4) there are bad guys, who are adults, and good guys, who are children, and 5) the hero and his family and his friends look just like the listener and his family and his friends and even have the same first names.

Naturally these stories end well and reflect great glory on the children in them, who use their quick wits and many tricks to catch the pirates and the burglars.

Now Mike makes up his own stories for the children he baby-sits and the formula is the same, although the victories are more vulgar and possibly more beloved: his small heroes always catch the villains the same way—they pee on them.

Book List

Many of these books we list are our personal choices—beloved by our children, by their friends and by us. Some of the books are prizewinners, many are in paperback, most are in the public library, and all are waiting to be read.

Authors and Illustrators

These are the names of authors and illustrators—classic and contemporary—that we've found are almost always associated with good books:

Aliki	Ingri and Edgar P. d'Aulaire	May Garelick
Edward Ardizzone	Laurent De Brunhoff	John Goodall
José Aruego	Janina Domanska	Kenneth Grahame
Frank Asch	Roger Duvoisin	Kate Greenaway
Jacqueline Ayer	Ed and Barbara Emberly	Virginia Haviland
Nathaniel Benchley	Marie Hall Ets	Lillian and Russell Hoban
Leslie Brooke	Louise Fatio	Tana Hoban
Marica Brown	Aileen Fisher	Ted Hughes
Margaret W. Brown	Marjorie Flack	Pat Hutchins
John Burningham	James Flora	Janosch
Virginia L. Burton	Michael Foreman	Ezra Jack Keats
Randolph Caldecott	Françoise	Phyllis Krasilovsky
Eric Carle	Don Freeman	Robert Kraus
Rebecca Caudill	Wanda Gag	James Krüss
Miriam Cohen	Paul Galdone	Albert Lamorisse

Munro Leaf
Edward Lear
Félicité Lefèvre
Lois Lenski
Leo Lionni
Anita Lobel
Arnold Lobel
Kenneth Mahood
James Marshall
Robert G. McCloskey
A. A. Milne
Else H. Minarik

Martha Moffett
Evaline Ness
Joanna Oppenheim
Susan Perl
Peggy Parish
Watty Piper
Beatrix Potter
Edna M. Preston
Ellen A. Raskin
Anne Rose
Richard Scarry
Maurice Sendack
Dr. Seuss
Peter Spier
Ianthe Thomas
Tasha Tudor
Janice M. Udrey
Judith Viorst
Rosemary Wells
Kurt Werth
Brian Wildsmith
Garth Williams
Dare Wright
Marie Winn
George Zaffo
Charlotte Zolotow

Science and Nature

Beaver Pond—Alvin Tresselt
Christmas Sky—Franklyn M. Branley
Curious Raccoons (with photographs)—Lilo Hess
Green Is for Growing—Winifred and Cecil Lubell
In a Running Brook—Winifred and Cecil Lubell
Lucky Ladybugs—Gladys Conklin
Machines—Anne Rockwell
Olly's Polliwogs—Anne Rockwell
Red Legs (egg-to-egg story of a grasshopper)—Alice
  Goudey
Remarkable Chameleon—Lilo Hess
See What I Caught—Ann Thomas Piecewicz
That Remarkable Creature, the Snail (with
  photographs)—Oscar Schisgall
Thruway—Anne and Harlow Rockwell
Toad—Anne and Harlow Rockwell
Toolbox—Anne Rockwell
What Makes It Go, Work, Fly, Float?—Joe Kaufman
*What's Inside: The Story of an Egg That
  Hatched*—May Garelick
Where Did I Come From?—Peter Mayle
The Wonderful Story of How You Were Born—
  Sidonie Matsner Gruenberg
The World of Push and Pull—Earl Ubell

Follett Beginning Science Books—Follett Publishing
  Co., Chicago, Illinois.
Science I Can Read Series—Harper and Row, New
  York, New York.
Let's Find Out Science Series—Thomas Crowell Co.,
  New York, New York.

Feelings and Foibles

You can help your child handle his emotions
better if he sees how other children handle theirs.
Many of these books exaggerate a child's feelings
enough to let him laugh at his foibles.
Elizabeth Gets Well—Alfons Weber
My Doctor—Harlow Rockwell
Tommy Goes to the Doctor—Gunilla Wolde
Exactly Alike—Evaline Ness
Go & Hush the Baby—Betsy Byars
A New Baby Is Coming to My House—Chihiro
  Iwasaki
*Nobody Asked Me If I Wanted a Baby
  Sister*—Martha Alexander
The Day Chiro Was Lost—Chiyoko Nakatani
One Dark Night—Edna M. Preston
No Kiss for Mother—Tomi Ungerer
Phoebe's Revolt—Natalie Babbitt
The Temper Tantrum Book—Edna M. Preston
We Are Having a Baby—Viki Holland
What Happens When You Go to the Hospital—
  Arthur Shay

Folklore and Fairy Tales

Fairy Tale Treasury—Compiled by Virginia Haviland
Kasho and the Twin Flutes (story about Sierra
  Leone)—Adjai Robinson
A Necklace of Raindrops—Joan Aiken
Princess of the Full Moon (African tale)—Frederic
  Guïrma
Twelve Years, Twelve Animals (Japanese folk
  tale)—Adapted by Yoshiko Y. Samuel
We Want Sunshine in Our Houses (Finnish
  tale)—Retold by Bernice W. Carlson & Ristiina
  Wigg
The Woodcutter's Duck (Polish folk tale)—Krystyna
  Turska

Poetry

All the Silver Pennies—Anthology of poems
  compiled by Blanche Jennings Thompson
A Child's Garden of Verses—Robert Louis Stevenson
Chinese Mother Goose Rhymes—Selected and edited
  by Robert Wyndham
Come Along—Rebecca Caudill
*Come Hither, Collection of Rhymes and Poems for
  the Young of All Ages*—Compiled by Walter de
  la Mare
A Family Book of Nursery Rhymes—Gathered by
  Iona and Peter Opie
Figgie Hobbin—Charles Causley
*The Golden Journey: Poems for the Very
  Young*—Compiled by Louise Bogan and William
  J. Smith
Illustrated Treasury of Poetry for Children—Edited
  by David Ross
In the Woods, in the Meadow, in the Sky—Aileen
  Fisher
*Lean Out of the Window, An Anthology of Modern
  Poetry*—Compiled by Sara Hannum and
  Gwendolyn E. Reed
*Listen, Children, Listen; An Anthology of Poems
  for the Very Young*—Edited by Myra C.
  Livingston
Meet My Folks—Ted Hughes
*Pick Me Up, Pick Me Up; A Book of Short, Short
  Poems*—Edited by William Cole
The Real Mother Goose—Illustrated by Blanche
  Wright
Small Poems—Valerie Worth
Toucans Two and Other Poems—Jack Prelutsky

Classics

Reading the classics aloud must be one of the
nicest customs for a father and a Five.
A Bear Called Paddington (series)—Michael Bond
*The Bumper Book—A Harvest of Stories and
  Verse*—Edited by Watty Piper

Music and Records

From the first day of life, a child absorbs every sound he hears, which is why we feel at least some of them should be beautiful. That's what music was made for. His introduction to it will be the lullabies you sing, the music box that tinkles, a soft piano passage. He'll be startled by any loud or sudden sounds and will be soothed best, we found, by chamber music—good reason for him to hear background music from the radio or the record player.

The smallest infant is entranced by just a few notes on the guitar or the bassoon, so if either you or your husband play any instrument we think you should entertain your baby with it at least five minutes a day. By three months he may smile to show you his preference for E Minor rather than C Major when you strum a chord, which will make you want to play more and more for him for the next few years. This will be the best audience you'll ever have. The charm of these little interludes will linger long after your child has grown.

Whether you can play an instrument or not, you still should whistle while you work and sing to your child too—sad songs, happy songs, any songs—and sometimes have your child feel your throat while you sing.

This won't be enough for a One. He wants simple melodies and clear rhythms so he can try to clap his hands and bounce to the beat. It's hard to believe, but this bumping and grinding focuses his interest, and this is what stretches a child's attention span.

Just as you want your child to respect musical instruments, so must he learn to respect people when they play them, but this, we tell you sadly, takes years longer—especially if you're the player. For some inexplicable reason, your child surely will feel he must hug your knees when you play the violin the same way he babbles when you read the paper. All your anger won't change it, but it will hurt your performance, so if playing is what keeps your soul in balance, you'd better do most of it when he's asleep or out visiting.

A Two doesn't sit still for music either (nor a Three, nor a Four)—nor should he. Music is to be enjoyed. Perhaps this is why outdoor concerts seem designed for a Two, for they give him plenty of room to move and he'll intoxicate all those around him with his enthusiasm for the music.

This child is ready for baroque music, hearty marches by Sousa and some folk songs and sea chanteys sung by Burl Ives, Woody Guthrie and Pete Seeger. The words in every folk song should be so easy to hear he can learn them if he wants.

You may be able to borrow more records from the library, or swap with friends, and if you have a true tape recorder, can tape the best of them. Unlike books for children there's a paucity of good records designed especially for them. Only a handful of recording companies bother to use top artists on the curious assumption that a child can't tell the fine from the indifferent. We think you must treat your child's ear with respect, listening to all new records as critically as you would watch a new television show and keeping only the best. Why teach a child to like dreck?

At Three your child will like Saint-Saëns' "Carnival of The Animals," Brahms' Hungarian dances, Prokofiev's "The Ugly Duckling" and Carl Orff's "Music for Chidren." Play these good scores for him on your stereo where the quality of the tone won't be lost. You also should play the best of jazz, of soul, of country and rock—any kind of music at all as long as it's first class. Let him play his records on his own player—which shouldn't be a toy, but an inexpensive turntable. It won't last more than a few years anyway. Because he'll want to keep it in his room so he can play the songs again and again or hop around to the rhythms with his friends, it must sit on a steady table.

We have a rugged, tree-climbing friend named Tom whose love of music was so great at Three that he was trusted to play the family's finest records on the family's fine turntable. Soon he was dividing his time between climbing trees and listening to music, until at Four, we watched him approach a young stranger—the oldest and therefore most important child at a birthday party—with, "You know what I like best? Beethoven's 'Ninth.'" To which the Seven astonished us all by replying, "Me, too." It turned out he also had played his first records at Three.

Your Four may not be ready for Beethoven's "Ninth," but he surely can enjoy Tchaikovsky's "1812 Overture" or Dvořák's "New World Symphony" or Bruch's "Scottish Fantasy." Certainly you'll want to get Prokofiev's "Peter and the Wolf" too. (We're partial to the Milton Cross narrative.)

We found that records of stories are most helpful to a child between Four and Six. They should be narrated by good actors with imaginative voices and played on his own record player during rest time, but they aren't, of course, a substitute for your reading aloud.

Records that teach colors, numbers and letters are no fun to be heard alone, which is why we think they should be limited to nursery school.

Sometime before Five, a child will be ready to go to an indoor children's concert, at least on an infrequent basis.

A Five enjoys songs in a foreign language, which he will imitate in an enchanting way. He also will like Mussorgsky's "Pictures at an Exhibition," Holst's "The Planets," Stravinsky's "Firebird" and Grieg's "Peer Gynt Suite," but for a good tone, they need your stereo.

Before first grade we hope your child will have attended not only that proper concert but also a ballet or two where he can watch the dance meld with the music, and a musical, like *Oklahoma!* or an operetta, like *H.M.S. Pinafore* or for a total fusion of the arts, a light opera such as Rossini's *The Barber of Seville* or Menotti's *Amahl and the Night Visitors*. Most children, to be sure, won't grow up to be musical giants, but all children should be exposed to so much music when they're young that they will love it for life.

Record List

"Abiyoyo and Other Story Songs for Children"
Folkways FTS 3100 (1968)
"Animals, Best In Children's Series"
Bowmar CL 19
"American Folk Songs for Children"
Folkways FTS 31501 (1968)
"Animal Folk Songs for Children"
Folkways FTS 31503 (1968)
"Birds, Beasts, Bugs and Little Fishes"
Folkways FTS 31504 (1968)
"Fables, The Best In Children's Series"
Bowmar CL 22
"A Gathering of Great Poetry for Children"
Caedmon TC 1235-1238 (1968)
"Hard Tack, He's a Fine Old Engine"
RCA Camdem Cal 1056 (1964)
"Music for Children"
Carl Orff and Gunhild Keetman
Angel Records 3582 B (1959)
"Music for Ones and Twos"
CMS Records CMS-649 (1972)
"Poems and Songs for Younger Children"
Spoken Arts 1060 (1971)
"The Red Balloon"
Nonesuch Records H 72001
"So Early in the Morning," Irish Children's Traditional Songs, Rhymes, and Games
Tradition TLP 1134
"Songs for Singing Children"
John Langstaff and Children's Chorus
Odeon CSD 1470
"Songs to Grow On" (Woody Guthrie)
Folkways Records FTS 31502
"A Treasury of Folk Songs for Children"
Elektra EKL 223 (1963)
"The Unicorn in the Garden"
James Thurber
Caedmon TC 1398 (1972)

Record Companies

Bowmar Records, 622 Rodier Dr., Glendale, Calif. 91201
Educational Activities Incorporated, Freeport, N.Y. 11520
Folkways, 701 Seventh Ave., New York, N.Y. 10036
Columbia Children's Record Library, CBS Inc., 15 W. 52nd St., New York, N.Y. 10019
Weston Woods Studios, Weston, Conn.

The Arts

Theater

Any legitimate theater—no matter how bad—has advantages over the best television, for the electricity of live drama is unforgettable. Also, when the cast takes its curtain call, a child can see that everyone is all right, whatever happened onstage.

At Two or Three we like to introduce theater with a puppet show (but not a Punch and Judy, which is grim at any age) and then at least one play a year for a Four, a Five and a Six.

While your child won't draw the same meaning from a play as you do (for he looks at everything from the underside), he still will feel its richness. You'll find he gets even more pleasure if you occasionally play a recording of the production afterwards—especially easy to find in the library if you have seen an old standard.

A child can discover Shakespeare in nappy style with the musical, *Kiss Me, Kate*, and go on to his comedies like *A Mid-Summer Night's Dream* or *As You Like It*. Again, this isn't hard to do if you live near a city, since so many now produce Shakespeare outdoors during the summer.

Any child, as early as Four, will be delighted with a comedy like *You Can't Take It With You*, by Kaufman and Hart, or one by that master, Molière, and by Six he'll be quite as thrilled by a mystery like Tom Stoppard's *The Real Inspector Hound* as he is with a children's classic like *Pinocchio*.

Of course, not all theater should be confined to plays and musicals. Besides modern dance troupes, there are classical ballets, which are often more appealing since they have story lines. We think your child is almost sure to like "The Dance Lesson"—that funny ballet—or one of the grand ones, like "Sleeping Beauty," and Balanchine's "Stars and Stripes" will make him march for days.

Sometimes you can find a good amateur production, but we'd rather scrimp for a professional company. This may be cheaper than you think since you'll buy balcony tickets, where your child can see better from above than he can from the orchestra, and you'll go to a matinée.

Even if the cost of the tickets bites into your grocery budget, your child will remember an afternoon at the theater a lot longer than he'll remember a week of spaghetti.

Movies

Of all the outings we've ever taken with the children, one of the nicest was a six-hour, air-conditioned orgy of the Marx Brothers in the middle of a heat wave. Generally, we're not so greedy.

A movie every month or two is a pleasant interlude if the quality is high, and a dismal one if it's not. We find there's no reason at all to endure a simplistic Walt Disney when both parents and child can be happy with a zinger like *The Yellow Submarine* instead. Adventures with a child are meant to be enjoyed by adults too.

Television

It's hard to imagine any influence that can be both so good and so bad for a child, but television is it. Nothing else is so easy to supply, so hard to deny, so intelligent when it's good, so dreadful when it's not.

Too loud, it can damage the eardrums, too near, it can hurt the eyes and too often, it can dull the senses. And after all that, we still approve of television. With its overseas competition, it gets better every year, as an art form, an entertainer and a teacher. Besides, it's an inescapable part of our society and one every child sees sooner or later, somewhere, so he may as well begin to learn how to watch it in moderation and how to judge its quality.

Sometime between Six and Twelve you'll be shocked to find your child—your bicycling, book-reading, games-loving, moderate child—wants to do nothing but watch the set all day long and the trashier the show the better he seems to like it. This too shall pass, but it will pass easier, we think, if you have thoughtful and consistent rules in the early years.

You shouldn't let your child sit any closer than six feet in front of the set, raise the volume above a normal level, keep it on during meals or let the bedtime slide "to the next commercial."

Although you may enjoy the freedom of an electronic baby sitter, you have to limit the time, alloting, we feel, no more than five hours a week, starting at Two, and seven to ten hours by Six. It also isn't wise for him to watch for longer than an hour at a time, for it can make him cranky to be inactive any longer. To be realistic, a sick child will watch more television, but he can't tolerate it for more than two hours at a time.

Sick or well, you won't want to let your child look at any program without permission. Before giving it, you should see one of the shows in the series yourself, rather than accept the recommendation of a neighbor or a neighbor's child. You're the arbiter, for it's your child who will be affected if the show he sees is too silly or too adult or too violent. While every child will see some violence in his life, the senseless fighting in a cat-and-mouse cartoon has as much impact on a pre-Six as a scary movie. A nature show, with its ritualistic bluffing and occasional blood, is about all he can handle.

Just as a child may be mesmerized by violence, so might he be transfixed by one bit of vacuous nonsense after another. Such blather is an assault on the mind and can hold a mother spellbound too—as we should know. It's so easy to use old movies and quiz shows to counter the lonely, rainy afternoons, but this expediency has its price. The more you watch television, the more your child will too, even while he's playing with his toys. This can make him passive as well as inarticulate, for it's hard to talk and watch television at the same time.

Television, if used wisely, isn't a constant factor but a small event—a supplement to the day's adventures.

When you and your child work together with letters, he begins to learn them but when he also sees the letters on the educational children's show, this lesson is enhanced. In the same way, the child who is taken downtown to see the parade in the afternoon and then sees it again on the evening news will have a slightly broader concept of the world and especially his important place in it. He'll be sure he's in the picture at least a dozen times.

Museums and Art Galleries

The best museums have special exhibits for young children, but you can add a lot to the adventure by the way you handle it. Plan to cover a small amount of territory, but let your child choose which display to visit and, with gentle guidance, which sculptures and paintings.

Point out how artists once used fruits and vegetables and egg whites to make and bind their colors, how they learned to paint pictures in perspective and paint portraits with such remarkable eyes they'll follow your child wherever he walks in the room.

Finally, although the day is a treat for you too, do go home before his interest flags. Like any other outing, you want him to want to come back for more.

Values

It's hard to cradle a newborn in your arms and realize that perfection isn't automatic. You're sure that anyone who can achieve such beauty in only nine months should have no trouble with his faith, hope and charity in twenty years.

This isn't so. You have to teach your child the virtues the way you teach him to dress himself or make his bed—by example, by insistence and by giving him the chance to make mistakes for himself. As long as he knows you love him, even when he's jealous and greedy and full of the faults that beleaguer us all, he'll be a better person for trying. It's maturity he's learning, not perfection.

If the values you try to live by are honest ones, they'll be your child's solace and his strength later; and if they're materialistic, hypocritical, rigid or simply never discussed, there will be repercussions too, for without this shield, his legacy is weak. As distressing as it sounds, we can never forget that the drunks in the park were all children once.

Although your child is born with hope—the expectation that he'll be fed and cared for—it's the love with which you swaddle him that will make him trust you and therefore trust himself. This faith in himself generates the self-confidence he needs to be daring at Two and also at Fourteen, when it takes a lot of chutzpah to be an individual, no matter how much teasing he gets from his friends.

A child learns to respect others if he is respected—not as a prince but as a person, albeit small. This teaches a child to accept others as they are and this is the essence of charity. The presents he makes, the kittens he cuddles and the work he performs are all tangible expressions of charity, which help a child learn to give that most important present: himself.

You will find your pre-Six is so egocentric he'll be able to recognize injustice instinctively, especially when it's applied to him, and in this way he understands about justice. The child who is treated fairly will be able to treat others the same way.

You do want your child to become a prudent adult who can handle money cautiously and weigh consequences before he acts. This lesson begins early and is learned not by your preaching but by his errors. When he starts to handle toys with some care and wear mittens in the snow, you'll know he realizes that a little trouble is better than broken toys and icy fingers.

The Carry Nations of the world have given temperance a bad name, but a child must learn moderation. He has to curb his love of candy and television the way he curbs his temper—the first steps toward self-restraint.

Your child must understand that it's not enough to be good and kind and prudent and true, since he still needs fortitude when the rest of the world is not. While a child must build the courage to finish the fights that he starts—even when he knows he's going to lose—he also needs the courage to face the tough realities of life and endure its small succession of sorry problems. As every mother knows, there are weeks and, heaven help us, even years when love is stretched quite thin. That's what fortitude is for.

Although your child must realize that he's responsible for every decision he makes, he can't make sensible ones unless he's supported by the old-fashioned virtues. Character is built, like a wall, brick by brick.

Generosity

The younger your child, the easier it is to live with him, but as he gets older, you'll realize that each member of the family pulls stronger in slightly different directions. The understanding that each of you has for the other will depend on the generosity

in your house, for giving in and giving are often the same.

Your child can be a giving person if you cultivate his empathy—that sixth and most delicate sense—so he can learn how to express all the love he feels. This is why we think a child, as early as mid-Two, should make a housewarming gift for a new neighbor, a bouquet of dandelions for the sick and have pets on which to squander affection. Later perhaps he can help you wash and mend the outgrown clothes to fill a huge Daisy Box, as we once did for our Aunt Kay. There all the clothes were collected for her friend Daisy who had even less than we did. As nineteenth century as this now seems, a child who is able to give hand-me-downs, as well as get them, can understand the essence of generosity. The more you give the richer you are.

Although your child may be unknowingly direct, his kindness can match his candor, as it did when we heard a Four ask solicitously of the neighborhood arthritic, his torso bent horizontal as he walked, "How are you today, Mr. Find-a-Penny?"

Your child needs some friends who are handicapped, not as a favor to them, but as a favor to himself, for he's the one who's enriched. It was Mali who said about one of our closest friends, "I know Charlie is retarded, but I really like him just the way he is." This acceptance of people is the essence of generosity.

The ability to accept others isn't limited to the poor or the sick. Your child needs to realize that eccentricities are as reasonable as red hair and, in effect, are not his business. Tolerance is expanded, for instance, when he chats with the old ladies on the bus—strangers though they are—for everybody has a story and the more stories your child hears, the more he understands about people. He begins to see that good health is not automatic, that poverty is not preferred by the poor, that some people are smarter than others (or kinder or prettier) and that, Pollyanna though we sound, there is good in

everyone. Sometimes, in fact, it's a sport in itself just to find it, and a child rather enjoys that too.

Gifts

A giving child doesn't simply sprout like a mushroom on Midsummer Eve. As much as he wants to share his love, he needs you to show him how.

You'll watch him instinctively experiment with the game of give and take (especially take) at nine months, when he hands you his teddy bear again and again, but always for you to return right away. The game gets more sophisticated by mid-One, when your child offers you one of his two precious cookies, but still he would weep if you ever ate it. Your effusive "thanks, but no thanks" may seem overdone until you realize that it's as hard for him to give away that cookie as it would be for you to give away your paycheck.

This appreciation you show helps him understand the joy of giving a little better. Soon your Two, if encouraged, will make some curried peanuts to give to the neighbor lady and find pleasure in her compliments. By Three he'll make a few presents for his favorite people, on his own initiative. A Four begins to see that a gift needn't be shiny and store-bought to be enjoyed, and in another year he can carry the custom of giving a little further. Now he recognizes that the work he does for others—in the kitchen, in the workshop, in the garden—is another way to give. By Six, a child is learning to give of himself, without expecting any immediate return. This is a sign of maturity.

Some of his gifts, like the Winter Blossoms, are so pretty you'll hate to part with them and others, like the Coat Rack, are so homely they require as much charity from the getter as the giver. Although the presents he makes may not be beautiful, each one he gives will help him give more freely the next time.

Curried Peanuts

There are those of us who are addicted both to curry and to peanuts and find these make a dandy combination. A Two can make this present but a Six still won't have the palate for it—which means you'll have as many gifts as you expected. Into a paper bag

Add   4 c. fancy peanuts
             1½ tsp. curry powder

Let your child shake the bag as much as he wishes. Lay newspaper on the counter, then dump the peanuts into a colander, rattling the pan to remove the extra spice. If the peanuts taste too strong to you, rub a paper towel among them to remove the excess, and if too bland, add a little more powder. Divide into four 8 oz. bottles for giving. No seal is required.

Kitty Wheel

Just as you provide toys for your child, so should your child provide toys for his pets. This one is especially good for the Three who still loves pull toys.

Assemble 6' string
1 empty thread spool

Have him poke the string through the hole of the spool for you to tie it, leaving a long tail for him to pull, like a wheel, to the giddiness of both your child and the chasing kitten.

Coat Rack

There once was that awful moment at his father's birthday dinner when we watched Mike instinctively realize that the bug collections he had heard about weren't quite like the one he had made for his dad: one water bug, four dead roaches, three flies (one squashed) and a doodle bug, all pinned to a ground of scurvy green. Actually, this present was an improvement, for he had found the bugs himself and painted the cardboard too, days ahead of time. Usually Mike—never one to plan in advance—made a coat rack every Christmas Eve and once on the very day itself, when he postponed his present making just a whit too long. This coat rack is quick for a Two to make, and it works.

Saw 1' length of 1" X 2" wood

Do this for him. Into it, have him

Hammer four 8-penny nails

He can paint the wood with felt-tip pens or color it with crayons or paint it with watercolors. Hang immediately and with love.

Potpourri

This is one of the easiest presents a Three can make, since it requires so many brief steps over a long period. It's also one of the nicest. The potpourri will last about a year in sachets or for a few months in an open dish as a room freshener. The newest blooms smell strongest.

In a measuring cup, and without packing them

Collect 5-6 c. rose petals

Have your child spread the petals on a window

screen and dry them under his bed for a few days. They will shrivel to about 2 cups. Put them in a quart jar.

Add ½ c. non-iodized salt

Cap tightly, shake and leave for a week.

Add 1 tbsp. crushed cloves
1 tbsp. mace

Cap again, shake and let steep for six weeks.

Catnip Toy

Children like frisky cats and this present makes a cat quite frisky indeed.

Cut 6" square of felt

In the middle of the square

Lay 3 tbsp. catnip

Fold the felt. A Three can staple it shut, a Four can cut the material too, and a Five can pin the edges and then sew the felt together with embroidery thread. Any age, however, will like to decorate it with bits of felt or braid pasted in place with white glue. Let dry 1 hour.

Scour Flowers

This fluff of net will scour dirty pots, pans and bathtubs and makes good gifts for aunties and grandmas. A half yard of net, 48" wide, will yield 12 flowers for your Four to give. Out of newspaper

Cut 4" X 18" pattern

You'll find it easiest to have your child do the cutting on the floor. Lay the pattern on top of the net, starting at one corner. Have your Four kneel on the pattern to hold it in place and cut around it, repeating until all the net is used.

Cut twelve 10" lengths of string OR yarn

He can gather the net lengthwise for you to tie in the center, leaving a loop at one end so it can be hung from a towel rack.

Dried Watermelon Seeds

Preheat oven 225°

Watermelon seeds dried in July make squirrel food in January. Let your Four wash them first in a strainer, then spread on a cookie sheet.

Bake 30 minutes

Stir every 10 minutes. Cool and package in plastic sandwich bags for winter.

Mediterranean Polish

Any Four who can make salad dressing can make this furniture polish. Use cider vinegar for dark woods; white vinegar for light ones. This is used instead of paste wax, to be applied lightly and buffed.

Mix 1 c. vinegar
2 c. olive oil

Bottle and give.

Transparencies

Preheat iron: Warm

A Four can make this, but under supervision, for it must be sealed with a warm iron. Between two sheets of wax paper

Lay   autumn leaves OR
             fern fronds OR
             pressed flowers

Iron both sides of the paper, trim the edges, and poke a ribbon through a hole at the top, so it may be hung from a window for the sun to shine through.

Play Clay

Since all neighborhood children seem to have two or three birthdays a year, you need a small supply of presents at the ready. We find this clay just right for a Five to help his mother make. You will need two boxes of salt. In a 6-quart bowl

Combine   3 c. salt
                6 c. flour
                3 tbsp. powdered alum

When well-mixed

Add   6 c. boiling water

Pour all at once—a job for you—and stir until well blended. Lay newspapers on a table and over them lay 2 large sheets of waxpaper. Dump the dough onto them and have your child spread it with a wooden spoon.

Cool   10 minutes
Add   1 tbsp. salad oil

Be careful to sprinkle the oil evenly over the dough. Help your child divide the dough into 6 portions.

Knead   7 minutes

Do this to each batch—a 20-minute job if you both work at it. As you work it the warm dough will absorb more of the loose salt and flour and make your hands tingle. When the dough is smooth

Add   several drops of food coloring

When the color is well mixed, store in a plastic sandwich bag, tie with a ribbon and refrigerate until the next party.

Driftwood Pictures

A Five can make this gift alone. On a small weathered plank

Staple   1-2 spring flowers

Daffodils look nice, but whatever the flowers, the arrangement should look like a bouquet. At its base

Staple   a bow ribbon

At first this picture looks great, and then it looks dead, but after a few weeks it dries with a primitive charm—or maybe you just get used to it. Another present for Aunt Rosie, but give after it's past its middling stage—which means it has to be made a month in advance.

Aluminum Foil

Aluminum foil comes in many weights and widths, but for the following recipes you'll need foil that is 35-gauge, 12″ wide and found in arts and crafts stores. It can be cut with a child's scissors, bends easily, holds its shape—and scratches, so your child should wear gloves when he works with it.

French Bread Pan

This pan—a nice present for the auntie who went to gourmet school—will bake two loaves of French bread and looks like a rounded W, because it's been shaped with a rolling pin. (She'll never guess what it's supposed to be.)

Cut   17″ length of foil

Fold the 12″ width in half and have your Five first press a firm crease in the foil and then pull it apart, so it looks like a tent. The rolling pin is laid down one side of the crease and rolled to the edge, forming a trough for the dough. Do this on the other side and fold down the tips of each of the four corners. The pan will squash easily but can be reshaped easily too.

Hurricane Lamps

Your Six can cut, curl and staple this lamp together in ten minutes, if you do the measuring first. It will look like an upside-down crown.

Cut   15″ length of foil

Mark one long edge of the foil every 1½″ and draw a line from each mark 9″ toward the other side. Have your child cut the lines into strips and then curl them around a rolling pin to make a fringe of them. Staple the short sides of the foil together, turning it into a tube, and rest it on its fringe. If the candle is low, curl the fringe tighter to shorten the height of the lamp.

Winter Blossoms

A lovely Virginia lady taught us how to bring cheer to a neighbor on a January day—a gift for no reason at all. Have your Six cut forsythia or fruit branches in November, when the tiniest buds have formed. With a hammer, let him

Mash   3″ base of stem

Put the stems in warm water, with no leaves or buds under the surface, and keep the vase in a dark closet for about six weeks. Replace the evaporated water with cool water as needed. When the buds are fat, transfer the branches to a well-lighted room, or for faster blooming, to a window sill. Use only a few at a time so you can have blossoms for many weeks and always let one branch bloom in your child's room.

Bookends

Two covered bricks make good bookends, as elegant or as casual as the material itself. Burlap or brocade are both handsome. Have your Six

Cut   11¼″ × 13″ of material

The fabric is glued to the brick—a messy step—so your child should cover the work table first with newspaper. Over it, have him stand a brick on its end and drip white glue down its four sides. Wait 5 minutes for the glue to get tacky. Have him cover the sticky newspaper with a fresh sheet, then lay the brick across the short end of the fabric, rolling it slowly toward the other, pressing it down hard against the material to make it stick. Smooth any wrinkles and have him seal the seam, but you should close each end with more glue, so that it looks as tidy as the back of an envelope.

Hair Ribbon Tree

This gift takes some forethought and is good enough for a Six to give to her best friend—for her to festoon with ribbons.

When you're on a walk, look for a small branch on the ground, no bigger than ½″ in diameter, with enough twigs on it to look like a miniature tree. Have your child put the branch in a large cardboard box or over newspapers and spray it white, aiming downwind (so the fine mist doesn't get in the lungs), and turned gradually for an even coating. In a bowl

Mix   ¾ c. plaster of Paris
                ½ c. water

Pour into a 2-3″ container, the kind that holds cottage cheese. You also can use patch plaster (page 210) but it takes longer to set.

Rest   10 minutes

Have your child imbed the branch, helping him hold it in place for 5 minutes or until it can stand alone.

Dry   30 minutes

Tear away the carton and let your child cover the sides of the plaster base with felt-tipped markers or instead, cut a strip of material with pinking shears and sew the ends to make a tube. Turn the fabric inside out and hold it in place around the top of the base while your child anchors it with a rubber band. Flip the material over the band so it falls like a gathered skirt.

Herb Garden

This makes such a great gift, you should plant an extra one for yourself. Your Six can plant the seeds in peat pots, but the present will look fancier if he plants them in egg-shell halves, and then puts the shells back into their carton. Identify the seeds on the flap, like a candy sampler, with a different variety in each shell—your job.

Mix   1 c. vermiculite
                1 c. scalded sphagnum moss

Your child can fill the egg shells and make holes in the base of each one with a pencil, for drainage. Water thoroughly. Into them

Press   parsley/basil/thyme and
                rosemary/sage/oregano

Germination   10-30 days

The garden will need little or no more watering if your child slips the carton into a plastic bag, ties it shut and keeps it in a warm place—an instant hothouse. He can give this present when the sprouts have 4-6 leaves and are about 1½″ high, so it can be transplanted either to a bed outdoors with full sun or to pots where the herbs can get 4-5 hours of indoor sunlight.

Swedish Rye Bread

Yield: 2 loaves

There must be a patch of heaven that smells like anise and orange. Since this bread keeps at least a week without refrigeration, it makes a grand gift for a Six to make. Read the general directions for making bread (page 249) and then, in a large bowl

Dissolve   2 pkg. yeast
                1½ c. warm water

When the yeast begins to bubble

Add   ¼ c. molasses
                1/3 c. sugar
                2 tbsp. softened butter
                1 tbsp. salt
                1 tbsp. fennel
                1 tbsp. anise

Grate   2 tbsp. orange zest

Stir it into the bowl.

Add 2½ c. rye flour

Stir the flour into the bowl one cup at a time.

Add 2 c. white flour

If the dough still sticks to the sides of the bowl, gradually add as much as 2 extra cups of white flour. Rest the dough, cover it for 10 minutes, then knead, adding flour if necessary. Stop when its color is golden, its texture smooth and the dough springs with a life of its own. Roll it in a greased bowl and cover with a towel.

First rising 2 hours

Poke for readiness, punch down dough, divide it and let it rest covered for 10 minutes. Butter pans and shape dough into loaves. Cover.

Second rising 1 hour

Preheat Oven 375°

Bake 30 minutes

Lower heat to 350° and cook 10 minutes longer. Butter tops, remove from pans, cool on racks and wrap in foil.

Responsibility

A child must learn to be responsible for four things: his toys, his clothes, his pets and himself. Frankly, it's much, much easier to forget about the pets and take care of the rest yourself, but it's quite unfair to your child. The longer he waits to learn the rudiments of responsibility, the more difficult it will be to assume them until one day he'll be looking around for his old mum to make his excuses, pay his bills and baby-sit his children.

It's your job—the hardest one of all, perhaps—to teach your child to be accountable for his actions.

When your Four spills the milk he must realize, as Harry Truman once said, "The buck stops here." It's his job to wipe the milk and no, he won't do it well, but when he's a few years older, he'll do it better and much more willingly than he would have if it had never been expected of him before.

Day-to-day duties, as well as the unusual ones, are simply part of the giving which must be expected of each member of a family. The more responsibility you encourage in your child, the more freedom he can carry. This is a connection to be stressed all his life, for no job seems too onerous when it has its reward.

The Five who can clean his hamster cage alone or the Six who can pick up most of his toys will be a self-confident child and proud to have earned the respect that comes with his accomplishments.

Pets

Just as there should be a boy in the world for every girl—a pretty notion—so should there be a pet for every child. It's easier to find the right one if you eliminate the wrong ones first.

Canaries and parakeets, we've found, aren't good pets for a child (although they're lovely for a mother), for the cage is too complicated for small hands to open without eventually letting the bird escape.

Most animals shouldn't be kept in captivity at all, no matter what they tell you at the pet store. There is the small dimestore turtle that lives in water and often carries salmonella, the exotic iguana that thinks the temperature in a hothouse is just warm enough and then there is the monkey, which has all the faults of a baby and few of the virtues. It doesn't coo, it has a fur full of allergens and it's sure to be, as the book says, "either shy or vicious" (ours was both). A monkey also must have a year-round heat of 80°, a huge cage cleaned at least four times a week and if you need one more argument, most likely a dead mother. According to our veterinarian, a baby monkey usually can't be captured unless his mother is killed first.

Your child can—and should—enjoy wildlife, but unless a species has been domesticated, it isn't ready to be owned. A fox, a raccoon and even a deodorized skunk can charm you, but they have powerful smells and revert to offensive habits easily when kept as pets. Instead, let your child fill the birdbath with water for the cardinals, toss grain to the chipmunks and, God forbid, the pigeons, and plant morning glories for the squirrels. Our favorite squirrel, a reprobate named Floyd, would nuzzle these flowers and hallucinate drunkenly every morning.

While we've ruled out many pets, there still is a long list left—the fish, the box turtle and the snake, as well as the gerbils, rabbits, guinea pigs, dogs and cats—every one an animal which offers a child a special bit of joy. You almost can see the electricity that flows between your little girl and her kitten, and her excitement when she watches the gerbils mate and her wonder when they birth. The life—and the death—of a pet is high drama to a child.

Even with the best of care, a pet usually has a rather short life expectancy, but his death, although tragic, is still a child's most gentle introduction to the natural cycle. The sorrow of death can never be greater than the gift of life.

A pet is easiest to care for if he's lively, happy and healthy, and for this he must have shots if necessary, a good diet, a clean home and enough room to move about. The bigger the animal the more often you'll have to clean after him and the warmer his blood, the more gentle the handling must be. In truth, you're looking not for an animal that suits your child, but one that suits you, for although he'll be in charge of the tender loving, you'll be left with most of the care.

Every child, as early as One, should learn as much about his pet as possible—how much food and sleep and exercise he needs and how he can help you feed him and clean his living quarters. The more your child helps, the better he'll learn the likes and dislikes of his pet, until by Four, he'll be sure he can care for him better than anyone in the world. By Six, he'll think he's doing all the work and if you're lucky, he'll be able to by Eight, but not without regular reminders—a custom to follow for years.

Like so many mothers, you'll find that pets instill a sense of responsibility and kindness and generosity in a child, teaching him that although love may be a lot of trouble, the trouble is quite worth it.

Fish

Fish make interesting pets, for you can start with a simple goldfish when your baby is only a few weeks old and graduate to schools of tropical fish before he's Six. If you treat fish with a certain reverence, your child will try to do the same, but a Two, no matter how accustomed he is to a fish bowl, will try to grab his fish with his fist, will feed it too much—and will be very sorry to see it floating on its side. He'll be better by Three, if he helps you care for the aquarium and feed the fish.

Any fish should be fed only twice a day and never more than the fish can eat in a few minutes, so the bacteria count stays low. If you have a tank with a pump, you only need to add more water when it has evaporated noticeably. Gravel isn't necessary, except it makes an aquarium prettier, hides any droppings, and anchors plants.

Goldfish

This flashy fish needs little oxygen, is happy with flake food and content to live in a small bowl of water at room temperature. Change the water every two to three days. Have your child draw the water from the tap twenty-four hours before you add it to the aquarium, so the lethal chlorine can evaporate. For a more exotic and equally easy pet, get a Siamese fighting fish, which can survive with just enough water to keep it wet.

Mollys, Swordtails, Guppies, Platies

Most fish lay eggs to reproduce, but these fish give live birth, which all Threes like to see. A large female will reproduce every four to five weeks.

Lodging—Use a five-gallon tank with a pump but have a smaller one ready for the babies, for these parents are so forgetful they may swallow their young as if they were bait. Transfer their children with a fish net and use an air stone in the small tank to provide oxygen, but no pump, for it can suck in such small fish.

Diet—Give twice-a-day feedings, alternating between flake and freeze-dried fish food.

Tropical Fish

These splendid fish are very expensive and all beautiful, with the red barbs and silver angel fish the cheapest and the heartiest. You'll want to buy a few of each because this looks more natural, and if they travel in schools, like the zebra, you'll need even more so your child can see the formations. However, the tiger barbs, the oscars and other aggressors should live in a separate tank, for they nip the fins of the more peaceful passers-by.

Lodging—A ten-gallon tank will house twenty to thirty fish, depending on their size. The water should be as it is in their native habitat: warm, running rapidly and acidic, with a pH factor between 6.6 and 6.8. For this, you need a heater to keep the temperature between 78°-80°; a pump to feed oxygen into the water and a pH kit to test the water regularly, so you can add the right chemicals to make it acidic enough. All these supplies are available from the pet store and are never cheap. Some fish look better in a dark tank, while others are seen best with more light. You can control this by the color of the gravel, the natural light near the tank or the electric light attachment on the top of it.

Plants aren't necessary; except as a place for the fish to play hide and seek, but they add beauty, so your child probably will want them. To grow, use the light attachment, but only in the evening and for no more than four to six hours, or they will photosynthesize too much and destroy the balance of the tank. Anchor rooting plants, like the amazon sword or the corckscrew valve, in gravel, but anacharis, cabomba and the hornwort simply float about.

For simpler decorations, your child can add the rocks, slate and even driftwood he collects, but scrub them first and check the pH content of the water afterward, for these additions can change it.

Diet—A tropical fish likes variety in his food, as he had back home. Alternate the flake food with freeze-dried foods or frozen brine shrimp, giving only two meals a day.

Cats

Mid-One is a good age for a kitten. A toddler seldom is nimble enough to catch him, and if he does, the kitten has twenty sharp ways to defend himself. There's nothing like a cat to teach a child what cause and effect are all about. By mid-Two, when a child is as quick as a cat, neither will want to tangle with the other.

Your cat is more likely to be healthy if you get him from a healthy, well-fed mother, but he still will need a vaccination for feline distemper at six weeks and if he spends a lot of time outdoors, a rabies vaccine too.

Lodging—A cat, that independent creature, will sleep where he wants and go in and out of the house three times while you're still struggling to get the baby and the groceries inside. A cat does need a litter box and will train himself to use it immediately if you give him a swat when he misbehaves and then scratch his paws in the litter a couple of times. However, accidents can happen when he's mad at you or when his box is too dirty.

Diet—A cat should have fresh water every day, an occasional bowl of milk, dry cat food (which is easy for a Two to pour) and, once a week, a scrambled egg.

Sex—Because of the explosion of the cat population, most veterinarians think cats should be altered. If you have a male, we definitely think he should be castrated, for he'll spray the same place again and again when he's sexually aroused and if he chooses an overstuffed chair instead of a screen door, you only can throw it away. The smell is that noxious. With a female, however, we think it only fair to let her sample the good life once and, besides, every child should know the wonder of a boxful of mewing kittens, looking like tiny lions with their eyes sealed shut and legs too limp to hold them. A female cat goes into heat at six months and every three to four months thereafter, if she's an outdoor cat, for with cats, as they say, "copulation controls the ovulation cycle." As far as we can see, this is another way of saying a female cat is either pregnant, mothering or in heat most of the time. Gestation takes fifty-nine to sixty-six days, and then the kittens will be born in some dark place, like a bureau drawer, and usually moved by the mother to a dry, clean, dark place, where she'll want them to stay until the kittens can see and walk. They will nurse about six weeks, and the mother can be spayed immediately after they stop.

Box Turtles

A mid-Two enjoys a pet box turtle because he can pick it up without hurting himself or the turtle. It doesn't bite, is quiet and unobstrusive and doesn't need to be fed regularly. At least, no one's ever seen a skinny turtle—or a fat one either. A turtle can live for weeks indoors without any obvious means of support, seems to last forever in the garden and is supposed to get a diamond in his carapace each year he's with you.

If your turtle gets sluggish indoors in winter, it means that the temperature in your house is probably too cold for him to want to eat but not cold enough for him to hibernate. Either put a light in his box to make it warmer or take him outside where he can hide.

Diet—A turtle will eat greens, strawberries, hamburger and an occasional banana.

Sex—It seems impossible to contemplate, but it must be true. Our Hilda proved it when she went to the beach with us, laid her egg in a blanket and left it—unnatural mother. Alas, we didn't know enough to wrap it in damp sand in the hopes that it would hatch.

Ants and Other Insects

All children are bug collectors at heart and none too selective about it. Roaches are quite as interesting to a Two as their cousins, the butterflies, and the ants that sneak in the kitchen are so fascinating they leave them sugar cubes.

Supposedly, you can fill an ant farm with ones from your back yard (rather than send away for them), as long as the ants come from the same colony, but our luck with ones homegrown has been very poor. We have found that a silk moth in a jar with mulberry leaves or a caterpillar with whatever leaves he likes to sit on will entrance a Four for a few days, but do keep the lid on tight, with a few holes punched in it.

By Six, books about insects usually interest a child more than the insects themselves, thank goodness. Books are so much more manageable.

Gerbils

A Four is ready for that bright, alert little rodent, the gerbil. Generally, gerbils are so friendly they want company, but unless you think they want lots of company, choose a pair of the same sex. They will play mostly by day, for unlike hamsters, they're diurnal animals.

With gentle treatment, a gerbil will eat out of your child's hand, but will try to slip out of his cage if he thinks no one is watching. Our Nadia and Mali have learned that curiosity is the downfall of the runaway, so one child taps her fingertips on the floor and the other grabs his tail when the gerbil comes forth to investigate. It takes some petting to settle him enough to go back into the cage again, for too much noise or rough play frightens a gerbil and then he may bite, which can develop into a habit. This doesn't hurt the child, but it does hurt their friendship.

Lodging—Use an aquarium with a heavy lid, for gerbils, like other rodents, can chew through plastic, wood or cardboard. Use fresh newspaper, which they will tear to pieces for bedding, but only clean the cage monthly since gerbils seldom urinate and they need the same nest as long as possible. The oil they exude on the paper is a protection. Add a tin can and an old shoe for them to climb into and a mirror to admire themselves.

Diet—They like dry seeds, shelled nuts, grain, cereals, crackers and bread crusts, as well as grass, fruit and vegetables—especially lettuce, carrots and apples. Either hang a bottle in the cage for water or add a cut potato, which supplies water too.

Sex—Gerbils are better at making more gerbils than they are at anything else, happily giving your child a litter a month after the first year. There usually are six to eight in a litter—tiny, pink, hairless and with their eyes shut tight, although Nadia has found there's only one in a litter if she's fed the mother dry dog food. The babies burrow into little nests of paper their parents have shredded and after three weeks of suckling, have wonderful brown eyes and brown fur.

A gerbil mother is such an elitist she'll eat any ill-formed child—a Darwinian example that is too graphic, we found, for a young child. If one of the litter is either lame or overly quiet, put him in another cage.

The babies also may be attacked if the cage is too crowded, if noise makes the mother nervous, if she doesn't have plenty to eat and drink and something to chew every day, and if you touch them, for she may not recognize their smell any more. Otherwise, Nadia assures us, gerbils make excellent parents. Because they do need some peace before the next litter, put the babies in their own quarters after the third week, with dry seeds and water and some paper from their parents' cage—a touch of home. Now your little girl has enough presents for the next six to eight birthday parties.

Guinea Pigs

A guinea pig can soak up as much affection as your Five cares to give. There is little else this dear animal can be except a terrific cuddle figure. If pampered he can live for seven years, although four months was our record.

A native of South America, a guinea pig (or a cavy, as it's also called) has either short or long hair, straight or tussled, and generally comes in white, black, orange, or mixes thereof. The Peruvian is the prince—the most expensive, the shaggiest and the funniest, for it wiggles along the floor like a big, fuzzy caterpillar.

His squeals and his grunts are his only protection and when he feels at home, he uses them to chatter to anyone who comes in the room and seems to think all conversation is directed to him. In fact, we found our cavy, who lived under the sideboard, talked straight through every dinner party.

He's a better talker than he is an athlete, for he can't jump or climb. However, he needs to run constantly, although not necessarily on a table top, for while he can scamper around and around it for quite a while he will, contrary to popular notion, fall off of it after a while.

Lodging—A guinea pig is sensitive to temperature changes and must live in an airy, draft-free, well-lighted house. Make a wooden hutch, which he can't gnaw, and cut a hole at each end and cover with screening, so he can watch the world. Inside put a skinny ramp of plywood to multiply his running space and cover securely if you have other pets.

Use a thin layer of sawdust, straw, cat litter or wood shavings to absorb the moisture and add a toy, like a treadmill, for him to spin. Clean the hutch weekly and occasionally wash it with a mild disinfectant.

Diet—The guinea pig is a vegetarian. Balance his diet with commercial rabbit food, apples, lettuce, celery tops, dandelions, grass and clover, but avoid onions, peppers and potatoes. Give him a salt spool, a bowl of water and, twice a week, a half teaspoon of linseed or codliver oil.

Sex—If you have a pair of guinea pigs, the boar and the sow must be separated when they are a month old, for they can begin mating this early. This may be fun, but it isn't good for the sow until she's six months old. For this reason, each sex will need its own hutch except for the month when you mate them and the new male babies will need a hutch of their own, since males will fight unless they've been living together continuously.

You can assume that a sow that's been in the mating pen for a month is pregnant, so put her in her own hutch to avoid premature delivery. It takes sixty-five to seventy days to produce a litter of one to six babies, but the wait is worth it. These children are born with hair, teeth and eyes wide open. They begin to run when they're only an hour old and can eat solid food in two to three days, but they'll continue to nurse for three to four weeks, when they must be separated from their parents, with the males going to one hutch, the females to another.

Rabbits

Your Five or Six is old enough to care for a rabbit, and it's a pleasant pet to care for. It's gentle, clean, quiet and big enough to romp in a fenced-in yard. A rabbit likes to be petted by its owner but he doesn't like noise, confusion or being picked up by his ears (who does?). Teach your child to lift him by the nape of the neck with one hand while supporting his rump with the other.

Lodging—The hardest part of rabbit keeping is the building of the hutch—and then the cleaning of it. It should be made of wood and hardware cloth, but if you keep a big rabbit indoors, the hutch shouldn't be made of chicken wire or be too near an electric cord, for big rabbits have big teeth—and together that meant the untimely end of poor Heather Lapin. Outdoors is better, no doubt about it. Build the hutch flush against the house and on stilts, 2 feet above the ground. It should measure 4' long, 2' wide, 3' high and have a sloped roof that extends over the sides to keep out the rain. One side should be hinged for easier cleaning and there should be a small room of plywood partitions for privacy. Rabbits like a clean cage, with a bed of cat litter, hay, straw or peat moss (but not sawdust, which sticks to the fur). This should be changed twice a week and disinfected occasionally, although a proper hutchkeeper tells us that a rabbit so civilized that he only dirties a corner of the cage should be rewarded with a clean cage every day.

Diet—A rabbit is a vegetarian who eats twice a day, preferring a deep bowl for his food, another for his water and a salt spool to lick. He does well on commercial rabbit food balanced with stale bread, lettuce, spinach, clover, pea pods, dandelions, carrots, potatoes and apples. It's tempting to give him other treats, but if a rabbit doesn't eat properly he'll get "pot belly"—a sign either of worms or a lack of protein or both in any animal.

Sex—A doe is ready to breed at eight months, but not earlier. Leave the doe and the buck alone for a few days until the doe begins to growl at her company. That's when she's had enough of the buck. Give her a hutch of her own for the thirty to thirty-two day pregnancy and expect her to want less affection, less noise, more food and a little milk. She'll start making a nest of her bedding about a week before she's due and must be left alone then and for the two weeks after she births, without being touched. When the babies are born—generally in a litter of eight or more—they are hairless, with their eyes closed. They mustn't be touched until they have fur and their eyes are open, for the mother either may kill them or stop caring for them. Give the babies solid food at three weeks and milk for the next three to nine weeks.

Snakes

A snake makes a nice and curious pet, although you shouldn't get it unless your child has handled one and asks for it, for even a Four has strong feelings about snakes. We've found a garter snake is best, for the female, while bigger than the male, is still small and gentle. No snake, however, is slimy and none seem to mind writhing in a small child's hands.

Teach your child to hold the snake midway along his body and use his thumb and index finger to hold his head, just under the ears (if he had ears). Like any nonpoisonous snake, it will stick out its forked tongue, not to bite but to feel about a bit. Don't be alarmed.

Lodging—Because a snake is almost solid muscle, he can push the top from any cage if it isn't heavy enough and because he's so squirmy, he can slide through the smallest opening—as we found after the big black snake slipped from his second-floor home and turned up in the back yard across the street, which was not considered funny by the lady in the back yard. That's why you need to have the cage ready before you buy your snake. An old aquarium is good, with a sturdy screen top and a hole cut in it to fit a 60-watt light bulb. This must be lighted all day to keep him warm enough. Have a hardy plant and a stick in the cage for him to curl around and a rough rock, so he can rub against it to scrub away his skin when he sheds—two to three times a year. Keep a 3″ layer of aquarium gravel in the bottom, which must be washed before using to get rid of the fine dust which can hurt his eyes. Dry the gravel for several hours in a 200° oven and cool it before putting it into the cage. Change the gravel every two months when you clean the cage.

Diet—Keep your snake on the same diet he had at the pet shop, which varies not from species to species, but from store to store. Ours liked to dive into a bowl of water every week to catch a live gold fish, which he chased with great cunning, tossing it in the air until he could swallow it head first so the fins couldn't scratch his throat. We found we could switch fairly soon to a much cheaper diet—a small

piece of frozen fish or some freshly dug earthworms placed in the water bowl every other week.

Sex—We had hoped a pair of garter snakes would produce babies, since they are among the few reptiles that have live births, rather than lay eggs, but captivity chilled that romance.

Dogs

If you or your husband want a puppy, fine—but don't pretend you're getting it for your child, any more than you'd get him a six-week-old baby. They need an equal amount of attention.

Even a smart puppy (the sort we've heard of, but never owned) requires a lot of time. Beginning at six weeks, you'll need shots for distemper, hepatitis, leptospirosis and rabies, and unless you want your dog to be a parent, either sex should be neutered. He also will need a course at obedience school with you, for he has to learn some acceptable behavior—and you have to learn to accept the rest.

Even the best-trained dog will bark (usually during the baby's naptime) at all those people who come to your door, but never enter, like the postman and the newsboy. Your dog will be doubly suspicious if they're of a different race from you, for although a dog is color blind, his other senses are keen and you can expect him to be prejudiced whether you are or not.

The younger the dog the more trouble he'll cause, since a puppy goes through stages just like a child. He'll teethe, not on rattles but on old shoes, new shoes, pillows, rugs and sometimes plumbers. This happens between three and six months and must be helped by much exercise, many toys and a lot of your time, or it will become a habit. Dogs, like children, get into mischief when they're left alone.

Housetraining will be your biggest problem, and it isn't possible to solve it until your puppy is about eight months old—the equivalent of a four-year-old child. To teach him, take him on six walks a day, and give him a dog biscuit when he performs. In the house, lay newspapers in a spot of his choice until he's old enough to last to the next walk. He'll use this same place every time if congratulated and given a biscuit, but if you act angry he'll choose another place, perhaps hiding his mistake so well you won't find it before the rug or the floor has spotted badly. During the night, put your puppy on a small porch or in the bathroom, with a rug of newspapers, both to train him and to protect his paws. They're made to walk on grass and dirt, not on a cold, hard floor.

Lodging—A puppy needs a ticking clock wrapped in a towel for consolation, to sound like his mother's heartbeat, and any dog should be put in a bed of his own. Most prefer to sleep in the house and often in a child's room, no matter who feeds him. To a dog, it's the playing that counts.

Diet—A dog should eat canned, dry or moist dog food with some additions, but they shouldn't be table scraps. These are so rich and tasty they make standard food seem boring. Canned food is good if it's a mix of cereal and meat but it's expensive since it can be 76 per cent moisture. Soft, moist dog food—the kind that's packaged in plastic—is fine for trips, because it needs no refrigeration, but the cheapest is dry food, which can be mixed with a little warm water. Supplement it with cooked meat, an egg or cottage cheese, but these shouldn't comprise more than a fourth of his food. An all-meat diet is especially bad for a dog and even can kill him.

A puppy can eat as much dog food as he wants, but don't give vitamin supplements for they can damage bone growth.

Sex—The female is mature enough to whelp after she's been in heat twice. If you're being formal, look for a gentle, prospective father in advance, so the offspring will be gentle too, and take her to his house twelve days after the start of the menstrual discharge. Leave her there three days to be sure of consummation (and to give her a good time) and check afterward with the veterinarian, for some like to give another round of inoculations then.

Gestation will last nine weeks. The puppies open their eyes at two weeks and can be weaned at five.

Work

For centuries people have blessed and blamed Calvin for his philosophy that all work is good as long as it makes you tired and gets you rich. Calvin and the pre-Three have a little bit in common.

Every young child glories in work, not as some puritanical penance, but for the sweet reward of doing a job and eventually of doing it well. You never heard a child say he wants to lie in a hammock all day when he grows up. Your child may want to be a trashman or a farmer or a bus driver, but he would never want to be a dilettante, even if he knew the word.

This is why it's important and productive—and initially quite troublesome—to use work to draw your child closer and closer into the family structure. Although it may seem easier, don't put off chores until he's asleep. For one thing, he doesn't sleep that many hours a day, and for another he wants to help you.

If you welcome his help his efforts will be positive, if bumbling, but the next time he'll do the work a little better. It may be some years before he does a good job but, fortunately, with his short attention span, he won't attempt anything for very long either. This won't detract from his pride, and his healthy attitude toward work will give him the stamina to endure those dreary classes and dull jobs that plague us through the years. As one determined mother told us, faith, hope and charity are all very well, but over the years, it's fortitude that counts.

After what amounts to a ridiculous ninety-six years of mothering between us, we've found our children have grown to like the work we like, as long as we've taught them to help when they were very young.

Many first-time mothers consider the only true learning to be academic and we couldn't disagree more. It's work that builds a child's coordination and sense of order and the success of this work which builds self-confidence—all necessary for arithmetic, reading and writing.

When Kate and Mike and Meg were six, four and two—often demons by day but almost angels by night—we sought our solace in many ways, including prayer. It was hard to believe that we would pass this way but once.

On their knees in nitey-nites, they earnestly said this prayer together, which made the next day seem possible to us and the last one not so bad:

Help me to work,
Help me to play,
Help me to learn a bit each day.
Teach me to wash,
Teach me to scrub,
To hang my clothes and clean my tub;
To put my toys upon the shelf,
Help me, dear Lord, to help myself.

If nothing else, this prayer will help your child realize that you weren't put on this earth to be a nursemaid, and it may help you see that your child is as eager to care for himself as you are for him to do it. He just needs a mother to guide him.

Mid-One
For a child to be self-sufficient, we believe in starting chores by mid-One, when he gets the morning paper for you and helps unpack a few groceries, working up to bigger and bigger jobs before first grade. Except for child-sized mops and brooms, we even think your child should use your tools, like your vacuum, and by Five, your iron, for this makes success that much likelier.

Two
The real jobs begin about Two, all of them small enough to be finished without pressure from you. It's better, we find, to have the closet floor cleaned well than to tell a Three to tidy his room, for one can get done and the other is impossible. By breaking a job into stages of time, the improbable, at least, is in sight. If he balks you're demanding bigger jobs than he can handle or thinks he can handle.

A child can understand the instructions best if you speak to him slowly, at eye level, and show him how to deal with his work safely and neatly,

dividing the job into segments so he can see each step clearly. The chores you have him do should be requested in a matter-of-fact, let's-go manner, and when the work is done you must inspect it and praise it promptly before he undoes it again (as he almost surely will). However, we think you should never give money for a job, even as an allowance, for then you're putting a price tag on cooperation. Within a family, a father, mother or child needs only the satisfaction of completing a job and not a cash bonus, since the feeling of accomplishment is its own reward. This is the difference between a business and a family.

A Two, as scattered as he is, will empty wastebaskets with you and tidy a little too. He also should help you undo many of those things he has done. He'll like some of the jobs, like washing fingerprints from woodwork, but don't remind him where they come from; he knows. It's obvious you don't want them there or he wouldn't be asked to remove them.

Three
By Three, your child wants to run errands and offers to help with chores—not picking up toys, of course, but real chores—like sweeping and dusting and polishing silver and shoes. If you've encouraged his help in the past his work will begin to be quite satisfactory, for his competence comes with practice.

Four to Six
A Four will step and fetch for adults and he'll rake the yard for you now and dig, both where you want him to dig and where he wants to dig, so you must work nearby.

Your child may learn some things far earlier than most children, depending on your own abilities. We once knew a chef who claimed his Four could separate a dozen eggs without breaking one and a seamstress whose Five taught herself to use a sewing machine one day while her mother napped.

A child will learn everything much faster if you let him learn by trying, and he'll fail sometimes too—just like you. When you let your child dare to try—and fail—you're showing respect, for it's a child's right to make mistakes too. Bear with his errors in judgment, whether it's making his bed or pouring his milk. If there are too many failures quit for a while, and you'll know the meaning of the old proverb: There's no use crying over spilled milk.

Your child gains self-confidence with each new chore he masters. He wants to learn more, do more, see more—because he knows he can. You'll find his capabilities increasing in direct ratio to the praise he earns, until one day you'll be astonished at the efficiency of your masterful Six. And you, dear heart, will face a revelation; your Six is more help than not.

Ordinary

No matter how you live, you have to do some routine housework every day and so should your child. It's nothing to feel apologetic about. The job may get boring after he thinks he's mastered it, but still he must be expected to do his share of what we call "the common good." At least it sounds more noble than housework.

Step and Fetch

Someone once said that if whales had thumbs they'd rule the world, for that's how smart they are. Teach your child, starting at mid-One, that it's smart for him to use his thumbs for something more than putting them in his mouth. He should clasp them over anything he carries, for he'll be much less likely to drop it. You also will teach him to carry anything with both hands, telling him approximately 117 times a year for the next ten years. He'll remember for himself most of the other times.

The House

A little child leaves you with little time or energy to clean house, but a tidied one will help you keep your psyche in order.

Go from room to room, wearing a big, pocketed apron to hold all the little things that are out of place, picking up and putting down items as you go. You can expect a mid-One to help you if you encourage him to follow you about and hand him each toy or box to return when you reach the place it belongs.

Do this casually and calmly for a half hour in the morning, if you do nothing else.

The Blitz

In the late afternoon, when the world seems so fragmented, set the timer for fifteen minutes and shout, "The Blitz!"

For this you and your child—a Three or better is best—should scout the room as fast as you can, picking up and putting down until, like a parody of Mary Poppins, the living room is tidy and the bell has rung.

When your life is stripped of clutter a couple of times a day, you can appreciate it more. The Blitz has other advantages, we found, for our husbands didn't mind helping if we had to wait until they got home, since they knew the time would be limited. Today, with any kind of warning from company, we still can shout, "The Blitz," and as a family, put the house together in fifteen minutes flat. If it's still a little chaotic when the bell has rung, we still stop just the same. Enough is enough.

Vacuuming

A One often is terrified that your noisy vacuum will swallow him as if he were an old paper clip, for sizes make no sense at this age. This fear both overwhelms and fascinates a child and he may follow you, rushing forth to touch the machine, shrieking, running away and then following you again. The reaction may get so bad you'll have to vacuum when he sleeps, but by mid-One, fascination

should prevail. Now he'll imitate you, eventually with the vacuum but first with make-believe props, perhaps as our Kate did the day the priest came to call. She came down the stairs, ever so politely, saying nothing but "buzz-buzz-buzz" as she pushed the nozzle around each balustrade. Unfortunately, she was using a douche bag.

Since a small child often is scared when he sees small items sucked into the vacuum, collect them first by hand, the way a professional cleaner does to prevent a blocked hose. Let your Two fit the attachment to the wand, push the plug into the socket and start the motor. He can vacuum for you, actively if not well, and by Four be expected to do a good job on the baseboards of one room a week. We think the living room is best so that company, once prompted, can praise such work.

The vacuum itself is such an awkward contraption, we find we hardly can expect a Ten to handle it well. Heaven knows we can't.

Dust Mopping

A dust mop must have been invented by a genius with a degree in childhood education. You need only teach your Two to run it around the floor without lifting the head (so the dust doesn't scatter) and to contain his cleaning to small areas or a hallway, so he doesn't skip as many boards. Carry the mop to the window for him, almost closing it on the handle, then let him twist and pump it up and down to shake the dust free.

Sweeping

This is an irritating job for a child, because he can see just as many mistakes when he's done as you can. Sweeping is easier if you give your Three his own child-sized broom and dustpan and considerable instruction too. Teach him to pick one spot in the center of the room and sweep toward it, starting from the corners, so he doesn't have to sweep the same spot twice—a technique he'll follow automatically in five or six years. It will take that long to get reasonably good results.

A child needs to see that the efficient way is the easiest way every time.

Mopping

A preschool child isn't old enough to mop a floor, or even part of one, by himself, but a Four should be expected to mop up his spills with a small mop of his own, even though you'll do it again afterward. He has to realize he's responsible for his own actions—and his mistakes.

The Child's Room

You'd never tell your child to "paint the house" or "go to the moon" but when you say, "Clean your room," it overwhelms him just as much. Truth to tell, it probably overwhelms you too, for it's hard to know where to start.

When just a few toys are out of place you put them back automatically and feel quite satisfied with your lot: that's what motherhood should be about. Unfortunately, that's your child's idea of tidying too.

You can expect your One to pick up his teddy bear sometimes without being told, and a Two may take care of his bear and a good truck. A Three may put away the tea set too, and a Four may have about four toys that he treasures enough to put away. To expect more of a child is to expect the impossible. Instead, you'll have to pick up the toys with him, doing almost everything when he's Two and almost nothing by the time he's Six, if you visit with him while he works, giving only occasional aid.

As in any other complicated job, you must break it into segments—"Now, let's put away everything that's under the bed" and then, "on the bed," then in it. Next it's the bureau top, then the night table, the chair, the desk. Finally you get a broom, sweep the rest into the middle of the floor, and sort the mess together.

You can make your child enjoy order by helping him tidy his room twice a week, so it never gets totally in shambles, and then seldom mentioning it in between. When you help your child keep his possessions reasonably in place, the clean-up will seem possible. If you can't, he has too many possessions.

Bedmaking

Along with the presents of a third birthday come the first real responsibilities, and bedmaking is one of them. If you handle it right your child will think it a prize for growing up—for a while.

For years his bed will be not just a place to sleep but a comfort in trouble, a trampoline, a tent, a zoo for stuffed animals. With this kind of wear he needs to learn how to put his bed together almost as easily as he takes it apart.

Three

Begin teaching him several weeks before his third birthday, not because it will take that long to learn, but because it takes that long to fit the job into his routine. He should do it when he makes his toilette—before he's ever entitled to breakfast—and he should straighten it after naps.

To give your child a chance to do the work well, the bed itself should be away from the walls on three sides, so he can get around it easily.

For any bed, use a fitted bottom sheet and square corner the top sheet and the blanket when you change the linens, for in his hilarity they are kicked away easily. Also, do use a quilt. It shows wrinkles much less than a bedspread.

To make the bed, help him pull the top sheet back to remove the toys, the pajamas, the apple cores and cookie crumbs. Next, have him pull the sheet forward again and then the blanket, folding back the sheet's wide hem so it will be on the right side. Help him tuck in the sides of the sheet and blanket but he can drag the quilt across the bed himself. By Four the job becomes automatic—more or less.

Five

Bedmaking becomes more precise for a Five and now he can learn to square-corner his own top sheet, like nurses do in a hospital. Little girls, we found, are particularly adept at this, not because they like housekeeping but because they like to play hospital.

Have your child tuck in the sides of the top sheet, as before, and fold the end of the sheet onto the bed. Each side of the sheet will have a tail, which your child should press against the end of the mattress with one hand, dropping the bottom of the sheet over it and tucking it in. This secures it and looks like the side of a triangle, as crisp as the flaps of a display package at the post office.

When your Five graduates to a spread, he can make a neat job of the pillows if you teach him to fold back the spread and lay the pillow slightly over the fold. This makes a tidy tuck when he pulls the spread into place. When you tell your child the reason for each step he will understand the job and do it better.

To be realistic, we find a child makes his bed perhaps four days out of seven, and for us, that's a lot better than no days out of seven. When you find he forgets, have him make it right then, even if he's just getting ready for bed. You should make it for him only when you change the sheets and a Nine, we discovered last week, can do that too.

The Table

The Pledge

Growing up in the deep South may have inspired Tennessee Williams to write remarkable plays but all we did was make remarkable promises in the style of Scarlett O'Hara.

There was that pledge to our Tante Margot to wear perfume, "always, ma chère, always," and to our dear Aunt Kay who said, in her moonlight-and-magnolia drawl, "Honey, if you're ever in a situation (and mind you, I don't know *what* that situation would be) when you can wear only mascara *or* underpants—always wear mascara."

These still seem like perfectly sensible promises and ones we'll pass on to our girls, but we already have insisted that all our children, like us, take the Carton, Can and Bottle pledge. Under no circumstances can these be on any table—not for breakfast, not for lunch, not for dinner. The manners your child shows when he eats is mirrored very much by the niceties of his surroundings. This small trouble is quite worth it—especially after you teach your child to set the table.

Setting

Once at a bazaar we bought a checked oilcloth place mat—pink and pinked to look like a pig—which taught Kate, at Four, to set a table much quicker than we could.

The mat had a brass ring sewed to its snout on the left, and with a waterproof marker, a fork was drawn to the left, a circle in the center for a plate and to the right a knife, a spoon and a circle for the glass.

We made more mats for the rest of the family, for it was hard for Kate to reverse the order when she set the other side of the table. We drew a kitchen picture of the other extras needed at the table—the trivets, the salt and pepper and the serving spoons—so she wouldn't be embarrassed by repeated reminders.

By Six, a child can learn about salad forks and soup spoons and how you set silverware from the outside toward the plate, according to the order they'll be used. A Six also can learn to serve on the left and clear from the right, and he should, for if a child is going to learn a job, he may as well learn correctly.

Clearing

A Three can clear a table, if you don't mind picking up the bones and silverware he drops. Personally, we do, which is why we wait until Four.

He should clear from the right, one dish at a time. You mustn't let him stack dishes, of course, both because it isn't pretty and it isn't safe. Your child will be Eight before he can carry a plate in each hand, but in the meantime, he should carry one plate in both hands, with one thumb on the rim and the other straddling the silver that is balanced across the middle. This prevents many accidents.

A Six will take away the unused knives, the trivets and the salt and pepper before dessert, but you'll have to remind him every time.

Washing Dishes

The most recalcitrant, into-everything Two will be pleased to wear a big plastic bib and stand on a kitchen chair for a half hour at a time for the privilege of washing dishes. Whether you have a dishwasher or not, take advantage. It's the best way we ever found to have a second cup of coffee in peace.

There will be reasonably little trouble if you prepare the scene, first by washing and drying all the breakable dishes and sharp knives—for a pre-Six should never wash these—then by covering the floor by the sink with newspapers, for much water will spill. Finally, set up one pan in which to wash dishes and another to rinse them.

Put the silverware, tin mugs and plastic dishes in one empty pan in the sink and teach your child to run warm water (which he'll run almost cold) and to measure soap (which he either won't use or won't measure). You'll have to show him how to rub the dishcloth on all sides of each cup and spoon and fork and to put them into the other pan on the counter when he's finished. When he's tired of washing, dump out the soapy water for him and put the pan of dishes into the sink for him to rinse under running water. And rinse. And rinse.

He can put the dishes in the drainer himself but don't expect your child to dry them or even to put them away when they're air dried, for there's little fun there. That's just as well, since you'll probably do them again when he's not looking. It takes a Ten to do dishes well—if you're lucky.

The Laundry

The Hamper

Mother's liberation begins at the laundry hamper. By Three, a child should pick up his own dirty clothes—automatically. Insist upon it.

Washing

A little girl at Three thinks hair ribbons and handkerchiefs are charming, but by now she should wash her own. Let her do it in the tub, when she bathes, and smooth them over the mirror. This irons them dry. A little boy will settle for washing his underpants.

Ironing

Ironing isn't dull to a child, and if it's taught right we don't think it's dangerous either.

A Two likes to use a little ironing board with a nonheating dimestore iron, but a Three quickly

Extra-Ordinary

graduates to one that heats a little. We had our Fours use this iron too, since they were so rambunctious, but a Five is ready to use your sturdy board, lowered to scale, and your regular iron, learning exactly where to keep the dial. He won't want to hurt himself and, in fact, will be even more cautious than you. The weight of this iron and today's synthetic clothes let him smooth any wrinkles, whether imaginary or not. Teach him to iron the sleeves and facings and the pocket and collar before he irons the rest of his shirt.

While every child should do some routine work every day, the unusual accomplishments are the ones that count. His pride in any job will last as long as the work looks good—which is why anyone would rather shine a window than make a bed.

Job Jar

We've found a simple, impersonal job jar appeals to the gambling side of every child as early as Four.

Taking an idea straight from the comics, we cut twenty to thirty strips of paper, printed on each one a little job that needed doing and dropped them all into a jar. The normal reluctance to work not only disappeared, but the children would rush to shake the job jar, even before breakfast. They would fish out the daily orders for us to read, like "polish Daddy's sandals" or "wash the fingermarks from the kitchen switch plate" and then act like we gave them a present. We don't know why, but the printed word causes fewer moans, much laughter and a zest for work.

Cleaning

Ten minutes of scrubbing anything will let your child release a whole morning's worth of angries. As in all work, don't expect much, be thankful for what you get and work alongside for less mess.

Walls and Woodwork

Use a sponge to clean walls and woodwork because a Two can squeeze it easily. This solution also cleans bathroom tiles, but your child will need a nailbrush to clean the grout, and even at Five he will need you to wipe the spatters.

Basic Cleaner
In a nonaluminum pan
Combine   4 c. warm water
                   4 tsp. washing soda
                   ¼ tsp. ammonia
Stir to dissolve the soda. The ammonia is included both for its cleaning power and its smell, which discourages a child from tasting it. The soda is the magic, erasing dirt but not color from both latex and enamel and leaving no trace to be rinsed. Make a fresh solution each time you use it, so the soda doesn't settle.

Furniture

A party needn't give your furniture a hangover too. The white rings usually disappear with this recipe, but if the cleaned patches make the rest of the furniture look dull, you may have to revive it (page 234).

Ring Remover
Your Three will think this job is a lark—briefly. In an ashtray, have him
Combine   cigarette ashes
                   lemon juice
Do this yourself, squeezing just enough juice to make a paste. Have your Two rub it on the ring, around and around with his finger, as hard as he can. The very light grit should remove the ring, but silver polish works too, for its base is rottenstone.

Windows

A Four can learn to shine a few windows so hard you'll scarcely know there is any glass there.

Have him crush newspaper into balls, a sheet at a time, to rub on the glass, but avoid the Sunday funnies, for the colors will smear it. Give him a plastic mister filled with Basic Cleaner and a cloth to wipe the sash and the window frame before starting, so the dust won't smear the glass more.

He needs you to show him how to wrap his finger in paper and poke the paper in the corners and along the edges first, since these are the hardest parts to clean, and then shine the whole glass. Explain that even a grown-up must spray and shine a window at least three times on each side to get it clean or he'll be disappointed in his speed.

If possible wash one side of the window pane while he washes the other, so you can admire each other's work and point out any dull spots as you shine. If he leaves smudges, polish them yourself when he's not looking, for you want your child to think what a great job he did, no matter how the sunlight hits the glass. That's how standards are made.

When your child has washed enough windows he may even stop making monster faces against the pane when it gets steamy, although we do know an otherwise charming Fifty who can't resist yet.

Pictures

This cleaner would interest any child, even if it didn't work. But it does. Let your Three use it on a gold leaf frame or an old oil canvas. Any paintings you get from the junk store can find a new life.
Halve   1 onion
Rub the canvas or the frame with the wet side of the onion, cutting a fresh surface as the juice evaporates. Wipe with a dry rag.

Polishing

A Four, we discovered, is a polishing fool. Perhaps it's because children like mirrors so much, but no work pleases a young child like shining wood, metal or leather enough to see his face in it.

Shoes

Twos, like Sixes, can polish shoes and belts—and tables and chairs and the ends of their noses. That's why we avoid colored waxes, either liquid or paste, and instead recommend saddle soap—a safe, colorless protection.

Have your child dip a damp cloth into the soap and rub the leather with it until the foam disappears. Let the leather dry for a few minutes, then shine it with a dry cloth. A Six will like to shine all the shoes in the house every week—for about three weeks.

Silver

The silver presents that may have seemed silly when you married seem mighty sensible when you have a Two. They're the only things in the house he probably can't break. This is why your child can polish them for you, but only give him one piece at a time, so he won't go to the next before the first one is completely clean. Silver polishing is one job that can be perfect and so it should be.

Cover the table with newspaper and give him some polish, an old diaper or a rag and a small, solid piece of silver, but not holloware, for we've had sugar bowls bend and crack like paper straws. Let him rub the silver as hard as he can, all over, then wash it in soapy water, rinse it and rub it dry for luster. Satisfaction is seeing yourself smile back in silver.

Copper

A Four wants immediate, obvious success when he works and this polish gives it. In a bowl
Mix   1 c. salt
             ¼ c. vinegar
Have him rub copper with a cloth dipped in this mixture and then rinse it. You may have to rinse it once again, since any residue turns to verdigris. When working with several children, let them add an extra ¼ cup of salt, so the polish makes a stiff paste, and pat it on the copper like a crust on a ham—an amusing task. This coating dissolves the tarnish in about 10 minutes, although they still will have to rub the metal to get a sheen, concentrating on any dark spots. Rinse well.

Marble

Marble cleans well, if your Four is willing to put a little oompah into his work. The powdered pumice and the chalk dust (or calcium carbonate, as it's called) can be bought at a drugstore. Your child

also can make his own chalk dust by putting a few pieces of his chalk in a paper bag and pulverizing them with a rock. In a pint jar
Combine   ½ c. chalk dust
            1/3 c. powdered pumice
            1/3 c. baking soda
Stir until all the shades of white are blended into one. To use, shake several tablespoons of the mixture into a bowl and have your child dip a

well-squeezed sponge into it so the dust doesn't fly as much as it would if you shook the powder directly onto the stone. Have him scrub the marble hard and in any direction. Rinse with a clean sponge.

Waxing

Paste wax gives furniture much more protection than commercial liquid wax and is much safer, for the liquid waxes on the market are highly toxic yet smell so nice a young child may be tempted to drink them. Paste wax is so much tougher it can be buffed to a shine many times without using more wax (and thereby hiding the wood itself) and will hold its shine longer. Also the petroleum solvent in the wax cleans the wood as it covers it. We like bowling alley wax best because it's so impervious that a drink won't leave a white ring on furniture and the floor won't spot in toilet-training season.

Floors

A child will be delighted to help you buff the floors if you skate up and down the waxed boards together wearing thick socks or pillows tied to your feet. Nothing is funnier to a Four than his mother taking a pratfall.

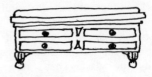

Furniture

Have your Five drop a plug of wax, the size of a quarter, into cheesecloth or an old diaper or a rag. The wax oozes through the cloth as your child rubs the wood, giving it a thinner coat and therefore a better shine. Have your child rub with the grain of the wood, let the wax dry for twenty minutes and then have him buff it with a dry cloth—again with the grain—until he can press the wood with his thumb and leave no print. Buff often and only wax when finger marks can't be erased with a soft cloth.

American Polish

If you want a matte finish, use liquid wax. We recommend the Mediterranean Polish (page 131), which is simply olive oil and vinegar, or this combination, which has no tempting color or odor. This one is the classic furniture polish found in "ye olde shoppes" at about five times the price it costs to make it. A Three with a funnel can do the job, but it takes a Four to apply it. Into a measuring cup

Combine   ¼ c. turpentine
                ¼ c. vinegar
                ¼ c. boiled linseed oil

Shake and rub on the furniture with a soft cloth and polish dry in twenty minutes.

Adventures

Every day you and your husband add a little more to your child's legacy, and money is the least of it.

It's the time you spend with him and the way you spend it that determine the richness of his heritage. The summer walks may seem a bother, the fishing trip too much, but they set the mood for talking—a habit once set that can never be lost.

The adventures you offer should be frequent and varied, with good planning for the special ones and spontaneity for the rest. Just as you prepare for his outings, so must he help you prepare for the family celebrations. When you let your child make a pecan pie for Thanksgiving or arrange the flowers for company dinner, you're giving him memories for a lifetime. Which is as it should be. They'll be your memories too.

Outings

Each day should have a focus of its own; no one wants to drift like flotsam. For you, the focus may be the digging of a garden bed or the teaching of a class—for the child, it's more likely to be an outing. Any size will do. The smallest baby will sleep better for having had a half-hour airing in the carriage.

As your child gets older, these excursions—from a ride on your bike to a camping trip—become essential and their quality will depend on you. We've found a happy outing with a child is no more accidental than a happy childhood. It takes good planning and good timing. If a mother appears casual on an outing it's because she's organized enough to feel free. Some organization is achieved through practice, but a great deal is the result of thinking a problem through before it becomes one, taking enough food and equipment to let you decide spontaneously to stay where you are a little longer but not so much that you'll feel too burdened to leave home.

The best excursions, at any age, have a goal but the goal needn't be designed for children. If it makes you happy to go to a garage sale to look for a table, your child will be happy to see if there are any puzzles there. As long as you're willing to visit with him on an outing, rather than treat him as a tag-along, he'll have a good time.

Children also need outings with people other than mothers. Grandpas, aunties, neighbor ladies and the teenage boy down the block are good companions, but fathers are even better. Each one of our children likes to ankle around the neighborhood with his father for a chance to talk alone. The children take turns in no particular order; the child who seems to need the visit the most gets the priority.

Just as outings shouldn't be only a mother's job, neither should they be limited to a certain time of day. Looking for the stars is as enthralling to a child as looking for morning glories.

Infancy to One
A walk is good for the soul, in almost any weather. Use a lightweight carriage or stroller so the walk won't become a chore and on cold, windy days, lay a blanket over your baby and under him too, for better insulation.

Wherever you go, you'll need to bring enough diapers, a bottle, something for your baby to eat, a blanket on which he can nap and a damp rag for his sticky fingers.

One
Although you'll use the stroller occasionally until your child is Four (at least toward the end of long walks), your child should do some of the walking himself, as soon as he can. The more he walks, the

longer the outing will take and the shorter the distance will be. Two blocks is a long, long trip for a One. If you want to get somewhere with this child, the happiest way to go is by bike and the best carrier for him is a plastic seat, molded so his legs will be protected from the spokes.

Two
Now you'll do anything to divert your Two and your house will reflect it. It either will be rather tidy, because you've gone visiting friends, or quite messy, because your friends—and their small children—have been visiting you. It all depends on which mother is organized enough to get out first. You and your friends can compromise once in a while and go somewhere else together. At this age your child will want to visit a firehouse, go to a band concert or begin the first of his many trips to the library.

Along the way he'll stop to gather, picking up fist-sized pebbles which he can scrub and oil for his window sill or bits of bark and moss for a terrarium. He'll dig for worms in the park and will like to keep a few in soil in a glass jar with a punched top, so he can see them aereate the earth. Tell your child what they're doing, for there is so much he wants to learn and he can't imagine all the questions himself unless he knows some of the answers.

Mid-Two
A long walk works very well now, leaving him as satisfyingly tired as an hour on the jungle gym. If you take more than one child—and you will, for a mid-Two is a sociable creature—you can hustle three or more across streets by stretching your fingers and having each child grasp one of them, then curling your fingers shut into a fist. You'll feel like a cow at feeding time, but safety comes first.

A mid-Two is energetic enough for an occasional, nap-free day, which permits a big adventure. You can drive to a hilly park for a short, backpacking trip, with fruit and cookies in his

knapsack or tied in a bandanna on a hobo stick. If you live near brackish water we suggest crabbing—an amusing family project—or a dig for mussels, using a table knife to cut the shells loose from the reeds along the banks at low tide (and far from sewers). If you're lucky enough to live near the Mississippi, you can catch crawfish in the ditches in spring.

Three
A Three is so full of curiosity and goodness, he'll like a parade (any kind of parade), can sit through a puppet show and is eager for the weekly story hour at the library, although it will be another year before he's ready for its movies.

This child will ask you about everything—and wait for the answers. A Three wants to know the names of the stars and the streets and with your help he'll notice the architecture and the fusty housetops of the city. We've found that walks help a child observe his world better than almost anything else. He can drive through the neighborhood twenty times with you and not notice as much as he will when he walks a single block.

When you go out with your Three take a lunch bag to hold things he wants to bring home. He's such a collector, in fact, that he needs his own museum: any shelf or cabinet that is strictly his own and too sacred to be touched by lesser people—like you. When you respect his precious bibelots, he can respect yours a little better.

Four
Your Four is a powerhouse of energy. He'll splash in the water until his lips turn blue and hike until he should be too tired to crawl. When he's not using his own energy he likes to see others using theirs: the monkeys swinging at the zoo, the cyclist on the high wire, the players at the high school baseball game. He's still delighted with the freedom of the countryside and he'll find a run in the fields just right.

Five
At Five, the countryside takes on a new appeal. He'll find the fields are full of a hundred wondrous kinds of weeds, good for gilding, for bleaching (page 153) or just for investigating. We've found it isn't the collection that sharpens his wits but the collecting. Your child never will forget how many kinds of daisies he once saw on a single day, particularly if you dry them. Snapshots aren't the only way to reminisce.

A Five likes to imitate grown-ups so much, he'll be delighted to go out to dinner or shop and will think it's a lark to spend part of a work day with you or your husband at the office. In fact, he's so contained now he'll hardly bother the other people who work there. This outing has another advantage. It helps your child see how you spend your time when he's not around.

The best outings he takes, however, will be the ones he takes alone, running errands for you next door to the neighbor lady, and farther away too, even if you have to walk him across the street and wait discreetly within eyeshot to guide him back again. We've found a Five enjoys these adventures even more if you send him on his tricycle or his scooter. This, we think, isn't for the joy of the ride as much as the sense of importance it gives him. As everyone knows, a person of affairs has a set of wheels.

Six

All children should have a purpose in whatever they do, but a Six demands one. He's a bit of a pain this way. He doesn't want to take a walk; he wants to take a walk to see the tulips in the park and he doesn't want to shop for a pair of jeans; he wants to shop for a pair of green jeans. This child will whittle his life until it fits into a neat, narrow slot, unless a good friend like you keeps him free.

He needs a variety of outings—from a fireman's carnival to the ballet—shared with a variety of friends. It's this flexibility that will make first grade easier for him.

Neighborhooding

Cold Weather Plans

If you're lucky enough to live in a snowy climate, take advantage of it. A One will like to sit strapped onto a sled and be pulled to the store, but a Two is ready to slide down small hills on a tray or a little sled, if the snow is well packed and not too deep.

Although it takes a coordinated Eight to roller skate, a Three can stand on ice skates and shuffle around the pond with only a few more falls than he'd have anyway (which is a lot of falls), but since it's a great adventure, there won't be many tears.

Warmth is the secret of a happy time in the snow and layers of clothes are the secret of warmth, for they trap the air. The layers must be thin, for bulky clothes will make a small wearer top heavy and clumsy and that is embarrassing. Dress him in several shirts and sweaters, two pairs of tights under his overalls and a pair of thick socks. He needs two pairs of mittens—the second to be given when the first pair gets wet—and a hat that covers the back of his neck.

Whenever you go on a cold weather adventure, take warm soup and hot chocolate with you, for the air gets mighty chilly when the sun is hidden. A hand warmer helps too and take many tissues, for a runny nose on a snowy day is as inevitable as a pratfall.

Foul Weather Plans

A child has such a great amount of energy he needs outdoor play every day and in almost any weather. He can romp in the rain just as he does in snow, if he's well bundled and booted and doesn't have a cold. For a child, there's hardly anything that beats a parade: stamping in mud puddles, marching underneath an umbrella or beating a pot with a spoon. For you, there's hardly anything more depressing than a week of rain. Endurance becomes a game, so you might as well play it. This is the time to widen your boundaries, invite more of his friends to visit and resign yourself to big, messy projects.

When the rain is light, you can walk to the library together or try to follow the arc to the end of the rainbow. By the third bleak day a pot of hot soup at the drugstore will be more enticing than any pot of gold.

Night Walks

It took our Nell to teach us that the dark is as magical to babies and first graders as it is to other romantics, for she was the one who said she hardly could wait to trick-or-treat on Halloween.

"Daddy takes me," she said, "and a walk in the dark with my daddy is the best sort of walk there is."

Which is what won her a walk with her daddy every night since.

Going to Church

You're bound to take your child to a wedding or a christening some day and unless he knows what to expect, he may create a scene. Explain the ceremony as best you can, but he'll understand it better if he's been to church before.

When you take your child to a regular service, take something quiet, like a book or a doll, to busy him. After thirty minutes, a pre-Six may cry, talk loudly or throw pennies in the air. Walk him outside at halftime—before he fusses.

Overnighting

Most parents leave their baby with friends for a weekend, to take a little vacation or to paint a room in peace, but they seldom think of it as a holiday for their child. While you won't insist on it unless it's an emergency, by Two your child may think an overnight with a good friend is one of the most exciting adventures he can have—even though he may back out at the last minute.

To be able to pack his own suitcase (diapers and all), will give your child a fine feeling of independence. It also teaches him that all mothers are not alike—or that, in some ways, they're exactly alike.

We remember one of our Fives who came home from an overnight and reported with relish, "You know Mrs. Walker? She calls her son a chowderhead too!"

There's nothing like motherhood to make a woman explode and there's nothing like an overnight to help a child accept it.

Finding

When you were pregnant, it seemed like every woman you saw was pregnant too. And then when you had your baby, something mystic happened. You never saw pregnant women any more, just other mothers with little babies. It's all in what you're looking for.

Children have their natural attractants too. With some it's feathers and some it's worms and one little boy we knew found beer can openers everywhere he went. In fact, we suspect that the Victorian custom of string saving wasn't started by

its scarcity at all but by an harassed housewife who had little time, a lot of children and too much imagination ever to say, "Go out and play." When you say, "Go out and find," you help a child keep busy and curious too. String is a good place to start. It's remarkable how much string there is in this world, just waiting to be saved: in parks, in alleys and especially near mailboxes. Help your child tie the ends together to make a growing ball of it. It's money in the bank to him.

Country Rambles

You may have to take a subway to get there, but every child deserves at least one tramp through the woods in the spring and in the fall—and a lot more often if you can. A country walk takes on new interest when your child is old enough to help you find moss, birds' nests and rabbit warrens in the woods and dragonflies and tadpoles in the pond or the bayou. Since you'll be doing the planning, you'll probably look for the things you like best and your child is sure to get interested in them too. You need to take a bag for whatever you collect and maybe one of the dandy little books to help you identify trees or rocks but probably not birds, because they fly away before you can get a good look at them. We preferred weeds and wildflowers and for this you'll need to take scissors and maybe a cake tin in case you decide to cut some. If you pick many, ask for permission first (some owners are very touchy about this), and only collect from a field of many, cutting no more than one bloom to a stalk to assure reproduction or take from an excavation site, where they would be destroyed anyway.

Since poison ivy often is found in the woods, bathe your child with a deodorant soap when he gets home and wash his clothes too, or the irritant will infect his skin the next time he wears them.

Weeding

This is a beautiful adventure in late fall and easy enough for a Two and you. By this time nature has dried the reeds and grasses, pods and burrs on their stems. Break or cut them near their base, choosing as great a variety of color and shape as possible and include many of the fluffy weeds for filler to make a winter bouquet—the sort popular in colonial America.

A Three can arrange them for you, if he uses three times more weeds than you think he should, for that's the secret of this dried arrangement. Let him add city flowers too, like hydrangea that's dried on the bush. These will last for years and the memory of the walks will be so vivid your child can tell you where he picked each one.

Bleaching Weeds
A Three can bleach some weeds for you, which gives more variety in color and still keeps to a monochromatic scheme.

Combine   1 qt. water
                  2 tbsp. bleach

Dip the heads into the solution for several minutes—until their colors change. Dry on newspaper.

Gilding Grasses
When you get home from weeding, have your Four spray some dry reeds and grasses with gilt—a few at a time, outdoors and in a box to contain the mist. This should be done lightly, since a complete gilding looks gaudy, and arranged with only a few in a vase for a Japanese effect. Large branches, like dried brown magnolia, look elegant with this dusting of gold, although your child might not think so unless you tell him.

Wildflowering

The wonder of the woods will stay with you longer if you keep some of the flowers in a bouquet (page 215). Most wildflowers wilt within an hour of picking, but some hardy ones like Queen Anne's lace, black-eyed Susans, ox-eyed daisies and the beautiful blue chicory are sturdy enough for handling and plentiful enough to pick.

If you're planning to pick flowers on a walk, take a cake tin with a tight lid or a plastic bag with a rubber band, either of which will keep the flowers alive for several days. However, if you're just going to pick flowers in a field near your car, take a bucket of wet sand and have your Five stick the stems in it to keep the flowers fresh until you get home. Once there, put the flowers in a glass.

Add   2" very warm water

Let them revive in a dark, damp place (under the sink is fine) and then either show your child how to press them in a book (page 216), dry them in the delicate silica gel method (page 217) or arrange them in a vase (page 159).

In a vase

Add   water
                  1 quick squirt detergent

You can use soap, too, including bar soap. Stir until the water clouds, then add the flowers. Change the solution every three days.

Transplanting Wildflowers
Very small plants will suffer less shock than large ones, for transplanting plants is as difficult as transplanting people. Still, a Five can do all the steps.

Have him draw a circle in the dirt with his finger about 2" around each plant he wants and then dig straight down with a spoon to catch all the roots. Pack each plant in its own bag, with as much of the soil as possible. Add a little water and close tightly with a rubber band.

Choose a place in your yard where the plants will have about the same amount of sun that they had back home. Have your child dig a hole for each plant—the size that he dug in the woods—and fill it twice with water. A plant goes in each hole with its own dirt around the roots. He should press the soil firmly to hold the plant upright and eliminate air bubbles and water again. Probably only 50 percent of these plants will live, which isn't a bad lesson for a child to learn.

Rock Hunting

Maybe it's because a Two is so close to the ground, but he always wants to pick up anything he sees—especially rocks. He'll find that some are sharp like coral and slate, some are round and smooth like pebbles and others are crumbly like sandstone, and once in a long time he may find one with a fossilized print of leaves or bugs or tiny creatures from the sea. With your help, it won't be long before he can sort the metamorphic rocks, like marble (and diamonds), from the sedimentary rocks that were formed by pressure and the igneous rocks made by a spewing volcano. If your child is going to have a rock collection (and they all do), he may as well know what he's talking about.

Berry Picking

"Doubtless God could have made a better berry, but doubtless God never did," said William Butler, the sixteenth-century poet.

We think every child should pick fruit (or vegetables) at least one time in his young life and, though you may have an affinity for raspberries, Mr. Butler's strawberries are much easier to pick, for they are ground level, very obvious, and have no thorns.

We've found berry picking is hot, dusty and unforgettable. Every summer for the rest of his life your child will conjure the smell of berries ripening in their beds of straw.

To offer this adventure, find a farmer who shares his crop on a pick-and-pay basis and go early in the day, when it's not so hot, and early in the season, when the fruit is best. Don't, however, go the day after a rain, for rain diminishes the flavor and texture of berries, if you make strawberry preserves.

A pre-Three should wear a shirt and hat, since the sun is strong in an open field, and he should at least arrive in a stroller, to mollify the farmer. Take shallow, lightweight pans, lunch, juice and a picture book. The flat pans—one for you and one for him—should have handles and be no deeper than 4" or the weight of the berries will mash the lower layers. Line them with paper towels before leaving home, to protect the fruit from bruises. Your child will enjoy the book and the treats in the shade when he's tired.

Before starting, teach your child how to pick the berries. They are ripe when the color is deep red and the stems break easily from the hulls. The smaller ones are generally more flavorful, although you can expect him to pick the biggest, fattest berries he can find. Pick the less vivid ones yourself, for underripe fruit contains more pectin and this is what you need for jam.

We've seen a One sit quietly for a half hour between the rows, picking berries with great care—and eating most of them. A Two and especially a Three will put most of the berries in the pan but he won't last longer than a half hour either. A Six can pick for twice that long and any child is content to amble through the rows for perhaps two hours if he has stopped for lunch. This is long enough for you to pick about ten pounds—as much as you can cook without wishing you'd never gone at all.

Once home (and these farms always seem to be at least an hour from home, no matter where you live), both you and your child will need a fat nap before making the preserves.

Strawberry Preserves

This experience will be as fresh to your child as the berries themselves. Your Two can help you hull the berries and your Six can cut out most of the soft spots, although you must remind any child to touch this fruit very gently. Don't expect a child to have the patience to help you make more than one batch. Four cups of berries are best, although we like to work on such a grand scale that we double it.

Old-fashioned Preserves

To cook these preserves, you'll need a pot three times higher than its contents, to prevent any hot syrup from splashing over the brim, and to bottle it, you'll either need glasses with paraffin or jars with caps and rings. In a colander have your Six

Wash and hull   8 c. berries

Drain. Pick them over yourself, cut the bruises and put them in a big bowl. In a kettle

Boil   6 c. water

Pour enough boiling water to cover the berries (your job) and let them sit in this bath for two minutes, to cook them slightly. Drain—again your job—and put the berries in the cooking pot. Into it

Stir   4 c. sugar
      1 tsp. lemon juice

Boil   15 minutes

Stir occasionally.

Add   4 c. sugar

Stir again. Although the syrup is hot now, a child can do this, if the pot is tall and he uses a long, wooden spoon.

Boil   5 minutes

You needn't skim the fluffy scum, since it will stick to· the high sides. To test for readiness, dip the spoon into the pot, cool it momentarily and let the syrup drip back into the pot from the side of the spoon, a step too dangerous for a child, we think. Show him how the syrup falls from the spoon into points like a "W." If you stop now, the berries will float in a soft jelly, but if you cook it longer the jelly will reach the thicker sheeting stage of 220° and the two drops will marry into one, like a "V." This gives a firmer base—a decision your child will want to make for himself.

Now you're ready for canning.

Sunshine Preserves

The most shimmeringly beautiful berry preserves are cooked by the sun. To do this your Five needs at least two glass baking dishes, three days of sunshine and if it rains (as it always does for us), a directional lamp with a 100-watt bulb. Have your child help you wash and hull the berries as directed above, and in a heavy saucepan

Layer   4 c. strawberries OR raspberries
                      OR blackberries OR blueberries
                4 c. sugar

Let the sugar extract the juice for a half hour in the uncovered pot. Cook over low heat (to prevent scorching) until the syrup boils.

Boil   20 minutes

Pour the mixture into a glass pan and cover with another—your job. Put the berries in the sunshine in the morning and bring them indoors at sunset, with your child carefully stirring the berries each morning and afternoon so that none are mashed. It will take 2-3 days of sun to have the syrup jell and turn brilliantly clear. In case of rain, put the dishes 6″ beneath the lamp for about 30 hours. Without reheating, bottle the preserves as directed below.

Open Kettle Canning

If you let your child can a few jars of preserves, his pride will be great, but it will be even greater if you use 4-ounce jars instead of the standard half pints. There will be twice as many.

Canning isn't as complicated as the cookbooks describe, particularly if you preserve jams or pickles or chutneys, which have a high acid content. Mold will be your big enemy and this is controlled if the jars are sealed well.

Because part of the beauty of canning is looking at it, the better you can see the preserves, the better they'll look. After the jars are filled and capped, scrub the outside of them because the glass usually clouds when they're boiled. This is what you need:

jars OR jelly glasses
lids OR paraffin
rings
funnel
tongs
dull knife
large wooden spoon
ladle
large pot
roaster with rack
many potholders

Lay a flat rack in the roaster and add the jars, upside down, with the metal rings, the tongs, the knife and the ladle tossed between them.

Add   5″ water

Cover. Bring to a boil.

Boil   20 minutes

Leave the top on the pan until you're ready to spoon the preserves into the jars, which your child can do with you if the preserves are cool—and you don't mind the mess. If you're using the old-fashioned rubber rings or the lids with rubber rings pasted in them (the prettiest kind), put them in a saucepan and pour boiling water over them 20 minutes before filling the jars.

Spoon the preserves into the jars almost to the top and have your child jockey the knife up and down to eliminate air pockets. Wipe any drippings from the threads of the jars and either cap them tightly or pour melted paraffin into them to form a seal. Refrigerate the jars sealed with wax, but you're supposed to put any others on a dark shelf to save the flavor. Personally, we'd rather keep them in the middle of the kitchen table where everyone can see them. So would a child.

Super Outings

No matter where you live, you mustn't let your neighborhood dictate the way you live; in fact, it should do just the opposite.

A child needs one zingy adventure a week in a completely different environment, whether it's walking the busy city streets or sitting on a riverbank.

Although a child has short staying power, he'll want to visit the places that interest you—but only for a little while. Let him investigate the monuments and fountains, the courthouse and city hall, the art galleries and the theater (page 127).

He also needs to see the wild animals at the zoo, the silly chickens in a barnyard and the galloping horses at the circus, just as he needs to see the rabbits and the birds in the woods, the frogs in the ponds and the seashells on the beach. It may take a thousand questions, but this is how a child learns how animals eat and where they sleep and why they look the way they do. It isn't that your child will learn so much but every exposure will make him curious to learn more.

The Beach

It's the planning that determines whether an outing with a child will be a success, and this is especially true at the beach.

You don't want to burden yourselves with a surfeit of equipment, yet your day may be spoiled if you forget some vital clothes or toys or the right food or drink. The beach, with its wind and water, its glare and sunshine, encourages extra hunger and thirst, and always, we're sure, more bowel movements for the child in diapers. There must be something about sea air.

For this reason, you'll need more diapers than usual and more to eat and drink, too—avoiding caffeine sodas and sugary snacks. This is what you need:

blanket
disposable diapers
tennis shoes
child's hat and shirt
sweater OR sweatshirt
life jacket
Wind Screen
toys
suntan lotion
food and drink

Having gone through a desperate hour when an Eight and a Nine were swept away in a riptide (good swimmers though they were), we strongly recommend a life jacket in the ocean and indeed near any water (except perhaps a swimming pool). It's such an easy precaution to take. Although the jacket is vivid so it can be seen at a distance, he may not be wearing it when he plays on the beach, which is why the bathing suit should be bright too. Since all patches of sand look the same to a child, it's mighty easy for him to wander away.

He'll also need tennis shoes if the sand will be hot or the beach rocky and the sweater or sweatshirt in case of sudden winds.

A baby's skin needs strong protection from the sun, both when it is dazzlingly reflected by white sand or water and when the overcast skies and soft winds make you forget how easily the skin can burn. He should wear a shirt and hat at all times and the playpen should be shaded by the Wind Screen, for a baby shouldn't have direct sun for more than a half hour at a time. Even so, a young child needs frequent applications of suntan lotion—your pediatrician can suggest the special type for his delicate skin—and much more water and juice than usual, as an extra precaution against dehydration.

A toddler can take the sun longer but still needs a hat and shirt, even wearing the shirt in the water. Give a new coating of lotion each time he gets out. A very tanned and tough-skinned Four—the sort who spends weeks at a time at the beach—usually can forego these precautions.

If your child does get a sunburn, put him in the shade and rub him quickly with ice from the picnic chest—for ice is the treatment for all burns—or cover him with a towel dipped in cold fresh water or one dipped in a 50-50 solution of vinegar and water. This may have to wait until you get home, unless you pessimistically packed the vinegar. If you're going to the ocean, that's not a bad idea.

Wind Screen

This piece of equipment is better than an umbrella, easy for an adult to make and considered a necessity on the Riviera—so it's said.

Assemble   3 yds. 45" sturdy cloth
           four 4' dowels, 1½" thick

Any heavy, closely, woven fabric, like canvas or vinyl, is fine, but the dowels must be at least a foot longer than the width of the material and sharpened with a hatchet at one end to stick into the sand.

Sew   four ¾" tucks

Do this across the width of the fabric, making one tuck at each end and the other two at one-yard intervals to form equidistant pockets for the dowels. Midway on one end

Sew   36" grosgrain ribbon

This should be done in the center of the ribbon only, but go back and forth several times with a small machine stitch, so it will be strong. Roll your supplies in the blanket, lay this bundle in the Wind

Screen and roll it like a sausage, securing it with the ribbon and carrying the whole screen under one arm.

When you get to the beach, jam the pointed ends of the dowels into the sand to form a wall to break the wind. Unless it's high noon, the screen will cast enough shade to protect your child and you too.

Marine Lab

Show-and-tell, the thrill of any nursery school, becomes more marvelous to the Five who has something notable to show. This lab is one of the best—or the worst—ideas, depending on the squeamishness of your child, since to make it he must drop live insects or small sea creatures into denatured alcohol. Although death is instantaneous and painless, you'll want to offer this experiment with discretion. To carry the alcohol, use a wide-mouthed jar with a tight lid. Into it

Add   fly/grasshopper/beetle
                sand crab/jellyfish

Your child—and all his classmates—can observe the specimens through the jar, with a magnifying glass to examine them from all angles.

Wall Hanging

One of the loveliest wall hangings we've seen was made by a Four at the seaside, because her mother had taken the patch plaster for a vacation. If you do, have your child

Gather   rocks/shells/crab claws
              leaves/grasses/reeds

Into his bucket he should

Stir   3 cupped handfuls patch plaster
            1 cupped handful sand
            3 cupped handfuls sea water

He should add more water if it isn't soupy enough and more plaster if it's too wet. Have him pour it into three paper plates and then arrange the shells and grasses into a collage, after waiting a few minutes so they don't sink through the plaster. Over each plate

Sprinkle   1 handful sand

Peel the plate from the plaster when it's dry, shake the extra sand loose and paste a picture hook on the back to hang it on the wall or simply prop it in the back of the bookcase.

Crabbing

This is a sport that suits our small talents better than fishing and it seems to suit our children too, perhaps because it gets so raucous. The investment required is quite small—but then so is the catch. Keep only those 5" across the shell—the legal limit—and expect more silliness than supper.

You also can expect your child to be bitten at least once (for crabs are craftier than children), for which you only can give sympathy. He probably will fall in the water too, a good reason to wear the life jacket. This is what you need:

crab net or box trap
line
sinkers
bait
knife
life jacket
tall basket

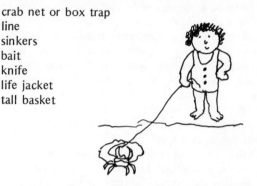

Plan to crab from a pier or a riverbank, in brackish water, preferably around a channel and when the tides are changing. A Two can operate a trap, a Three can manipulate a line, a Four thinks he can net a crab, a Five sometimes can and a Six can do both jobs at once. When using a crab net, cut several lines for each person, long enough for the string to reach bottom when weighted with a sinker or a rock. Tie the bait—such as a chicken neck or some fat back—just above the sinker and tie the lines at intervals to the pilings or to small sticks that you jam in the sand. Reel in the lines often, using both hands. Do this gently and quickly, with the net held just below the water to swoop beneath any crab that might be hanging on. We think it's best if a parent holds the net and a child pulls in the line. It's a wacky way to teach cooperation and you'll catch more crabs too.

If you use a box trap, tie the sinker and the bait in the middle of it and drop the trap until the line is slack, the sign that the four sides of this box have fallen flat on the sand for the crabs to walk inside (for crabs are more greedy than crafty). Once the line is jerked taut, the sides flip back into place and capture the crab—all principles of crabbing which a child must understand if you want him to do it well.

Keep any crabs in the basket, without water and lightly covered from the sun. They take about ten minutes to cook in a covered pot of boiling water. A Four can season as you would for Boiled Shrimp (page 245), but transfer the crabs yourself, using long-handled tongs to grab each one from the rear. Still, you can expect at least one crab to escape for an unforgettable chase in the kitchen. Your child will like that very much. You can tell by the way he screams.

Fishing

As soon as your Four finds that someone has invented fishing, he'll want to try it. No matter how little he knows about it, in his mind fishing is the sport of kings.

It took a handsome grandfather to teach us how to make it the sport of small children too, instead of the disappointment it so often is. Our gentleman friend, a perfectionist like all good fishermen, feels you need to do some fishing yourself before you try to teach its techniques, while we belong to the "let's bumble along together" school. Whether you practice first or not, this outing needs some preparation with your child, even if you're an expert.

Your child will want to know the names of the fish he might catch, and he also should know about the innate courtesy anglers have for each other—speaking quietly so the fish aren't frightened from your hook (and from theirs) and even showing courtesy to the fish, tossing back any that are too small to eat.

In fairness to your child you'll want to tell him that fishing at times will be uncomfortable and boring and tiring and, truth to tell, it may be unsuccessful too. This not only won't daunt him, he'll still plan a fish fry for the whole nursery school.

In fairness to yourself, you should know that when a parent and a child go fishing, the child fishes—and the parent explains, untangles and pours juice, with little time to drop a line. Some outings, like adult fishing, are simply not made for children, which is why you leave your Four at home when you really want to fish. Apartness has its place.

The equipment you use when you fish together should be simple and the same for both of you. If you bring a fly rod, your child will want to cast and since it's too complicated for him to handle, it becomes a weapon. This is what you need:

metal tackle box	screw driver
2 bamboo poles	first-aid kit
line	life jacket
several sinkers	juice and snack
several bobbers	bait
several leaders	
assortment of hooks	
stringer	
knife	
nail clipper	

The night before you go, spread your equipment about the living room and show him how it works, rather than waiting until you reach the water, for it will be hard for him to learn in the midst of such excitement. With your child's help, thread the poles with the bobber midway on the line, to be adjusted as you fish to suit the depth of the water. Tie the hook on the end to the leader—the wire that makes it easier to change hooks and keeps the line less snarled. The sinker is just above it, to hold the bait deep in the water. Your child should be told the reasons for everything, although they seem obvious to you. When you're finished, wrap the line around the pole, stick the hook into the bobber for safety and let him stow the extra supplies in the tackle box.

You need the stringer to keep all the fish you catch and the knife, the screw driver and the nail clipper to remove them from the hook and to cut new line—a regular duty when you fish with a child, for he tangles it often. We find it's better to throw away a few pennies' worth of string than have a child dance around while we spend a half hour untangling his line.

In this modern age, worms are still the best bait, for a child can slide them onto the hook easily and they stay in place better than meat or dead insects. If possible, help your child dig the worms before you leave, for he'll think it's a lark, but you may need to buy some too, for you should have at least two dozen.

Fish seem to bite best on a clear day and since it probably will be sunny, have your child wear a hat. He needs a life jacket too, whether you fish from land or from a boat. It's one less thing to worry about.

We prefer the dock or the shoreline for a novice fisherman, choosing a place with few reeds or logs to tangle the line. An older, more experienced child can fish from a boat, but only if you know the currents, the channels and the day's weather report.

To bait the hook, thread it through the worm, hiding the point within it. Drop the line over the edge, keep quite still and talk, if you can, in whispers. When fish begin to nibble, the bobber starts jiggling. Wait until the fish takes a few big bites (which you can see by the way the cork plunges), then pull the pole sharply and quickly upward, so the hook becomes imbedded in the fish's mouth. This single, sudden action, successful or not, is so exciting to a child it will make the waiting worthwhile.

Take the fish off the hook for him, for he may scratch himself trying, but he can run the stringer through its gills and toss it into the water to keep it alive, because the freshest fish always taste best.

To be realistic, you probably won't catch enough fish for the nursery school—or for dinner—but you'll know the pleasure of a quiet, lazy day when whispers bring secrets to life.

The Circus

One thing we learned by experience is how to take children to the circus. It isn't that we are such circus buffs, but when you take your own flock and their friends to see the clowns every year, you learn a lot about children and circuses.

Children find the circus is a great adventure but a scary one. This is one time when food is a good diversion. We brought enough to give a treat before every high-wire act, when they might be frightened. You'll need a wet washcloth to wipe sticky hands, and for each child take:

roasted peanuts
popcorn
candied apple
peanut butter and jelly sandwich
soda

Although some of this is available at a circus the cost is prohibitive and the hawkers are never there when you need them. Save the soda as long as possible, and if you must take your child to the bathroom go in the middle of an act. At intermission the bathroom is like the fourth ring of a three-ring circus.

When you take more than one child, you can expect at least one to wander. For this we recommend a helium balloon—their only treat—tied to the wrist, or have them wear vivid hats or sweaters so you can follow them more easily.

Camping

Camping gives you time to hike and fish, find rocks and wildflowers and generally fall in love with nature again, for all you have to do is simply eat and sleep. There are as many styles of camping as there are styles of living, and it can be as encumbered or as free as you wish.

We like it somewhere in between, relying on our old station wagon, a top carrier to hold the gear on the roof and few fancies. You can find much of the equipment you'll need in your kitchen, and you may be able to borrow a good deal of the rest in the beginning. Avoid extensive purchases until you know if you like camping and, if you do, the style you prefer.

A camping trip, we found, is a pleasure if everyone helps, but a bore to anyone, including a young child, if he must watch others work and has nothing to do himself. Since we find it hard to assign jobs when we're busy setting up camp, we plan the work before leaving when we sort the paraphernalia on the living room floor. You'll find this is a good time to teach your Five the square knot—an invaluable lesson—and to show your Two how to zip and unzip the screen door of the tent. Otherwise, you'll have a tentful of mosquitoes. This is what you'll need:

tent, with floor
plastic tarp OR ground sheet
nylon rope
sleeping bags
2 firm rubber pads
blanket
3-5 changes of clothing
towels/washcloths/dish towels
packaged pre-moistened towels
hatchet
large flashlight/lantern
large water jug
large wine jug
canteen
cold chest
propane gas stove/matches
skillet/saucepan with lid
large plastic bowl/plastic bags
plastic trash bags
plastic dishes and flatware
aluminum foil
long-handled fork/spatula
sharp knife
oven rack
life jacket
collapsible fishing pole
liquid and bar soap
laundry powder
insect repellent
food
salt/pepper/herbs

If camping with an infant, you also will need a portable crib or playpen, a collapsible stroller or sling and the same necessities outlined in Travel (page 88).

An older child will need sturdy shoes, rubber boots for wet ground, a sweat shirt with a hood (for the nights and early mornings can be chilly), a friendly toy and the canteen, both for hikes and for that midnight drink of water.

He also should have the fishing pole and the life jacket if you think you may camp near a stream. The tarp is to lay over the tent floor to keep rain or dew from creeping up from the ground.

We only bought the waterproof, torso-length foam-rubber pads for the adults since a child accepts the hard ground as his lot in life.

The insect repellent should be the one sold at camping stores—a cream which doesn't burn the skin or the eyes.

You can mix food in the plastic bags and wash dishes in the bowl. By taking the oven rack, you can cook more food over the wood fire—a sensational taste. Since it's harder to prepare meals when you camp, you should serve the most satisfying foods—the best breads and natural cheeses, the freshest of roadside fruits and vegetables and eggs. Because of the space shortage, you'll need to buy perishables every few days but you can carry the dried foods, like potatoes and soups, and the staples. We also recommend taking Banana Cookies, Homemade Biscuit Mix and Granola, all from our Cooking section, for camping seems to call for the heartiness of natural foods. It also calls for a sense of festivity—hence, the wine.

At the Camp Site
After making an initial one-night trip—to see if we actually could do it—we made many trips, lasting from two days to two weeks.

This experience taught us that it's easiest to stay two nights in the same place and to choose a secluded campsite, so our children didn't disturb other campers—nor they disturb us. We found most campsites sell dry wood, a few of them have laundry facilities, all have trees to hang the clothesline and many are close enough to town for you to find a supermarket and a laundromat.

Pitching the Tent
To give you an idea of your child's capabilities, a Two can be in charge of the tent stakes, unpacking them and handing them one at a time to his father. A Three can lay out the tent poles, a Four can fit them together, a Five can help to pitch the tent and a Six can bang a few stakes in place, if the ground isn't too hard.

Once the tent is pitched and the tarp is laid, decide where each person will sleep, lay the bedrolls in place and hang the flashlight. This gives a child great comfort for as soon as this is done, the tent becomes his home.

Cooking and Fire Building
Whatever you do during the day, return to base at least three hours before dark. This will give you time to prepare dinner (for everyone is much hungrier, much earlier than usual) and time to wash dishes, brush teeth and build the campfire before dark.

When you camp, almost all the work involves cooking the meals or cleaning up after them. With more than one child, we find we must alternate the jobs for everyone wants to pour water from the big, squeezable jug and no one wants to gather the sticks. The cooking is done on the propane stove, which your Five will like to pump, although he only can do a few strokes.

Everything you cook at camp has its own touch of glamour and dinner is the focus of the day. If it's too simple or if your child has nothing to do, he'll be bored. We find there's bound to be some dish a child can prepare, whether it's Grilled Corn or Bean Salad, so long as you use the same safety precautions that you do at home. As for yourself, you can cook almost anything at camp that you can at home, depending on your spirit.

Before dinner, your child can begin to lay the bonfire. A proper fire has the most inflammable material at the bottom with drafts to fan the wind. A Four is ready to assemble the paper in the center, with a pyramid of small sticks over this heap and a bigger one of larger kindling over it all. After you've lighted the fire and it's caught well, lay the logs—an adult's job. Before dark, have your child find green sticks on which to roast the marshmallows.

The prize of our day comes when we lie on the blanket with our children to watch the falling stars and point out the constellations with a flashlight.

Problems

For us, getting to sleep is no trouble in the brisk, outdoor air, but getting up in the morning is difficult. The ground is wet with dew, the bed is warm and it may be a long walk to the bathroom or, if you're a more primitive camper, the slit trench. If you think your child would be embarrassed to walk around in pajamas let him sleep in his clothes. It may be that—or a wet sleeping bag.

Water, in one way or another, is the menace of every camper. Children splash in ponds, sleeping bags get damp, rain drips in the stew and the best of tents will leak a little in a downpour. That's all part of the Great Adventure.

If you find you must cook in a slight rain, you can cover the area by throwing the tarp over the clothesline and tying each corner to a tree. When water comes in the tent in a storm, we recommend towels bunched to absorb it and a meal in town while the clothes and the sleeping bags are in the laundromat drier. The treat is almost worth it.

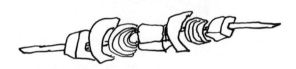

Shishkabob

Serves 6

This recipe is one of the most adventurous ones a Four can cook, for it gives him a dozen important jobs. Have him make the marinade at home, but he'll soak and cook the meat at the campsite. You may want to buy the meat at home. In a plastic bag

Pack	1½ lbs. lamb or beef cubes
	2 green peppers
	4 yellow onions

Use a jar to make the marinade. In it

Combine	1/3 c. salad oil
	3 tbsp. soy sauce
	3 tbsp. vinegar
	3 garlic cloves, minced
	1½ tsp. sugar
	¼ tsp. pepper
	¼ tsp. steak sauce

At the campsite, remove the green peppers and onions and add the marinade to the bag of beef, but do it after lunch because it takes a few hours to tenderize it. Hang the bag from a branch so the animals can't reach it. In the meantime, have your child

Collect	four 2′ sticks, ¼″ in diameter

Whittle one end of each stick (your job) for your

child to thread the ingredients more easily. Soak the sticks briefly in water (his job), so they won't burn. On these skewers

Alternate	meat cubes
	green peppers, in eighths
	onions, quartered
Roast	20 minutes

Turn to brown on all sides. The onions can be cooked separately, sealed in a package of foil with 3 tablespoons of butter and laid over the coals. Shishkabob is served with rice, cooked on the propane stove.

Bannock

Serves 6

If you take Homemade Biscuit Mix (page 250) with you, your Six can make this bread on a stick for dinner. Have him find 6 straight green sticks 1″ thick and 2′ long. Sharpen one end of each stick yourself as a stake to drive into the ground. In a plastic bag

Mix	2 c. Homemade Biscuit Mix
	½ c. water

Have your child knead the dough 20 times, adding a little more mix if it's too sticky. Snake a piece of dough around each stick, near the top. When the coals glow, poke the pointed ends in the ground at an angle over the fire slowly turning them so the dough will brown evenly on all sides.

Campfire Beans

Serves 8

Sometimes campfire dinners need all the help they can get. In a saucepan have your Four

Mix	two 30-oz. cans pork and beans
	one 10½-oz. can tomato soup
	1½ tbsp. dried minced onion
	1 tsp. instant coffee
Simmer	10 minutes

Do the small amount of stirring yourself, since a camp stove is not so steady.

Potatoes in Mud

This is a great project if you have time, a fire, a shovel and a Three. Build a fire either outdoors or in a campsite fireplace. Dig thick mud or have your child make it with dirt and water—enough to cover medium-sized potatoes with a ½″ of it. Into a fire of hot coals

Drop	mud-covered potatoes
Bake	1 hour

Turn them with a stick midway. The mud will get darker in some spots as it bakes as hard as a clay pot and you'll be amazed to find it leaves only a trace of dust on the skin when your child breaks them open.

Grilled Corn

Try this recipe only with fresh-cut corn, still in their husks. Drop the ears in a bucket of water.

Soak   15 minutes

The rest of the jobs are yours, although a Two will feel he's completely responsible. Lay the corn over gray coals.

Grill   20-30 minutes

The bigger the ears and the wetter the husks, the longer they'll take to cook. Turn the ears every 10 minutes and, when tender, peel back the hot silk and husks.

Add   salt
              butter

Brown Bean Salad

Serves 6

You may think this recipe has odd ingredients to take on a camping trip, but living in the woods is no reason to eat dull food. Let your Five

Stir   one 21-oz. can red beans
           1 green onion, chopped
           2 tsp. oil
           1 tsp. vinegar
           1 tsp. cumin
           ¼ tsp. salt
           ¼ tsp. garlic salt
           dash pepper

Add   2 tbsp. chopped parsley

Grilled Cinnamon Apples

Serves 4

It takes a Six to count as high as this recipe requires.

You can use ripe pears instead of apples and in either case, the dessert will be fresh, pink and bubbly.

Quarter   4 apples

Remove the core—a job for you. On 24" heavy-duty foil

Lay   apple quarters

Over them

Sprinkle   150 cinnamon candies
             2 tbsp. butter

Fold shut and seal by folding the edges together. Lay the foil package on the grill over a smoldering fire.

Roast   30 minutes

Backpacking

Backpacking, far more adventuresome than camping, is a long, long hike, with at least one night spent outdoors and every person carrying his share. That's why a child who backpacks either must be a steady walker, generally no younger than Four, or an infant you carry in a sling.

Even so, it's only practical to backpack with an infant if your baby is breast-fed and if your husband can distribute your load of food and equipment between at least two other adults, for only the most experienced backpacker can handle more than a forty-pound load and you have the baby to carry.

To prepare an older child for backpacking, you must help him get into condition, preferably starting as early as mid-One when you put away the stroller and have him walk everywhere. This helps a child develop the muscles and stamina he will need.

A good walker is ready for a one-mile hike at Two, but he should wear rugged boots and carry his lunch in a small knapsack on his back—props that aren't necessary yet, but they make the woods seem more exciting.

When you graduate to hiking long enough to cook a simple meal, your child should have small jobs to do, as he would in camping. He also must be responsible for more equipment, carrying his own fork, spoon, tin plate, cup and canteen in his gear.

By the time your child can walk five miles without any bellyaching, your family is ready to start backpacking together.

It seems to take as much precise planning and preparation as the coronation of a king. You can backpack in national forests, national parks and some state parks, all of which have maps of their trails showing the terrain, the sources of water and where you can build a fire and pitch a tent. These maps are found at the information centers in the national and state parks, but to backpack in the wilder, less crowded national forests, write the United States Geological Survey, Map Distribution Office, 1200 South Eads Street, Arlington, Virginia They'll send you the index of the state where you want to hike so you can send money for the right map.

It's best to choose a trail that brings you back to your starting point, so you can return easily to your car, and one where you can camp near a spring or lake, so you won't have to carry water too far. (Water from a spring is always drinkable, but chlorine tablets will make any water safe enough to drink.) You'll want to avoid areas with steep climbing, not because your child can't climb up, but because it's hard for him to climb down.

Adult's Backpack

This is what you need for backpacking. You can borrow many of these items until you find your own priorities.

backpack	nylon rope
2-man tent	large plastic trash bag
plastic sheet OR tarp	pliers
sleeping bags	flashlight
canteen	toothpaste/brushes
stove	soap
wineskin OR collapsible plastic jug	insect repellent chlorine tablets
aluminum pot	raincoats
aluminum skillet/lid	bandannas
tin plates/cups	matches
flatware/sharp knife	toilet paper
small plastic jars	dried foods

Child's Backpack

Backpacking, like nothing else we know, forces your child to decide what is essential in life—the big, old teddy bear or the scraggy old blanket. After he's carried one heavy pack, he'll be glad to lighten his load.

diamond-shaped backpack	2 pairs of socks
sleeping bag	sneakers
raincoat	toothbrush
1 change of clothes	cup/spoon/plate/canteen

Since the gas is in your feet when you backpack, you must have shoes that fit well and either cotton or wool socks, thick enough to be absorbent. A two-man tent is big enough for parents and a pre-Six, if all the gear is stored outdoors. True backpackers tell us that the pliers have many uses, especially for picking up live coals when you make an oven to bake bread. The bandannas will be your potholders, scarves, dishtowels and washcloths, for they are much lighter than terrycloth, and the plastic jars will hold food like honey or jam.

Backpackers follow the same procedures for setting up as campers, but since they have no ice chest, all food is hung in the big plastic bag on the nylon line (too high for raccoons to reach). Also, if there's no portable toilet nearby—and there usually

isn't on these rugged trails—you'll need to dig a small hole with a stick for potting, at a respectable distance from camp.

Cooking

All the food you carry should be put in plastic bags with the finer ones in double bags. Carry powdered milk, dried vegetables, potato flakes or lentils, dried soups, fruits, some onion and garlic flakes and spices, as well as packages of powdered drinks like lemonade as well as margarine in plastic tubs, which don't leak.

For meat, carry canned fish or sausage that needs no refrigeration. Good cooks find these foods have enough variety to let them be imaginative.

The Trail

When you hike with a full pack, you'll want to teach your child to distribute the weight evenly on his back, to hunker down a little when he goes up a hill and to list slightly backward when he comes down, planting his feet sideways, rather than forward, with each step, as he would on a snowy hill.

You should walk at a steady pace and rest whenever anyone is tired, for you're not in a race to see how far you can travel or how fast. Drink a little water from the canteen, have a bit of Hiker's Snack for energy and take the time to rub elbows with nature. That's what backpacking is all about.

Hiker's Snack

In a plastic bag, before leaving home, have your Four

Combine	1 c. raisins
	1 c. Spanish peanuts OR walnuts
	1 c. semisweet chocolate morsels OR candy-coated chocolate bits
	1 c. chopped dried apples

Celebrations

The first holiday may have been invented to celebrate fertility or planting or harvest, but we're sure a mother was behind it. Even then she must have known that nothing could cure her day-to-day drudgery as well as a holiday or brighten the eye of a small child so quickly.

We have touched on the main holidays in this section but have skipped Mother's Day and Father's Day since they are capers a child should initiate and also in deference to firsttime parents who no doubt are as appalled by their commercialism as we once were. As our children grew older we learned to take anything we could get and found ourselves happy to exchange our principles for the guarantee of a late sleep and breakfast in bed once a year. There were also the rewards of ill-made treasures and, one joyful year, a two-wheel bike all our own: not bad for a nonbeliever.

Whether you encourage these holidays or not, we don't think a month should go by without a celebration of some sort, even if you have to invent it. However, the only thing worse than having a month without a holiday is having a holiday without your child's help. He has every right to be a part of the preparation of each festivity, as he is a part of everything else that happens in a family.

When he polishes the silver bowl, roasts pecans or draws the place cards, he'll anticipate the party that much more—and that's where most of the fun comes from. The celebration itself will be over in hours, but the memory of those giddy days of preparation will last for years.

Birthday

When your child has his first birthday party, he needs only his doting family and perhaps one young guest, the "happy birthday song," a little help blowing out the candle and then the cake itself, placed right on his high chair tray. You can expect him to burrow into the icing with two hands and a face: a spectacular snapshot.

By Five, the happiness of a party is in the weeks of anticipation, the hours of planning, with lists and invitations, the surprise of the cake cut into the shape of a sewing box or a train (with candy for the trim and boiled icing to cement the pieces together).

Some mothers dread these parties, but we think they're great if you plot them well in advance. We finally learned that everyone has a better time if the party is limited to two hours (most of which will be spent eating and opening presents), if you invite no more guests than the birthday child has years and if you drive the children home. We never met a mother who fetched her child on time, including us.

However you handle the invitations, you should tell each mother not to spend more than a dollar on a present, for you want your child to realize that the present from a guest is not as important as the presence of a guest. The limit should be kept when you give too. For peace of mind, keep a few gifts in reserve, for a pre-Six is invited to more parties than a New Orleans debutante.

The joy a birthday party brings a child beforehand and the sweet memories afterward completely erase the anxiety he may feel during the party. Be prepared for a deathly quiet for the first hour, punctuated by the guest who weeps when he surrenders his gift—typical of a Two—and the host who says "yuk" when he opens it—typical of a Six.

Turn the music high and have a favor for every child—wrapped like a present—to give in return for the one he gives. We don't recommend competitive games often, particularly in this situation, for a child may be ready to win publicly but not even a Six is ready to lose. If you give prizes every person should get one for whatever reason you can concoct.

If you have one balloon per child he will cry when it breaks, but if you have several he should have one left to bring to his little sister (who will cry when it breaks). For extras, rub inflated balloons on your hair to generate static electricity and stick them to the wall to be plucked down as needed.

For the first few years one mother is necessary to help, but if all the mothers stay, they may deaden the party since they are sure to spend some of the time correcting the children's behavior. By Six your child will want to invite a few of his grown-up friends—both men and women—and this is a grand idea. A mixture of ages and sexes miraculously turns a party into a celebration.

Ice Cream Pots

The chocolate "dirt" on top of these pots is much too realistic for a very young child to eat, but a silly Four will think it's so funny he'll want to make these pots for his equally silly friends. First he should plug the holes of small clay flower pots with aluminum foil and into them

Pack   ice cream
Over it
Grate   chocolate candy bar
Freeze until the party begins. Poke a hot skewer into the ice cream and stick the stem of a fresh flower into each pot—both your jobs, for he has better things to do—and serve one to each guest.

Penny Pitch

To pass time simply at a birthday party, have the children stand behind a starting line and, one at a time, have them toss pennies into a wastebasket. This is much harder than you might think. A Two may be successful at a distance of 2' and a Six may manage at 6', but if it's too hard, make the distance less and give them all another turn. As at all parties, each child must be a winner—either for accuracy or distance, noisiness or style, and they'll want the pennies as well. To the victors belong these spoils.

Your child also may like to play this game on an ordinary day, using a deck of cards, and either playing alone or with company.

Copycat

Giggling little girls of Five like to stand in a circle while one of them shakes her arm for all the others to imitate. The next child adds another motion, for both to be copied, and so it goes, around and around, until you have a roomful of St. Vitus dancers. Anyone who forgets a motion is out of the game.

Dining Room Ping-pong

This game requires one ping-pong ball in the middle of the table and two Sixes facing each other, hands behind their backs. One child tries to blow the ball over the opposite edge of the table to score a point while the other child blows against it. It takes five points to win, or less, if one of the children can't stand this much competition. If balls dent, they usually reinflate when dropped in boiling water.

Passover

The Seder, to open the eight days of Passover, has to be one of the most inspiring—and dramatic—of all religious feasts, especially for children, for the significance and the history of each step are explained in this dinner table ritual.

In the Seder, everyone takes part, from the young child who asks the four questions of faith to the patriarch who answers them, helping each person relive the saga of the Jews' flight from Egypt. It's a child's job to open the door for the prophet Elijah—the sign that any stranger away from home is welcome on the sabbath—and to end the festivity, there is the wild search for the afikoman—the broken matzoh. This is what the father hides at dinner for all the children to seek later and then gives a prize to the winner (and often to the losers).

A child can help prepare for the Seder, as sacred as it is, by setting the traditional fine glass on the table for his father to pour the wine for Elijah and by helping to make the individual Seder plates.

A Two can roast the dry shank bone of lamb—a recollection of the ancient Passover sacrifice of the pascal lamb—baking it in a 325° oven for several hours. He also can prepare another symbolic offering—the roasted egg—by baking a boiled one (wrapped in foil, in case it explodes), leaving it in the same oven with the bone for about an hour until its shell is streaked with brown. A Three can mix the salt and water in little bowls for every plate, to represent the tears shed, and cut the top of the horseradish root to dip in this water: bitter herbs to represent the bitter lot of the Israelites. He also can give each plate its sprig of parsley—the green vegetable usually chosen to mark the festivity of the day—and at Four is trustworthy enough to make the charoses, to signify the mortar that Jews had to make to build the pyramids for the pharaohs. Finally, in the most symbolic of all foods, there is the matzoh, the big square cracker made without leavening so everyone will remember the haste of the flight, when there wasn't even time to get the yeast. Three matzohs are placed on the table under a folded linen napkin—the middle one to be broken and the afikoman taken from it.

Like Christmas, we think any child should celebrate at least one Seder, even if it's not part of his faith. It's unforgettable.

Charoses

This doesn't look much like any mortar we've ever seen, but the story of the Jews and their enslavement by the Egyptians is so dramatic your child will think this simple recipe is the most significant part of the Seder. In a bowl

Grate	½ lemon
Add	1 c. chopped apple
	¼ c. chopped walnuts
	1 tsp. honey
	1 tsp. cinnamon
	1-2 tbsp. Passover or sweet wine

Add enough wine to bind the mixture together.

Easter

Rituals are built into all cultures—some sacred, some silly—and a child should have a chance to sample them, especially Easter. It comes just when nature erupts with such a miracle of life that there should be a way for your child to celebrate it. What could be better than to wake up once a year to find dyed eggs, chocolate eggs and jelly eggs hidden everywhere?

You either can dye the Easter eggs yourself the night before (which can be a bother) or let your child help you the day before (which will be a mess). Even when he leaves them openly in the basket, he'll understand it's only a favor for such a busy bunny.

Buy much less candy than you're tempted, particularly chocolate, since pre-Sixes don't digest it too well, and forget about serving Easter breakfast. Even one hard-boiled egg with some milk or juice will be a fine meal, if strange.

Hide the candy and eggs, either indoors or out, choosing obvious places in a confined area for a pre-Three—and have a camera ready. An older child likes to look a little harder, will stay cleaner and be less picture worthy.

Watch carefully that your child collects all the dyed eggs and stores them in the refrigerator. We once smelled the results when our flock left an egg between the cushions of their dear Aunt Mary's fancy sofa. Unfortunately, it took three weeks.

Baked and Stuffed Chicken

Serves 4-6

It's hard to match the pride a little girl feels when she presents the chicken she has roasted for Easter dinner. It is much, much easier than it looks and combines interesting jobs, like cutting the bacon strips with scissors, tearing the bread and poking the dressing inside—all work a Five can do.

| Sauté | 2 bacon strips, cut up |
| | 2 tbsp. chopped onion |

Remove from the heat when the onions are clear.

Add	4 slices bread, torn
	1 stalk celery, chopped
	1 egg.
	¼ tsp. sage
	½ tsp. salt
	¼ tsp. pepper

Stir. If the mixture is too dry

| Add | ¼ c. hot water OR |
| | chicken broth |

Let cool.

Preheat Oven 400°

Wash and dry a large fryer, inside and out. Inside the bird

| Rub | ½ lemon |

Poke stuffing into the cavity, a handful at a time, and leave open. It will puff out, but little will be lost. Into your child's hands

| Pour | 1 tsp. oil |

Have him rub the chicken and over it

| Sprinkle | ½ tsp. salt |
| Bake | 1-1¼ hours |

When it's ready, the meat should pull away from the bones, the joints should wiggle when touched and the juice should run clear, not pink, when the breast is poked with a fork.

Strawberry Icing

This frosting is easy for a Three to make and as pretty as an Easter bonnet. Use it over the Pound Cake (page 253), or substitute raspberries and serve it on top of the Ultimate Chocolate Cake (page 253). Make this icing shortly before dinner, for it loses its pep in about two hours. Your child can do everything except separate the eggs. With a mixer

| Beat | one 16 oz. pkg. frozen strawberries |

Use partially thawed, sweetened berries. When well crushed

| Add | 2 egg whites |

Beat until thick and frothy.

| Add | ½ c. sugar |

Whip until stiff peaks form. Heap over the cake, spreading with a rubber spatula and refrigerate until serving.

Easter Egg Tree

After Easter, when your Six still is intrigued with colored eggs, teach him how to blow raw eggs right through the shells and into the skillet, saving the shells for this egg tree. Have him poke each end of the shell with an embroidery needle or an ice pick, deep enough to break the yolk. He'll blow the small end like a whistle and the egg will slide out of the bigger one. About half the eggs will break, for children are not too adept, but save the rest until you have a collection. You can paint these for him with clear shellac which toughens the shells enough for handling, then let him color them with felt-tipped pens or paste gold stars or sequins on them. To hang these eggs

Cut   6" lengths of thread

You need one length for each egg. Fold the thread in half and knot the ends to make a loop—your job—and lay the knot over the fat end of the shell for him to seal in place with dripping candle wax. Hang the eggs gently from a branch, tied from some high place like a stairwell, or from the Hair Ribbon Tree (page 133).

The New Baby

Every newborn deserves a party, whether it's to celebrate a baptism, a bris or simply the birth itself. It's especially important if you have an older child, for with forethought you can give him a role to play. He's the one who needs to grab a little glory.

For Christians, the christening is generally in the first six weeks, while Jews have a bris on the eighth day (but only for a baby boy, since it's the rite of circumcision). In either case, it involves a weepy baby, a weary mother, a few old friends, a little wine and whatever goodies the grandmothers and aunts are willing to make, with perhaps rogelach—the rolled pastry—at a bris and chicken salad or a ham at a christening. Whatever the occasion, there's sure to be a fine dessert, like a cheesecake, which a child can make with a little guidance.

Cheesecake

Serves 16   Preheat Oven 475°

A Three can make this recipe because there is no need for a complicated crust. It does need a greased 9" springform pan, so it can be removed easily before serving. Have him make the cake before his nap, because it needs an extra amount of quiet while it cooks, and bake a day in advance, for chilling makes it firmer.

Beat   2½ lbs. soft cream cheese
                  1¾ c. sugar
                  2 tbsp. flour
                  ¼ tsp. salt
                  6 eggs
                  ½ c. heavy cream

Add ingredients in order, beating well after each addition and adding the eggs one at a time. The total mixing time is 8-10 minutes, but the mixture is so thick at first, he'll need your help to free the beaters.

Bake   10 minutes

Lower heat to 225° for 1½-2 hours, until the center doesn't jiggle any more and it shrinks from the sides. Cool in the oven 1 hour with the door partly opened and then cool on a rack for another hour. Refrigerate or freeze. Because a cheesecake cracks easily, cover it with Currant Glaze to hide the crevices.

Currant Glaze

In a skillet, have your child

Melt   ¾ c. currant jelly
                  2 tbsp. water

Add   1 c. fresh berries or sliced peaches

Pour over the top of the cake. The glaze will jell again in about 10 minutes. If you whip some cream and put it into a small plastic bag with a hole cut in the corner, your child can pipe a design, of sorts, to cover any bad cracks. Remove the springform and present the cake on your very best plate.

Christening Hat

Your Four will need 6 straight pins, a threaded needle, some ribbon, a beautiful lace and linen handkerchief and a lot of help from you to make a christening hat for the new baby. A 12" square, when pleated and folded, will fit a newborn.

Have your child first lay the handkerchief on a table, then fold each corner to the center and pin it into place. The four points should meet.

You now have a smaller square. Pleat it into 4-5 parallel rows, which makes accordion-like folds that will cover the head, from ear to ear.

Pin the ends while your child holds these pleats in place. He has now fashioned the hat—narrow over the ears (where it's pinned), and expanded in the middle (where it isn't).

Your child can sew the corners in place and tack the four corners too, but you must tie the knots. Pin, and then sew, a ribbon over the pleats on each side, so the hat can be tied under the chin, and a bow to cover the top where the four points meet.

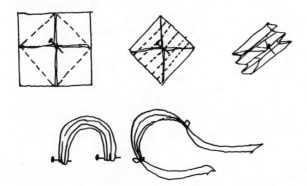

At the risk of sounding sentimental, the hat can become a handkerchief again, to be used by your daughter on her wedding day or for your son to give to his bride.

Halloween

Some mothers can handle Halloween efficiently—and then there are people like us. We're the ones whose jack-o-lanterns draw fruit flies on October 28 and whose children, year after year, are dressed only as unimaginative ghosts or tramps.

Still Halloween is a marvelous event, if only for the amazement it will bring your toddler when he opens the grumpy neighbor's gate and for once you don't say, "Come back." He marches up the front steps and suddenly the lady who frowns so much is giving him candy by the handful. It's as surprising as winning at numbers.

By now we've learned a thing or two, mostly from all those mothers who've done Halloween right. Following their example, we think you should go on a pumpkin hunt a week ahead of time, with your child making the choice. Once home, have him draw a face on the pumpkin with a felt-tip marker, but do wait to cut it until two days before Halloween, so it won't rot. After it's carved he can clean the inside, refrigerating the seeds until he's ready to roast them, and put a candle inside. Any jack-o-lantern looks all right with a candle shining inside.

You'll want to prepare the costume in advance and together, either buying one of those dreadful ones from the dimestore, which every pre-Four prefers, or making it at home. It should be funny or beautiful, but never truly scary, for the only person who'll be afraid will be your child and he'll be terrified. Let him wear his mask for days ahead of time, because it's so exciting and because he'll need

practice to become accustomed to it. Claustrophobia, we've found, is automatic with a store-bought mask, unless you enlarge the holes for the eyes.

By Halloween itself, excitement is so high you may want to contain it better by having a few children over in the morning, either for them to dunk for apples in a roasting pan of water—a nice, wet thing to do—or to bite into ones you've hung by strings from a doorway. In either case, their hands must be clasped behind their backs.

A nap is impossible on Halloween, even for the children of mothers like us, for the anticipation is overpowering. Put him down to rest at least, so you can do the same, then dress him in costume and take him door to door to the homes of people you know, and preferably with one of his friends, who will be sure to giggle better than you do. We've found if a child goes trick-or-treating before he gives candy away at his door, he'll be in a more giving frame of mind.

Some of our children hoarded their Halloween candy for months, others would eat it in a remarkable forty-eight hours, but we never knew a child who wasn't eager for a taste of salt instead of sugar the day after Halloween. For this we recommend roasting the pumpkin seeds.

Roasted Pumpkin Seeds

Preheat Oven 250°

Help your Three wash the seeds in a colander—a tedious job. Drain them and pat dry with a paper towel. In a large skillet

Sauté 2 c. pumpkin seeds
2 tbsp. butter OR 1½ tbsp. salad oil
1 tsp. salt

Stir 3 minutes, until all seeds are coated with butter.

Bake 30 minutes

If not roasted enough, bake 15 minutes longer, or until brown. Crisp on a paper towel and eat them, shells and all.

Thanksgiving

This poor holiday, so arduously arts and crafted in school, is scarcely mentioned at home except in terms of cooking, cleaning and company. When the day does arrive, most little children are cross to find it's just one big dinner. It's sure to last too long, because any meal longer than twenty minutes is too long for a child, and have too many vegetables, for one vegetable is often too many.

Some of the disappointment is lessened simply by talking about the holiday in advance. It may seem like an old story to you, but the classic tale of the pilgrims will be a wonder to your child. We've found a museum visit is helpful too, but nothing makes a modern Thanksgiving better for your child than to feel a part of it. We assign the flashiest, fanciest little jobs we can find, like the relish tray, for it's praise that keeps pre-Sixes good. One of the simplest and most praiseworthy of all recipes is Curry Dip.

Curry Dip for Raw Vegetables

A Four can make this sauce very easily, although he may like the compliments better than the taste.

Blend
- 1 c. mayonnaise
- 2 tbsp. green onions, chopped
- 2 sprigs parsley
- 1 tbsp. green pepper
- 2 anchovies
- 3 tbsp. ketchup
- 1 tbsp. curry
- dash cayenne

Make a day ahead to ripen in the refrigerator. Serve with peeled and quartered carrots, cucumbers and celery sticks and cauliflower broken into flowerets, all of which you'll prepare yourself. Crisp them in cold water and dry before serving.

Pecan Pie

Preheat Oven 425°

Southern cooking became famous with recipes like this. And so will your Five. In a bowl let him

Beat
- 1 c. light corn syrup
- 1 c. sugar
- 3 eggs
- 1 tsp. vanilla
- ¼ tsp. salt

Pour into unbaked pie shell

Add 1 c. pecans
Bake 10 minutes

This seals the top and crisps the pecans. Lower the heat to 325° and bake another 40 minutes. Serve cold.

Christmas

The commercialization of Christmas may offend many of us, but a young child never sees it. To him, each decorated store window, each advertisement, make expectation all the sweeter. For once the world is turned upside down and it's decidedly a better place.

Slowly you'll help your child realize that Christmas is a celebration of charity, when the joy of giving is at least as fine as the joy of getting. A Two, however, can't hear enough about such dazzling ideas as a tree in the living room and elves who know how to make wagons. We think you also should explain the religious history of Christmas, even if you don't advocate it, for a child deserves to know what any hullabaloo is about.

Whether Christmas is a spiritual holiday for you or not, to a child it's the ultimate in family unity, like a vacation at the beach or a trip to Grandma's. He feels wrapped in a cocoon of closeness that comes from sharing so many good times and special traditions. These traditions will be your own blend of the customs you and your husband inherited and others you've evolved together. This is what makes Christmas a unique experience for each child.

There will be cookies to bake and presents to make, carols to sing and popcorn to string until, on the night before Christmas, when stockings are hung and the poem is read for the last time, the electricity of your child's excitement almost shocks you. You may be exhausted on Christmas morning—for what mother is not?—but his poignant expectancy on Christmas Eve will catch your heart: one of the more obvious blessings of motherhood.

Giving

It will be your job to emphasize the charity of Christmas, by asking your Three what he's going to give for Christmas, before you ask what he's going to get. Help him make his list and count his money and then take him on at least three trips to the museum shop and the dimestore for the presents he can afford—the sea shells, the flints for a lighter, the address book. Most of the gifts, however, should be homemade, for it only takes money to buy presents while the drawings and bookmarks and sculptures of wood are presents that come from the heart. When a child sees how much they mean to you, he'll want to give presents all year long.

We reactivated the custom of candymaking, as we did in our childhood when there was little for gifts but a sack of sugar and pecans from the trees. It was, we found, as horrendous and hilarious as we remembered. We organized our children by having one child in charge of his own recipe for the evening, and the rest of us working as assistants. Although we read the instructions and checked the measurements, it was the chef for a night who would assign the jobs, giving orders with all the frantic pomposity of a bad French general just before his next defeat. The mess was major and the voices shrill, but somehow the candy was great, the memories better. Each child would put a few pieces of his candy in the small baskets to give to their grown-up friends, and, alas, to eat sometimes, as we discovered at the end of the long ride to see Uncle Jim, when Mike sat absolutely still in the back seat, aghast to find himself holding an empty basket. This was the candy that lured him on.

Butterscotch Crunch

When we were retesting this recipe we offered some to a pretty Three and asked for her opinion. She put the candy in her mouth, solemnly pronounced, "Yumm," and picked up two more pieces to take home to her daddy.

The ingredients are so pure no child can fail, but since the sugar mixture gets so hot when it cooks, only a Six should stir it. Line a jelly roll pan or a 15" X 10" X 1" baking dish with foil, and crack and blend the nuts in advance, because this

recipe allows no time for these steps after you combine the ingredients. In a 1-quart saucepan

Melt   ½ lb. butter
Add   1 c. sugar
Cook   8 minutes

Do this over medium heat, stirring with a wooden spoon. It will look like bubbling bread dough after 3 minutes and be pale caramel when it has cooked the full time. Remove from the heat and spoon evenly into the pan—definitely a job for you.

Cool   2 minutes
Over it
Scatter   6 oz. butterscotch morsels

The hot butter and sugar layer will melt the morsels in about 4 minutes. When they are shiny and soft to the touch, spread them with a rubber spatula, covering the first layer completely—definitely a job for your child.

Sprinkle   ¾ c. Brazil nuts, finely blended

Chill until firm, about ½ hour. Break into tiny pieces, for it's very rich.

Getting

Before Christmas, retire a few more toys to the closet shelf than usual and repair all the broken toys and torn books. Discard those that are outgrown or irreparable. By making this inventory, you have a clearer idea of your child's needs—which are never quite as much as you think they are. In fact, we recommend you cut your shopping list in half at least once, for too many toys baffle a child of any age.

Your Five will need some help for that letter to the North Pole (the one you'll keep in the Bible for years) with cutout pictures of the things he'd like and not too many of them. You must tell your child to expect only some of the things on his wish list, and then stick to that, for a parent shouldn't be in the spoiling business.

Anything you give should be sturdy and of good quality, so your child won't feel he's a destructive person. The promotion of ill-made toys, particularly on television, has devastated many a Christmas morning, including one of ours, when we bought Mike a flashy, short-lived mechanical monster, his heart's desire. The next October we mentioned, casually of course, how sad it was that TV toys never worked and we certainly were glad to hear that Santa wouldn't give them any more. By November, he began to believe us and by December, as much as he may have hankered after the red, white and blue robot, he had the good sense not to ask for it. We found this technique so infallible our children would turn off the set if they thought their special toy might be advertised.

Santa

You can give the Santa Claus legend as much or as little emphasis as you want—one of us thinks it should be a lot, to stimulate the imagination; the other, very little, to keep it in perspective. We do know, however, that if you deny the fancy of the elves completely, your child will not.

We remember a Six, reared with unbending realism, whose parents told the sitter to forget about reading "The Night Before Christmas" on Christmas Eve. "David," they announced, "has never believed in Santa Claus," and yet, the minute they left, David chortled and said his parents pretended every year that they bought all the presents but, of course, he knew better. Santa Claus had. He had no doubts at all.

A child will believe in elves (and bunny rabbits and the tooth fairy) if he needs to believe and as long as it makes him happy to believe. No matter when a child accepts the truth, he always is wise enough to recognize the Santa Claus story for what it is—another guise of your love.

The only bad effects seem to be caused by some department store ringers who misinterpret their job. Although your child will rationalize— without any help from you—that this man isn't the *real* Santa Claus, it's better to tell him beforehand that all the Santas he'll see in the stores and on the sidewalks will be only "helpers."

We've found the best helpers work in the swankiest stores, where they don't dare push or promise certain toys. The richer the customers, apparently, the softer the sell. To have this visit run even smoother, call the store first to check Santa's schedule and avoid a wait.

We almost can guarantee that your child will be stricken with a chill of conscience late in the day on Christmas Eve, even though you've never mentioned charcoal and switches. Suddenly he wonders if he and Santa Claus really have the same standards for goodness after all. We find it helps to tell a child he's wonderful—about fourteen times— and then let him prepare the cookies and sugar cubes for Santa Claus and the reindeer. A little giving can assuage a lot of last-minute doubts.

The Tree

In some families, the parents put up the tree on Christmas Eve, after the child goes to bed, so that Christmas will be one big ball of magic the next morning. We think that's a terrible idea. It isn't just because the buying and decorating of a tree is a family project which thrills a child, but because you'll be starting a tradition.

The most docile child will expect you to repeat everything you do, Christmas after Christmas, and this can turn the holiday into chaos.

In a few years you and your husband not only have the breakfast cart to prepare, the stockings to fill and the presents to arrange, but you'll have the tricycle, the twenty-four cardboard blocks and the doll's crib to assemble, and as years and babies progress, at least one frantic trip to the all-night drugstore when you realize that one child has less presents than another. To decorate a tree between bedtime and dawn would be just too much. There's such a thing as too many traditions.

If you plan to keep the tree in the house more than ten days, you may want to fireproof it. Do this before you bring the tree inside, by spraying the needles with the Fireproofing Solution (page 41).

Where and how you place the tree may decide on how smoothly Christmas will go. We found it best to place it in a bucket of wet sand, either on a sturdy table or in a playpen, held firmly in place near the top by picture wire or string attached to anything that is fixed, like the window catch or a nail driven into the bookcase. There's no fun in having the tree fall down. It's trouble enough just decorating it.

At least one parent is sure to scream at the other, the way it happens before a dinner party, and the Four takes an age to string popcorn and cranberries. It will be the blowing of the tinsel, strand by strand, that makes adults pleasant if breathless again, but you'll find your child ignores all dissension. He'll let nothing spoil this good time.

We allowed our children, beginning at late Two, to help hang the unbreakable ornaments around the bottom of the tree and we put the breakables near the top, but after all these children, only the unbreakables are left, top or bottom. These scruffy family favorites still look beautiful to us, but the ones our children like best are the ones that belong to them.

The Dowry

Every year we give each child one decoration, all his own and unlike any other we have. He hangs it where he pleases and wraps it in his own box to put in the trunk after Christmas. We figure a good education and a box of memories are as much a dowry as any child needs. We also make other ornaments of bread.

Ecuadorian Bread Dough

Preheat Oven 250°

These are charming, seldom break, last for years and make good holiday presents for your Five to give. For reasons unknown to us, this recipe can't be doubled or halved and must be mixed, shaped and put in the oven within 2 hours. It will make 10-15 decorations. In a bowl

Mix	2 c. flour
	1 c. salt
	¾-1 c. water

If the dough still doesn't hold together, add a tablespoon of water.

Knead	7 minutes

Shape, according to suggestions in Handbuilding (page 207), and poke a small hole in the top for the hanger. To make a bas relief to hang on the wall all year, open a paper clip partially and press half of it into the back of the decoration, before baking. Lay all decorations on a lightly greased cookie sheet. They may puff a little, so you should smoothe any edges with a wet knife before baking or they may look rough when cooked.

Bake	2 hours

Paint with acrylics and then with clear shellac.

Candy Ornaments

Preheat Oven 300°

These are the prettiest, easiest, tastiest decorations a mid-One can make—and not bad for a Thirty either. Lay any hard candies on a cookie sheet, but the delicate ones with flowers in their centers will look best, for the flowers will bloom as they expand.

Bake	10 minutes

Let cool a few minutes, then turn a nutpick or the point of a pencil near the edge of each candy to make a hole for the ornament hanger. These decorations can be stored from year to year—if they're not eaten first.

Christmas Dinner

Christmas Eve is the best time for a child to prepare his treat for the Christmas dinner. We think this one is best and even a Two can make it.

Roasted Pecans

Preheat Oven 300°

This is likely to earn more compliments at Christmas dinner than the turkey. The nuts can be reheated 10 minutes before eating, while the meat rests to draw back its juices. In a pan

Combine	8 oz. pecan halves
	6 tbsp. butter
	½ tsp. salt
Bake	15 minutes

Take the pan from the oven midway so your child can stir the pecans with a long wooden spoon. Let them crisp on a paper towel. Serve in small dishes at the dinner table, as you do the green onions and celery sticks.

The Slump

The post-Christmas slump can be almost as bad for a child as the postnatal blues for a mother. To make it a little less slumpy, we think you should plan two to three low-key activities for your child for the week after Christmas, so he can simmer down slowly. We've found it pleasant to go to a movie matinée, see the animated displays in the store windows, drive through town to look at the decorations on other people's houses—in short, those adventures we never found the time for before Christmas.

Company Dinner

The pleasure in giving a dinner is mostly the pleasure of giving yourself. The effort you take is your way of showing your company that you care about them enough to give them a good time. Your Three wants to be a part of this too, even if he's never met the guests or if he must go to bed after passing the hors d'oeuvres only once. When you let him help with some of the preparations, you're letting him share your gaiety.

Cold Artichoke

No one keeps as busy as a child, which might be why even a Two will eat a whole artichoke. It's ten times more work for him to eat it than cook it—plucking each leaf, dipping the base in the sauce and scraping it between the teeth for just a little pulp. Cut the stem yourself with a knife and use scissors to cut the pointed tips, but let your child stand the artichoke in the pot.

Add   1″ water

Simmer covered 20 minutes. Serve hot or cold with Hollandaise or Lemon Sauce and when the leaves are gone, remove the fuzzy thistle yourself. Have your child slice the heart and serve it with toothpicks and the sauce. This hors d'oeuvres serves four—if your child allows it.

Lemon Sauce
It takes a Four to make this sauce.

Melt   6 tbsp. butter
Add   juice of 1 lemon
            1 tsp. salt
            ½ tsp. dried dill OR tarragon

Eggplant Caviar

Preheat Oven 425°

Once we knew a fellow who, when our Nell offered him this fine hors d'oeuvres, heartlessly said, "My Gawd, she's serving rat." We've camouflaged the eggplant's distressing gray color with chopped parsley ever since, which simply makes it better.

Let your Six put a large eggplant in a pan and prick it with a fork before cooking or it will explode.

Bake   1 hour

When cool enough to touch, slash it lengthwise and scoop it out of its skin—a mother's job—and put the pulp in a bowl. Have your child

Add   2 tbsp. olive oil
            2 tbsp. chopped green onions
            1 tbsp. chopped parsley
            2 tsp. lemon juice
            1 garlic clove, pressed
            1 tsp. salt
            ¼ tsp. pepper

The eggplant will absorb flavors better if it's still slightly warm when these ingredients are added. Your child should squeeze it through his fingers until well mixed.

Cover   2 tbsp. chopped parsley

Serve at room temperature with chunks of French bread.

Luminarios

Spanish
Spanish lanterns turn a neighborhood barbecue into a fiesta—and a Two can make them out of brown paper lunch bags.

Sit your child in the sandbox with as many bags as you'll need to light the table, the garden and the edge of the driveway. Have him fill each bag halfway with dry sand and poke a candle stub into it. They'll look magical by night but a little scruffy until the sun goes down. If that bothers you, use fancier bags, which your child will like, or bring them out after dark, which he will not.

American
Our teenager, having no sandbox to call his own, invented luminarios that last from one party to the next. We've found a Six can make them just as well with an 8-penny nail and two 4″ scraps of wood for each luminario.

Have him nail the scraps together in an X, working on the lawn, so he can pull the nail out of the earth easily. Heat each nail over a flame—your job—so it will be easy for him to slide a fat candle stub onto it and drop the candle and its holder into a brown lunch bag.

Arranging Flowers

Flowers are sure to win praise at a party—which is reason enough for a Five to arrange them. The job is done best in the afternoon, before you feel pressured. With your guidance, he can do almost every step himself.

If the stems are tough, like those of daisies, have him smash 2″ of the base of the stem with a hammer. Cut any other stems diagonally—your job—and have your child put them in a bucket of very warm water for 1-2 hours to harden the stems so they last longer.

Spread newspaper on the table (a child makes this messy work much messier) and have him remove all the lower leaves and at least half of the others, since they foul the water and rob the flower of energy. He can pour sand in a vase to hold the flowers or mash his oil-based clay into the bottom of it and press either a styrofoam block or a frog in it. Before arranging the flowers, have him add water and one squirt of detergent or soap, which extends the life of the flowers.

You need to teach your child the rudiments of flower arranging, and the reasons. First, have him

count the number of blooms—since the best bouquets have an odd number of flowers—and then have him stuff only one flower into the frog at a time, so the arrangement looks natural, with the bigger blooms at the bottom and the tallest one in the center. Have your child keep the setting of the vase in mind. It matters whether the flowers will be seen up on the mantelpiece or down on the dinner table, so he may have to crouch and stretch as he works. When done, provide him with filler of ivy or hedge cuttings to poke into the inevitable gaps, just like a florist.

Flowers, like parties, don't last forever, more's the pity. Have your child change the water every 3-4 days, adding new soap. The flowers can be rejuvenated if you trim. the stems, mashing again any tough, woody ones. Dip them in very hot water for 1-2 minutes to shock them into new life, then return them to cold, soapy water.

The Non-holiday

When the weather turns foul or friends are away, melancholy may strike your child too. These days are no fun at all, and when you have a string of them you have to manufacture a good time. Use any small milestone—your son's new molar or your daughter's first go on the potty. Life is meant to be celebrated and here are three fine ways.

Sidewalk Sundaes

This is called a sidewalk sundae because you'll be sorry if your child eats it inside the house. In an ice cream cone

Pack	ice cream
Add	chocolate syrup
	coconut
	nuts
	cherry

Wrap a napkin around the cone and send him running.

Ice Cream Sodas

This home treat shouldn't have gone out of style.

Mix	¼ c. milk
	3 tbsp. chocolate syrup OR
	3 tbsp. strawberry jam OR
	5 tbsp. frozen fruit
Add	1 scoop ice cream
	2 ice cubes
	club soda to fill

Stir quickly.

Cream Puffs and Eclairs

Yield: 12   **Preheat Oven 375°**

This will seem almost too simple to a Five. It's easier to make than a cake from a box and requires only six utensils. Cream puffs can be used in a main dish—as in the Chipped Beef—but add no sugar.

Combine	1 c. water
	½ c. butter
	1 tsp. sugar
	½ tsp. salt

Bring to a boil in a heavy saucepan. Remove from the heat.

Add	1 c. flour

Stir with a wooden spoon for several minutes until smooth and return to a low fire. Stir constantly until the dough leaves the sides of the pan and rolls into a ball, then remove from the fire again.

Add	5 eggs

Drop one egg at a time, but show your child how to beat the batter firmly with the spoon, so the egg disappears. He should mix the batter well after each egg, but he may need some help from you. Drop 12 spoonfuls on a greased sheet and for éclairs, trail long spoonfuls.

Bake	45 minutes

The puffs are ready if the first one doesn't fall immediately when you take it from the oven. Cool on a rack and split them—a job for you—but let your child fill them with whipped cream or ice cream. Cover éclairs with Chocolate Icing I (page 254).

Expressions

Expressions

A baby is curious about everything, creative about some things and capable of almost nothing. His curiosity and his creativity will grow or shrink, depending on the limits he meets, and his capabilities will never develop well unless they are nurtured.

The more your child is allowed to expand, in every direction, the better he can express himself. These expressions take many forms. While one child might speak best with words, another uses his easel or his carpenter's kit, and still another prefers clay or needle and thread or a suitcase full of dress-ups. This doesn't mean he'll automatically be an actor, a writer or a builder when he grows up, but his preferences often point out his talents. Unless he has the chance to sample a little bit of everything, he may never find out where these talents lie.

He clearly has likes and dislikes from the day he is born. Simply the way he snuggles in the bassinet, tummy up or down, is a matter of choice. You'll want to accept as many of his preferences as you can, for this is how you show respect for him as a person, just as you do later when you let him choose which flavor he gets in an ice cream cone or whether he'll wear the red sweater or the blue one. The more a child realizes that he can be different from other people—including you—the more original he can be.

Any expression your child attempts will need some help from you—sometimes just a little, as in drawing, sometimes very much, as in carpentry. You're the one who'll show the world to him, pointing out the ants on a stick and the moon in the daylight sky. Later it will be the fractions he makes when he cuts his apple and the letters he finds in the headlines. It isn't that you're trying to nurture the superchild (a scary idea), but there are degrees of ability, in originality and in intelligence, and any help he gets will make him just a little bit better—and, therefore, a little bit happier too.

You'll gasp at his curiosity when he probes the first mysteries of science just as you will at his lip-biting concentration when he cooks and at his imagination when he plays store. All of his activities, as well as his adventures, his friendships and his toys, give his intelligence a tug every day. The mind is not taut like the skin of a drum, but

rather like taffy. The more it's stretched, the farther it can reach. Each time you help him look for the nest when he sees a tree and look for the eggs when he finds the nest, he'll be more likely to grow up with a zesty "What's next?" view of life. He'll be able not only to see beauty in the world and try to create more, but also to see its problems and try to find answers.

Curiosity

Curiosity is the basis of creativity. A baby's fresh mind strives to make sense of the world from the day he is born, gulping every sensation. He begins life as hungry to know as he is to eat.

From the first he pieces his ideas together into a patchwork of knowledge—however erroneous—which he reorganizes every time he draws a new conclusion.

Every mind-stirring thing he meets will add to his wonder, which is as it should be. The more a child wonders, the more inventive and resilient his mind will be. Each new idea will make him more capable of thinking for himself, of exploring his own head for answers. At this age, he'll look at life from the underside, not only finding the unusual but expecting it: a viewpoint to be encouraged for the rest of his life.

We try not to be sentimental, but the flowering of a child is a triumph of nature. When you feed his senses and his mind, you feed your own soul. This is the flowering of a mother too.

Imagination

Imagination brings glory to some—to architects like Eiffel, to statesmen like Lincoln—and it brings satisfaction to all, from shoemakers and plumbers to very young children. It's imagination that turns the mundane into the marvelous. With it, a smart child conceives with brilliance, a normal child displays extra perception and a slower child delights you with a special, original turn of mind.

Everyone is born with imagination, but no flower in the soul of man is more easily crushed—or more easily nourished. You nurture this imagination when you let your child explore, when you trust in his ability—to climb a tree, to create a song, to dress up like a king and to simply sit and dream. In these ways, you're giving him the right to think for himself.

Your own inventiveness can stretch his imagination. The questions you ask, the fancies you suggest, the problems you pose, all put visions in his head. When you encourage your child to substitute the unusual for the obvious—a rock for a hammer, a can of beans for a rolling pin, a different mug instead of his favorite—you're stirring his imagination too. Every time you offer him a choice between a trip to the park or a trip to the zoo, or even between an apple and an orange, you're asking him to exercise his imagination, for he must use it to recall the adventures he's had and the fruits he's tasted before he can reach a decision. The child who is asked to shut his eyes and listen hard enough to describe every sound he hears—the blue jay and the diesel brakes; the drier tumbling clothes; scissors clicking—will not only have a better awareness of sounds but a richer reservoir of words, for he becomes more conscious of them. Each time he's pushed to be clever with words, he can express himself better and he can think better too.

The music he hears and the stories you tell also broaden his ideas, but he'll get even more from an activity if he takes part in it—singing, dancing, painting and especially in games of make-believe. For the same reasons, the best toys are also the ones that invite participation, like blocks, a tricycle or a puzzle.

While the potential of each child is different, his need for ingenuity is the same. Imagination gives wings to the intellect.

The Senses

In his early years a child learns only by specific example, never by concepts, and this is most obvious when you help him stretch his sensitivity.

You begin the day he's born, with the teasing of his senses, for even a day-old child can follow moving objects, feel temperature changes and turn his head to sound.

Soon his fingers want to reach whatever he sees and then he wants to smell it, taste it and squeeze it too. He'll make every possible noise, screeching his voice up the wall and dropping it down to the floor simply for the pleasure of hearing such sounds. The joy of each new dawn brings exquisite knowledge to a child. He'll be amazed the first time he rubs satin on his cheek, smells cloves, listens to raindrops or licks a spoon of honey. Every new sensation, every new idea, gives him something else to wonder about.

Sight

Visual stimulation is easy to give, for all things are new to a baby's eyes. Although his sight is blurred in the first weeks, it's still much better than many people assume and he has a strong preference for bright colors. In the hospital, your own face, the glow of a lamp, the movement of people are almost as much as you can offer, but from his first day, you can light a match and, from a distance, pass it back and forth across his vision, so he can try to follow it. This makes the muscles work and there isn't a part of the body that doesn't profit by exercise.

A young child will revel in the pictures and mobiles in his room, but he'll be just as intrigued by the picture on the bread wrapper in the kitchen, the foil gum wrappers in the park, the stop light on the corner. He is so visually oriented he needs picture books before six months are past and at One a full-length mirror, because it always has a picture of his best friend in it: his mirror image will be his favorite conversationalist for the next year.

A child will see the world in technicolor but it's for you to point out the hidden surprises—the pigeon's nest (and the fact that it's almost impossible to catch sight of a baby pigeon), the weathervane on a barn, the "eyebrows" on old brownstones. He needs you to show him that each kind of flower has its own kind of petal, every type of spider its own type of web and every animal a different gait. Once you help a child see the unseen, he'll always see it again.

"I Spy"

You can teach concepts and colors and still prevent trouble with this game. When mischief looks imminent, shout, "I spy something blue," picking the obvious blue chair. Your child will touch everything, while you say no, that's red or brown or whatever, but eventually he gets to the chair and learns the color of blue—indelibly.

You also can spy something square or metal or soft or something that starts with a "t" but use its sound, rather than the letter itself, so he can guess better.

Even a brand-new talker can play if you choose a new word, like "I spy a ruler"—or a rug or a candle. This is a painless way to expand a child's vocabulary and is ideal in a doctor's office or a traffic jam. A Three will want you to guess too.

Touch

Touch is better developed in a newborn than any other sense and is the one most responsive to your attention. Your baby grasps your finger automatically when you put it in his palm and within a few weeks he'll poke his thumb in his mouth, try to squeeze his toes and soon may treasure a terrycloth toy or a magic blanket to tickle his lips.

As he gets older, you'll watch his delight when he rubs his finger along a rubber tire, tries to pinch running water, scrambles his hand through garden soil. A Two can be irritating when he stops to touch the bark of every tree on a walk, but he does it because each texture is different and he wants to touch them all.

A Two sees with his fingertips when he glides them over the contours of a banister, a bench or the edge of a kitchen table. He'll enjoy going with you on a nature trail for the blind and touching the trees with his eyes shut (at least most of the time). The sense of touch is always arrested to some extent, first when you (quite rightfully) stop your baby from yanking your glasses or from bumping a playmate and later when you stop him from picking zinnias in the park.

To touch in freedom, however, helps a child develop the gentleness he needs to cup a flower in his hands or pat a baby's head, so we think you should curb him by rules rather than warnings. If you insist that snacks be eaten at the table and hands be washed before leaving it, there will be fewer fingerprints to wash from the walls and less need to fuss, and when you keep breakables out of reach, you seldom must say, "Don't touch."

Some cities have barnyard zoos where animals can be petted, and museum exhibits where children can feel the sculptures and touch the dinosaur bones: all lovely places to go.

Since touch is the sense that makes sex so sexy, we think it's unwise to start limiting it now.

Grab Bag

A grab bag heightens the sense of touch in a child's fingertips and makes a good guessing game too, with no more reward than the promise of being right.

A Two can feel inside a paper bag, naming easy objects first, like a ball and a nail, and then more difficult ones, like a grape, a square of sandpaper, a napkin ring, a hard-boiled egg, a piece of elbow macaroni (yes, uncooked). As he gets older, he can learn to discriminate between six objects, all about the same size, or only between ones that are round or ones that are square.

Sound

You automatically introduce sound to your baby when he's in the womb, as he listens to your heartbeat—like no other heartbeat in the world—and to your body's noisy symphony.

When he's born, he has the shock of hearing his own cries and begins to adjust to a whole new set of noises. The best will be the music of your own words and your lullabies as soon as you feel less self-conscious about being a mother.

When you get home from the hospital, give your baby more music, through the radio, records, wind chimes, soft bells. Let him have a long, skinny rattle to clutch in his fist, which he can shake for several minutes. The tinkling of a music box or a soft musical toy is excellent and the one toy a newborn should have. If you have an older child let him turn the key: a small task to diffuse some of the jealousy.

Your baby's need for new sounds increases rapidly as he gets older, but he needs to hear these sounds singly and not in unison. Studies show that the child who hears a voice, a record player, a radio and a television simultaneously hears only noise. If he hears one sound, he absorbs it and can develop into a quality listener. A child can't learn in cacophony and, in fact, he savors individuality in all the senses.

Sound Sets

One of the best ways to teach a Four to listen closely is with a game from Montessori, the school

system that stresses the senses so much.

This game is played with a handkerchief and sixteen pairs of small containers, each pair filled with something different. You can make this game yourself by buying one-ounce plastic medicine containers with child-proof caps from your druggist and filling the pairs halfway with rice, water, syrup, gravel, peppercorns, orange pips, 4-penny nails, birdseed, peanuts, lentils, spaghetti sticks, dimes, chips of glass, buttons, bells and bolts—whatever pleases you. Offer only three sets at first, letting your child look at them and shake them, then cover his eyes with the handkerchief so he can shake each container blindfolded, pairing them by their sound alone. Add new pairs as his ears become more attuned to the old ones.

Smell

The stimulation of the sense of smell is often ignored, but it shouldn't be. A child is never too young to learn about lilacs.

Your child will like the smell of his baby lotion and the breath of perfume you wear every morning (and therefore both should be used). Wave a blossom under his nose when you take your carriage walks and in the kitchen let him smell the ingredients you use—the onions and garlic, the apples and oranges, the cinnamon and celery salt.

A mortar and pestle do more to enhance smell than almost anything else. Let your Three pulverize a cinnamon stick or some allspice; a tomato, a strip of green pepper or a handful of rose petals. Other spices, like ginger, are too hard for a child to pulverize but heat can release the smell too.

Odors have a vocabulary of their own and a child wants to learn all the words. In forty years he'll be bathed with warm memories of his father's face when he smells eucalyptus in the shaving cream or of a childhood summer when he smells a vine of warm grapes.

Ginger Tea

We've found this especially good for a cross child with a stuffy nose. In a teacup, have him

Measure   1/8 tsp. powdered ginger
Add   boiling hot water
Pour the water yourself.

Steep   5 minutes

Let him add as much honey and lemon juice as he'd like—the basis of so many good, safe cough medicines.

Taste

This is one sense that's sharper in a baby than in his mother. Salt is saltier, sugar is sweeter, for his taste buds are unsullied.

For the first year a baby uses his mouth as he uses his fingertips, trying to touch his tongue to everything he · sees, tasting every surface, every texture. He often will spit out food, not always because he doesn't like the taste, but because his tongue is savoring the touch, rolling it around his mouth as if he were using it to explore a cave.

Because of possible allergies and because you want eating to be a happy, nutritious experience, you should stimulate the sense of taste quite slowly. A child usually prefers a sweet taste from the first day of his life, perhaps because he needs, and is given, dextrose shortly after birth—or perhaps because sugar tastes so good.

As tempting as it is, beware of giving even a "taste of a cookie" or "just one lollipop" to a six-month-old, for your child is *smart*. He'll never see another cookie or another lollipop again without screaming for it. We think it's no use asking for a tantrum any sooner than you must.

Alcohol seems to cause the same reaction. When you casually offer a sip of beer to your mid-One, you can expect him to reach for any drink he sees—no matter who's drinking it—for years. Although we can't believe alcohol is good for a child, we don't think you should share your cranberry juice either, for his badgering will be a pain. It's easier to give your child his own juice in his own cup when you have a drink.

All children develop some eccentricities in their diet, but the pattern of a truly poor eater is set early, when he's given too many candies or cookies or repeatedly given food he doesn't like, with gritty textures, like fish roe, or dishes with more than one flavor at a time, like stew. This is the way a child learns to say no to his food.

By the time he's mid-Two, he's old enough to be tested on difficult foods like melon and peanuts; in fact, at this point, there's nothing your child can't taste. This is when you begin to stretch his sense of taste, letting him lick not only the bowl of frosting, but also the bowl of chili. Let him eat bagels and lox, some gumbo, a raw clam. He'll never know what he likes until he tries it.

Your child's taste—adventurous or cautious or finicky—will depend on the way you cater to it.

One of our favorite Twos, whose mother buys pomegranates by the case and whose sister gives kosher pickles for birthday presents, was enchanted to find a jar of stuffed olives in her stocking at Christmas. Since they had to be shared (for this was as expected in Suzannah's house as good eating), she couldn't bear to open them until March. This treat, she felt, was just too tasty to share.

Taste Test

If someone could freeze liver in an ice cube, we think a child might like it, for taste is affected by touch as well as smell. He rolls his tongue around anything he puts in his mouth, examining every surface with it, and generally the slicker and smoother it is, the better he seems to like it. After the first year, when most food has been tested, you can let him lick the spoon of anything you cook, shutting his eyes and guessing what it is. Later, have him hold his nose too and see how hard it is to tell what it is without any smell. He'll like this game if you offer only the tastes you think he'll like, for, after all, this is a game to help him discriminate, not to trick him into eating new foods—although he will be a more experimental eater because of it.

Empathy

When a child is born, his senses fairly vibrate with response. There isn't a sensation he doesn't savor, and yet, for all these inborn reactions, he still needs you to arouse his empathy—that sixth and most important sense which only will bloom if you nurture it.

"What If?"

This is a game that brings empathy home to a Four. Ask him what would happen IF

People had wings?

The car was never invented?

You knew what dolphins were talking about?

There was no gravity?

You lived on a bay

or in a castle

or on a farm

Or in a tarpaper shack without plumbing or heat or much to eat?

Mind

The better a child uses his body, the better he can use his mind, because all basic mental skills are built on physical accomplishments. When he transfers his rattle from one hand to the other, reaches for his ball, rolls over, crawls, stands, falls, climbs and walks, he's programming the circuits in his brain in the same patterns he'll need one day to read a story, add numbers or draw abstract conclusions.

Your child registers these patterns when he fights against the obstacles you never knew were there. The battle is repeated intensely each time he grasps a wooden spoon in his fist or coordinates his thumb and forefinger well enough to pick up a scrap of paper, and it continues when he climbs a step over and over or teeters on a little stone wall—both stunts that help his sense of balance and perception. His coordination becomes significantly better as soon as he decides whether he's right-handed or left-handed, for this lets one side of the brain dominate. Until this is set, any learning will be harder.

Slowly your child will begin to master his equilibrium, first by crawling, then by walking on the balancing board (not just forward but backward), riding a scooter, walking on a twisted rope and imitating the gaits of different animals—all of which are preludes to reading.

A child must be given the chance to practice each skill again and again, from learning to stand to tying his shoes. This stretches his attention span and the longer it is, the better he can observe and concentrate. It's this concentration on a task—and the repetition of it—that makes a child so articulate with his body that his mind is freed to think. You can expect your Two to focus intensely on an activity for as long as ten minutes; your Six, as long as thirty.

This concentration is part of his drive for independence, which is why you let him do things for himself. Since anything he does requires a fusion of mental, physical and emotional readiness, he'll need a lot of practice before he can use the potty, clean his closet or learn to read.

Your child gathers the concepts of math when he sorts blocks by sizes or aligns row after row of beans, and he'll get a feeling for science, not just through simple preschool experiments, but through the notice you call to small details—in pictures, in buildings, in people. This gives your child a good eye for observation—the heart of scientific study.

Every young child is logical, not because he knows so much, but because he knows so little. Each day more information will clutter his mind, but if he can pigeonhole his knowledge he can digest it and keep his mind logical and precise all his life.

A child needs both physical and mental order. The first he gets from clearly drawn boundaries, limited choices, the encouragement to finish what he starts, and such specifics as a place to put his toys. Mental order comes from logical questions, which help him use his memory and his imagination to arrive at logical answers. When a child finds his own answers he remembers them better.

He will put himself through many physical exercises, big and little. The more complicated they are the more circuits he'll energize and the easier it will be for him to think. When he connects plumbing pipes and strings beads he's helping his eyes and his hands work together, when he plays Follow the Leader or Simon Says he's coordinating his whole body with his mind, and when he moves his eyes from side to side, rather than up and down, he's preparing them unknowingly for the printed page.

It's tempting to play the schoolmarm at home, teaching your child reading and math as if they were separate entities rather than knowledge woven through life, but he learns from his own actions rather than your lectures and he only learns when his body says it's ready. It is, after all, as hard for a child to identify numbers and letters as it is for you to decipher a code. If he isn't interested in these symbols, fine. That's the way he says that his body and his mind aren't in tune yet for this kind of learning. He'll get there in his own dear time, after he's perfected the physical skills he needs to do it.

The body and the mind are one package. A child can't rush or skip the physical—or the mental—stages any more than the psychological ones.

Symbols

Despite our fascination with computers today, it's important for a child to feel comfortable with letters and numbers, for these symbols are the cybernetics of the mind. A child usually can translate numbers into tangibles and tangibles into concepts long before he can identify letters, but he'll be more interested in the alphabet when you draw the "S" that looks like a snake that goes "hiss" and the "M" that looks like a river, humming along. It's all part of a child's insatiable need to know the reason why.

Mathematics

One child can be as nimble with numbers as another is with paints, but this doesn't happen as often as it should.

An agility for math would be more common, we think, if arithmetic were woven into a child's world before first grade and if so many parents didn't pass on their prejudice against it as if their dislike were genetic. If this has happened to you, we think you should look at math in a fresh way. It's like scanning a column of figures in your checkbook to see if the answer is sensible, rather than adding one digit to the next and perhaps repeating the mistakes. By looking at arithmetic as a mosaic, not a series of unrelated bits, your child can use it as an exciting pastime, whether he has a flair for it or not.

As in anything else, if you do a job with zest, so will your child—a truism demonstrated to us well by one scientist we know who weaved numbers through the minds of her boy and girl until Ben and Missy, at Nine and Eleven, think math is as fascinating as a Nancy Drew mystery.

And she started when they were One.

One
To do this, train yourself to be specific. Instead of promising a walk "in a few minutes," or "after a while," be exact. Say fourteen minutes. It doesn't matter if the time isn't quite accurate, since we have never met a One (or a Six) who could tell time anyway.

Be equally specific about the plane and solid geometry in your life. Give every shape a name—a triangle, a cylinder, a cube or a sphere. Show the logic of math by cutting a cake and pointing out that the wider the angle of the knife, the bigger the slice will be. The more a child can see the rationale of math, the more sense he can make of it later.

Mid-One
This child enjoys counting if you teach him how. Name each object as you count it—one apple, two apples and, of course, only count those objects that are the same, so he won't add apples and oranges when he can count by himself. He'll need this reminder for years.

Most children like to count food best, but our Kate, the chatterbox, regularly counted the steps in her row house: one step, two steps, right up to seventeen, not because she knew what the numbers meant, but because the words amused her.

Two
A Two recognizes that a part is smaller than a whole, as every mother knows who has tried to give her child a cookie that's been broken in half. Even if you fit the parts together, it won't taste as good.

Now your Two begins to fathom concepts. He speaks in numbers, not parroting them like a mid-One but thinking like a primitive tribesman who understands one, two and many. For this you help him by counting together: "one blue car, two blue cars, three blue cars." The concept of zero is clear now too. When he finishes a banana, for instance, he has none left and the example is graphic. This idea is the basis of negative numbers, which is why we think you should say "zero" quite as often as you say "all gone."

Three
Fractions come alive to a Three, for now he can see that a fraction is a number too, coming between

whole numbers like the colors in a spectrum. He can see that an apple cut into fourths is 4/4 of an apple and can be put together and that a pear sliced into fifths is 5/5 which makes a whole pear. Amazingly, he can grasp that 7/6 of a pecan pie is one pecan pie and an extra sixth of another, but they should be pies he can see and touch and eat and, even better, pies he has made.

He won't be able to read fractions of course, but he can recognize a few written numbers, like the ones on his house or the "3" on his cake. He also can count up to ten, but not understand the meaning of a number bigger than his own age.

We have watched mid-Threes in a Montessori school juggle binomial and trinomial cubes, not as a geometric exercise to decipher the formulas of cube and square roots, but as amusing three-dimensional puzzles. However, a child will benefit from these cubes or an abacus only if you know how they work and will explain them as games and not as lessons.

Four
Inexplicably, children love to learn numbers in another language. Our Mali, no genius in math but comical as a clown, learned to count in Spanish. We remember watching her stand on a fence counting uno, dos, tres cows until, instead of eight or "ocho," she shouted "fuchi"—a rather scatological bit of Mexican—to make her family laugh. Mildly dirty words are every child's inspiration—and for her they made math almost spicy.

A Four adores to play store and can add and subtract with beans, marbles, apples, pencils, pennies, fingers and toes. This isn't because he has memorized 3 + 2 = 5 but because he can align the beans, for instance, adding two beans to three beans to get five beans. Slowly he begins to see that each time he adds one bean to the total he is counting one number higher, and if he removes a bean he has one number less. This is the basic concept he will need for arithmetic.

A mid-Four starts to appreciate a little algebra, for he can grasp the concept of variables (a word that still terrifies us), realizing that two oaks can be the same size but each have a different number of leaves.

A child keeps his fresh awareness of mathe-matics as long as it is applicable and practical. This is why you measure the shadow with a yardstick together, pour water by the tablespoon into a graduated cup and make a game of finding parallels in a room.

At this age he'll play store for hours with friends, a cash register, a card table and all your canned goods, which he'll leave strewn about as if you're the worst housekeeper since the Collier brothers' mother.

Five
A Five can learn to find the area of a room not because he can multiply but because he can count. If a room is 10 X 15 he can lay out 10 beans in a row and make 15 rows of tens. He will count every one of them for he has great patience now.

Your Five will like to shop for you, and should, buying bread and counting the change. He'll be much more impressed, however, with the number and weight of a handful of coins than he will be with paper money.

Six
A Six should feel so comfortable with arithmetic when he starts school that he'll savor the new math and even stomach the rote as a way to get his answers in a hurry. Since every mother likes to look ahead, remember that a child who is articulate with numbers develops a sense of logic and a respect for precision—the backbone of dozens of careers, from music to architecture.

Money
The concept of money teaches arithmetic better than anything else. It's tangible, it has a purpose—and adults respect it. As long as you treat it as a commodity, and not the most important thing in your life, a child will use it for the tool that it is.

The Penny Candy Store
When we had three children under Five, such a sense of what-the-hell inevitability overcame us that for a year we invited two more pre-Fives from an orphanage to join us each Sunday. Although they

endured the museums and were amused by the zoo, it was the weekly trip to the penny candy store that delighted them.

The five walked, stiff and tense, palms sweaty from squeezing their pennies. Each got an equal number—four or three or six—but never a nickel or a dime, for the concept of change is impossible now. Once in the little store, they pressed their noses to the glass like Norman Rockwell figures, choosing candies and then exchanging them, almost as fast. At home they opened their small paper sacks, smelled the candies, licked an occasional one and traded some more: five children who learned what pennies meant.

Although these stores and their patient owners are vanishing—small reason why—the dimestores and supermarkets have penny selections, and self-service works almost as well.

Playing Store

By now your Four may start saying, "Buy me" to everything he sees, which you won't do, of course, but playing store will satisfy him a little bit.

The props need be no more elaborate than a card table and some canned goods, but you'll want a sturdy cash register, for it will get hard use. It should jingle, its numbers should jump and its door should pop open sharply as a jack-in-the-box. The earlier you let your child use real coins, the quicker he can understand how to make change.

The One Dollar Game

On one long, long car ride, we instituted the One Dollar Game—100 pennies if our Five could count to 100 without falter or flaw. This wasn't given, we tell ourselves still, as a bribe for good behavior or a payment for work, but because money translates 100 more graphically than anything else. For Mike, we gave a 50-cent piece, a quarter, a dime, two nickels and five pennies, which explained it even better. Anyone would rather count money than beans.

Cards

A deck of cards, with its symbols, colors, pictures and numbers, teaches a child to classify—an essential part of learning. First he separates cards into reds and blacks, then into suits, but even

before he's old enough to put them in numerical order he's ready for some card games.

Battle

A Four is ready to play a simple game like Battle where winning and losing are obfuscated by all the action and the hours it takes to play. Two players split a deck, each playing one card at a time with the higher card taking the match, and a rematch in case of a tie. Since the winner must take all the cards, the game is seldom finished.

Concentration

This game reinforces a child's memory skills at the same time it teaches numbers. A Four can play Concentration with you if you use only five pairs from a deck, but a Six can use them all.

Lay the cards singly and face down, in orderly rows. Each player has a chance to turn over two cards at a time and at random, and if he finds a pair he gets another turn. If the cards don't match—which they seldom do at first—they're turned down again in the same place. When the next player chooses his first card he hopefully remembers where to find its mate. The player with the most pairs wins, but it better not be you. A Six isn't ready to lose to anybody.

Reading

When a child can read even a few simple words, he experiences the same glorious boost to his ego as he did when he learned to talk.

There's nothing in the chemical or biological make-up of people that prevents reading before Six. Some children—the ordinary variety, mind you—can translate speech into sight reading if taught in simple, relaxed games. Later when a child recognizes the letters in a word and can connect their sounds, he is reading. He may learn sight reading as early as Two (a rare occurrence) and phonetic reading as late as Seven, which happens more often. By the start of second grade, a child should be able to read simple books with some ease and if he can't he should be tested to find out why. When the reading problem is defined, it's easier for a teacher to choose the right approach to help that particular child.

A child's ability to read depends on his control over his muscles—the coordination of his hands with his eyes—but he must be interested too. This depends not only on how he's taught, but how important books are to you, how many he has and how often you read them to him.

However, never teach a child to read—or to do anything else—for your own pleasure. This not only will be damaging, but it won't give him a head start in school either. Just as an early walker doesn't predict an athlete, neither does an early reader reveal a genius.

Pre-reading

We never figured how to teach our children to read before they went to school, but the alphabet was a cinch. The daily newspaper was the best tool, as it allowed us to point out letters by sight, by order and especially by sound—the basis of phonetics.

Pick out a capital "A" in a headline, say it by name and by its short sound, for a child can't learn more than one sound and the short one is the simplest. Let him draw over the letter, then circle all the other As on the page. In a day or two, when he has a fair grasp of the letter "A," go on to "B" and have him circle both As and Bs in the headlines. Continue this routine at his pace until he learns the whole alphabet. Unless he was pushed, he'll be very pleased with himself for he'll see letters everywhere, pointing them out for you on signs, in books and by singing about them with his alphabet record.

Another mother had great luck with stiff letters she made of corrugated cardboard so big her child almost could play through them as well as with them.

It helps any child to involve his whole body in the making of letters, even if he only imagines them. To do this, let him use his arms to draw them in the air, as children with dyslexia are taught to do.

We recommend the consistent use of capital letters in all these techniques, simply because most schools do the same. If he's learned all the upper-case letters before first grade you then can introduce lower case.

As your child learns his alphabet, he will want to stick magnetic letters to the refrigerator or felt letters on a flannel board. This keeps him familiar with letters, although he may not try to combine sounds until first grade.

Sight Reading

We once knew a mother who taught her Two to read many simple words within a year. She created a book for her daughter, drawing and coloring pictures of simple nouns like MAMA, DADDY and BALL, printing the words beside them in capital letters and binding the pages in ribbon. Annie carried her book everywhere, for anything a mother makes for her child has enormous impact. She would ask her mother to write down a word or two wherever they were, just for the joy of reading them again. Her interest flourished with these relaxed, one-minute lessons and as the book got fatter, she was able to read many simple words. Because it was treated so casually, Annie never realized how extraordinary that was.

Even without making a book, any child will like to see you write simple words when he says them—especially if you put them on a postcard, for him to get in the mail the next day. These first lessons in sight reading will trigger his interest in all reading, but you shouldn't expect him to get beyond this point until he starts first grade.

Phonetic Reading

If you expect to teach reading phonovisually, as it's done in any good school, you should use phonovisual charts, records and about six months of lessons—more pressure than we think a prekindergartner should feel. Just knowing letters, sounds and a few sight words is enough to enchant most children.

Reading Clocks

You can't expect a preschool child to tell time but you can help him grasp its concept better if you use precision when you talk, like "fifteen minutes after twelve," rather than "around noon," and if you let him set the timer for the rice and put the money in the parking meter. When your child knows his numbers by sight, he may understand that the little hand points only to the hour, but the big hand will baffle him. You only can hope that he'll remember which is the before side and which the after. It helps if you give him a cardboard clock from the stationer's—the kind with a face that says "Be Back at ——," so he can spin the cardboard hands the way he's told and hang it on the front door when you take a walk.

Reading Maps

So your Six can learn to use streets and numbers too, draw a big freehand map of the few blocks around your house. Name the streets and let him color the stores and churches and the places where friends live. Naturally, his house will be in the center.

Science

Once a bright, bright child named Eliza, a mid-One, amazed her parents when she pointed to the first real horse she ever had seen and said, "Horsey!" Clearly, the picture books her mother had shown her, and the prancing and neighing like a horse had been a success. And then the next day Eliza, sprawled on the kitchen floor, pointed to a train of ants and said, "Horsey, horsey, horsey."

The conclusion was as logical as it was erroneous. Until a child knows that horses, ants and dogs are called animals, he has to find a word that fits; no puzzles are permitted in a small child's head. Instead, his conclusions are based on the little he knows and the many things he sees.

A child needs to examine all things closely and find their points of similarity and their points of difference so his knowledge can rest on firm foundations. This testing, either by experience or by observation, is the heart of science and he must do it as much as he can. He'll feel tall next to a seedling, almost equal to a sapling, small near an oak, but dwarfed beside a television tower. Every new fact, every new experience make him sort and reclassify his information, so that each fact is relative to the next.

When your child organizes his collection of cars, beads or shells, he's sorting them by size, by color or by favorites, as carefully as he sorts the ideas in his head. You'll find him classifying the intangibles too, curious about the dandelion that's alive but doesn't move and the wind that moves though it isn't alive. He'll wonder what happens to the sugar in the lemonade, to the milk when the batter is baked or to the moon when he goes to bed. The answers, so obvious to you, are a discovery to a child.

You'll not only want to answer his own lively questions but also the ones he hasn't thought to ask. This is when you teach him about concepts like gravity, explaining how the spinning earth keeps his feet on the ground, that all the world is made of matter and all matter is made of molecules; that energy comes from a hundred sources and that gasoline is an unimportant source compared to the sun. When your child jumps, runs, scrubs a table, kicks a ball, kneads dough or picks up his toys, he's using energy, but energy is also used when the rays of the sun make the plants grow, the current in a stream carries a log and the campfire roasts the marshmallows.

If his experiences are broad he'll have a smattering of every science. He'll learn some botany when he gardens and some biology through the care of pets, while the blocks he stacks teach him about physics, and cooking can explain chemistry. It will be the basic experiments of science, however, that help your child understand and value the laws of nature. When he can examine air, heat, light and water as separate entities and use the same sort of wheels, ramps and pulleys that built the Roman roads, he'll recognize one day that concrete examples are the basis of abstract concepts.

You'll want to use scientific terms when he does the experiments in this section because symbols, either in words or on paper, help you be precise and they help him express himself accurately. You also should have him use small containers to hold the ingredients he adds, since any child becomes so interested in the pouring that he can forget the point of the experiment.

Some of these experiments require many steps, like lifting a weight with a pulley or making a volcano erupt, while others, like tracing shadows or making a water lens, are very simple. The best experiments are the ones your child can do almost entirely alone. This is how he makes sense out of science.

Water

Water is sure to make a baby laugh more than anything else, but as much as he enjoys splashing in it, nothing will baffle him quite so much. He can sit in it, pour it and shake it, yet he can't pick it up in his hands. It's in the faucets, the ocean and the skies, sometimes fresh or salty; sometimes clear, green or brown—an astonishing creation.

A Two can spend hours pouring water back and forth from one cup to another, letting it trickle through his fingers. When a Three tries to float dishes and toys in the kitchen sink, he'll discover that glass and crockery fall to the bottom; that a sponge will float and so will crayons and blocks (because wax and wood can float), but only some metals, and only in some shapes, can ride the water.

Later he can check this if you help him roll, bend, fold, wad and flatten foil, finding, like every sailor before him, that the shape of a boat floats best. A Four wants to understand how the water can only be horizontal and how it seeks its own level. By now he's most curious to find why sugar and salt and baking soda dissolve in water but pepper, sand and cinnamon don't, and why some liquids, like milk and chocolate syrup, will unite and others, like oil and vinegar, are as unfriendly as some people and avoid each other as much as possible.

Evaporation and Condensation

When a Five starts to wonder what happens to the mud puddles or where the dew comes from, he's ready for experiments on evaporation and condensation.

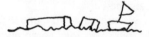

Humidity
The air in an average-sized room usually has eight cups of water suspended in it. Although no one can see the water floating about—since it's been broken into molecules—a child can believe it when he makes his own humidity. In a pot

Measure   8 c. water

Let him place it near a radiator or a sunny window and measure it daily for the next few weeks until there isn't any left at all.

Dew
Your child can bring some of the evaporated water back by filling a metal pitcher or a glass with ice and leaving it untouched for a few minutes, until the container is covered with dew. This begins to teach him that the cold air around the pitcher has cooled the wayward molecules of moisture and turned them back to water again. The chill from the ice turns mist to moisture, just as it does outdoors when the cool night squeezes the air dry and leaves dew on the grass. Your child may be surprised to learn that the grass really has nothing to do with the dew. It will settle on anything that's handy—the house, the car in the driveway or himself if he is out in the cold night air.

Rain
Any child who has seen steam rising from a boiling kettle has seen heat change liquid into a gas. If he pretends that the steam is a cloud in the sky your Six can see how the cloud carries water and with your help, he even can make it fall from the steam again like rain.

Boil a kettle of water and fill a sauce pan with ice, choosing a long-handled one so you won't burn yourself. Hold the pan about 4 inches from the spout, tilting it enough so the ice doesn't spill. Almost immediately the chilled pot will change the steam back into drops of water—the way cold air changes a cloud of humidity into raindrops. If your child puts a cup under the saucepan, he can measure how much rain he's made.

Water Levels

The report of a study of college students found that most boys pass this test and most girls don't. We don't believe that for a minute—even if it did work that way for us.

Have your Four partly fill a clear glass with water, showing him how the level of water is parallel with the table. Tip the glass for him and then ask if the water is still horizontal. If your child thinks the water tips as well as the glass do the experiment again, holding a pencil even with the surface so he can see that the glass tips, but the water always remains level.

Skin Test

In science a child learns—but only if you tell him—that everything in the world has an invisible skin, which is called surface tension. Nothing proves it quite so well as water. This skin, as delicate as it is, stretches over water like a rubber sheet. Show him how insects can skate across the surface of a pond, how a superthin razor blade can be dropped flatly and lightly to rest on top of a bowl of water and how the water in a teacup can curve slightly above its rim without spilling.

Your Five can use any kitchen spice and a bar of wet soap to prove that water does indeed have a skin. When he sprinkles the spice into a bowl of water, the tiny grains will rest on the skin. If he pokes his fist or a spoon into the water the spice hardly budges, but when he dunks the soap into it, the spice skitters away before the soap molecules weaken the surface tension, releasing the energy to chase the grains away—the same way they chase dirt from the clothes in the washing machine.

Light

A child's eyes track light from the day he's born and they'll keep doing it for the rest of his life. He'll follow the glow that filters from the moon, a street lamp, the night light, the luminous hands on a clock or a firefly. As he gets older you can help him experiment with light.

A Two will like to work in a dim room with a flashlight of his own (taped shut so he won't dismantle it). Just by shining it about he'll discover that light travels almost forever in a straight line, cutting through glass or paper, but not around corners or through wood or foil. He'll find it magnified when he flashes it in a mirror and that it turns his face into a horror show when he stuffs the lighted end in his mouth—a trick he'll enjoy again at Six, and by then he'll be brave enough to do it alone in the dark.

Brilliant sunshine can give color its full depth as he'll find when he looks at multicolored fabrics under the noon sun. Some, like tan, hardly change. Some, like blue, soothe the eyes. And others, like yellow and orange, are dazzling. But when night falls, colors fade into a common drabness—which is why all cats are gray in the dark.

Your child also can learn how to splinter white light into a spectrum, using a prism or a spray of hose water against the sun to bend the rays until they open like a fan, separating into a rainbow of purple, violet, red, orange, yellow, green and blue.

Shadows

When a child plays with shadows, he's really playing with light. A Two will enjoy reflecting his fingers on the walls to make pictures at night, and a

Four will find his shadow is a friend on a lonely day outdoors: someone to chase when he's silly and hit when he's mad. With company, a shadow becomes a foil in tag, as children catch each other by stepping on their shadows—a particularly good game for the late afternoon, when shadows are longest and tempers are shortest.

By Six, your child will be skilled enough to chalk the shadow of some immovable object, like a fence post, on the sidewalk. This lets him see how big it is at the start and the end of the day and how small it is at noon—changes that are apparent even in fifteen minutes. In this way a child gathers his first concept of the movement of the earth around the sun—but only if you explain it.

Lenses

Lenses come in six basic shapes and every one of them bends light, not enough to make a rainbow, but enough to make the eye see better. They may be made of glass or plastic or even water, but at least one side must be curved.

A Six may be able to understand that sometimes only one lens makes an eyeglass and sometimes more must be fused together to get the right correction, but even a Two can see that a convex lens will enlarge a picture, whether with a magnifying glass, the side of a jar, a silver spoon or a drop of water.

At first he'll be less interested in the lens than in his own reflection. When he looks into the concave bowl of the spoon, he'll be upside down and when he turns it over to the convex side he'll look broad, chubby and silly enough to make him feel the curve of each surface and peer into the shiny sugar bowl, the toaster and the refrigerator handle as if they were fun-house mirrors.

Magnifying Glass

Giving a child a magnifying glass is like giving him an extra eye; there seems to be no limit to what he can see.

A mid-Two puts it up to his thumb and yours, his father's big nose and the baby's little toes. The glass is taken on more outings than anything else, for it gives him the chance to examine leaves, grains, rocks and wood. For this you'll want to buy the inexpensive magnifier with a handle, which is easier for him to focus. The better the lens, the more carefully he'll have to hold it, since it must be

held exactly the right distance above the specimen for him to see clearly. The best magnifier, beginning at Three, is a large one set in the center of a child-sized stool, so the legs regulate the distance.

Sponge Sprouts

You almost can see some seeds sprout, particularly if you use a magnifying glass to watch them grow on a sponge. Set one in a cake pan with 1" of water and on it have your Three

Sprinkle   1 tsp. grass/radish/birdseed

Set the pan in a warm place and have your child add enough water to keep the sponge wet. This garden will sprout in about 48 hours.

Magnified Matter

A child has a hard time believing in molecules, but the idea seems more sensible to a Four when he can examine a sugar cube, charcoal, chalk or a clay shard by breaking it to pieces to study under a magnifying glass. First have him crack a cube of sugar, then break it into small chunks, then crumble it into grains and finally pulverize it with a hammer until he can see that even powder is made up of particles. Like most of his laboratory work, this is best done outside.

Water Lens

Your Five can make a lens out of a drop of water and because the surface is convex, the lens becomes a magnifier. Since the water wobbles if he moves it, this isn't too practical, but it does teach the principle of a convex lens very well. To make it

Assemble   1 dark crayon
                  eyedropper
                  a piece of window glass (any size)

Lay the clean, dry glass over a newspaper. Have him use the crayon to draw a freehand circle on it, about the size of a penny, pressing hard to make the wax stick to the glass. He should fill the eyedropper with water and release a drop of it at a time until the circle is filled and the letters in the paper beneath it look bigger. If he adds too much water it will spill over the boundary and there will be no curve—and therefore no magnification. Dry the glass so he can make many more lenses and discover that they come in all sizes. The fun of this experiment is more in the making than the looking.

Air

Since air is invisible, a child never stops to think about it unless you mention it first—and even then he may think you're fooling. Somehow he's supposed to believe that he can't see it and yet it's there and that it's terribly strong and yet—as little as he is—he can push right through it.

If he believes all that, he's a trusting child—and you're a powerfully fine teacher.

While your child has seen the wind bend treetops and bang the back door shut, he'll need some experiments before he can understand that the air that surrounds him on a still summer day is the same as the wind that whips his hat away. It just isn't going anywhere.

He begins to believe it's a substance if he can lock it inside a bubble, and for this he can blow through a straw into water. He also can water the soil of an extremely dry flower pot and watch bubbles collect on top. If you blow up a balloon for him he can see that air takes up space, and when you tie it and put a lightweight toy or a couple of socks on top of it, he can see that the balloon is strong enough to support it. This is the way a child learns that there is no such thing as nothing. Air fills the empty wastebasket just as it fills his shoe when his foot isn't in it and his cup until the milk is poured, with more returning every time he takes a swallow.

When he realizes that air is all round him, he can accept the idea that it's pushing against his head, his fanny and his ribs, with a pressure that would be strong enough to crush him if he didn't have enough air inside him to balance the force—the same principle that keeps all things from exploding or collapsing, from the box turtle to the boxwood.

If you start early enough and simply enough a child can understand almost anything.

Experiments with Air

When these tests are done, your child still may wonder if air is really everywhere but he can't have any doubts about water and neither will you. After he finishes playing with a dishpan full of it, water will be everywhere. Work outdoors.

Experiment I

To make this experiment work, let your Four use a dishpan and a slightly shorter glass to put in it. Have him turn the glass upside down and plunge it straight to the bottom of the pan. The water will try to rush in but the air pressure in the glass will fight to keep it out. The air wins and only a very little bit of water will enter the glass. Your child can put his finger inside it and check for himself that it's still dry. If he tips the glass as he plunges it into the water he'll see air bubbles escape from the jar and rise to the surface.

Experiment II

Instead of a glass, give your Four an empty plastic carton with a small hole punched in the bottom and have him plunge the carton upside down into the pan with his finger a half inch above the hole, so he can feel the air coming out of the container as the water rises in it. If you dry the carton he can try the experiment again, plugging the hole with his finger. The carton with its plugged hole will stay as dry as the glass in the first experiment.

Parachutes

A Five knows that all things fall down eventually, but he doesn't know that the same things fall at different rates of speed if they are in different shapes—all because of the air's resistance. To show him this principle, give him two sheets of typing paper and have him crumble one into a wad. He can let them go at the same time to discover that the flat sheet takes longer to fall than the crumbled one because the flat sheet has a bigger surface and the air resists it more, slowing down the fall. He'll understand this better if he makes a parachute out of cloth and string, with a small block of wood or a key for the weight.

Cut   15″ square of fabric
               four 16″ lengths of string
Help him tie each string to a corner of the cloth

and tie the four loose ends around the block like a package. Your child will toss parachutes into the air and watch them fall again and again for the next five years. So far Nell has made 127.

Sound

After a child learns that light can travel in a straight line, he's ready to learn that sound does not.

A pebble tossed in a pond explains it best, for the shaky rings of water radiate from the splash like sound waves, engulfing twigs and rocks but getting less and less distinct the farther they travel. The bigger the stone, the bigger the splash and the more distinct the vibrating waves. A shout is like a big stone; a whisper like a pebble.

Your Two will be pleased to find that some sound vibrations—like those of a guitar string—can be both seen and heard. When he sings he can hear the sound with his ears and feel the vibrations if he stretches his fingers to touch the side of his throat, his nose and his jawbone. He also can hear the difference between a noise and a note of music and, even though he can't count the number of vibrations in a note, he'll be curious to know that each one must have a set number of them in a second to ring true.

Unlike light, which can travel through a vacuum, sound waves must flow through a medium. Some media, like air and water, are very good conductors of sound, and others, like cotton batting, foam rubber or feathers, muffle it.

A Four finds that metal, glass and wood conduct sound too, if he puts his ear against a door, a metal cabinet or a glass pane while you rap on the other side. To test air as a conductor, let him collect sound waves from it by putting a cone of cardboard to his ear; he also can put the cone up to his mouth to amplify the waves of his own voice.

Water, however, makes the best test of all, if only because it's a child's favorite toy. Have him sit in a full bathtub and rest his ear on the water while you splash a few pennies into the tub. When they strike the bottom it will prove that water not only carries sound but amplifies it, which is why whales can hear each other talking three hundred miles

192

away, even though they have no ears poking out of their sleek heads.

Tuning Fork

Your Five can make a classic telephone by connecting two cans with a long piece of string. Unfortunately, children have been disappointed by such toy phones for decades, since the voice is barely carried and a child usually can hear his colleague as easily without this phone as with it. To make the principle clearer, cut one yard of string and tie a fork in the center. Have him hold one end of the string in each ear while the fork hangs down, keeping the string taut. He then walks around, striking the fork against a desk, a stove, a table leg—whatever's around. He'll be amazed how loud and clear each bump sounds and how well a simple length of string can carry vibrations directly to his ear.

Thunder

A storm is the finest show that nature can produce, releasing vast quantities of energy as it scrubs the air as clean as an hour in the tub cleans him. To many children, however, it's about as scary as a spook show.

We've found science takes some of the mystery—and therefore the fear—out of thunder and at the same time teaches a child that light does indeed travel faster than sound.

Use a globe and a watch with a secondhand to show your Four that light is so fast it could go around the earth seven times in just one second. And then take a four-block walk and tell him that sound is so slow it takes a second to go just that far. Once he accepts the idea that the sound of a thunderclap comes long after the sight of the lightning, he's ready to measure the distance to the point where the lightning struck. He can do it if he counts slowly from the time he sees the flash until he hears the thunder, measuring a mile for every five seconds, so that fifteen seconds are three miles, ten seconds are two miles, five seconds are one mile—and one second is unfortunate.

Heat

Heat is as ubiquitous as air, but unless it's uncomfortable, it almost goes unnoticed.

Quite properly you've warned your baby against "hot" before he can talk, but by Three he can begin to treat heat more as a friend than an enemy. Without it, his food couldn't cook, his plants couldn't grow and when he gets sick his body couldn't burn the germs with its fever.

The more your child understands about heat,

the more curious he'll be to do experiments and learn to read the thermometer outside his window. It will be years, however, before your child truly realizes that everything in the world has a temperature—not just the fire in the barbecue and the ice in the freezer, but the heat in his kitchen, in his pencil and certainly in himself. He'll be surprised to find out that the 98.6° temperature that registers on the thermometer outside his window in July is the same as the temperature inside of him, all year long.

Heat Energy

The energy of heat will stir water, as your Five will find when he dyes water near a sunny window. Have him fill one glass with cold water, the other with hot. Into each

Add   2 drops food coloring

The color acts as a tracer so he can see that hot water is a swirling force, for it mixes the dye evenly, while most of it sinks in cold water.

Conductors

Everything has heat, but it has it in different degrees, and everything conducts heat, but some things, like metal, conduct it better than others. Even the metals themselves differ, as your Five can find with a quarter, a nickel, a dime, a penny and four ice cubes.

Have him lay a coin on each one, leaving them alone for a few minutes—until the heat of the room can transfer through the metal and into the ice. Help your child lift each coin with a knife blade (a trickier feat than you might think). He'll find the nickel is the worst conductor, because it makes the least imprint of all, and the penny is the best, for the copper etches deepest.

Insulation

Unless there's some insulation to block it, heat flows like water to make all temperatures equal. A child can understand this flow when he watches his ice cream melt in a warm room and learns that as the ice cream gets warmer, the air above it gets colder.

The observation becomes more graphic when you have him put an ice cube on a plate and one inside a mitten. He'll find the one on the plate melts quicker, because the mitten keeps the warm air in the room from entering just the way it keeps the cold air out of his mittened hands in wintertime.

When your Four wraps his hands around a cup of hot chocolate he's learning that his hands take heat away from the cup and into themselves, but when he puts them around a glass of iced water, they'll raise the water's temperature enough to melt the ice.

Hot Air

At one time or another, your child is sure to ask why cigarette rings and campfire smoke go up; why those wavy lines squiggle over a hot pavement and what good are chimneys anyway.

A Five can feel for himself that heat rises, by putting his hands first above and then below both a light bulb and a radiator. There is always more warm air above.

The proof is more memorable with a plastic sandwich bag, a jar, a saucepan and a stove. Fit the bag over the neck of a jar, wrapping a rubber band around it to make it fit tightly. Have him set the bottle with 1" of water in the pan and put it over low heat for five minutes. Indeed it is true. As the air in the bottle gets warm, it will rise and inflate the sandwich bag. It won't puff completely but it will puff enough for him to feel the pressure. Hot air rises and—the experiment has a double lesson—it also expands.

Friction

A little bit of friction holds a family together and too much will tear it apart, just like it does to anything else.

If you have the sort of Four who wears down the heels of his shoes before they ever need a shine he has had a clear lesson in friction. On the one hand it's a culprit—always rubbing away at a surface—and on the other hand it's like glue. If the

nails that hold the heel in place were as slick as icicles they would fall from the shoe, for there would be little friction, and without friction there would be no bond.

Your child either can erase some of the friction around him, by making a surface more slippery—or he can create more. To prove it, have him examine the ridges and whorls on his hands that give him the friction to open a jar, then have him erase the friction by rubbing them with wet soap, so they are too smooth to turn the lid.

He also can sharpen a stick by scratching it to a point on the sidewalk until it's warm to the touch, an experiment which helps him understand that friction can create so much heat it even may send sparks.

And then on the day he falls and scrapes his knee, you can tell him that the friction between the knee and the sidewalk wore away the skin. And he'll cry, just the same.

Tools

Like you, a child can multiply his strength with tools and do work he couldn't possibly do alone. Some tools are big, powerful and complicated like a concrete mixer, others are fragile like a straw or pretty like a teaspoon. Most tools were designed for just one purpose—a hammer, a garlic press or a needle—but if your child understands tools well enough he can be inventive with them.

All hand tools combine the principles of the five basic ones: the lever, the inclined plane, the wheel and axle, the wedge and the pulley. Every child is interested in tools, but he'll like them even more if you identify them by their technical names and give him the chance to use each one.

Lever

A pair of shears, a shovel, a nail clipper, a spoon, a seesaw, a car jack and even your child's lower jaw are levers, for a lever is any tool that moves to lift or pry. A child know that his scissors won't cut if the blades are apart, and the seesaw is no fun unless it rests on a stand—or, as it's called in the tool game, a fulcrum.

Your child can dig with a shovel, eat his ice cream with a spoon and even borrow his father's jack to raise the coffee table, but he won't understand how much work a level and its fulcrum do until at Five he makes his own. For this he'll need a wooden plank about four feet long to serve as the lever, a large rock, a sturdy box or a concrete block to be the fulcrum and a bag of something heavy from the garden shed or the kitchen as the weight he will lift.

Have your child rest the lever on the fulcrum with the weight on one end, but for safety you'll have to steady it. Like a seesaw, the plank can hit him when he lets the other end go. After a few tries he can slide the plank up and down the fulcrum to understand that the longer the lever extends, the more force it has.

Inclined Plane

An inclined plane, as stuffy as it sounds, will intrigue a Four by its very simplicity. It's the bedway of his slide and the gangplank to a boat as well as the ramp that carries furniture into a moving van, wheel chairs into the museum and toy cars down the box he tilts. As your child will learn from the hills on a hike, the longer the incline, the gentler the slope and the easier it is to climb it.

Wedge

A wedge is a little inclined plane, like the ones your child has in his box of blocks, but a wedge can be as skinny as a blade or as fat as a doorstop. The chisel that cracks a brick, like the hatchet that splits a log, are wedges too, but so is a dull knife slicing through cheese—and that's a wedge that is safe enough to use.

Wheel and Axle

While a child tries to push every chair, every toy, every shoe box around the house from the time he can toddle, he'll automatically invent the wheel and axle when he gets his first wooden construction set—a glorious day. You'll watch him painstakingly fit a rod through a disc (which you'll call a wheel and axle), but it will be months before even the most mechanically minded Two will put a disc at each end of a rod to make a set of wheels (which you'll also call a wheel and axle). By Five, when your child is a champion truck pusher, you can show him how the axle turns the small hub of the wheel to make the big rim turn. Although they both will turn the same amount of times, the rim will go much further. The moral of this story: the bigger the rim, the faster the wheel will go—although it does take more energy to push it.

Pulley

The principle of the pulley—the oddest of all the tools—is the most complicated for a child (or a mother) to understand. The fact is, a pulley enables your child (or you) to lift a weight with half the effort it would otherwise require.

Start by letting your Two lift an encyclopedia in his hands to see how heavy it is and then tie some twine around it, leaving a long tail for you to drape over the pole in the closet. When he pulls on this string he can feel how much easier it is for him to lift the book, although it will be years before he can understand the neat relationship between the distance an object is moved by the pulley and the effort it takes to move it.

A Five is ready for a back yard experiment with real pulleys and a rope from the hardware store, so he can try to lift something too heavy for him to move alone. When you add another pulley, he'll find he can lift twenty pounds and it will feel like five, because every time one more pulley is added, his effort is halved—comforting information for the child who spends hours figuring how to move mountains and monuments. Now he knows.

Magnets

A magnet is one of the best friends a curious Two can have. At first the Chinese used lodestones for magnets, but the ones today are made of hard iron or steel that have been permanently magnetized. Their strength will vary from the industrial magnet, so powerful it can lift huge girders, to a child's horseshoe magnet, just strong enough to gather slag in the street. It's one tool of learning that seems to have a touch of mystery, and the more a child learns about a magnet, the more mysterious it becomes.

While you know that only iron and steel are attracted irresistibly to magnets, your child does not. Let him try the refrigerator door, the tacks on the carpet, the scissors, needles, pins, pliers, hammer and nails. He only can be certain that a piece of metal contains iron if he touches it with his magnet and feels a pull.

Even though a magnet isn't attracted to cloth, glass, paper, plastic, pottery or wood, its magnetic force passes through them. To test this, have your Five lay a paper clip on a stiff sheet of bond, moving the magnet beneath the paper to pull the clip. He also can repeat the experiment by putting the clip on an aluminum pan and running the magnet beneath it or by putting it in a jar. Even if it contains water, the clip will skate around the glass.

Magnet Making

A Six can make a magnet himself, although it will be temporary. Teach him to rub a nail against the end of a permanent magnet about twenty times—always in the same direction—until the nail can attract a paper clip. When the nail loses its magnetism, he can recharge it by rubbing it on the mother magnet.

He also can make magnets with only a momentary life span by using his permanent magnet to attract pins, paper clips or any lightweight iron that is easy to bend. It will lift them up like a row of elephants, with each paper clip hanging onto the other one's tail, because each clip becomes a magnet and draws the one next to it. The clips lose their magnetism as soon as the magnet is removed.

Magnetic Poles

A Six first discovers that a magnet has magnetic poles and then a magnetic field.

All magnets, no matter their size or shape, have more force at their ends than at their centers. To test this, have your child lay a piece of brown paper over a magnet and sprinkle the paper with as many as a hundred pins, which will skitter to either end of the magnet.

If you lay a paper plate over a magnet and crumble steel wool all over its surface your child can see the radius of its energy—the magnetic field.

Bar Magnet

If your Six has two bar magnets he can discover not only that a magnet is strongest at its poles but that one pole is different from the other. Have him place the two magnets end to end, almost touching each other, so he can see if the magnets pull together. If they do he's put the opposite poles next to each other and learned that great truth of love and science: opposites attract.

To show your child how each magnet has a north pole and a south pole, help him tie a string around the center of each bar magnet and hang one string from one end of a clothes hanger and one from the other, far enough apart for the magnets to swing freely without interacting. When they've

stopped twirling and hang parallel, show him that one end points north and the other points south (which you can figure by the rising of the sun). Let him mark the poles "N" and "S" and, facing north like the magnet itself, he can learn that west is to his left and east to his right.

Energy

Energy comes in many forms, but the experiments your Five likes best are either dramatic or goofy.

Homemade Gas

Air has energy and a child can see it if he makes a fuel of carbon dioxide. In a paper cup

Combine 1 tbsp. baking soda
    2 tbsp. vinegar

Volcano

This combination of vinegar and baking soda, if mixed with powder paint, will look a little like an erupting volcano—especially since your Six never has seen one.

Cover the table with about 8 layers of newspapers, put a small, inverted flower pot on them—to serve as a pedestal—and set a mug on it. Staple a piece of construction paper into a cone. Trim the bottom so the volcano will be level and adjust the top of the cone so it fits the size of the mug. To make the lava, use a 6-oz. paper cup for every color. Into each one

Blend   4 tbsp. baking soda
    1 tsp. powder paint

Drop the cup through the cone and into the mug (which keeps it steady), and into it

Pour   ¼ c. vinegar

When its overflow stops, add another quarter cup of vinegar to prolong the eruption. After this display, remove the paper cup and drop the next one into place and add the vinegar, continuing until all the colors are used. You may be ready to quit, but your child wants to use every color—and still will be ready for more.

Dancing Garden

This same carbon dioxide form of energy can provoke a lot of laughs. Make the garden in a goldfish bowl of stones/buttons/beads. In a jar, let your Five

Mix   3 c. water
                2 tsp. baking soda
                1 c. vinegar

Pour it slowly into the bowl to make the gas.

Add   20 mothballs

Do this yourself, for mothballs are poisonous. The balls will bounce up and down, fizzing as they go. When the bubbling stops, reactivate the garden with an occasional sprinkle of soda.

Crystal Garden

These snowy salt crystals grow for three days, clustering together like little cauliflowers. Have your Six prepare the bed first and then in a pie pan let him

Combine   6 charcoal brickettes
              6 clay shards

In a glass

Mix   4 tbsp. noniodized salt
                4 tbsp. liquid bluing
                4 tbsp. water

He should mix the ingredients in this order, stirring with a wooden spoon until the salt is partially dissolved. You must use regular salt, since any trace element inhibits the growth of crystals.

Add   1 tbsp. ammonia

This is needed because crystals grow best in an alkaline solution. There will be a dramatic change in color—from blue to a muddy brown. Have him stir it some more, then drizzle it into the pan, making certain that the sediment of salt falls over both the coals and the shards. The crystals begin to grow immediately and last about three days, but the strong odor of ammonia disappears in about an hour. For bright (but tacky) colors, your child can add a few drops of Mercurochrome or food coloring on each lump of coal, right after he's poured the solution.

Rubber Egg

This experiment in quiet energy produces a fascinating, if short-lived toy. It doesn't even smell bad when it breaks. Have your Six slip a raw egg, still in its shell, into a clear glass jar with a mouth wider than the egg since it will expand. Fill the jar with white vinegar, cover and let it rest for two weeks.

As the shell and the vinegar combine, your child will see tiny bubbles form on the shell—a sign that the acid is acting on the alkaline shell and slowly dissolving it. Your child may open the jar regularly to test very gently how it feels; if he's rough at first he may crack the shell. The egg will grow slightly in size and in time the vinegar will dissolve the shell and cook the membrane so that it's as firm as a little balloon full of water.

Let him empty the jar in the sink, rinse it, rub away the residue of grit and hold the egg to the light to see the yolk floating in the white. After that he can roll it gently and bounce it a little too. Our friend Kathy even bounced it on the ceiling (once).

Creativity

Every child must express himself every day, with words and music, with dance and make-believe, with the pictures he paints and the dolls he makes. Somehow he has to tell what's on his mind and he doesn't care if he has talent or not; it's what he says that counts. His work may not be beautiful, but it will be creative, for it is his own.

Since no two children follow exactly the same interests or the same timetable, you'll want to offer your child a little bit of everything. The help he needs will depend on his age and what you suggest.

In the beginning most of his self-expression will be simple and as brief as it is giddy. He'll draw for a few minutes, run around in his fireman's hat or plink his xylophone, but by mid-One, he also needs you to plan at least three to four special creative activities a week. Naturally, these aren't the only moments that let his imagination soar. Some of the best times will be the ones you have together as a family: the "What Am I?" guessing games of charades, the dancing and even the writing, when you encourage your child to singsong the poems and stories he invents while you or your husband take down those brilliant words.

Other expressions of creativity take more guidance. The supervision of art projects will vary from a lot, with plaster casting, to very little, with pasting. Sewing and other complicated crafts, like dyeing cloth or pressing flowers, require a calm morning and much of your attention. The more time you must give the more likely you are to get cross about it. Unless you have the nerves of a sphinx, your dear little child and a mound of papier-mâché may be your undoing. Paradoxically, we've found company helps. A young guest more than doubles the chaos but he also can inspire you with a what-the-hell spirit. The project will be noisy, confused and memorable even with firm rules, so at first only ask one extra child at a time. You eventually can invite as many as five, but don't expect the children—or you—to last more than a half hour and still enjoy it.

You'll be more apt to promote creativity (with or without company) if you have good work space and handy supplies, if you make the cleanup a part of the project and if you explain the techniques. As a child gets more adept with a paintbrush and play dough, he can concentrate more on the results. He'll paint the same picture a dozen times in a week and roll out snake after snake of clay—practicing until he's figured out how to paint the best tree and make the finest cigar. In the process of repetition he learns to accept small setbacks—the only way he can sample the pleasures of success. If a child could paint his best picture and dance his best dance the first time he would never be challenged to grow.

While creativity is a vital release to a child, it's also an absolute lark. Little else gives him more day-in, day-out good times and therefore more good times to you too. A happy child is mighty nice to have around the house.

Art

Art is not only the food of the soul but the one form of self-expression that bewitches every child. A One, young and inept as he is, wants to fiddle with it as soon as he's coordinated enough to squiggle a crayon across a page.

Drawing precedes all other art forms by at least a year and probably is enjoyed longer than all of them too, as a worldful of doodlers knows well. No other art causes so little trouble, because it can be done almost anywhere and anytime.

To many mothers, creativity not only is limited to art, but art is limited to painting. It's easy to see why, for almost any broad, swooping strokes with a paintbrush will be beautiful to you and a great physical and even spiritual release to your child. But other art does this too. Although pancakes of clay and blobs of paste may not appeal much to you, the tactile pleasure they give a child is just as important to him as the pleasure he gets from a colorful picture.

Sculpting—in clay, mâché or plaster—gives a child the chance to create everything from a medallion to a horse and even a preschool child can handbuild well enough to make thumb pots.

Pasting may not seem like an art form to you, but to a child, it's a brilliant accomplishment and the basis for many crafts and most collages. Here he learns how to give a picture an extra dimension, combining different materials into a single composition—considered one of the most sophisticated talents any artist can master.

Whatever medium you offer, you'll have to teach your child the techniques, so he can feel comfortable enough to express himself well, and you'll have to teach him to wash his tools and himself when he's done. If you don't you'll resent his dependence so much that the art supplies will become a treat instead of a routine. It's easier if you're near him when he works, both because most art is messy enough to require supervision and because your conversation will pique his fancy.

Even though his talent and his originality come from within, you refine it every time you help him notice a ladybug on the lily or the cumulus clouds in the sky, for then you can ask if the flower he's drawing has a bug on it or if his sky has clouds. While your questions will be casual (for anxiety has no place in art either), they can inspire his work and make it livelier.

By Five, your child still will be proud of all his art, but you can tell that he leans either toward sculpting or painting by the way he handles the medium. The painting style of one child may stay the same while his clay figures suddenly become wonderful creatures, but another child—even in the same family—is content to roll simple snakes of clay and yet paint complicated murals on the freezer wrap. This is classic. Almost no one is equally adept in both two-dimensional and three-dimensional art because the painter and the potter have a different set of abilities.

Although your child may have more of a bent for drama or music, any child who has wrestled with clay and swirled color on paper not only knows its joy but he'll appreciate Rodin and Van Gogh a little more too. Every effort of his own trains his eye to see more clearly, and all the museums in the world can't stretch a child's love of art any better than this.

Drawing

Drawing isn't just an easy expression of creativity, but an exercise as necessary to the development of a child's small muscles as running is to his big ones.

At nine months a baby falls in love with paper and pencil—a romance that lasts about five years. He begins with dull pencils, in either graphite or color, and crayons and then prefers felt-tipped pens. These are the most satisfying of all drawing tools for their colors are so vibrant and their lines so crisp. Still, every child has a special loyalty to that green-and-gold box of crayons—a love that will last as long as childhood.

The first drawings at mid-One will be formless but by late Two your child will graduate to stick men to whom he'll give pants and shirts, curly hair and cigarettes at Three—if you suggest them and are willing to recognize them, no matter how hazy the resemblance. Generally, however, he'll draw a sun, because it's a sign of happiness, and a tree, because it's a phallic symbol and that's a sign of happiness too.

A Three also can make three letters—O, X and T—which you should call by name and with enthusiasm, even if they were accidental. You won't expect much at the start, for a young child will only "scribble-scrabble," as our Six haughtily said, but he likes to savor the experience quietly, imitating you at your desk.

A Four can make most of his letters and print his first word—his name.

By Five, his name is such a mania he writes it everywhere, as you'll see even ten years later, when you find it etched into the bedpost.

A Five, bless his heart, culminates his love for writing by treating his tablet and pencil box—with its five pencils, its sharpener and its eraser—as if they were his best friends. They often are.

The older your child gets, the more he'll restrict his pictures, in both size and fluidity. You can prevent this somewhat by spending a few minutes outdoors encouraging him to draw great, sweeping pictures in the air with his arms—both of the things he sees and the things he would like to see. This helps a child draw with new scope, so his trees, while they still will look like phallic symbols, will look like BIG phallic symbols.

Pens and Pencils

By the time a child is nine months he's likely to use ballpoint pens and pencils, both because they're handy and because they help him imitate you and other important people. While it's restrictive to draw with them, you always will want to keep one or two in your purse; they've carried many a child through the doldrums of a waiting room.

Rubbings

A hundred years ago members of the English gentry laid parchment over brasses and tombstones and rubbed the paper with lampblack and beeswax to transfer the silhouettes.

Your Four can make rubbings too, with no more than a pencil, a penny and the back of an old envelope. Have him put the coin on anything flat, like a table top, cover it with a single thickness of paper and scratch it lightly back and forth with the side of the pencil until the picture emerges. This is an especially good trick if you're stuck somewhere you don't want to be, like an airport. However, if your child is getting fussy, don't try to show him the trick—just do it. The crossest child will be too curious to resist trying it.

Crayons

Your child is ready for crayons as early as mid-One or as soon as he's stopped putting everything in his mouth; even if he eats one, he won't get sick. You'll want to begin with the flat-sided jumbo crayons for your pre-Three, working up to magnificently elaborate boxes with sharpeners for the kindergartner. All should be of such high quality that your child can get good results.

We've found the so-called erasable, washable ones make waxy, muddy colors on paper, and they're hard to remove from the walls too, since they leave a film of wax. Besides, if you give your child washable crayons, you imply that drawing on the walls is in the same category as leaving fingerprints on them. Instead, expect the best from your child, use regular crayons and when he has an occasional accident, have him help you remove the marks with soapy water and scouring powder.

A beginning artist will draw for only a few minutes at a time, using several sheets of paper and a choice of several colors. He must work under very close supervision and in a confined space, like a high chair, so he won't slip away and draw elsewhere. Of course, put the crayons away in some clever spot when he's done, because it's cruel to tempt such a young child.

A Three can take care of his own crayons fairly well, but he still should work at a specific place. like a work table, since some crayons will drop and you'll want to be more careful where you walk. You also must check your child's overall pockets, for only one crayon melted in the dryer can stain a whole load of clothes.

A Four is ready for you to teach him to cover paper with quick little dots, to rub crayons sideways and to lay one color over another gently to create a third color. Like any other techniques, these aren't automatic.

Contrary to all nursery school precepts, a Five is happiest when he colors between the lines of a dimestore coloring book, for he likes to impose limits on himself now. This is part of his new conformity, and no, it won't stifle creativity if you have other art forms available. Also, it's the same exercise for hand control that prepares him to write in school.

Your child can stay within the lines easier if you teach him to make the long strokes within the picture just a little shorter and to use a series of tiny circles around the edges, so the marks won't slop across the lines.

A Six creates his own pictures again, although they're seldom as original as they were at Four, and

he often fills them in heavily and completely. Now he can etch designs on these pictures by drawing on them with an empty ballpoint pen, which shaves away some of the wax. To a child, that's magic.

Crayoned Batik

Preheat iron: Warm

Your Four can do this if you supervise the ironing. Have him draw a picture or a design on a white handkerchief or a piece of a plain sheet, pushing the crayons down hard to sink the wax into the cloth.

Dampen   2 paper towels

Lay the fabric between them and iron until the paper is dry and the melted wax has set.

Picture Window Pictures

Preheat iron: Warm

The sun will filter through these pictures as if they were stained glass. Use any broken crayons, in any colors. On a newspaper have your Five

Grate   crayons
Cut   2 squares of wax paper

Cover the ironing board with newspapers to keep it clean and lay one square over the other with the crayon shavings sprinkled in between like a sandwich. Cover with more newspaper and have your child press the paper with the warm iron until the wax is melted. Trim the edges for him and hang by a cord in the window.

Transfers

A Six can transfer pictures without carbon paper. Have him fold a small sheet of your notepaper like a book, filling the inside left page completely with crayon, shutting the book and then drawing a picture with a pencil on the front page. The drawing is duplicated, in color, on the inside right page when he opens the book.

Chalk

Chalk is one of the most imaginative, if impermanent, of all art forms.

A Two will be fascinated with it. At last he has something he can make appear and disappear, over and over—something he can control. For your sake, the chalkboard should be near your work space. The best we ever saw belonged to our friend Guy

whose mother covered every low cabinet door in her kitchen with blackboard paint and hung a rag for an eraser.

However, you may want to keep at least the colored chalk under your care, because chalk is so fragile that one mashed red stick can cause a remarkable amount of mess and tears.

A Three will like to use white chalk on dark construction paper and learn to make swirling patterns by rubbing a stick on its side. A Four certainly can handle his own supply, in any color, with no more than the usual problems, and he'll be happy to draw pictures with his friends on the garage floor for a half hour at a time, although the sidewalk is preferable, for everyone can admire it there. Little old ladies may object, but that will just delight the children more.

A Five, with his great admiration of school, likes his chalkboard on an easel, so he can play teacher, and a Six is quite ready for his own box of pastels to use on brown wrapping paper. Spray any work he wants to keep with a fixative like hair spray or it won't last. We wish Picasso's mother could have done the same.

Felt Markers

These pens must be one of man's finest inventions, for they flow so easily and respond so well that a child as young as Two feels like a winner when he uses them. For best results, buy pens with broad tips and fat cases, and for your sanity, buy only water-based ones. You also must supply plenty of newsprint and much supervision, because it's hard for a child to contain himself to the paper. If he goes too far remove the ink from the walls with strong detergent.

Keep these pens capped when not in use, but if they're not too dry they may be rejuvenated with a ten-minute soak in a cup of warm water. Water-proof pens need denatured alcohol or nail polish remover to bring them alive again, which also removes most of the traces when they're left where they shouldn't be left.

Painting

No one is as logical as a child—even a Two—which may be why he likes painting so much. This medium, more than any other art form, forces a child to look for logical answers to problems—in composition, in color, in perspective.

You'll see him paint his version of a tree, day after day, with little variation, until he feels he's mastered it, much as he climbs a stone animal in the park over and over until he thinks he can do it blindfolded.

The trees he paints between June and September may look the same to you, but he'll want you to notice the differences and comment on some aspect of each painting, as thoughtfully (and as kindly) as you would to an artist at his show of twenty landscapes. A child adores to be taken seriously.

You also show your respect when you tell him how to hold the brush, how to catch the drips and later how to mix the colors. This doesn't hurt his creativity, it simply makes him more adept. The better a child can handle his tools, the more he'll enjoy working with them.

There are five kinds of paint available, but we think a child should skip oils and watercolors entirely, even though they're cunningly boxed. Oils are not only indelible and messy, but they take weeks to dry, and watercolors are so subtle they must be laid on with a small, delicate brush, each color blending into the next. A child, accustomed to vivid poster paints, can't resist rubbing the brush into the paper to enliven these pale colors—one of the hardest habits to unlearn if he ever should become a serious artist.

You'll find acrylics have spectacular colors (and prices), which a Five or a Six can use on his sculptures or crafts, but he might think the paint is too thick to glide easily on paper.

This leaves the two paints made from powdered tempera: fingerpaints, which most young children unaccountably like, and poster paints, the classic choice, since the brush fairly flies across the paper.

Whether your child uses poster paints or acrylics, he never needs more than red, blue and yellow—the source of every color in the prism—and white to make the shadings. If you buy pre-mixed paint, he'll not only become a lazy painter, but he'll miss the mixing and that's half the fun. It's particularly good for a child to make his own dark shades, because they'll be more interesting than any you can buy. You'll notice he instinctively avoids black—a good idea. It's the most dominating and therefore the most difficult color for anyone to use.

Even when your child mixes paint—a trick he'll begin about Four—you can keep a painting session simple if the supplies are always ready. You'll need slick paper you can dampen, like freezer wrap, for fingerpaints; simple newsprint for poster paints and good brushes with long handles and bristles of various thicknesses—one for each basic color. For poster paints, buy fat, pointed camel's hair brushes. Acrylics, which have a plastic base, are trapped in these natural bristles and will ruin them. For these paints, you'll need a set of special blunt brushes with synthetic bristles that can feed the paint more smoothly.

He'll poster paint best at an easel and needs a table for either fingerpaints or acrylics, but you always should use newspapers or an Art Mat on the floor and his father's T-shirt on him; paint is a pain to scrub.

While these measures help your child to be a somewhat independent painter, he'll have some work to do when he's done—capping his own paints, folding his Art Mat and washing, drying and standing his brushes upside down in a tin can—and if he's not ready to do these things for himself he's not ready to paint the next time he asks.

Art Mat

This mat will depress you less than a littering of newspaper on the kitchen floor. To make it

Cut   4' X 4' vinyl

Lay on the floor under his work space when he's painting, fold in a cupboard between use and hose clean when it looks too mangy.

Fingerpainting

Fingerpainting is a delight of the very young, the bold and the messy, but it also is grand for loosening the shy and proper child. Where else can he smear paint with anything from his elbow to his fanny and be applauded for his creativity? Unfortunately, we ourselves never felt comfortable with fingerpainting but then we began late in life.

The Techniques
Sit your well-smocked Two at a well-protected table and give him thick, slick paper, like shelf paper, the matte side of freezer wrap or, as a last resort, wax paper. Wet it first, either with a sponge or by

skimming it under the tap, for this makes the paint slide better.

Drop a blob of the special paint onto the paper, and with some initial encouragement from you he'll make swirls and splats, dot and squiggles, using his elbows, his fingertips, his nails, his palms or, if he wants to be less physical, a cork, a sponge, a comb.

Fingerpaint I

Liquid starch makes a fast and adequate fingerpaint and your Two can make it himself. In a cup

Mix   ¼ c. liquid laundry starch
             2 drops food coloring OR
             1 tsp. powder paint

Fingerpaint II

Let your Three help you stir this to see the starch go through its magical change when mixed with boiling water. You can find the starch at the supermarket; the glycerin at the drugstore. In a 2-quart pan

Combine   ½ c. laundry starch
              ½ c. cold water

The mixture will be sticky and hard to stir.

Add   4 c. boiling water

Add this yourself, a half cup at a time, but your child can stir it with a long wooden spoon. To keep it soft

Add   1 tbsp. glycerin

When blended, separate into small baby food jars and into each one

Add   3 drops food coloring

You can make it as intense as he likes. Liquid or powder paints may be substituted, but they will leave color on his hands. Cap tightly and refrigerate between use.

Poster Painting

Poster painting encourages more freedom of movement—and therefore more originality—than other painting, partly because the exquisite tip of the brush makes the paper almost reach out to greet it. Newsprint is the paper you'll usually use, but a roll of brown wrapping paper is a good investment. It invites a big picture and forces a child to use vivid colors for contrast.

Almost all premixed poster paints are good—especially the ones that come in the big, squeezable bottles—but you can make an excellent paint with powder if you use flour or detergent to give it body.

While a Two may like to lie on his Art Mat to paint, any child will do better at an easel. We found we could make a simple one by tacking a sheet of newsprint onto pressed wood, leaning it against the back of the kitchen chair and putting the paint pots over newspaper laid on the seat. If you can afford to buy an easel, however, it should be the best: sturdy, so it doesn't bring grief and make your child feel awkward; double, so a friend can paint too, and with a rack on each side to hold the paint without tipping.

The best paint pots are plastic jars with screw tops, baby food jars or even small juice cans, but if he's painting on the kitchen chair, use tuna fish cans. They're harder to tip, although you must cover any open can with foil between use or the paint will harden.

Because the mechanics of poster painting are hard to coordinate, a Two does better with only one color at a time at his easel, but an early Three can handle two colors at once, and a late Three can use all the primary colors at the same time.

To keep any color true, show him how to clean his brush between colors, dipping it first into a water pot and then wiping it on an old rag—a custom he'll learn to follow when he sees it makes sense.

Your Four is ready to mix his own colors. To do this give him small amounts of red, blue, yellow and white paints and a few extra cans so he can pour the colors back and forth—like a mad scientist. At first all his colors will turn mauve, but by Five he'll be a fairly competent mixer and soon will like to fiddle with a color wheel from the art store. It teaches him that some colors are warm, others are cold and the combinations that look best to him are usually the ones that look best to all the other artists too.

The easiest kind of poster paints your child can use are sold in small jars at great cost, but you can make cheaper paints at home with powder paint. The results are better too, but you must mix the powder with more than water or the colors will be dreary. These powders are sold with art supplies in department stores, in hobby shops and in some toy stores. We recommend the brands that come in pint-size cans—a mighty supply of creativity. You need only four colors—the three primary colors and the white to tone them.

Flour-based Poster Paints

Your Three can mix his paints himself if you have the stamina to stay with him and explain each step. To store them, have small wide-mouth plastic jars ready, one for each color. Measure all ingredients over the sink. In a saucepan

Stir   ¼ c. flour
                 1 c. water

Add the water slowly to make the paste smooth.

Heat   3 minutes

Stir constantly, removing the pan from the fire when it begins to thicken. Cool. Into each jar

Mix   ¼ c. flour paste
                 3 tbsp. powder paint
                 2 tbsp. water

If the mixture is too dry add more water, a teaspoon at a time. Store in the covered jars and stir each time your child uses them. For a more opaque finish

Add   ½ tsp. liquid starch

Or for a glossier finish

Add   ½ tsp. liquid detergent

Detergent Poster Paints

This velvety mix makes each color as vivid as an acrylic, a dramatic paint for a Five. These proportions make enough for one color and one painting session. In a paper cup

Combine   1 tbsp. clear liquid detergent
                    2 tsp. powder paint

Painting to Music

We once endured a duty day at the cooperative nursery school by experimenting with music and art at the same time—a dandy way to stimulate a bored child and a bored mother too.

Without any direction, each child painted blue skies and sunshine as they listened to some soupy Hawaiian love songs and added darker colors and more detail with "American in Paris," but when we switched to "Slaughter on Tenth Avenue," they slowly covered their pictures completely with browns and blacks. While we don't recommend such drastic mood changes regularly, we did find that any child likes to translate sound into sight.

The Wash

A Six can draw a picture with a fine-lined felt-tipped pen, a pencil or a ballpoint pen and make it look almost professional by giving it a wash with poster paint. To do this, have him dip a wet cotton ball into any pastel shade, press it lightly against the side of the cup to remove most of the paint, and pat or wipe it over or around the picture. The touch must be gentle and the drawing must be waterproof so it can't smear.

Designs

Your child can get a wholly new effect with paint if you introduce other materials to use with it.

Texture
Texture comes through if you have your Three lay net, burlap or any other loosely woven material on a piece of paper and brush paint over it. Lift it carefully for him.

String
To make this abstract design, let your Four dip a length of string in poster paint, then hold one end taut in the center of a sheet of paper and sweep the other end around the paper like a hand on a very fast clock.

Stencil
Have your Five make a stencil in reverse by cutting a piece of construction paper into any shape and laying it on drawing paper. Have him paint its edges with short, feathery strokes that leave a design when he lifts the shape.

Block Printing

This art form brings instant success and requires little but an interesting stamp, a pad, some paper and a steady bang-stamp rhythm, which a Two can master. For paper, use newsprint, shelf paper, brown bags or wrapping paper, freezer wrap or a piece of an old sheet, but by the time your child is Six, he may want to use manila paper and make his own stationery.

To block print, he can use a cork stopper, a piece of sponge, a scrap of smooth wood, the base of a bunch of celery or a head of lettuce or any firm fruit or vegetable, like a potato, which you first slice in half. A Five is ready to scoop a design ¼" deep from the heart of the potato or trim the edges to make a shape, but at any age the child simply bangs the block he's made on the Stamp Pad and then on the paper.

Stamp Pad

Wet one section of a paper towel, fold it and place it on a flat dish. On it
Sprinkle   1 tsp. powder paint OR
                 1 tbsp. liquid tempera paint
Use the back of a spoon to blend the powder or paint into the pad, adding more water and more paint if it dries before he's done.

Acrylics

Acrylics are the most beautiful paints of all—shiny, vivid and true—perfect for decorating crafts.

Like oils, they're not diluted but squirted directly from the tube to the palette. Unlike oils, however, a coat of acrylics will dry in just twenty minutes and the paint is water soluble.

To use, your child should have brushes with synthetic bristles and the easiest palette of all: a paper plate with dabs of white, blue, red and yellow on it. He can mix more colors by using the brush to lift some of the paint to other parts of the plate, stirring each new color with it. Teach him to rinse the bristles before touching the next dab to keep the colors pure.

You can make the paint go further if you add a gel medium to each color. This also retards the drying time but it doesn't change the color.

Even with gel, these acrylics are thick, so your child should dip the brush into water and then into the paint to make the strokes smoother. He can skip this step if he wants to drop the paint in blobs—a technique that takes longer to dry but gives a three-dimensional look.

Acrylics must be washed from clothes or brushes before they dry or they can't be washed at all.

Pasting

Pasting is integral to a child's creativity, for it gives him another way to build. Besides, paste actually feels good to a child, which is one more way you can tell the difference between him and a grown-up.

The younger your child, the less he minds the smears of paste left on every picture. Thinned White Glue leaves the least trace, but the flour pastes are cheaper and easy to make. All must be stored in airtight containers, and the flour pastes must be refrigerated.

A child applies a paste better with a 1" brush than anything else, although a pre-Four may like to dip his collage materials into a saucer of paste instead. Have him work on newspapers and in his father's T-shirt, for a child and his paste are soon parted.

When he gets older and uses the White Glue recipe, he'll find it easier to glue two sides together if they're covered first with the glue and then given a 10-minute rest before pressing them together.

Uncooked Paste

This paste is good for an emergency and not much else. Into a cup
Mix   ½ c. flour
            ½ c. water
Always add the flour to the water so it won't lump.

Cooked Paste

The heat blends this paste well. In a 2-quart saucepan
Mix   1 c. flour
            1 tsp. salt
            2 c. water
Add the water slowly, stirring until cooked.
Simmer   5 minutes
Cool and refrigerate in an airtight container.

Thinned White Glue

This cold-water glue lasts longer than the cooked paste, is just as safe and doesn't look crusty when dry.
Mix   ½ c. white glue
            ½ c. water

Cutting

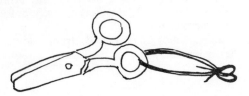

A child judges himself by the way he handles his tools, particularly a pair of scissors. Nothing else brings such pride if he's successful or such despair if he's not—which he surely will be if their quality is poor or if he's offered them too soon. It takes the skill of a Four to manipulate scissors perpendicular to paper, but not even a couturier could cut a pattern with clean edges if he used a pair of child's scissors from the dimestore. It's much more sensible to buy decent scissors from an art, surgical or school supply house—two pairs, in fact, in case of company or loss—and if your child is left-handed, the scissors must be too. For some reason, you usually can find good southpaw scissors at a toy store.

Your child's frustration will be even less if you teach him to sharpen the blades by cutting sandpaper or trying to cut the neck of a soda bottle, which hones the edges too.

Still, the best scissors will bring despair unless you hang a long, bright ribbon on the handle so they won't get lost so easily, and unless you hide your scissors, in case they do. As we remember too well, once a child learns to cut, he doesn't quit easily.

Since every child will use pointed scissors sometimes, the safety rules apply to all. Explain carefully that he mustn't run with them or wave them and he must carry them with the blades wrapped in his fist and the tips extending just below the palm to avoid a cut.

When your Four begins to cut, he'll make endless chains of construction paper and can cut simple swatches of crisp cloth for collages and for sewing. Scissors become the biggest mainstay of the school-happy Five and he practices with them almost continuously. A Six becomes adept enough to cut out paper snowflakes and the simplest paper dolls—not well, but well enough for the costume to hang on the figure.

Collages

A collage is a three-dimensional picture made from any combination of textures, weights and shapes, pasted into an abstract design at first and perhaps later, a realistic mural.

Although early collages may not win a wholehearted "Wow" from you, your Two is learning to judge the feel and dimension of different objects and slowly he can harmonize a paper doily, a piece of fur, some ticket stubs and a pussywillow into an interesting, balanced composition.

The material will come from your kitchen cabinets, your sewing box and those slow walks to the park. Help him collect anything that's vivid, shiny, soft, brittle, geometric, common, rare— anything as long as it's reasonably clean and can't choke him. Give him a few empty oatmeal boxes to hold his collections, but don't let him keep buttons, stones or beans if he's a pre-Three and don't save paper or cloth that will need cutting until your child is Four and old enough to handle scissors.

A young child pastes collage material on anything stiff, like construction paper or paper bags, and by Five, uses glass jars and wood as well, with more expensive felt or burlap for a special tapestry.

As in any artwork, your child should wear his father's T-shirt and work over newspaper. Work alongside him at first, to explain the technique— particularly of pasting. He can take it from there. A Two will dip the scraps into Cooked Paste, but a Three will want to use Thinned White Glue to hold the heavier mosaics of beans, stones or pasta.

First Collage

Choose anything that's easy and safe for a Two to pick up and paste.

Collect   cottonballs/leaves/feathers
                  eggshell bits/fabric and ribbon

Pour Uncooked Paste in a saucer and teach him to dip scraps into it and press them onto paper.

Geometric Collage

On that rare day when you have extra time, cut a dozen sheets of construction paper into rectangles, circles, triangles and squares, ranging from 1" to 4" in size. Your Three will need only one lesson to see that two circles and a rectangle make a car, but if he adds another, skinnier rectangle, it's a handle and the car becomes a wagon. He can glue the shapes onto a piece of paper with Cooked Paste and a 1" brush and save the rest in an envelope for that ordinary day when he has extra time.

Gravel Mosaic

Let your Four dye gravel with various colors of poster paint, by dropping the stones into shallow tin cans of paint and then scooping them onto newspaper with a slotted spoon, where they can dry. While he waits, have him draw a picture or a design on a stiff paper and cover one section of it at a time with Thinned White Glue, then cover each section with stones of a different color.

Tissue Collage

This collage looks best with paper scraps about the size of a Five's hand.

Tear   3-6 colors of tissue
Using Thinned White Glue
Paint   a wine bottle OR a block of wood

When it's completely covered, have him wash the glue from his hands, then paste overlapping scraps of paper on it. Wait about 10 minutes and wipe with a damp cloth to remove the extra glue and to stick the edges firmly in place—a delicate job you may have to do yourself.

Glass Collage

A crafty Five we know invented collages made from the broken bits of colored glass he collected on his walks. Some were lovely, some ghastly, but he never cut himself, and he always had presents to give. A plastic lid made both the backing and the frame. On the inside of it, have your child

Smear   Thinned White Glue

Let it rest until tacky—about 10 minutes—then he can arrange the glass bits in the lid.

Fabric Collage

This only looks handsome if your Six uses your good sewing scissors, for all edges must be clean.

Collect   yarn/string/twine
               fabric scraps
               trimmings/ribbons

Staple burlap or felt to a thick section of the daily paper to keep the surface firm—a job for you. Your child can paint the back of each scrap with Thinned White Glue and press into place, adding pieces from day to day until he's made a picture. Unstaple the paper for him when the glue is dry.

Sculpting

Sculpting takes many forms, and if the medium is soft enough a young child can handle it. You'll want to offer the clays as early as Two, the plasters at Three and, finally, at Four, the papier-mâché.

Clay

The tactile joys of pounding, rolling and flattening clay can strengthen a child's sense of touch as much as painting at the easel expands his sense of sight.

There is the Flour Clay and the Cornstarch Clay in this section (as well as the Play Clay and the Ecuadorian Bread Dough elsewhere), all of which are homemade, and the splendidly messy oil-based clay from the dimestore, which you'll want to buy only once a year—but no more, since it sticks so well to the floor. Finally, there is natural clay, that blessedly tough earth in the backyard where you thought the topsoil would be.

All of these are pliable enough to be shaped again and again and all, except the oil-based clay, can be baked and painted with powder paints or acrylics which you can spray with a fixative later.

Your child can help you make the recipes but he needs you to give offhand suggestions and many compliments to learn the techniques.

Handbuilding

A Two automatically shapes clay into a ball, which you'll call an orange, and flattens it with his fist, which he'll call a cookie, imprinting the circle of clay with a fork, a key or a piece of your jewelry.

At Three he'll make paperweights, pressing clay over and around a rock and sticking a collage of shells, stones and dried flowers on it. He also can make snakes—if you teach him to lighten his touch enough to roll a ball of clay into a skinny rope. From there he learns the coil construction of a potter, circling the rope around and around from the center to make a basket.

A Four can make a gingerbread man—fixing the eyes and a mouth onto a ball, adding hair that's been squeezed through a garlic press (the one trick that won't work with natural clay) and twisting a body out of snaky clay, pressing it with a rolling pin. Almost any figure can be hung on the wall or on a Christmas tree if you imbed a paper clip in its back before baking. At this age, your child can make and bake ropy rings and threaded beads of Cornstarch Clay—fragile gifts indeed, but the love they carry fortunately outlasts them by years.

The Five achieves real sophistication in his figures, dressing them in skirts and pants and hats. They can perch upright (if they're squat enough) and like to be painted. He'll lay snakes on the table in the outline of the pussycat and the neighbor lady, glasses and all. The more classic handbuilding starts with natural clay when, with much help, your Six can dig for his own clay and make his own thumb pots. Teach him to do this by shaping the clay into a ball the size of his fist, pressing his thumb in the center and then pressing it against the sides until it turns into a pot.

Flour Clay

This is easy for your Two to make, but you still must help him measure and knead as directed in breadmaking (page 249).

Combine	4 c. flour
	1½ c. salt
	2 c. water

Add the water slowly, stopping when the dough is still a little dry, and begin to work by hand. While the salt keeps this recipe pliable, it dries the skin, so you and your child should rub a little salad oil on your hands first.

Knead 10 minutes

When it's soft and smooth, divide the dough into batches and add food coloring into each one. Refrigerate leftover clay in airtight containers between use, but have your child oil his hands whenever he sculpts with this clay.

Cornstarch Clay

Your Four will appreciate the smooth texture of this clay, for it's a pleasure to touch and it can be worked into delicate shapes. It also absorbs colors better than any other clay. In a 2-quart saucepan over a low fire

Stir	2 c. baking soda
	1 c. cornstarch
	1¼ c. cold water

Add the water slowly to prevent lumps and help your child stir, because the job is hard until half the water is mixed.

Cook 6 minutes

Stop when it looks like mashed potatoes and spread the dough on a cookie sheet to cool—your job. Cover with a damp cloth to keep it moist.

Knead 10 minutes

Divide the clay into batches when it's pliable and add food coloring unless your child plans to paint it later. Store in airtight containers, one for every color, or let your child shape it as soon as it's cool.

These decorations will harden in 24 hours if exposed to the air at room temperature or if they're left overnight in an oven that was first preheated to 275° and turned off, but most children would rather see the results a little quicker. To bake the clay

Preheat oven 200°

Place the decorations on a lightly greased cookie sheet.

Bake 2 hours

Cool in the oven for 2 hours longer, removing when the decorations are hard underneath.

Natural Clay

Probably the nicest reason for having your child work with natural clay is that you get a chance to do the same. Like making bread, anything that's been done for thousands of years is irresistible. You also don't need a potter's wheel, tricky tools, glazes or a kiln to know its joy. A young child is much too inept and impatient to throw clay on a wheel, but he can handbuild with a few kitchen utensils and his own ten fingers. As for glazes, we think natural clay is meant to look natural, for it lets a child concentrate on the texture and the shape and this is where the pleasure lies. Finally, an oven is much handier than a kiln and although success is less certain, you can salvage enough to be proud. At this age, his cups are meant to be admired, not used.

There are many clays available, including the plasticized (and comparatively expensive) clay at the art supply stores, which can be air dried without crumbling, or the ready-to-use and much cheaper clay sold in five-pound boxes, but your child probably would like to dig it for himself, at least once. It's a nice thing to do on a country vacation.

Clay is found everywhere—in tan, gray, white or red—depending on its minerals. Dig along the edge of a stream or near a construction site—wherever the topsoil has been cut away—but be careful of broken glass. Before taking some clay, add a little water to it, twisting and squeezing the clay to see if it's pliable enough to hold a shape. Good clay is almost as springy as half-kneaded dough. Plan to take no more than half a bucket of clay, because the preparation is hard work.

You'll have to help with both the digging and, when you get home, the spreading, for it must dry in thin layers and then be crumbled into tiny pieces. Put them in a big bowl with enough water to turn the clay into "slip." This stage, about the consistency of pea soup, is so gloriously messy your child will want to do the next job himself: pouring the slip first through a colander and then through a window screen several times, which is necessary to filter the debris. Let the slip settle, drain the excess water and store in sealed plastic bags, where it will mature and perhaps smell sour as the organisms decompose. This adds some plasticity to the clay but it still can't be used until it's wedged—a nice potter's term that means to pound it and slam it down hard, again and again, both to make it pliable and to knock out the bubbles that can splinter clay as it dries. Your child will help with this hard work (but not much), but he will like to wrap a piece of heavy thread around both hands, pull it taut and slice the clay in half. If no bubbles show, it's been wedged enough.

Generally a potter wedges and handbuilds on a "bat"—a slick, 2" plaster of Paris slab that absorbs extra moisture—but the wrong side of oilcloth works just as well and the clay won't stick to that either. The clay stays moist if the cloth covers it between use.

If the clay should get a little dry before you use it, add only a sprinkling of water to make it elastic. No matter how old or hard it gets, it will come to life if you soak it in water and roll it with a rolling pin, putting each layer between thicknesses of newspaper to get that plastic consistency. However, any clay that has been wedged—either by the factory or by you—should be kneaded a little before using it. This your child can do for himself.

Any of the handbuilding techniques can be used to make figures, boxes, animals or thumb pots, but if you and your child stop between shaping, cover your works with the oilcloth or a damp towel so you can work with them the next day. A fairly thin piece—less than an inch thick—can be baked in the oven but clay shouldn't be too thick, even in a kiln, for it fractures easily under heat. That's why a potter leaves his finished sculpture uncovered overnight to dry a little and then scoops away some of the innards before he bakes it.

Papier-mâché

No art requires as much imagination as papier-mâché—or as much faith. It's hard for a Four to believe that water, paste and the classifieds ever could look like a cat. While a Five can't make the classic mâché of absorbent paper that's been torn, soaked, boiled, drained, squished and perhaps mixed with sawdust or plaster of Paris, he can dip strips of paper into wheat paste or starch. This sculpts quite as well, as long as he learns some techniques from you.

The Armature

Since a good sculptor makes an armature first, your child should do the same—a subtle way to compliment him, for any child likes to feel he's doing adult work. This mâché armature is simply a few sheets of newspaper rolled into a primitive shape (his job) and bound with string or masking tape (your job). It won't look like much until he's molded the wet strips of paper around it.

The Snake
Roll 4 sheets of newspaper into a tube and tie.

The Horse
Roll 5 double sheets of paper into a tube, tying to make the head, neck and body. Make two more tubes for the legs, using 2 sheets for each one and sealing the paper shut with masking tape. Leave room at one end for the head and neck and bend the legs across the top of the body so they go down straight. Tie with string in a secure X, under and over the body. The same armature makes a dog, a cat or a pig, but you must make shorter tubes, for the neck and legs must be much shorter.

The Puppet
Have your child wad newspaper into a ball for the head, doing it around a toilet paper tube (so half of the tube extends to become the neck), while you wrap the head with string to keep it round. After the puppet has been sculpted and painted, cover the neck with a skirt of material, held in place by a rubber band.

The Mâché

A mâché sculpture should please most children and mothers too, for it not only can be stretched over several days—it must be. Your child has to tear the paper, make the armature, make the paste, wet the paper with it, press it on the frame, dry it and finally paint it. To begin,

Tear   8 sheets of newspaper, 3" wide
The paper rips straighter if several sheets are torn at once. To stick it on the armature, your child should drop each strip, as needed, into a bowl filled either with an inch of undiluted liquid starch, which is handy, or with wallpaper paste, which bonds better

and can be sanded when done—a step some purists follow. To make the paste

Mix   2 c. wheat paste
                    2½ c. water

The Sculpture

Have your child cover any armature by dipping one strip of paper at a time into the solution and pressing it over the frame, repeating the process again and again until the body, legs and head are covered. As layers accumulate, the figure will be wet enough for your child to pinch and poke the nose, the ears and the eyes into shape—or to transform a two-legged animal into a fat duck, for instance, by puffing his chest, pulling out his beak and flattening the ends of his legs, covering them until they turn into web feet.

If your child is making an animal with a tail, have him cut paper ¼" wide and poke the lengths into its behind with a pencil, which will cause wicked laughter from scatologically minded children (and all children are). Broom straws, yarn or serpentine confetti will give as many yocks. Keep adding more strips until the animal has the right shape, then add a layer of paper towel for final smoothness.

Harden   2 days

This may take more time, or less, depending on the humidity of the room and the size of the sculpture. When completely dry—it will feel very light—the sculpture is ready for him to sand any rough edges and to paint with acrylics or poster paints. He can decorate, if he wants, using Thinned White Glue (page 205) to stick buttons for eyes, glitter for grandeur and elbow macaroni (or feathers) for feathers.

Mâché Masks

Our younger children hit an artistic peak in Kate's art class, making masks imbedded with mirrors, fur, feathers and fancies and painting them in brilliant colors—too fragile to wear but each a knockout on the wall. Your Five can make a mask, but your Six can make it better.

Assemble   8 sheets of newspaper
                  1 c. wallpaper paste
                  1 balloon

Tear most of the paper into pieces the size of playing cards and the rest into strips, 5" long. Drop the squares into the paste, inflate the balloon and cover half of it with the wet paper. Add fangs, beaks, noses and ears by holding balls of paper in the proper places while your child covers them with wet strips.

Dry   2 days

He can pop the balloon—an exhilarating step—then trim the edges with scissors, but you'll have to cut holes for the mouth and eyes. Have your child sand the rough edges and paint the mask with poster paints. When dry, paste the decorations with Thinned White Glue.

Laminated Shield

A knight, if he's Five, can make this shield and he can laminate a crown too, in case he gets promoted. In a bowl

Mix   1 c. wheat paste
                  1¼ c. water

Dipping a 2" brush into it,

Paint   6 sheets newspaper

Press one sheet on top of the other and cover with a layer of paper towels. He'll need your help to trim and bend it in the shape of a shield, rolling the edges under. Dry before painting.

Plaster

Since plaster is about the messiest art form of all, you'll want to use it on your more tolerant days.

Unless you're mixing your own exotic blend of lime and gauging plaster (a bother), you can choose between plaster of Paris, patching plaster and spackling compound. They differ in color and in drying time, but any can be used to cast a handprint or repair a wall, and all may be found in the hardware store.

Plaster of Paris (which naturally was invented in Paris) is a crisp, snowy mixture made mostly of gypsum. Because it's slick and white it's still the favorite of some old-time plasterers and because it's so quick to dry, it's also preferred by impatient Twos. As your child becomes more adept, he probably would rather work with patch plaster, which takes twice as long to set. It's much cheaper too, since only 3 1/3 cups of plaster equal a pound, and you can buy it in 25-pound sacks. The spackling compound is the slowest to dry and to a child it seems to take forever, which makes it best to fill nail holes. It's a little gray in color and has more lime, sand and hair than the others and very little gypsum.

The drying time of any plaster can be retarded

by adding some extra water or sand. Use a tin can to mix it and never, never dump the leftover plaster down the drain unless you want to cast your pipes.

Plaster Mix

You can use these proportions to make any casting plaster, but don't mix more patch plaster than you can use in an hour or more plaster of Paris than you can use in several minutes. In a big tin can have your child

Stir   2 c. patch plaster OR
               plaster of Paris
               1¼ c. water

It should be as thick as pea soup so it can cast without air bubbles. Plaster of Paris goes to the consistency of thick stew in 3-4 minutes and dries in 10-20. Patch plaster takes 20-40 minutes to dry, but all drying time depends on the humidity, the size of the mold and how much the plaster was stirred. The more air you whip into it, the quicker it sets.

The Mold

Plaster casting enchants the Three who first uses his hands as a mold. Make a small batch of plaster of Paris, wait about 2 minutes and then pour it into his cupped hands. Help him hold them together for several minutes more until the plaster feels quite warm and the shape is set. He'll think it beautiful.

Handprints

A new handprint (or footprint) every six months makes a nice frieze around a child's wall, as fascinating to him as his growth chart on the wall. It's all part of the No-Belly-Button-Is-As-Interesting-As-One's-Own syndrome. Start at any age, but it seems to have a special appeal to a Three. Into a paper plate

Pour   1" Plaster Mix

Wait 2 minutes for plaster of Paris; 6 minutes for patch plaster.

Imprint   1-2 minutes

Have him press his hand gently into the plaster so it doesn't go right to the bottom. Let the handprint sit overnight, peel the plate from the print and paste a picture hook on the back for hanging.

Plaster Medallion

A Five can make a free-form medallion pretty enough to be proud of.

Cut   27" thong OR yarn OR string

Spoon thickened Plaster Mix onto a piece of wax paper or a plastic lid. Let him use an opened paper clip to make a hole for the thong. When plaster has set, he can paint the medallion with a felt-tipped pen or poster paint and scratch a design on the medallion with a nail when the paint is dry.

Birdcage Balloons

This is a recipe that needs plenty of time, help and compliments, but your Five will be rewarded by airy make-believe birdcages to hang from his ceiling or small Christmas ornaments for the tree, made of plastered yarn that's been dried around a balloon. Have your child make enough to ensure some success and, if possible, make them outdoors, because the yarn is so drippy.

Assemble   6 round balloons, large and small
                 3 c. Plaster Mix
                 six 12' lengths of vivid yarn
                 six 2' lengths of string

You'll need less yarn and less string for the small ornaments. Have your child inflate the balloons, securing each with a 2' string, so he can hang it later to dry. He can cut the yarn into lengths equal to the diameter of its inflated balloon and then dip them into the plaster. The thinner the yarn and the less plaster it attracts, the more delicate the cages will look. The yarn should be wrapped lengthwise, but the pieces must cross securely at the top and bottom, even if you have to reinforce them with a teaspoon of wet plaster. Tie the balloons by their strings to a hanger, suspending it from a door frame indoors or from a tree branch outside.

Dry   30 minutes

Your child should clean the mess while waiting, which he'll scarcely mind in his excitement to pop the balloons. When the scraps are pulled out of the cage, the rigid yarn should keep its shape.

Crafts

Since crafts are once again a part of our culture, every child deserves the chance to become adept at them. While a young child can't have the ability of an artisan, each of his attempts makes him appreciate the value of handwork.

His best work will spring from ideas of his own, which will be prolific if he has scissors, paste, tissue, yarn, paper doilies, straws, pipe cleaners and those blessed scraps of telephone wire given by the repairman. The tiny, brightly colored wires, which you'll pull from the casing for him, can make everything from sculpture to jewelry (of a sort).

Your child will need your guidance to follow most of these craft recipes—at least until he understands the techniques—but the time is well spent. It's important for a child to know that he can capture the beauty of the flowers in a meadow with more than a memory; that he can gather berries and roots to dye cloth in rich, if muted, colors; that the doll he makes himself is quite as good a friend as the one you buy and that, with needle, thread and a little skill, he can make simple clothes for it or make a beanbag to toss. A child is never too young to learn that everything in life doesn't come from a department store.

Dolls

Since dolls are among the few toys that are cheaper than they used to be, children are likely to have many more than they need—and yet, they'll all look alike. Tell your child how it used to be, long before you were born, when rich children had china dolls from the store and the rest had dolls they made with their parents from a hundred odd things.

Some they stuffed with rags, some they whittled of wood, some they made of cornhusks and some they carved from apples into wonderful, awful old crones. With your help, your twentieth-century child can also make dolls. Although some may not last long, like the foil doll, others like the yarn doll will hang on the wall for years. The joy, we find, isn't just in the making but in the chance it gives a child to breathe some life into a creation all his own.

Life Mask

Aluminum foil holds a shape, bends easily and can be decorated with poster paints. A Three can use it to make his own life mask and, in fact, wants to make so many you'll think he found his face in an assembly line.

Cut   18" length of foil

Double to make it stiffer. Help him press it evenly over his face, molding it against his eyes, nose and mouth. Lift the fragile mask gently for him, poke holes at the temples with a knife and run string through them to hang it.

Aluminum Foil Doll

By Four, a boy sometimes won't play with dolls but he likes to make one out of foil—especially if he can make a bosomy girl.

Cut   9" length of foil

Help him roll it into a cylinder and pinch twice: once in the center for the waist and then higher for the neck. Press the foil into a ball for the head and wrap a pipe cleaner once around the neck with ends extending for arms. Probably without any prompting he'll strategically plump out the cylinder above the waist and flatten it below. If his girl wears pants he can rip the lower half in two, but for a dress, he must press an extra piece of foil around the middle for a skirt. So much for the life of a couturier.

Nutshell Creatures

A hundred years ago, when children were more prevalent than toys, the walnuts they ate became fine and fanciful creations. With clay, your Four can transform a shell into a basket for tiny dough fruit, a turtle shell with clay feet, head and tail or into a sailboat. To make this one, he should cut a triangle from the corner of an index card, thread it with a toothpick and anchor it in the shell with clay. The boat will float, because the shell is waterproof.

Orange Doll

One orange and a piece of material about 24" X 36" make a doll, would you believe, as cuddly and floppy as any little girl could want. We saw a Five named Molly, lonesome for her doll back home, ask for an orange, cover it with a dish towel, tie it with her hair ribbon and draw a face on it. The day wasn't done before she had embroidered the eyes and mouth, not too well, but well enough for the doll to be her constant companion for the rest of the week.

Yarn Doll

A Five can wrap yarn around the width and length of a book to make a fat, old-fashioned yarn doll, but you'll have to count as he winds and tie the ends for him too. The width becomes the arms; the length becomes the head, the body and the legs.

Choose a thick book that is roughly 5" X 8", and wrap the long side of the book 80-100 times. Slip a 5" piece of yarn underneath one end of the book to tie the loops so they stay together when he slips them from the book. Make the head by tying a knot 4" from the top.

To make the arms, wrap more yarn 40-50 times around the width of the book, slipping it from the book carefully for your child and tying a short piece of yarn near the ends to form the hands. Have him slip the arms under the head through the strands and use a short piece of yarn to tie under the arms to bind the waist. If your child wants the doll in a dress, it's finished when he cuts all the loops; if the doll must wear pants, he'll have to divide the yarn into legs for you to tie at the feet.

Octopus

Braiding is an important and tricky skill for a Five to learn, and the Octopus teaches it well. This stuffed animal is made with the fattest yarn you can find and in three colors, so a child can see what he's doing.

Assemble
    twenty-four 30" lengths of yarn
    one 3" styrofoam ball
    10 rubber bands
    ten 3" lengths of ribbon
    2 felt discs
    white glue

Have your Five band all the yarn an inch from one end and smoothe the strings evenly over the ball, if possible keeping the colors in sequence for easier braiding. Tie them just below the ball with another band to make the head of the octopus and hang this head on a hook or a nail so your child can have both hands free. He'll plait three strings, each a different color, stopping near the end while you band it, for he mustn't let the braid go. Do this 7 more times—and by then they may look right. Tie a bow ribbon on each arm, around the neck and at the topknot to cover the bands—another job for

you. Your child can paste the felt in place for eyes.

Cornhusk Doll

Any cornhusk doll charms an adult; but your Six will be enchanted by the one he makes himself. Creating the doll is a project which thrives best in a gentle atmosphere, when both of you feel like being together, for he'll need your help to bind the husks with heavy-duty thread and glue the corn silk hair.

Dry the inner husks and the silk in a brown paper bag months ahead of time and take them out on a quiet winter's day. Have your child soak the husks in warm water for 5 minutes to make them pliable again.

To form the head and body, have him choose the biggest husk and fold it in half over a small wad of thin husks to round out the head. Tie at the neck with thread. To make the arms, fold a long husk lengthwise 4 times and slip it through the body just below the neck. Tie the thread under the arms to make the waist. The doll can stand by itself if you cut the husks straight across the bottom when dry. Your child can cut another husk and tie it around for a skirt.

When the doll is dry, have him draw the face with a felt-tipped pen and cover the back of the head with white glue, pressing corn silk onto it.

Apple Doll

An apple doll needs to cure in a dry, warm house as we discovered one September when it grew a beard of mold after three weeks of rainy weather. So the head won't mildew, make it in late winter when the fruit is dry and rather cottony.

Peel a whole apple—one without bruises—and help your Six use a corer to dig out two small holes for eyes and a crescent for the mouth. Shape the nose into a bump by whittling bits of apple from each side—a job too tricky for a child. If your child wants the doll to have a rather fair skin he should paint the apple with lemon juice. To dry the fruit, poke a popsicle stick into the base, drop the stick in a soda bottle and place it in a well-ventilated place, but not near a window or you may get fruit flies. If you put it near a radiator in the winter it will dry a little quicker.

Dry   5-7 days

When the apple begins to pucker and form a skin, it's time for your child to pinch and poke the features to exaggerate a smile or to make the cheeks sag.

Cure   2-3 weeks

After the face has set, help your child gather a ruffle of material around the stick with a rubber band to make the dress. Tie a bow ribbon around the neck. Raisins are glued in place for eyes and cotton is the snowy hair.

Now he won't think Grandma looks so old any more.

Dyes

Over three thousand years ago some clever Phoenicians built their fortunes on snails, taking a tiny gland from each one and baking it in sunshine before making the best, most expensive and one of the most complicated dyes in the world. Your child can make dye too, although it won't make him rich, it won't be kingly purple and unless you set it first with a mordant, it won't be colorfast either. Nevertheless, he can make a dye with almost anything—except perhaps snails.

Dyes come from chemicals, minerals, fruits, vegetables, roots, barks and, although you won't want to use them, insects.

Whatever you use must be boiled long enough to reach a deep color, then strained, measured, salted and cooled enough for your child to soak the cloth in it—a dripping job best done outside. It's the experiment that pleases your child and in the process he realizes that every color has a different source. At least he'll never wonder if sheep come in pink, blue and plaid.

Since synthetic fibers take natural dyes so poorly, your child should use natural cloth: linen, wool or cotton. Cotton is the cheapest and a good first choice and old cotton is the best, because if it's new its sizing must be removed by a washing in hot water before the dye can be absorbed.

We've found an old sheet is ideal, since it can be ripped into small squares and dyed in many colors. These either make rather wretched, ragged but much treasured handkerchiefs or can be pieced together into a drape for the playhouse, which is much prettier. A patchwork cover like that, machine-stitched by their mother, delighted Sarah and her sister Rachel.

Mordant

If you child dyes fabric in cooled water—the safest way for him to do it—the color will bleed unless you treat it first with a mordant to bind the dye to the fiber. Boil the material in an enamel pot with a metallic salt, like chrome or potassium or the much more common aluminum potassium sulfate, known as alum at the drugstore. The salt you use will affect the color of the dye, which makes the results even more interesting. A Four can do this measuring and return to help you when the water has cooled.

Cotton and Linen

To prepare these fabrics

Combine   1 gal. water
                           1 oz. alum
                           ¼ oz. washing soda
Add   material
Boil   1 hour

Cool, rinse and dry before dyeing.

Wool

To prepare this fabric, substitute ¼ oz. cream of tartar for the soda.

Natural Dyes

While your Three can dye cloth simply by wetting it with vinegar and laying it on damp clay to draw the stain, he's ready for more sophisticated techniques at Four.

All dyes must be made in an enamel pot, 2 quarts or bigger, with enough water to cover the leaves, flowers, berries or roots. Each takes a different length of time to release all its color and all must be stirred with a wooden spoon, cooled, strained and measured. If the cloth hasn't been treated with a mordant you'll need to add table salt, but even then it won't be very fast. To each cooled pint of dye

Add   1 tsp. salt

When the dye is cool, have your child drop the cloth in the pot.

Soak   10-15 minutes

Rinse the excess color in clear water and lay the material in the shade to dry.

Onionskin

For a dark honey color, have your child peel the brown shells from 5 pounds of onions.

Boil   30 minutes

Goldenrod
When the goldenrod has just begun to bloom, pick about 3 dozen flowers. Chop both stems and flowers into small pieces.
Boil   15 minutes

Cranberry
A half pound of cranberries bleeds a lovely magenta.
Boil   30 minutes

Beets, Dandelions and Sassafras
The beets make a red-violet color; the dandelion roots are magenta and the sassafras roots and bark are pink.
Boil   45 minutes
This is one dye that requires salt, with or without a mordant. To each cooled pint
Add   1 tsp. salt

String

There's something about string that elicits inventiveness in a child. Since primitive times, people have used leather strips and grasses to bind tools and thread ornaments, and we still follow the same techniques today.

Your Two will begin by stringing a thick cord through his big wooden beads, gradually learning by Four to move the string to the bead and never the bead to the string: a basic exercise of coordination he'll need when he wants to thread a needle or read. Such ability seems to come naturally to a child if he's given a ball of twine and a few casual lessons in the simplest knot tying. He also can use long leather shoelaces, a packet of pipe cleaners, some delicate telephone wires—or, of course, long grasses.

String Designs

Three-dimensional geometric pictures can be very pleasing. Into a block of pine, let your Four
Hammer   twenty 8-penny nails

They should be driven 2" deep, at random, although you may have to give the final rap to keep them steady. To any nail he chooses
Tie   5' colored twine
Your child takes the string from nail to nail, twisting it once under the head to hold it in place. Tie the tail to the last nail when he's done. A Six can do it all, using a variety of lengths, colors and textures of string to create complicated geometric patterns—and also to look pretty.

Yarn Pictures

If your Five soaks yarn or string in glue and pastes it on tissue paper, it can become a mobile, a sculpture or a window decoration. Cover the table with newspaper and have a washrag handy, because this is messy.
Cut   4-6 lengths of yarn
They should be about as long as his arm. In a bowl
Mix   2 tbsp. water
          2 tbsp. white glue
Have your child soak the yarn in the glue, squeezing each piece through his fingers and then pressing it on the tissue, with each piece of yarn snaked across another so the picture will hold together. To make a mobile or a sculpture, use plain tissue, tearing it away when the glue dries, but for a window decoration, use vivid tissue and trim the edges. It will catch the sunshine rather like stained glass.

Flower Keeping

The child who can dry flowers will never be insensitive to beauty. This is the art that makes him notice each petal, each leaf, until every flower in the field becomes unique in his sight.

Although flowers and foliage need water to keep them fresh, it must be removed as quickly as possible to dry them. Some hardy flowers can dry upside down in the closet—simple enough work for a Two—but others can be pressed in a thick book, which requires a Four. Drying them in a medium, like sand or silica gel or dipping them in wax, is the work of a Six (and a most patient mother).

Unless your're buying the flowers or cutting them from the yard, it takes some foresight to keep them fresh until you can get home from an outing in the country. If you want to press flowers you should take a phone book with you, so you can slip a few between the pages wherever you stop, but if you dry them you'll need to put them in a well-banded plastic bag, a canister with a tight lid or a bucket of wet sand, so they won't wilt. If they do they'll dry badly. Finally, you'll have to get the owner's permission to take any flowers from his field, but wherever you are, only cut one wildflower from each plant, so it can reproduce itself.

When you get home, remove the leaves and either hang the flowers immediately, or if you're drying them in a medium like sand, put the stems in very warm water for 1-2 hours to harden them. If you're still not ready to work with them poke the stems into a damp sponge, so they won't get any wetter than necessary, but for best results, try to dry them before the day is done. Most weeds and many flowers will cure well in air, but only expect good luck with half the flowers dried in a medium. If you collect them often enough, the losses won't matter so much.

Cured Flowers

This is an easy method for a late Two, but it only works for hardy, fresh field flowers with long stems and small flowers, like goldenrod, and never with petal flowers, like ox-eyed daisies.

Have your child remove all leaves and help him tie the stems into loose bunches. Hang upside down from clothes hangers in a warm, dry place, like an attic or a utility room, so they won't mildew.

Cure   10-14 days
They can, of course, stay longer.

Treated Foliage

There is as much subtle beauty in a finely veined leaf as there is in a flamboyant flower. Your Three will see it well when he soaks branches in glycerin, for this drugstore chemical makes the leaves turn color dramatically. Some become deep brown, some mahogany, some bronze, depending on the species and the season, but the dogwood, that maverick, turns a bright green.

Not all foliage works and not every time but the experiment will fascinate a child. He'll have best luck with deciduous hardwoods like beech, birch, crabapple, maple and oak, but holly usually works too and so does bayberry, blueberry, forsythia, privet, rhododendron and rose. Once treated, the foliage keeps indefinitely in a vase without water, without shriveling and without losing its color. Our record is three years for ligustrum—a little dusty but still a rich chocolate brown.

Cut foliage when the leaves are green—a sign that the sap is running and the solution can run with it. Your child should crush the bottom 2" of each stem with a hammer, which is a job he'll do enthusiastically. In a jar

Combine   1 c. glycerin
                    3 c. hot water
Add   foliage
Soak   1-3 days
They're done when the top leaves feel oily to the

touch and all the leaves have a startlingly different color. The hotter the water, the quicker this change will be. You can use the solution over and over if it's reheated each time.

Pressed Flowers

Some pretty—and pretty expensive—pictures today are made with pressed flowers. A Four can press them with a fifty-fifty measure of success, if the flowers have only one or two layers of petals, like pansies or vinca minor. Fat flowers, like roses, carnations, hydrangeas or geraniums, should be pulled apart and pressed as petals.

Flowers press best in a telephone book, since its paper is so absorbent, or within a 3" stack of newspapers. Don't use the Sunday comics, because they may stain, and don't use paper towels or napkins, because the embossed design may transfer.

Collect   flowers/ferns/leaves
The flora mustn't be damp or cold—which means a sunny day, perhaps as late as noon—and the book shouldn't be cold either, or the flowers will be brown when they dry. Remove stems and leaves and lay the flowers in the book carefully, smoothing the petals so they don't crease and adding an entry every 4-6 pages.

Weight the book with a six pack of beer or the family Bible (whichever is handiest and heaviest) so light won't enter, and keep in a dry place.

Press   7-10 days
It's best for your child to keep the flowers in the book until he's ready to use them. If he removes them too soon they'll wilt and the leaves and fronds will curl, although these can be rescued by ironing them between two sheets of waxed paper.

Pressed Flower Pictures
Your Six can make a picture of his pressed flowers if he dots the center area of construction paper with Thinned White Glue (page 205) and waits 10 minutes, until it's quite tacky. With tweezers, have him lift a few leaves and fronds gently, one at a time, dropping them on the glue as a background. The flowers go on top of them, each slightly overlapping the next like a bouquet and any petals are scattered among them for balance. This is a case where too many are better than too few.

These flowers will fade unless you frame them under glass so air can't reach them. However, if you're going to that much trouble, glue the flowers to a ground of velvet or taffeta, which looks much better. Seal the back of the frame with tape.

Paraffin Flowers

It takes only seconds to wax fresh flowers and success is instant though not everlasting. Fresh flowers contain so much water they'll only look beautiful for a week or two, then they'll wither and brown like a pansy in Dorian Gray's lapel. Truth to tell, most fresh flowers last just as long, but this is such a wacky thing to do you'll be glad you did—once. Since paraffin melts at a low temperature, it's safe enough for your Five to work with you, but you need many papers on the counter to catch the drips.

Choose fresh flowers which have only a single layer of petals—like daisies—so that every surface can be covered and have your child cut off the bottom part of each stem that's been under water so the wax will stick. Set a 16-ounce tin can in gently boiling water. Into the can

Add   1 lb. paraffin

Melt the wax slowly and turn off the flame when it's clear. Use an imperfect flower to check the temperature of the wax. Too cool, it will show on the petals; too hot, the flower will shrivel. When the temperature is in between—about 130°—let your child dip a stem quickly into the wax, let it dry, then hold the stem to twirl the flower in the wax, coating it well. He should shake it slightly to lose any extra wax and then drop each stem into its own soda bottle to cool.

Remove any wax on clothes or counter by rubbing it with ice and peeling it free, and never, never pour leftover paraffin down the drain.

Dried Flowers

Although it may take a delicate little girl to arrange dried flowers, we've found the huskiest little boy will like to dry them.

Almost all flowers can be dried in sand, silica gel or in a mixture of cornmeal with borax, using the same technique with each, but petunias are too sticky for success, violets too fragile and bulb flowers too wet. Other flowers will be a little smaller and paler, although just as beautiful as before.

Some flowers take as long as two weeks to dry; but most take two to four days, depending on their delicacy, the size of their seed pods (which store water) and the humidity and the temperature in the room.

Dried flowers either can be used to make a picture, as with pressed flowers, or arranged in a bouquet, if wire stems are used.

Most of these flowers will last at least a year, and some, like pear blossoms, will last two, because the woodier the stems the longer the blossoms keep. Seal all dried flowers in plastic in summer for the humidity will ruin them unless you have an air-conditioned house.

Drying Media

Sand is the oldest method and the favorite of purists. You'll need sterilized sandbox sand, builder's sand or sharp quarry sand, which is sold in toy stores or garden centers. Sea sand is a bad substitute; it's not only salty but dirty and the bacteria in the dirt will spot the flowers.

Silica gel, sold in garden centers and through seed catalogues, is the newest, quickest drying method, as well as the easiest and most expensive. The deep blue gelatin bits scattered in this fine sand will turn pale lavender as they absorb the moisture.

Although the cornmeal medium fades flowers more than the other two media, the ingredients are at the grocery store, and it's quick to prepare. To make,

Mix   5 lbs. cornmeal
                 2 lbs. borax

All mixtures can be used again if baked and poured into airtight containers while still hot. Bake the sand for 1 hour at 200°, the gel for 30 minutes at 350°—until the beads are dark blue again—and the cornmeal mix for 1 hour at 150°. Stir all of them occasionally. Because the borax may harden in the baking, it must be stirred twice as much and then poured through a colander to screen any lumps.

Technique

Before your Six goes flower picking,

Assemble   lidded canister or suit box
                 drying medium
                 #20-#24 florist wire
                 florist tape

Have your child remove the stems, for they usually can't support the heads when they've dried. Also, foliage is much wetter than flowers and the petals would be burned before the leaves could dry. To make new stems, help him bend one end of each wire to look like Bopeep's crook. Cup the blossoms in your fingers while your child pushes the length of the wire through the flower so the crook is imbedded in the center.

Your child will need a large, lidded canister for smaller flowers, burying them vertically and upside down on a layer of mix and adding a layer of sand for each layer of flowers, bending the wires to fit if necessary. When you near the top of the container, poke the wires into the mix so these blooms are upright. Cover with 1″ of the medium.

Use a large suit box for tall, spiky flowers or for branches of fruit trees or dogwood (your own, since most states conserve theirs). Pour some mix in the box, make trenches to lay the flowers in them and cover with another inch of mix.

Seal any containers with tape, to keep out damp air, and keep them in a warm place. Help your child check the flowers after two days, for they can disintegrate if left too long in a medium. Flowers with a single layer of petals should dry in 2-3 days and multilayered ones in 4-5 days. If they take much longer, you may have packed too many in the box.

When petals are crisp, lift the top layer of flowers for your child and gently empty the container into a colander, so he can collect the rest. He can blow the dust from the blooms, while you brush any residue with a poster paint brush.

Twirl the wire so the florist tape will wrap around it—a task we found too tricky for our children and almost for us, but, fortunately, it isn't essential.

Arranging

Your Six should arrange these dried flowers as he would fresh ones, choosing a container a third as high as the tallest flower. Fill it halfway with sand, pebbles or sea shells, instead of water, for a tall arrangement and use a frog, florist's clay or a styrofoam ball for a short one. Small arrangements require a variety of shapes in flowers and a good frog, so that flowers can be poked from any angle,

but these flowers are so brittle they must be handled gently indeed. Use cured flowers or dried grasses as filler.

Sewing

In other countries, a child is taught to tat, embroider, knit or crochet as early as Four and yet in our culture the simplest sewing is often considered too hard for a child under Eight.

There are, of course, exceptions. When our good friend Leah was Four, she asked her mother to thread a needle for her and she's been sewing ever since, learning almost every step on her own. Today at Eleven, Leah makes skirts and shirts and weaves cloth on a loom, and if they're not perfect yet, they show as much creativity as any picture or any pottery her friends have made.

Your child's first attempts at sewing should begin at late Three, we think, with yarn, sewing cards and a crewel needle, which is blunt and has a big eye. First use blank index cards, in which you've punched some holes for him to make his own designs, and later use the follow-the-picture cards from the dimestore, which are harder.

A Four is ready to work with cloth if it's a small piece and if the material is stiff and crisp. He also needs a table, a good pair of scissors—and a mother nearby. At this age your child can learn the basic Running Stitch—the key to all hand sewing—and will like to sew scraps of cloth together for no reason at all (except perhaps to him). As in all his hand sewing, have him use a doubled thread, which you'll have to knot at each end, a job too complicated even for most Sixes.

A Five begins simple embroidery and uses the stitches to make toys, like a beanbag, but a Six is ready to handle a sewing machine if you keep it threaded.

The mechanics of either hand or machine sewing aren't easy to master, but if you have patience, if you stop the lesson before one of you cries and if your child believes that everyone else has trouble at first (and they do), he'll feel confident enough to pursue this avenue of expression too.

Unweaving

Some children enjoy precise work and this is one of the precisest. To make cocktail napkins, use any loosely woven fabric like burlap. The smaller the child, the looser the weave should be, for it's the removal of various threads that makes the design.

Cut   3″ × 6″ pieces

Have your child wrap two threads around his forefinger and pull them at the same time, so they won't break so easily. The unweaving of one napkin needn't, and probably couldn't, match another. We call that creativity.

— — — — — — — — — — — —

Running Stitch

This simple stitch is as essential to hand sewing as it is to embroidery and is no more than the weaving of a needle in and out, in and out, as evenly as possible, so the thread is tight enough to lie flat on the cloth but not so tight it could pucker it. To help your child keep it like that, have him smooth the material across his bent knee every time he's taken a few stitches.

The Apron

An apron is an admirable thing to sew; it brings out the virtue in us all. To make,

Assemble   1 yd. ribbon, 1″ wide
                      1 terrycloth tea towel

The ribbon covers one end of the towel to make the sash and the other end is folded to make pockets—all steps which use the Running Stitch. Have your child sew across the top of the towel and then pull the thread a little to gather it, but you'll have to knot it in place. Lay the towel on the table and help him pin the sash over these gathers. To make pockets, fold the bottom third of the towel over on itself and pin in place. Have him sew the sides together with No. 50 thread and sew the pocket down the center so it won't flop open. The ribbon should be sewed in place twice, to withstand washing.

The Pillow

Every dolly needs a place to rest her empty head. To make a pillow, have your Four

Assemble   two 9″ squares of cloth
                      many old, clean stockings

Any elastic on the hose should be cut away and the stockings heaped between the squares. Help your child pin the squares together and, using embroidery thread and a needle, sew them together with a Running Stitch 1″ from the edge. Knot the thread yourself and pink the material to prevent raveling.

The Beanbag

The beanbag is almost as necessary in childhood as the storybook and a child can make it himself. With a funnel, have him pour any small beans, like lentils, into an odd mitten or sock until it's about two-thirds full—still heavy enough to carry through the air but not so packed it could hurt anyone if it hit him. Have your Four sew the bag together with embroidery thread and a crewel needle, using a small Running Stitch.

Doll's Serape

The moment your child can cut with scissors, he can make this serape, which boy dolls and girl dolls wear with aplomb.

Assemble   1 strip of cloth
                      10″ length of ribbon

The material should be slightly wider than the doll's shoulders and twice the distance between the shoulders and the knees, for that's how long this costume reaches. The serape slides over the doll's head, through a cross cut in the exact center of the strip. Your child can do this by folding the material in half horizontally and then vertically, cutting perpendicular to each fold, as deeply as necessary. The ribbon becomes the sash.

Headdress

Your Four will take longer to collect exactly the right feathers on his walks than he will to make this headdress. Help him measure the cloth but he can cut it himself.

Assemble   one 6″ × 12″ strip of cloth
                      9 feathers

Help him fold the cloth in half, then fold again, until the strip is only 1½″ wide. Your child should slide the feathers between the folds, with the biggest in the center, and pin them in place.

Because the quills are tough, push the needle once or twice through each one yourself, to secure them, then have your child sew tightly around each quill to finish the job. Tie around his head.

Embroidery

All hand sewing is improved by the skill of embroidery, which your Five can learn if you teach him the stitches and let him sew his own design as he goes. Keep the supplies tidy, as the skeins are a mess to untangle, and have your child sew with three strands of embroidery thread, doubled, which he'll cut first for you to separate from the rest. A hoop is essential to embroider the Running Stitch and the Cross-stitch but not the Blanket Stitch.

XXXXXXXXX XXXXXXXXXX

Cross-stitch

To begin, let your Five draw a line of Xs on the top of the cloth, then follow this pattern by crisscrossing two Running Stitches over each X and moving on to the next from the underside. The only thread that shows should make an X

⊔⊔⊔⊔⊔⊔⊔⊔⊔⊔⊔⊔⊔⊔⊔⊔⊔⊔⊔⊔⊔⊔⊔

Blanket Stitch

This is much harder and is used only on a border, forming a series of square U's. To make each U, have your child poke the needle from the underside of the material, about 1/8" from the edge, then stick the needle through the loop before the thread is tightened. He'll make three stitches before he sees the pattern.

Machine Sewing

The sewing machine is such a clever invention that it won't break if your Six uses it—so he should.

It will be awhile before he cares how it's threaded or how the tensions make the threads knot in the cloth every time the needle meets the feeder. These are incidentals; right now he wants to run it.

When your child presses the starter foot it will be quite as exciting for him as the first time you pressed the accelerator of a car and, like you, your child will want to know how to stop it. Let him sew on scraps of cloth to practice starting and stopping the motor, both to give him the feel of the machine and to help him realize that it doesn't have a will of its own.

He can slip the material beneath the presser foot and lower it, pull the balance wheel to bring the needle down into the fabric to keep it still, then hold his left hand behind the needle to hold and guide the material as it moves. His right hand must be far in front of the needle, so it won't hit his finger.

After this practice, he's ready to learn the gentle one, two, three, four process that finishes a seam: lifting the presser foot, lifting the needle, pulling away the fabric and cutting the thread.

To begin real sewing, choose a simple idea, like a bag to hold his marbles, using a pretty, crisp material that has obvious right and wrong sides to make the pieces easier to match. Draw a pattern first on smooth brown paper and have your child cut and pin it to the material and then cut the material itself. Help him pin the pieces together (there should be no more than three) and baste the seams with a Running Stitch to make the machine stitching smoother and easier. It also lets him remove the pins before he starts to sew—a good idea for they can cause a novice a lot of trouble.

You can expect to tie all threads yourself, although a late Six is ready to secure the seam by reversing several stitches at the beginning and end of it—if reminded. When he's done, have him pull the basting threads from the seams and sew any hems by hand, using any of the basic stitches. This not only looks prettier, it's also the way for your first-class child to do a first-class job.

Doll's Coat

Your Six can make a simple three-piece coat for a doll, varying it in size according to the size of the doll. Cut one thickness for the back and cut the front twice—once with the sleeve facing right, once with it facing left. Have him sew the sleeve seams, top and bottom, then the side seams. The rest is done by hand. Your child should fold and pin the raw edges at the neck, the sleeves and the hem, sewing them with embroidery thread in the Blanket Stitch.

Drama

The child with a dramatic imagination has a hundred playmates and a thousand games. Like many other expressions, it all begins in infancy. A baby is a consummate actor; he knows exactly how to make his audience laugh or how to wring their hearts. He'll flirt and sigh, giggle and coo, scowl and shriek, experimenting with every emotion and technique. He'll improvise, pretend and invent, but how far he goes depends on the sights, sounds and ideas in his memory bank and how rich those images are.

A child can't hop like a bunny if he's never seen a rabbit or at least seen its picture, and he surely can't imagine what it's like to row a boat if he's never heard of a boat. His frame of reference is stretched with each new experience you offer and when you heighten the experience it's stretched even more. You do this with dress-ups and props and with your questions and suggestions. To tie a helium balloon to your child's wrist and ask if he thinks he can float to the stars will focus his imagination on that slight tug so sharply he can dream of a dozen balloons sailing him anywhere.

It isn't that you'll make-believe all day long, but if his imagination is jostled enough, he'll seldom be bored—or boring.

His first planned brush with make-believe is around three months when you play peekaboo, covering your face and quickly appearing again, first behind a handkerchief, then as he understands the game, behind the sofa, the chair, the curtain.

To let your child act his dramatic best, he'll need props. By six months, he'll start to play with a latch-free pocketbook, a set of old keys and a comb to rub over his head (whether he has any hair or not). In a few months he can respond to peekaboo, crawling behind the skinny avocado plant or under the receiving blanket, and then inventing a whole new game, he pretends the blanket is first a hat, then a handkerchief in which he blows his nose.

By One, he improvises in earnest and everything in the house is likely to become something else. Ramon would push a carrot stick around his high chair tray, humming as if it were a car, and Nadia used the cotton balls to dust—a chore she must have learned in heaven for she couldn't have learned it at home.

Since "moo-moo" and "arf-arf" are among a child's first words, it will be no surprise when he imitates the way animals walk, run and eat, and you can expect him to imitate "Mama" too—scrubbing when you scrub, talking on a toy telephone whenever you answer the real one. A mid-One will copy the way you stand, the way you take off your glasses or raise your eyebrows. At times he'll want to wear your gloves and shoes and want to carry your briefcase too. Different children have different fixations. We had one child so addicted to hats that she even wore one in the bathtub and Kate would have walked naked past the White House as long as she had her rubber beads around her neck. It's fine, we think, to let these eccentricities flourish, as long as they don't hurt anyone, for the drama your child puts in his life helps shape a distinct personality.

A pair of tall boots, you'll find, will make a performer of the most timid child, and high heels turn a tree-climbing tomboy into a mincing, prancing lady—briefly. Day-to-day clothes, in fact, affect a child so much that we relied on party clothes and patent slippers to make little Meg behave and found our quiet Nell became twice as outgoing when she wore her tough-guy jeans.

A Two spends hours pretending to be all the grown-up people he's ever seen—another reason for him to see many people. For this he needs one flexible costume, like a shawl which he can drape forty-two ways, or perhaps a piece of fur (either real or fake) with its silky, sexy texture. Whether he's wearing a costume or not, he'll still spend many minutes a day before his beloved mirror and this is dandy. A mirror not only encourages a child to make bizarre faces but it makes him be good too. No child can cry or even stay angry in front of one, proving once more that children are no different from adults.

A Three needs props, as he begins to play mother and father with a doll and a carriage or a tricycle. He wants to sit on a large cardboard box—a train—or under a card table covered with a sheet—a playhouse—and he's ready for his first charades, pretending to be a stop sign, a car and a chair, as well as a tree, a gust of wind, a flower or the seed itself. All he needs is an occasional suggestion and an audience who may laugh at his antics, but never at him.

A Four needs costumes too. One day he's an Indian, the next a cowboy, the third a sailor and, while he'll be expected to improvise most of his outfits, he'll be very happy to have one that's beautiful, complete and by all means of good quality. A cheesecloth Halloween costume will fall apart quickly, no matter how well your child takes care of it, and then he'll be sure to think it's his fault—a lesson which makes him wonder why he should take care of anything.

Between now and Five, your collection of dress-ups will be much bigger and you'll find a suitcase holds them best and even is a prop in itself. Your child will want to enact his fantasies with his friends. Together they'll develop elaborate stories and they're sure to dragoon a smaller child to play the baby because every children's play has a baby just as surely as it has tears, misery and at least one fight. Pathos is the trademark of all young actors.

A Five will translate his dramatics into puppet theater, making figures out of anything from peanut shells to paper bags, and for this he'll like the simple stage our friend Priscilla used so much. It's the easiest design we've ever seen.

By Six, charades can become a family ritual (we hope it does) with everyone enacting the simplest titles from your child's library. Now he becomes so self-confident about his abilities that he and his friends will produce a show, any time, with many props, a curtain, a great opening line and then a collapse into an unintelligible script, giggles and then recriminations, all of which are forgotten before the next production—seldom more than a week later.

For our children, this love of drama made them beg for old-fashioned home theatricals. This has led to an annual production for neighborhood children, wittily written and improbably plotted by one of the fathers, stage-managed and costumed by two of the mothers and fantastically acted by children from Five to Twelve who don't mind the hours of rehearsals so long as they're treated like professionals—and so long as they all have the same number of lines.

Dress-ups

While a child doesn't need a set of props for every role, he does need a selection from many—enough to tickle his fancy.

A secondhand shop is a fine source for pocketbooks, jewelry and especially canes, which teach children to strut; but of all the imaginative dress-ups, we've found hats are best. A hardhat, and a plastic fireman's hat from the toy store, a baseball cap, a football helmet and a cowboy hat all will spark hundreds of Walter Mitty games. You'll find a big selection of authentic hats for soldiers and sailors, workmen and trainmen at a surplus store, which apparently acquires leftover sizes, for many are very small. You can find a magnifying glass here too—for your detective—and a real stethoscope, which encourages the more positive side of that great favorite—playing doctor. This is a game where children are wont to strip and take temperatures, bottoms up; a game, therefore, that you'll want to supervise more carefully than almost any other since their thermometers are likely to range from pencils to popsicle sticks.

You also will want to consider not only how a prop will be used, but how safe it is and the younger the child, the more careful you'll have to be. He can't wear neckties or necklaces to bed, nor have props that contain harmful dyes, sharp edges or pins, or shoes that have straps or high heels and, of course, he can't stomp the stairs in any dress-up shoes.

The props he likes best will be the ones that make him feel heroic, for no young child is ready to pretend to be a villain. To make fairy tales come alive, children enjoy a sword, made of one long piece of lathe with a shorter piece nailed across it for the guard; a baton, which is both a scepter and a magic wand and a royal train: three feet of fabric with a grommet at one end to fasten the cloak under the chin and a mantle made by doubling the materials back over the shoulder and pasting cotton to it. He doesn't know what ermine looks like anyway.

Sarah, ordinarily one of our most magnanimous friends, could only let another child wear her gauzy fairy princess gown from Grandma for ten minutes without agony, so we suggest you might make two of any simple but glamorous costume. Harmony is its own reward.

All of these dress-ups should be kept together in a trunk or a big suitcase, where you'll also want a false beard (hard to find, but a dramatic delight); a wig; a chapstick (but not a lipstick, since that's asking for trouble); powder and rouge puffs; aprons that can turn into Superman capes; one of your husband's old hats, a vest and a pair of his pants; several pairs of discarded slippers, tennis shoes and boots—yours and his; an old dress that reaches to the floor like an evening gown and gloves—the longer the better, but they don't have to match.

These all help a child play the role he thinks is the most heroic of all: the role of parent.

Playing House

When a child can play-act the everyday role, he feels more in charge of his destiny—and certainly nothing is as everyday as housework. While he'll do most of his cooking at your stove, it's nice to have this one just for make-believe. Choose a box that's as high as his elbow, remove the flaps and turn it upside down. Paint the box the color of your own stove, with four black circles on top, four knobs on the front for decoration. Cut out an oven door and screw a knob to the front for a handle. Keep the flap shut by poking a cotter pin just above the door, from inside to the outside, so he can slide the prongs horizontally to open the oven and vertically to keep it shut. Later you may want to get a real toy stove—not the metal sort that heats (for their safety is questionable), but a wooden one. However, these stoves are in most good nursery schools and generally that's enough for a child.

Broadcast Game

It's a little ridiculous to describe this game, but if you give a Four a hairbrush and call it a microphone, he'll sing, broadcast, tell a story or just gab—a particularly good game of drama when you're on a car trip. Even the quietest child becomes garrulous in front of a mike.

Fortune Telling

Once you've tied a scarf on your head and read your child's palm, he'll re-enact this scene a dozen times with his friends. To get him started, explain

the head line

the heart line

the life line

Predict anything as long as the forecast is happy and he lives one hundred years. Let any little wrinkles represent the children and promise as many as he has in his nursery school, which will please him. He won't care a whit about marriage, however, since every little boy knows he'll marry his mother and every little girl will marry her dad. Instead, concentrate on his heroic future. If you're like other mothers, you'll just be dreaming out loud.

Charades

Props, let us emphasize, needn't and shouldn't be part of all drama, because you want your child to know the joy of creating through action alone—the essence of all good stagework.

It won't take long before your Three can be an animal, a vegetable or a mineral at the merest hint. He is at once a stationary, solitary rock; a pinwheel flailing his arms; a bud opening its petals.

As we learned from Jennifer, a fascinating Four whose mother schools her in sensitivity the way another mother might teach reading—a child can pretend to be any animal from a ferocious lion to a sweet mouse, stalking first through a shag rug whose pile feels taller than bamboo, then nibbling real cheese held tightly in tiny front paws.

You help your child learn to feel from within himself each time he can pretend to be something else—even a lima bean. After he's seen one sprout in a clear plastic pot, clinging its tendrils around a popsicle stick, he can imagine he's been planted in some nice, rich earth where it's cozy and warm, growing plump in his shell beneath the earth. Suddenly he can burst out of it pushing through the soil with a well-bent head and wrapping his arms around a sturdy broomstick. He begins to flower and then to fruit, every step of which he can enact as you talk about the story of a seedling and imagine what it's like to grow up green.

We've found it takes little practice before a Five can perfect his improvisational techniques well enough to take part in a simple family game of charades. For this game, use book titles he knows, limited to three words, and place little emphasis on winning. No Six is ready for competition like that.

Puppets

A child can create drama in many ways, but as he gets older he often feels more freedom if he can have puppets do the talking instead of himself. For the classic puppet of papier mâché, see page 209.

Paper Bag Puppets

A Two can bring two small paper bags to life, one on each hand. Draw a face for him on each bag and fasten them on his wrists with a string, some tape or a rubber band. He can make them himself by Three.

Animal Puppets

Your old glove can become a rabbit for your Four if you sew the thumb to the palm and make ears out of the fingers by sewing or stapling the first and last two fingers together. Sew buttons on the other side for the eyes and the mouth and then have your child wear it backward, with his fingers wriggling in the ears and his hand twitching his face: a rabbit.

Finger Puppets

Although these sound simple, it takes the steady hand of a Six to put a face on a peanut shell. To make, have him fit ten shells on his fingers like thimbles, then draw the eyes and mouth with a fine, felt-tipped pen. He'll cover his fingers and thumbs with these puppets so they can bow and talk to each other—the only players in a single-member cast and good company on a nothing day.

Puppet Theater

This theater has a double dividend. It's so inviting it encourages frequent use and the rest of the time it stands flat against the wall looking pretty.

Assemble one 2' X 3' piece of plywood, ½" thick
one 16" length of 2" molding
one 2' length of 2" molding
2 small cabinet hinges
four 1" No. 8 roundhead wood screws
one 4" length of 2" X 4"
30" length of string
two 12" X 15" panels of fabric
paneling adhesive
jigsaw
enamel paint

The theater will stand 3' high with a window across the top of the stage and simple braces in both front and back, so it won't topple.

Measure and draw a 6" X 16" rectangle on the sheet of plywood, leaving 1" of wood along the top

and 4" on either side. Cut it cleanly with a jigsaw.

To make the pair of side braces, use this rectangle and diagonally cut it into two triangles, 6" X 16" X 17". To attach them, hinge the short side of each brace to the front of the theater—one alongside the lower right corner and one alongside the lower left, so the 16" side of each triangle can swing forward and distribute the weight of the plywood.

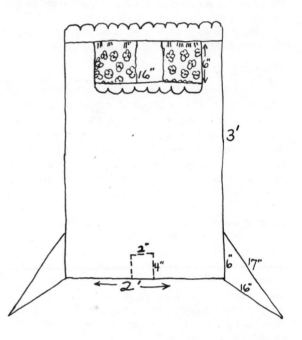

The theater still needs another brace in the back, and for this you'll use the simple scrap of 2" X 4". Glue its narrow side vertically against the center of the base, which gives it a 4" support on the floor so it can't fall backward. For extra strength screw the block in place from the front. To trim the theater, glue the 2' piece of molding across the top to cover the narrow strip and the short piece along the bottom of the window. Then paint it. Make the curtains by hemming the top of the material and running a string through it. The string is held from cup hooks, which should be screwed into the upper corners of the stage, but from the back, so they won't show. Your child can slide the curtain open for his productions.

Dance

To a child, dancing is as natural as laughter. He bounces to the beat of music from the time he can stand, for dancing is bred in his bones. It's been a part of every civilization, every culture, for all ages.

You encourage this love of rhythm when you bounce him on your knee and twirl him about the room in your arms, and when he's a toddler you and your husband will dance with him while he sways and spins to music without any self-consciousness at all. He learns to move his whole body in any way the music affects him: hopping, tiptoeing, jumping, crawling or rolling into a ball. Only dance releases so much energy so creatively and spontaneously.

If dancing has been a natural outlet for your child, by Three he'll like to dance regularly with other children, not as a show-off, but as if he were painting a picture with his body. All you'll need is a cleared room, a smooth floor, bare feet, a record player and music with many moods and beats. Leotards, perhaps a flashy scarf, a peasant shirt for a boy, a full skirt for a girl all help make it much more exciting.

If your child pines for a pair of dancing shoes the best you can give him are rhythmic shoes, those ugly suede sandals, because they do give good leverage and they last much longer than the snug-fitting ballet shoes. We think tights are best, for they're safe, as long as you rip the seams in the soles so he can dance barefoot, and because they keep his legs warm and help him pretend he's a real dancer.

You may want to advance to lessons at Four, for they can counteract the bad posture and clumsiness that sometimes begin at this age. Tumbling, modern dance and especially eurhythmics help a child feel more in command of his body, but the contortions of acrobatics are too strenuous for him, and ballet requires the concentration of an older child to swivel the whole leg from the hip joint. Even a Six uses his foot to direct his leg and this will cause bulging muscles and poor posture later.

Toe shoes, as fetching as they are, cause trouble too, since young bones aren't developed well enough to take the strain. Even the most gifted ballerina must wait until she's at least Ten, has had several years of ballet—and the teacher says she's ready.

If your child does take lessons the time he spends on them should be just a fraction of the time he spends dancing, for dancing is meant to be as much a part of life as art or sunshine.

Dancing School

If you plan to send your child to dancing school you'll want to visit it first, as you would any school.

Beware of high-pressure salesmanship which indicates that the business of the school comes before the pleasure of the children, and avoid schools which insist on fancy recitals. They may make a mother happy, but we never saw a young child who enjoyed them.

The building should have well-lighted rooms, big enough for easy movement, but not a ballroom. This is unnecessary since the classes should be limited to twenty.

The best dancing schools have a good pianist to accompany the children, but the teacher may make or buy her own special teaching tapes and records which substitute well. She also needs a bongo drum or some percussion instrument to emphasize the beat.

In a good class, a teacher extracts each child's individual expression, giving only enough direction to create the order the children need to respond to the music as well as to each other. You can judge the teacher's ability by the grace and ease of her own body, the warmth and encouragement she shows the children and how well she understands how they're built, so that none of the movements she suggests will strain their muscles—the most critical knowledge she can have.

Music

Long before your child ever begins to play a musical instrument or even to sing, his ear will record a dictionary of sounds, categorizing noises, imitating them and creating new ones.

If songs and music are part of your baby's life he'll perform before he can talk, ahhhhing strings of sounds, and even at six months, shaking a tambourine and blowing into a wooden horn. He only needs you to blow the horn in front of him first, with great, obvious breaths, then hold it in his mouth for him to copy. Sooner or later he'll produce a magical toot. Once he can do this he's ready for a huge and, therefore, quite safe police-man's whistle, although you may not be. It's much too loud for frequent use, but an occasional blast certainly delights a child.

You'll want these and the tambourine to be your baby's first musical instruments. After that we think he'll profit by simple, one-note percussion instruments because they let him concentrate on pitch. A primitive bongo drum is a good starter, followed by small cymbals, bells and a triangle (any of which cost less than a child's hardcover book), and by Three, sandpaper blocks, one of the first musical instruments he'll make.

A Four is ready for something more complicated, like a wooden xylophone or a marimba, and if his interest in music is strong enough you might consider tone bars too. Again, make sure the pitch is true. Your child will like to play any of these instruments with his friends, but he needs to practice alone too, discovering, experimenting and repeating the different sequences he invents. When you encourage music you also must set limits. A fine musical instrument needs a loving touch, just like a little baby. Although you'll let him sound the notes occasionally, he must be expected to do it gently.

We don't think these limits will curb his creativity any more than it will curb a future writer when you expect him to scribble on paper and not on the walls. A child has to learn to express himself and still be able to respect all things, from pianos to people.

You probably will be able to notice a musical bent in your child by the time he's Five or Six, just by the way he behaves. This child will talk about music more, move his body in time with the songs in his head, ask for records more often than books and perhaps beg to learn to play a particular instrument. Do what you can, but you should realize that standard lessons are not ideal for a young child. Not only are they expensive, but a child usually isn't ready for them until he's old enough to read well.

There are, however, some very successful methods which teach a child to play before he can read notes, the way he learns to talk before he can read letters. Both the Carl Orff and the Suzuki systems use group lessons, believing that children find the same pleasure in making music together in a class as adults do in a symphony orchestra.

In the Orff approach, a group of children learn to play the simplest songs in unison. In Suzuki, the widely taught Japanese method for violin, a child as young as Three is given a tiny fiddle and plunged into sophisticated musical scores, concentrating first on making music and then refining it later. Here a child studies both in individual and group lessons, with the mother not only supervising the practice and attending the classes, but often becoming so involved that she studies the violin with him.

When he's ready for traditional training he'll need a teacher so good she can stretch his potential to its limits and still make the half hour happy.

Homemade Musical Instruments

A baby absorbs some sense of sound when you give him a wooden spoon and a metal one so he can hear the different tones they make when they're banged first on a metal pot and then on a wooden salad bowl.

A mid-Two will like a primitive maraca you make by filling half of a small tin can with dried beans, covering it with a plastic lid and taping it shut. A tambourine is made by safety-pinning small bells around a sturdy paper plate, which any young child will shake (and shake and shake).

With some help he can make other instruments himself, and he should, for it's the making of them that helps him learn how sound is made and pitch is changed.

Water Pipes

A Three can fill six heavy glasses with water, each at a different level, and tap tunes against them with either a metal or a wooden spoon for a drumstick. Different amounts of water make different tones. When he's Six he can align the glasses so the levels are graduated to make the scale.

Sandpaper Blocks

These wooden blocks, which sound rather dreadful to us, are rubbed together to the beat of the music and are popular with children and nursery schools. For your Four to make a pair

Saw   two 5″ lengths of 2″ X 4″
Cut   2 pieces 00 sandpaper, 4″ X 5″

You'll do the sawing but your Four will do the cutting and can paint one wide side of each piece of wood with Thinned White Glue and paste the paper to it (page 205).

Dry   30 minutes

Harp

A Five can combine eight large rubber bands and a little shoe box to make a harp. Have your child wrap the empty, topless box with bands, roughly equidistant and, if possible, using both thick and thin ones to produce different tones. For a Six to make a more elaborate harp

Saw   one 10″ square of wood shelving

Cut it diagonally, saving only one piece. Along one 10″ side have your Six

Hammer   eight 8-penny nails

You'll have to pound 8 more nails into the other 10″ side so the nails will be in line with his row. To string it

Cut   two 4″ lengths of nylon fish line
            three 10″ lengths of nylon fish line
            three 14″ lengths of nylon fish line

If your child can tie a knot let him tie a length to every nail he's hammered, with the short ones near the right angle, the long ones at the far end. So the harp strings will be tense enough for twanging, you'll have to tie them to the other side yourself, giving any string a few extra loops around its nail-head if the line slackens. He can cut the tails when the strings are secure.

Writing

Making Books

Your Three can make his own book if you collect a few pictures he draws and write the captions, helping him tie them together into the simplest story by the discreet questions you ask. Later you can turn the tables on his "Tell me a story," by asking him to tell you a story of his own. It may be his own version of "The Three Bears," or it may be a dream or a nice bit of fantasy, but if you take it as dictation and type it onto several sheets of paper, he can draw the pictures to illustrate his text. Give any of these books a title page and either staple the sheets together or bind them with yarn. He'll be so impressed he'll memorize the words and read them back again and again.

Poetry

At Four, when every child rolls words on his tongue as if they were lollipops, you'll find that many of them are as sweet as poetry. At this lyrical age, his conversation often has an instinctive beat, his ideas are as free as space and his words so simple and direct that they can be precise as a poet's. Since this almost excessive pleasure with words doesn't last, you'll want to keep a record of it, just as you would a photograph. We found long family car trips could become quite passable when we'd scribble Kate's prattle into the format of verse. If poems didn't have to rhyme for T. S. Eliot they didn't have to rhyme for her either.

Round Robin Story

To tell a story in the round is almost as exciting to a Five as going to a movie—and possibly a lot more memorable. You'll need several children sitting in a circle while you invent maybe the first two paragraphs of a story and then, in midsentence, point to a child to continue it, letting him talk for two to three minutes before you point to the next child, again at random, again midsentence, so the plot takes wacky turns. By Six, the children need no more than "A boy named Ramon went to the circus and . . ." to follow with an idea. If you take notes and type the story for them the treat is compounded. The charm of a by-line begins very young.

Synonyms and Other Nyms

Every time a mid-One masters a word, teach him another in its place. Use only that one for a while, then switch back and forth. Our Kate and Mike, at Five and Four, used to race each other to find synonyms for the easy words we'd suggest, like happy and sad, which occupied them on long, crosstown bus rides. Antonyms and homonyms work just as well.

Cliché Game

In our writing family, each child knew what synonyms and antonyms were by the time he was Four (but nothing, alas, about fishing or baseball).

It was the Cliché Game, however, that pleased our Nell best, for it bailed her out of any argument. When the insufferable little boy said, "Naah, naaaah, you're a . . .," she could counter with exquisite sophistication, "That's a cliché." This was such a surprise it let her leave the scene in dignity.

Your late Three can understand clichés when you tell him that some phrases, like "black as night," are used again and again because they mean the same to everyone. Together you can pick out old ones and invent new ones, for if there's another way to describe the blackness of night, you can expect your original Four to find it. A nice game for a wet day.

Typing

It's as hard for a child to write before he can form letters well as it is for him to run with a weight on his back. We found the faster our children learned to put words on paper, the more creative they could be. Cursive letters are quicker than printed ones for a Six and calligraphy makes them more fun to learn, but since we weren't patient enough to teach either one, we taught typing instead. It was a small miracle; the touch system turned out to be a cinch.

A child masters typing the same way he masters printing, which is not very well. Still, it makes him more eager to learn the other forms of writing and that's what it's all about.

Unlike the sewing machine, a typewriter does get out of kilter easily, but you can fix it easily too, unless you're using a toy, which is an impossible contraption. Instead, use either an electric typewriter or a manual with a very gentle touch, for the keys must be light enough for a child to strike.

To teach typing, color your child's fingernails with waterproof, felt-tipped pens in five colors—each hand the same—and then paint the typewriter keys, including the space bar, to match the pattern his fingers will follow: left forefinger in orange and the letter "F" too. The code lets a child use the proper finger to hit the proper key.

Set the left hand on **ASDF** and the right hand on **JKL:** and remind your child to return to them every time he hits a letter, so he won't jam the keys. Although he'll look at them before he strikes the letters, he'll almost always use the correct fingers and after two or three lessons, he can remember the system for months. As for spelling, we don't worry much about that. A child is mainly interested in typing his name and a few three-letter words, which you'll spell for him if he asks you. While your child will never be a speed typist until he takes one of those dreary courses in school, he probably will do better than you expect. As our friend Andy announced after his first lesson, "I really typed fast when *she* left the room."

Capabilities

Any capability a child acquires—even in the smallest degree—will help him feel more comfortable to develop it as he grows older. Although your child still will learn to carpenter or cook as an adult, he'll be much less clumsy if he's had a chance to practice as a child.

To help your child be as self-confident in his skills as he is in everything else, he needs a chance to garden, to cook and to handle tools. When a child can know the pride of painting a baseboard or transforming a packet of seeds into a row of lettuce—or a head of lettuce into a salad for supper—he'll find that there is a joy in production just as there is joy in creation.

To be sure, it's a bother to begin to teach a Two these skills, but this is another way you show respect to a child—an unspoken compliment that tells him he's smart enough and adept enough to be a part of the work in the household, as well as the play. While his efforts won't be perfect even at Six, they'll be a real help at Twelve, but there are psychic rewards at any age. A family is strong not for what the parents give to it, but for what every member gives.

Workshop

Whenever you accomplish something permanent, you feel better about yourself. Your child is just the same, which explains the joy that manual labor brings him. Refinishing, plumbing, carpentry, bricklaying and plastering all develop a child's dexterity and self-assurance and satisfy his drive to feel part of the real world, which is particularly important for girls, for they need extra help to break our social conventions.

We give more advice on the restoration of furniture than anything else, both because we know

a lot about it and because tangible accomplishments win compliments—the bread and wine of life.

You'll need to take more safety precautions in these activities than in any others we suggest, and to keep yourself and the rest of the house safe, you'll need to work alongside your child except when he uses the Plumber's Box or, when he gets more adept, the carpentry tools. At the same time, you must let him do as much of the work as he can, for the more you intrude, the more you chip away his ego—exactly the opposite of your goal.

Beginning at Two, your child can guide the electric sander, oil the squeaks out of hinges, help you revive dirty furniture and, before the year is done, can use his Plumber's Box—an assortment of pipes and joints he likes to fit together. Most of this is about as productive as painting the pavement with water and a 2" brush and he should do this too. It's one more workshop triumph.

A Three is ready for a Carpenter's Box, for he can handle many workshop tools and he can help you with more of the odd jobs: scrubbing carved wood with hot red wine and a toothbrush, feeding furniture with oil and soaping the runners of bureau drawers.

The masterful Four, always his own favorite hero, can lay bricks if you mix the concrete and sink the first course with him. He also can help you strip some furniture with denatured alcohol (and a lot of fresh air), wipe a stain—a pleasantly messy job—and paint the first wash coats of shellac, but he won't do any of these for more than twenty minutes and, of course, he won't do them very well.

A Five and a friend can saw three-inch logs with a bucksaw, but he should work with you and no one else when he cuts with pruning shears, because in his enthusiasm he may move too fast and hurt a little child. He also might hurt the bush, unless you keep a sharp eye, for pruning is a hard job to quit, but don't withhold the shears, for nothing inflates his ego so much. One day he'll discover that the length of the levers governs the power of the tool, but now it teaches him that he's the smartest, biggest, strongest person around.

A Six can give a prime coat of latex to a radiator or a fence, patch small nail holes in plaster and hold the wood you saw—all with enough skill to be rather helpful.

Plumbing

A late Two can assemble and reassemble pipes into a dozen designs with little help, and by Four can work for thirty unsupervised minutes—a joy for both of you. A little boy especially enjoys the role of a master mechanic and is often about as successful as his father. His interest is stimulated by one of the big events of his life—the Great John Overflow, which usually leads to the Coming of the Plumber. Later you can commemorate the occasion by giving him some pipes and fittings.

Plumber's Box

In a carton or a wooden box

Assemble   plunger
                   6-12 lengths of pipe, 6-24" long
                   12-24 fittings
                   petroleum jelly
                   striped cap

Have the pipes cut at the hardware store and rub all threads with the jelly, so your child can screw the pipes into them more easily. The fittings, you'll find, have lovely names—crosses, bends and elbows—and nipples, unions, eccentric couplings and female adapters. This should appeal to his sense of silliness. The box itself appeals to your worker's sense of order (which he does have) and because a worker puts away his tools. If your worker doesn't, put them away yourself and keep them away for a time. A plumber can't leave his tools about and still go to the next job.

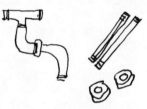

Some may argue that the striped hat—available at surplus stores—is not essential, but it does give that element of staging your child likes. The same thing is probably true for plumbers.

Bricklaying

As you've discovered on many walks, construction fascinates a child—boy or girl. The roaring of trucks, the scooping of earth, the hoisting of beams all mesmerize him, but simple bricklaying has a special appeal. It's so much like blockbuilding that he thinks he can do it—and he can.

At Two, he watches with fascination as the hod carrier balances a load of bricks across his back and a mason lays them in rapid, one-two-three motions.

If you buy twenty to thirty bricks from a demolition or construction site and then leave them in the back yard, your mid-Three will lug them, stack them and lay them without waiting to be told. He also will drop them, and since each brick weighs four pounds, he'd better wear shoes.

He'll soon be ready to lay a flat square of bricks in sand and by Four can set them in mortar. He even can build a little wall, although it will take days. When he gets to the wall-building stage, you'll want to explain the reason for each step and the correct technical terms; he'll savor every bit of such exotic information. He may want to know what mortar is made of (sand, cement, lime and water) and that the end of the brick is called the header, the flat side the stretcher—names which also make it easier for you to give clear instructions. You can tell him that bricks are laid in different patterns, called bonds, not just to be pretty but to reinforce each other.

Patio Square

This square of bricks looks well under a big potted plant or a portable barbecue grill, where the grass won't grow. You'll do the digging, but your child will do the rest.

Assemble   30 lbs. building sand
                   8 common bricks
Dig   17" square, 4½" deep
Fill   2" sand

He can lay the bricks flat in the sand in two parallel rows, although a true construction buff may work

out more complex patterns. Over them

Pour   sand

Have him sweep the square clean when the cracks are filled completely—and then quickly cover it with the plant or the grill before he takes the bricks out again.

The Wall

A low brick wall in the corner of the yard offends no one and it's one of the biggest ego builders your child ever will know. We recommend a wall that's three bricks long, with five courses of brick—two below ground for the foundation and three above—and laid in the most basic pattern: Simple Running Bond.

Assemble   15 common bricks
20 lbs. prepared mortar mix
small pointing trowel
hammer
chisel
broomstick
bucket
paper bucket

Use bricks without holes, because they're prettier. Before starting, break two of them in half with the hammer and chisel, so the joints can be staggered to be strong. You also have to dig a foundation trench—6" deep and 25" long—across a corner of the yard to give the wall a firm anchor in the earth. Both these jobs will be yours, but in the meantime your child can prepare the bricks. If they're old he has to knock any mortar from them so the new mortar can stick and soak either old or new ones in water so they won't draw moisture from the mortar and crumble it. To do this, have him drop 3-6 bricks in the bucket of water—as many as he probably can lay in a day—and leave them there for about 15 minutes.

The joints also will crumble if the mortar sets too soon, which is why it's mixed in small batches. Make no more than he can use in a half hour. In the paper bucket

Stir   5 lbs. mortar mix
1¼ c. water

This consistency is fairly stiff, although you may add more powder if it seems too runny or more water if it's too thick. Much depends on the dampness of both the bricks and the weather.

Without using any mortar in the trench, have your child lay a brick flush against one end of it. Before laying the second brick, he should butter the header with mortar, ½" thick, and then zigzag the tip of the trowel across it for a better grip. Help him press the buttered end of this brick against the first one, tamping it hard with the butt of the trowel, and then lay the third (and last) brick in the row the same way. He'll use two half bricks at each end of the second course (as well as the fourth), so each brick in the wall can overlap half of the one beneath it. To lay this second course, have him smear and score mortar on the first brick he's laid and press a broken brick on it. From then on, the bricks should be laid as before, with mortar splatted on the course below and each brick tamped into place. Because mortar drips everywhere, your child should clean the bricks that are above the ground as he goes, wiping the excess with his trowel. The wall is finished when he has pounded the earth close to the foundation, rubbed oil on his hands (for mortar will dry them) and been given many, many compliments.

From then on, your child will scrutinize every brick building he sees, noticing the fancy Victorian fret, the arched doorways and the different bonds. He'll trace the patterns with his forefinger as if it were obligatory and seriously tell you how the shade or the pointing in the mortar of one house is quite different from the one down the street. Professionals have to start sometime.

Carpentry

To pretend that a young child could make a bookcase would be fatuous, but the simplest carpentry gives him both pleasure and a sense of dignity. It also gives a child enough coordination in the handling of tools to feel familiar with them for the rest of his life.

Carpenter's Box

As your child knows, building is a serious business and for this he needs real tools and a box in which to keep them. You'll feel more comfortable (and so will he) if he uses his tools when he has no company. We don't include pliers, because they're too complicated, or a screwdriver, which can be lethal in a fall, but other tools are dandy. In a wooden box, gradually

Assemble   simple block plane
10 oz. claw hammer
10-point crosscut saw
brace and bit
small monkey wrench
wood chisel
hinged rule
yardstick
assortment of nuts and bolts
8-penny nails
lightweight aluminum discs
2 doz. scraps of pine

In the beginning, your Three will make designs with wood, nailing discs and nuts and wood scraps together as if they were trucks and boats and other curiosities. Although the wrench is of no use to a Three (nor a Six), it causes no harm, it weighs enough to make him feel important, it can't come apart and the bolt is big enough for the most awkward fingers to manipulate. Hammering, however, is the big entertainment. The hammer should have a flat face and a tight fitting handle of wood, for an all-steel hammer is very tiring. Above all, the hammer must be heavy or it will bounce back as if the nail is being sunk into ironwood.

Nails should be big, so his fingers can grasp them, and they should have heads so they can be hit more easily. You may have to make a hole first to rest the nail while he drives it, but a Six should be able to hammer one without bending it and to pull it out with the claw. A Three can begin to cut wood with your help, if the saw has a good set, and by Six he can saw with the whole length of the blade. A Four can use the hammer to split a length of wood at intervals with the chisel, can shave the edges smoothly with a plane and wants to measure everything with his hinged ruler and his yardstick. Your Five can operate the brace and bit, just to drill holes. Of course, you should be in the same room with a Three or a Four while he works, but a Five or Six who's familiar with tools can be left

alone safely—which is more than you can say for some carpenters.

Plastering

A mother we know, whose home had been full of plumbers, carpenters and plasterers for months, was startled to see her mid-One begin some renovation of his own. This child examined a small hole in the wall in silence, then toddled up and down stairs three times: first for his brother's chalk, then for his wooden hammer to beat it to bits and finally for a cup of water to pour on the chalk. Still flabbergasted, she watched him stir it to mush with his fingers and poke it into the hole.

Padraic had made plaster.

Patching

Like Padraic, we think nail holes are meant to be filled by young children, although a Six does it much better than a mid-One and spackling compound does it much better than chalk. Cover the floor with newspaper and in a tin can

Pour   1 c. spackling compound
Add   ½ c. water

Let him stir until the paste is smooth and stiff. You'll find it's thinner and easier to handle than prepared spackling and it takes longer to dry than patch plaster, which is good too; a young plasterer needs all the time he can get. He should press the plaster into the hole or into a small crack with his fingertip, until it won't hold any more, then dip a sponge or a paintbrush into a cup of water, wiping it back and forth over the new plaster until the patch is exactly even with the wall—a professional trick. If the plaster pulls out of the hole while it's being patched, add 1-2 tablespoons of water to the plaster mix and fill the hole again. The next day—when the spackling is completely dry—he should wipe the excess dust from the wall with a wet cloth. Later you can sand it if it's necessary.

Painting

You may say that giving a child real paint is silly and it probably is, but it will make him feel twelve feet tall—a noble height for a Five. Although your child surely will make a mess, some things are worth it. Besides, the child who has the chance to help you when you paint either will 'get bored in ten minutes, leaving you to work alone for an hour, or he'll like it enough to be quite helpful, painting for perhaps thirty minutes.

Latex paint, because it's water soluble, is best,

but it won't hurt him to try acrylics and oil-based paint too. We've found a Five can cover a small area like a door panel or a simple piece of furniture with a thin prime coat of enamel and can help paint closets with latex, but by Six he can paint a two-inch latex border above the baseboards, in the corners where the walls meet and around any window and door frame he can reach while standing on the floor. This border makes it much easier when you use a roller, for there's no temptation to go too close to the edges and your own job will be neater and faster.

To be a successful painter, your child will need the floor covered with newspaper, his father's T-shirt covering him, a brush that sheds few bristles and a few holes punched in the lip of the can, so the drips fall into the bucket rather than down the label. You also will have to remind him, rather regularly, that each side of the brush must be wiped against the lip of the can each time he gets more paint, that two thin coats are better than one thick one and that if he steps in a blob of paint it will track him around the house like a shadow, so he must clean the soles of his feet each time he leaves the room.

When he quits painting with latex, have him wash his own brush in soapy water and himself in a tub of warm water with a squirt of detergent to soften the paint on his skin. If he used enamel remove the paint from both his brush and his skin with petroleum solvent before putting him in the tub, but never bathe him in very warm water or it will sting wherever you have rubbed the solvent. Whatever paint he used, coat his skin with mineral oil after his bath to keep it soft.

Even though your child has left most of the painting for you, he still should help you clean the room when you quit, for a good worker must finish his job. The more mess he has to clean, the more careful he'll be the next time; he sees the reason why.

Refinishing Furniture

A child finds that cooking and gardening have their place, but working with wood brings a pleasure all its own. It's such a grown-up thing to do.

Like many women, we were as inept as Twos with hammers and nails and instead found that refinishing furniture suited us exactly. With our children trailing behind we would look for pieces from one seedy junk store to the next, plunking Meg for safety in the great toy box at our favorite, the Alley Store, until at eight months she said her first words—not "Mama" or "Dada," but "Alley Store."

We think you'll find, as we did, that the revitalization of the treasures is easier than you'd think. Most furniture needs only revival, not refinishing, which is. fortunate, since stripping is hard to do around a child and, while he enjoys helping you sand and add the many coats of finish, the job can outlast the enthusiasm.

While your child will need more precautions and more supervision in this work than in any other we recommend, we found it safe for a child to strip and paint shellac. In fact, there never was a time when any of them were tempted to drink the solutions we used or to splash them around—perhaps because we warned them of their dangers and kept them out of reach between use or perhaps because they didn't smell like cherries or lemons and they weren't kept in bottles that looked like soda pops.

The restoration of furniture fascinated the children and it was a blessing to us too, psychologically and financially. It not only fitted into those fragments of time we called a schedule, but it was a cheap way to furnish a house. More than that, it made the children so aware of the beauty of wood they've never been blind to it since.

You'll find it's like magic to see the lines of a tree reappear as you strip a piece of furniture, watching it glow stronger and stronger with every coat of finish and wax you add.

This is the kind of magic a child can understand.

Revival

Five-year-old furniture, like any Five, is bound to be dirty, even if it hasn't been playing in mud. Your child can help you rejuvenate wood by cleaning white stains with the Ring Remover (page 146) or rubbing a piece of furniture with either American Polish (page 148) or Mediterranean Polish (page 131) to give it a fresh matte finish.

The scruffiest table may just need a good cleaning instead of a new finish. Either of these revivers will remove most of the checks in an old finish and make the grain of the wood come alive again.

Reviver I

A Three can help you restore the warm color of dark wood while cleaning it. In a saucepan

Heat   1 c. red wine

Dip a soft cloth into it and squeeze it, so the wine will be cool enough for your child's touch and warm enough to melt the wax. Have him rub the wood with the cloth and use a toothbrush, dipped in wine, to scrub any carvings. Apply paste wax and buff—a job for you or a Five.

Reviver II

A fine Swiss cabinetmaker we knew claimed that all furniture, whether varnished, shellacked or oiled, should be washed twice a year, then oiled to feed the wood and waxed to protect it.

For a time estimate, it took us three hours to revive a large antique grandfather's clock, from the bath to the final shine, but we worked alone. If your child helps double the time (as always) and stretch the job over several days, to suit his attention span.

Washing Wood

You'll need a well-squeezed cloth diaper or a terry-cloth towel and this solution to clean the wood. In a bowl

Combine   1 qt. warm water
                   2 tbsp. detergent

Let your Five start in the most conspicuous place you can find—just to make him feel proud—rubbing a small patch with this solution until a clean cloth shows no trace of dirt. Rinse with clear, warm water and dry thoroughly. Wash the rest of the wood to match the color of the cleaned area, rinsing and drying each part before starting the next, or the water will swell the grain of the wood.

Feeding Wood

This treatment completes the cleaning, lightens the wood a little more and smooths away light crazing. We find paraffin oil the best, because it's thin enough for a Five to help you wipe away the excess easily and it doesn't show our housekeeping like boiled linseed oil, which attracts dust. Paraffin oil is available in big hardware stores or old-fashioned ones. Rub it on the furniture with 0000 steel wool, working in tiny circles with the grain. Rub one patch down to the finish—but not hard enough to remove it—and match the next patch to it. Let the oil soak into the wood for an hour or more, then rub dry with a clean cloth. Apply paste wax thinly and buff.

Stripping

Your Four can help you remove shellac—the protection on almost all furniture built before 1910 and much of it built afterward—but paint or varnish is too dangerous for a child to strip.

Some furniture, in fact, shouldn't be stripped at all, like an antique with its original painted finish (for that hurts its value and its charm), or one with an unappealing wood, but most pieces look best when you can see the grain. To tell the difference between varnish and shellac, touch some nail polish remover to the finish. Shellac softens immediately.

Strip the wood outdoors or in a well-ventilated room, working for no longer than a half hour at a time, and don't worry if the wood has some painted or stenciled designs. It won't budge them. Paint, as well as varnish, requires removers usually based on lye. If you do use them work alone and, to get the job done quicker, use a marine grade. Like marine paint, it's much stronger.

Shellac Strip

Speed, an old rag and denatured alcohol melt shellac as an oven melts ice. This solvent won't hurt the skin but it will dry it, for which you and your child will need hand cream afterward, and you also may want to wear simple gauze masks to avoid the fumes. Cover the floor with newspaper, open all windows for ventilation, don't smoke, and into a bowl

Pour   denatured alcohol

Give your child a piece of a diaper in each hand,

one to dip in the alcohol, the other left dry to wipe away the softened shellac. Have him work with the grain of the wood, dipping and wiping in a quick 1-2 motion that takes less than a minute—not easy for a pre-Six to coordinate. Help by wiping after him before the shellac hardens again, wherever it's been smeared. Repeat many times, adding more alcohol to the bowl occasionally, and sand when a clean cloth still looks clean after the wood is wiped with fresh alcohol.

Sanding

While your child can sand by hand, he'll like a machine better. The most timid Two unfolds at the chance to run an electric sander, for it's such a heavy, noisy, masterful tool and it's the only power-driven one that's safe for a child to handle. Use an oblong sander (a circular one is too difficult) and let him turn it off and on, over and over, and help guide it with the grain.

Use   0000 aluminum oxide sandpaper

This production paper is best, because it lasts longer. Also this grit is so fine and his pressure so light that you can erase any cross-grain scratches he makes by a little more sanding with the grain. How long it takes depends on how hard the wood is and how bad the damage. The wood is ready for a finish when it's as smooth as a baby's bottom. Onto a clean cloth

Pour   petroleum solvent

Wipe the wood lightly with it to remove any dust and let it dry before applying the stain, if necessary, and the finish.

Finishing

Any wood that has been stripped must be protected again, either by paint, varnish, shellac or oil. Wax alone can't give enough protection and the wood can't stay shiny without a protective base.

We've let our Twos—and our visiting Twos—apply both oil and shellac finishes with us and never had a problem. Their help also has never lasted more than ten minutes nor amounted to more than 2 per cent of the work. In the next four years, your child can learn to apply the first coat of paint, to wipe a stain, to rub oil into wood and brush on thin wash coats of shellac—all with your constant help—but no young child can apply varnish well, for it must be laid on rather than brushed into the pores.

However, by Six he can steel wool and paint the shellac finish for 20-30 minutes at a time—the longest this job takes unless the furniture is very big—and will do maybe 20 per cent of the work. Still you can expect him to grow up and remind you of the time he refinished that picture frame in the hall "all by myself."

Finishing furniture is a great image builder for him too.

The Stain

Let your Four spit (once) on bare wood to see the color it will be when it's shellacked. If this color isn't dark or warm or soft enough to suit you he can help you brush one of the many oil-based stains on the wood and wipe it away again with cheesecloth, before you apply the finish.

You also can make a stain in any color by cutting enamel paint in half with petroleum solvent. Brush this solution, rest it a few minutes and wipe with cheesecloth. All paint and most of the stain can be removed with pure solvent if you think the tone is too blatant. Always work with the grain.

Cover with either an oil or a shellac finish.

Oil Finish

This is durable and subdued, well suited to modern furniture and painstaking mothers. A good oil finish is impervious to heat, alcohol, water and stains. Give your Four a wad of cheesecloth, saturated with boiled linseed oil, and have him rub it into the stripped wood, going with the grain, catching all the places he has missed yourself. Wait 20 minutes and, with dry cloths, rub and rub the wood—again with the grain and especially in corners—until it isn't sticky any more.

Apply a new coat every few days for weeks, but never give another treatment until the first one is absolutely dry or the furniture will draw dust. Quit when the wood has a warm matte glow and can absorb no more oil.

Shellac Finish

A Two can rub this shellac finish with steel wool and a Four can brush on the shellac itself. Altogether, stripped wood needs five of these wash coats to be well protected, but don't use shellac straight from the can; it's too thick. In a paper cup

Mix   1 part orange shellac
             1 part white shellac
             3 parts denatured alcohol

The orange brings out the richness in the wood and by diluting it with alcohol the layers will be thinner and easier to apply and the finish will look deeper.

Stir gently to avoid air bubbles, then have your Four paint a light coat with a 2" brush, going back and forth but with the grain—a reminder to be given often. Wait 24 hours—so the shellac is dry beneath the surface too—then, still going with the grain of the wood

Rub   0000 steel wool

This slices the tops of the tiny bubbles in the finish to make it smooth. If you don't do this the next coat will make the bumps look even bigger. Your child should know the reason for each instruction before he asks, for anyone feels silly when he has to follow rules and he doesn't know why.

After rubbing the shellac with the steel wool—very quick work—have your child blow at the dust and then wipe the wood with an old diaper dipped in petroleum solvent, to catch the rest of the dust. Let the solvent dry and repeat all of these steps with each succeeding coat. When complete, add two very thin coats of paste wax to protect the finish, for shellac can be damaged by alcohol, by vinegar and by water.

French Finish

For a special treasure, our Fives have helped us paint as many as twelve coats of this special finish—a recipe invented, it's said, by a craftsman in Marseilles. This recipe, applied daily, gives a depth and a sheen to wood that's only improved by applying it with the French Polish, but still it will look grand if you use the conventional 2" brush instead of a wad of cheesecloth.

Start using this recipe after you've applied three coats of the Shellac Finish. To make it,

Combine   1 drop olive oil
                 1 c. Shellac Finish

Add 2 drops of oil to this mixture for the second coat, 3 for the third, increasing a drop a day until you add a dozen drops to the cup on the last day.

French Polish

In our collection of little European cabinet-makers, we found one from Spain who insisted that this technique—the prince of them all—was simple enough for a child to do. Consequently, he was able to teach it to our Six, who found it easy, and to us, who did not. It takes a wad of cheesecloth, instead of a brush. Dip the cloth into the shellac or the French Finish and press it against the side of the cup to get rid of the excess, then have your child rub it on the wood in tiny circles, going with the grain. Dip and press each time the cloth dries, which happens very quickly. We recommend polishing something quite small, like a picture frame. You'll find it very messy, very successful and worth trying—once.

Cooking

The same mother who can find words in the babble of an eight-month-old will take a cake to the table and say her Two made it. And we think she should.

Even though you'll read the instructions, gather the ingredients, explain each step and check each measurement, the person who measures the flour and beats the batter is the cook. If your attitude to his accomplishments is positive he not only will grow up thinking he can do anything, he'll think he's already done it.

We believe a child can gain more self-esteem in a kitchen than anywhere else, for to him, cooking probably is the most important job in the world. Although you may have an office job eight hours a day, he still sees you spend most of your time in the kitchen—so it must be important. Every moment you allow him to cook with you is one more sign of his own worth.

A child also is learning a lot about creativity, about cause and effect, about arithmetic—even about sex. To us, a child whose sensitivity is encouraged in any way, including the cooking and savoring of many foods, will be an adult alive and sensitive in all ways—including sex. Which is as it should be. When he splashes the walls with his Hollandaise, be cheered. The cause is good.

We can't pretend that cooking with a child is always jolly and if you truly don't like to cook, you should do little of it together. Conversely, if it's a skill you enjoy it's much easier to work intensively with him for ten to thirty minutes in a day than to work by yourself for an hour while he whines and plucks at your skirt. There's another advantage. Although it will take twice as long to cook with your child (as it does to do anything else with him), the joy of a shared experience will be the joy you remember twenty years from now.

We think you should start cooking with a child when he's very young. Many mothers think a hot stove and a rowdy Two are a dangerous combination, but we never found a child who behaved foolishly when he was given a small but grown-up job to do and we never saw an accident when the

Safety Rules were followed. Besides, most of the kitchen work is in the preparation and not at the stove at all.

We've directed all instructions to you (since you're the one who reads), but unless we've specified otherwise, a child will be able to do each step himself with some assistance and advice—and as little of both as you can manage. The recipes offer a variety of tastes and textures, all chosen because they're easy to make, nutritious to eat and most people like them. Some are adult favorites—good to make and serve to company since a child is enriched quite as much by compliments as by vitamins.

You may notice that few of our recipes have chocolate, for this, like cola, has such a high caffeine content it can kill B vitamins, but don't deny your child the joy of the Ultimate Chocolate Cake. That would be going too far.

Because a child needs a purity of tastes, we use no substitutes for butter and cream, natural cheese, fresh eggs, pure vanilla and top grade soy sauce and instead find our economy in less expensive meats or in egg or fish dishes. The optional ingredients we suggest are listed parenthetically, but even these trimmings aren't for looks alone. A child needs his parsley and almonds for magnesium, raisins for iron, walnuts and cashews for protein, wheat germ for vitamin E.

We use no mixes in our recipes, because the directions are on the boxes anyway, because it's much more fun for a child to cook from scratch and because, like potato chips and candy, they fill the stomach only briefly and whet the taste buds for more.

We particularly object to toy store "mixes," for their flavors are so synthetic and stale that no child could be proud of the results. Also, we totally oppose dressing up everyday foods to look like animals or faces or cooking with miniature pans in toy ovens. A child doesn't want to think his cooking is a joke.

When your child is between Two and Six, you'll demonstrate, casually and often, that two tablespoons make an ounce and that a pint and two cups are just the same. You'll show him the degrees on the oven knob and the way the broiler flame is high for the ten minutes it takes to reach the right temperature. Children are very logical people, and they need to understand that cooking is logical too—that meat must be dried before it can brown, and eggs help a cake to rise. You should give a child the reason for each instruction and identify each ingredient, encouraging him to taste and smell as he goes and reminding him that he's expected to eat a little of everything he makes—and also everything you make.

Two

At this age he can hold the portable electric mixer with both hands if you're ready to push it deep into the bowl every time he forgets. He can roast bacon, snap the ends of the beans and wash the salad greens, but not very well, and decorate a cookie with a nut but not with icing. He can take out utensils now and knead hamburgers, but be cautioned: his attention span will last about ten minutes in a job, whether it's cooking or cleaning.

Three

He'll gather most of the ingredients and drop very few. He can make applesauce—with skins to keep the food value—and crack eggs, squeeze lemons (if he has no cuts) and shake stew beef in a paper bag with flour. Now he'll bake bread and be fascinated with the properties of yeast, and you'll spend a lot of time explaining kitchen safety.

Four

This child makes granola for the family and because he's such a show-off now, he may eat it. He'll cut parsley and green onions with scissors—the only way they should be cut—make salad dressings, bake a cake and be very daring if you don't watch out. This is a good time to let the Great Experimenter bake just one loaf of bread without yeast—the biblical way—although no one may want to eat it.

Five

This child makes his own Lost Bread (left over from the bread he's baked), fried bologna sandwiches, a daube and, with a blender, makes a Hollandaise

Sauce or a chocolate mousse. By now he should be cleaning as he goes and not even minding it too much.

Six

Now he can make any of the recipes we've included, but even if he can read and is a genius at organization, you still must check his accuracy, do the steps he doesn't like to do and, generally, be around for safety and so he doesn't feel like a slavey. Of course, you can't expect him to gauge his time or prepare dishes for simultaneous serving.

Any child who contributes a little to the meal, even the salad dressing, will feel more responsible for the conviviality of the dinner itself, for he's part of the work as well as the play. Every time you help your child achieve an ability of his own, you have put a stone beneath his feet where only sand has been.

Kitchen Code

A child has the right to learn each skill with as much simplicity and safety as you can give him. He learns best when the instructions are simple and the action verb is the same every time. Below are the rules and techniques a child needs.

Rules

- ☐ Wash hands before starting, so they can be used to mix anything.
- ☐ Wear an adult T-shirt to keep clothes clean.
- ☐ Assemble all ingredients on one side of the working area, all utensils on the other—before you start.
- ☐ Use only one bowl, if possible, rinsing and reusing, to prevent a huge cleanup—a practice you may one day learn to copy.

Techniques

Measure—Spoon dry ingredients lightly into a measuring cup and level with a knife. To avoid a mess, work over wax paper, and when measuring wet ingredients, do it in the sink.

Sift—Omit this standard step; it isn't necessary in any of our recipes.

Chop—Work on a cutting board, slicing as much as possible with kitchen shears, which takes the coordination of a Four. A younger child uses a knife, holding each end of the blade with his fingertips and walking it away from him, working it

up and down like a seesaw.

Pare—Peel as few fruits and vegetables as possible, since most of the nutrition is just below the skin. Scrape away the thinner skins with a pot scrubber and use a peeler on the thicker ones, working away from the body, but the healthiest, easiest way is to cook the foods in their skins, then let your child peel them with his fingers when they're cool.

Grate—Hold any object with the fingertips to avoid the curse of the kitchen: grated knuckles. Grate only the colorful zest of citrus, not the bitter white beneath it.

Stir—Use a wooden spoon and stir gently, so the bowl can contain the ingredients.

Beat—Use a mixer on medium speed with the blades deep in the bowl to avoid spatter and the bowl on a wet dishcloth so it won't spin while mixing.

Blend—Use a blender as directed.

Safety Rules

You should

- ☐ Avoid all recipes involving hot grease or boiling syrups, which cause the worst kitchen burns.
- ☐ Stand your child on a kitchen chair, with its back to the counter or stove, so he can hang on while he works.
- ☐ Turn on the stove yourself and always stay with him in the kitchen if he's cooking on the burners.
- ☐ Give him a long wooden spoon for stirring, so heat can't transmit.
- ☐ Have him hold the pot handle with one hand, with a pot holder if necessary, while he stirs with the other, which gives the extra balance a small child needs.
- ☐ Aim all pot handles to the back of the stove when he isn't stirring, so he can't knock over the pots—a rule for all the family to follow, for a child's height is handle high.

Breakfast

Spanish Granola

One afternoon Nell brought dismay to her mother (the sort who says, "So eat," so often) when she announced, "Guess what! Today I wasn't hungry until lunch."

That was the morning we served not fish or eggs and certainly not cold cereal, but our own homemade Spanish granola. It's as filling as it is nutritious and, ounce for ounce, it's cheaper than any puffy, commercial cereal. It also makes a good cookie base instead of oatmeal, it's a fine snack and a Four likes to make it.

Preheat Oven 250°

In a saucepan
Heat   ½ c. oil
           ½ c. honey
Add   1 tsp. vanilla
In a roaster
Mix   4 c. rolled oats
           1 c. raw wheat germ
           4 oz. chopped almonds OR pecans
           1 c. unsweetened coconut
           3 tbsp. soy flour
Add the honey mixture and stir until all ingredients are sticky.
Bake   30 minutes
Stir every 10 minutes. When cool, store in airtight plastic bags. This makes seven cups, but servings are smaller than usual. Like any cereal, it should be served with milk to make a whole protein.

Milk Shake

Serves 1

Appetites fall enormously between the second and fourth year and the standard foods lose appeal. Mothers have used this breakfast substitute for generations—both because it's so nutritious and, we suspect, so quick. Have your Three
Beat   1 c. milk
           1 egg
           1 tsp. vanilla
           1 tbsp. sugar

Roasted Bacon

Serves 4   **Preheat Oven 350°**

Even an early Two can handle this if the bacon is room temperature.
Separate   ¼ lb. bacon
Lay strips on a cake rack over a baking dish.
Bake   10 minutes
For crisp bacon, bake 20.

Lost Bread

Serves 1

The frugal French have turned stale bread into a treat and so can your Three. In a bowl
Beat   1 egg
           ¼ c. milk
           1 tsp. sugar
           ½ tsp. orange flavoring
Add   3 slices stale bread
The more stale it is the more it will absorb and the better it will cook. In a skillet
Melt   2 tbsp. butter
Help your child lift the slices with a slotted spoon, frying them first on one side, then on the other. Butter and serve with honey.

Cinnamon Toast

Serves 1   **Preheat Broiler**

We hate to admit it, but only the Health Bread (page 250) or one made of a whole grain makes this recipe nutritious. Still the taste and the smell are worth a great deal. Your Five can
Mix   ¾ tsp. cinnamon
           3 tbsp. sugar
In the broiler
Toast   4 slices bread
Do this on one side only, spread the other with butter and sprinkle with the cinnamon sugar. Broil until bubbly, lifting it with a spatula yourself and serve when cooler, because caramelized sugar can cause a bad burn.

Eggs

We once knew a college professor who, despairing of modern youth, applied for a job as a houseman on an estate. He listed such a grand spread of skills that he was hired, even though he said he "would have nothing to do with eggs."

This is understandable. A person can become quite uncomfortable with an egg, particularly a very small person. The best way to overcome this reaction is to teach your child to cook his own.

Soft and Hard Cooked Eggs

The most inept toddler can make these eggs, and they are more digestible than boiled ones. In a saucepan

Combine   cold water
                 eggs

The rest of the job is yours. Bring to a boil. To cook a soft egg, reduce boil to a simmer and remove in four minutes. Scoop the egg into the fat end of an egg cup, for its gentility will delight him.

To cook a hard egg, turn off the heat when it boils, cover and wait 20 minutes. Your child can peel a cool egg under running water, for slick removal, but we think unshelled ones are meant to be colored by a small child, so you can identify them in the refrigerator. Let him use crayons, paints or felt-tipped markers.

Scrambled Eggs

Serves 4

If scrambled eggs are beaten first they lose the stringiness a good chef insists upon, and besides—there's another bowl to wash. A Three will enjoy cracking the eggs directly into a skillet, but a Six likes to blow them into it and save the shells for an Easter Egg Tree (page 167). Over low heat

Sauté   2 tbsp. butter
               5 unbeaten eggs

Add   1 tbsp. water

The water slows down the cooking process. Have your child stir the eggs with a wooden spoon, but take the skillet from the fire before the eggs are done. They'll keep cooking until he spoons them into the serving dish.

For variety, he can add parsley, chipped beef or crumbled cheddar cheese instead of chopped green onion—or none of them, depending on the whim of your child.

Poached Eggs

Serves 4

Surprisingly, a Four can poach the breakfast eggs. In a skillet

Simmer   2 c. water
                1 tsp. vinegar (optional)

The vinegar helps older eggs hold their shape. In a bowl, have your child

Break   4 eggs

Help him slide the contents into the skillet—an extra step that usually keeps the yolks from breaking—and cook 3-4 minutes, until the whites have set. Remove the eggs yourself with a slotted spoon. Serve on buttered toast or on English muffins as in Eggs Benedict.

Eggs Benedict

Every Six should have the chance to eat this dish at least once—and even to make it.

Toast   2 split English muffins
Sauté   4 slices Canadian bacon
Poach   4 eggs

In a double boiler to prevent curdling

Heat   leftover Hollandaise

Butter the muffins, lay a slice of bacon on each one and then an egg. Cover with the sauce.

Hollandaise Sauce

Nothing is sacred any more. Even a child can make Hollandaise if he has two helpers—you and the blender—and with this recipe, he can make it in advance. Serve over meat, fish or vegetables, hot or cold. Separate the eggs yourself. In a small pan

Melt   ½ c. butter
Blend   3 egg yolks
               2 tbsp. lemon juice
               ¼ tsp. salt
               1/8 tsp. pepper

Blend at high speed. A child then can add the butter very slowly through the hole in the top or by stopping the blender repeatedly to add a few drops each time. It will begin to thicken after two thirds of the butter is added. If this Hollandaise should curdle

Add   1 tbsp. hot water

Blend again for a second. Reheat slowly in a double boiler.

Lunch

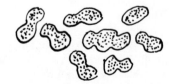

Homemade Peanut Butter

Old-fashioned, unhydrogenated peanut butter is a cinch for a new-fashioned Three to make. The hulling should be done outside, away from the wind and over a bag.

Blend   1 c. hulled, roasted peanuts
               1½ tbsp. peanut oil
               1/8 tsp. salt

Have him start the blender on a low speed, while

you hold the lid down, then switch to high, stopping it once or twice for you to scrape the jar with a rubber spatula. Stop when it's as smooth as he likes. Make 1 cup at a time but never more than 2, or it might jam the blender. Refrigerate.

Banana and Peanut Butter Sandwich

This sandwich will surprise you. It tastes good. It also combines two of the most nutritious foods available. On one slice of bread, let your Two

Spread   2 tbsp. peanut butter
Add   ½ banana, sliced lengthwise
Fold the bread over itself, like a hot dog roll.

Egg Salad Sandwiches

Serves 4

A Four's favorite because all the ingredients can be mixed by squeezing them through the fingers until the whites are broken into small pieces.

Combine   4 hard-cooked eggs
         3 tbsp. mayonnaise
         1 tsp. Dijon mustard
         ½ tsp. Worcestershire sauce
         ½ tsp. salt
         dash pepper

Have him spoon it on a slice of bread and cover it with another. Be sure to wash your child's hands again when he's finished making the sandwiches, or he'll leave a trail of egg prints.

Fried Bologna Sandwich

For some inexplicable reason, children adore this sandwich—possibly because it was invented by a child. A Five makes it well. Use a skillet but no grease.

Fry   1 slice bologna
Remove when the bologna puffs in the center. Lay it on a slice of bread and roll it like a taco.

Grilled Cheese Sandwich

This makes a Six feel skillful. Have him
Butter   2 slices bread
Put the slices together, with the butter on the outside.
Insert   1 slice cheddar cheese
Fry the sandwich in a hot skillet, about 4 minutes on one side, two on the other, to melt the cheese and toast the bread. For a change, you also can insert sliced cold cuts, tomatoes, chopped olives or apple slices before cooking.

Celery Boats

This recipe gives your child almost every vitamin he needs as a lunch supplement, and a Two can do it all.
Clean   celery stalks

Into their scoops
Spoon   peanut butter OR
         cream cheese
Skim a knife across the top to level the boats.
Add   raisins OR
         nuts

Applesauce

Suzannah, a neighborhood favorite, could make this recipe at Four, although she needed her big brother to help her stir and strain. Into a heavy soup pot
Add   12 uncored apples, quartered
Since apples contain so much water you don't need to add any if you cook them covered over the lowest fire. Stir every 5 minutes with a wooden spoon—a job that needs your help—for about 20 minutes, or until the apples are soft. Squeeze through a food mill or use a colander, pressing the pulp through with a small wooden bowl or a tin can. Most children like this without any sugar or spices.

Dinner

Soups

French cookbooks have introduced more mystery to the soup pot than Sherlock Holmes did to Baker Street. We can't imagine why. Although we've never known a woman who could spare a burner to simmer her stockpot around the clock (and, consequently, a stockpot that didn't turn sour in a week), we've found it very easy to turn out a good soup. The smell alone is reason enough to make it.

Soups require two or three hours to cook—not necessarily consecutively—including short spurts of time when your child lobs something into the pot.

A Three only needs to know what to add and when.

Children generally like to eat thick soups better than thin ones and soups that keep them curious, with bits of meat and fresh vegetables and certainly a pasta like alphabet noodles floating in them. There are so many soups and so many flavors of each one that anything your child makes will be right. If it has a pallid flavor, add more salt and pepper or a few bouillon cubes and boil to reduce the liquid. If it's too strong add water, and if it's too salty add a few extra potatoes to absorb the salt.

Any canned vegetables (except tomatoes) should be drained if the soup is to keep its homemade flavor and they should be added during the last few minutes of cooking.

Soup Base

This base can be used for either beef or chicken, depending on the protein you add. The turnip is essential for the sharp-sweet taste it gives, whether it's eaten or not. The carrots are added for their nutty flavor and the pasta or potatoes or rice for their thickening powers. This is a base to make yourself, and later let your child make the soup, which, as you both will discover, is much less formidable than it seems. In a heavy soup pot

Combine   2 qts. water
                1 large onion, quartered
                1 turnip, quartered
                3 whole unpeeled carrots
                2 stalks celery
                1 bayleaf, crumbled
                1 bunch parsley, tied
                2 tbsp. salt
                6 peppercorns
Bring to a boil.
Add   1 lb. stew beef OR
                2 lbs. beef bones OR
                1 cut-up chicken

Simmer covered for two hours. Remove the haggard parsley and celery, the beef or chicken and any bones in the pot. You should have 6-8 cups of broth left.

Fancy cream soups always are made from a strained chicken base. Any extra meat can be used in salads or sandwiches or for baby food when blended with a little broth.

Vegetable Soup

Yield: 18 cups

The ingredients are listed in order of the time it takes them to cook and the flavors to marry. In a heavy soup pot
Combine   6-8 c. beef base
                1 c. boiled beef
Bring to a simmer. Now's the time to tell your Three what to toss in the pot and when.
Add   3 potatoes, peeled and quartered, OR
                2/3 c. pasta OR
                1/3 c. barley OR
                1/3 c. uncooked rice
                one 28-oz. can tomatoes
                2 tsp. basil
                1 tsp. oregano
                2 celery stalks, chopped
                2 carrots, sliced
                ¼ lb. snapped beans
                one 10-oz. pkg. frozen limas
                one 8½-oz. can shoepeg corn, drained
Simmer covered 20-25 minutes, until the potatoes—or whatever starch you use—are tender. Add salt and pepper to taste. Leftover soup can be frozen.

Chicken Soup

Yield: 8-10 cups

After making a soup base with chicken, cool the bird enough for your child to pull away the skin and bones, a gruesome, 20-minute task every Four strangely enjoys. In a heavy soup pot
Simmer   6-8 c. chicken soup base
                ½ c. cooked chicken

In a skillet
Sauté   1 carrot, chopped
                1 celery stalk, chopped
                2 green onions, chopped
He'll need your help to do the chopping, because the vegetables should be fine—and because it's boring to work alone. When the onions are translucent
Add   2 tbsp. flour
Ladle a little hot soup base into the skillet and stir to dissolve the flour, so it won't lump. Empty the skillet into the soup pot (a job for you) and bring to a full boil.
Add   1/3 c. pasta OR
                1/3 c. uncooked rice
Simmer covered 15 minutes before serving. You can add dumplings of Homemade Biscuit Mix (page 250).

Pistou

Yield: 12 cups

If you managed to plant an herb garden, try this "pea stew." And if you didn't, use dried herbs and still feel blessed. This has the triple virtue of tasting good, requiring short segments of working time—about as long as a small child's interest can stretch—and sounding obscene enough to delight a Five. In a soup pot have him

Combine	1½ qts. water
	1 c. dried white beans

Boil two minutes, then simmer covered for 1½ hours. In a skillet

Sauté	2 medium onions, chopped
	¼ c. olive oil

Add these onions to the soup pot and boil 5 minutes.

Add	one 16-oz. can tomatoes
	2 potatoes, peeled and chopped
	½ lb. snapped green beans
	2 zucchinis, chopped
	½ c. fresh basil OR
	2 tbsp. dried basil
	5 whole garlic cloves
	2 tbsp. tomato paste
	2 tbsp. salt
	½ tsp. pepper

Simmer covered for 15-20 minutes, until potatoes are done and colors are still vibrant. Over it

Sprinkle	¼ c. chopped parsley

Main Dishes

Hot Tuna Sandwiches

Serves 4   **Preheat Broiler**

This is a fine, fast supper for a mother and a Six to make together.

Mash	one 7-oz. can drained tuna
	2 tbsp. mayonnaise
	1 hard-cooked egg, chopped
	1 green onion, chopped
	1 celery stalk, chopped
	½ c. diced natural cheese

Stir well and spread on bread. Broil until bubbly—about five minutes.

Chipped Beef on Toast

Serves 4

The best thing about this recipe (besides its good taste) is how quickly it can be put together. It requires about 10 minutes of stirring, which a Four thinks is dandy. Serve on toast or a baked potato.

Sauté	2 tbsp. butter
	½ medium onion, chopped
	½ green pepper, sliced

Stir until the onions are clear. Turn off the heat.

Add	2 tbsp. flour

Stir over a low fire for 2 minutes, until there are no lumps. If they develop, beat them with a whisk.

Add	1½-2 c. milk.

Do this slowly, stirring until thick.

Add	4 hard-cooked eggs, quartered
	4 oz. chipped beef, shredded
	½ tsp. salt
	¼ tsp. pepper

Cheese Soufflé

Serves 4   **Preheat Oven 425°**

This recipe should be tried once, because it's very easy, it doesn't fall if dinner is late and because most children love it. The rest of them hate it. There is no in-between. Have your Four start this recipe in a bowl.

Mix	3 eggs
	1 c. milk
	1 tsp. dry mustard
	½ tsp. salt
	1/8 tsp. pepper

Butter a 1-quart baking dish, and into small bits

Tear	4 slices bread

Lay the bread in the bottom of the dish

Slice	1/3 lb. (1 c.) cheddar cheese

A child does this best with a vegetable peeler. Lay the cheese on top of the bread. Pour the egg mixture over the bread and cheese and bake 20 minutes, or until lightly browned on top.

Spiced Chicken

Serves 4

There is a large if dreary school of housewives who think food shouldn't be touched. Children know better. This is the touchiest recipe we know. In a large bowl have your Three

Combine	1 cut-up fryer
	1/3 c. soy sauce
	3 tbsp. salad oil
	1 garlic clove, pressed
	1 tsp. ground ginger
	¼ tsp. pepper

Rub the chicken completely with this marinade and let it soak in it for a half hour to overnight in the refrigerator.

Preheat Oven 350°

Arrange chicken in a baking dish, with no overlapping so it will cook crisply. Cover with the marinade and baste three times with it during baking, a mother's job.

Bake   50 minutes

Chicken with Fruit

Serves 4

If children get enough natural sugar they won't crave sweets so much, but don't skimp on the onions here. They balance the flavors. A Five is quite old enough to make this. In a Dutch oven

Sauté
- 1 medium onion, sliced
- 2 apples, unpeeled, quartered, cored
- 2 tbsp. butter

Cook until clear and remove onions and apples with a slotted spoon, which you should do. In the same pan

Brown   1 cut-up chicken

This is another job you do yourself.

Add
- ¼ c. raisins
- 2/3 c. mixed dried fruits
- 1 c. apple juice
- 1 tsp. salt
- ¼ tsp. pepper
- sautéed onions and apples

If you're using a very large pot you may need to add more apple juice, for it should be about an inch deep when all the ingredients are added.

Simmer   1 hour, covered

Serve with Baked Rice, which is in this section.

Grilled Hamburgers

A Two likes to smash these into shape.

Knead
- 1½ lbs. ground beef
- 1/3 c. water

The water prevents dryness. Make patties 1½" thick for rare hamburgers, less thick if you want them well done.

Broil   5 minutes

Turn and repeat—a job for you. Season with salt and pepper.

Chili

Serves 6

We never knew a Six who didn't like to make chili, perhaps because it dresses up so easily.

Brown   1 lb. ground beef

Add
- one 18-oz. can tomatoes
- one 18-oz. can red beans
- 2 tbsp. tomato paste
- 1 tsp. cumin
- ¼ tsp. chili powder
- ¼ tsp. garlic powder
- 1 tsp. celery salt
- 1 tsp. salt

Simmer uncovered for a half hour. Serve with Baked Rice or in a bowl with saltines or in hot tortillas to make tacos, every child's delight. To make them, spoon the chili inside and

Add
- chopped Munster cheese OR Monterey Jack
- sour cream/chopped parsley/chopped green onions/shredded lettuce/diced tomatoes

You can use any or all of these ingredients.

Daube

Serves 6   **Preheat Oven 350°**

The layering involved in this beef dish intrigues a Five, who is as orderly as he is inept. The gin tenderizes the meat and then evaporates, as all alcohol does under heat. Into a large bowl

Combine
- 2 c. sliced carrots
- 2 c. sliced onions

This is your job—the only one—for the slices must be thin.

Add
- one 28-oz. can tomatoes, mashed
- ¼ c. gin OR vodka
- 1 beef bouillon cube
- 2 tbsp. olive oil
- 2 garlic cloves, pressed
- 1 bayleaf, crumbled
- ½ tsp. thyme
- 2 tbsp. salt
- ¼ tsp. pepper

In a paper bag

Combine
- 2 lbs. cubed stewing beef
- ¾ c. flour

Shake the bag to coat the cubes.

Separate   ½ lb. bacon.

Line a Dutch oven with bacon strips. With a slotted spoon, scatter a layer of the vegetables and then of the beef. Add another three layers and end with the rest of the bacon. Pour the gin marinade over it and, if necessary, enough water to reach the top layer. Cover.

Bake   1 hour

Lower heat to 300° and cook two hours longer. Serve with Baked Rice or buttered noodles.

Pizza

Serves 4   **Preheat Oven 450°**

In an Italian household, this is known as "Mama's pizza"—good, plain pizza with no frills, the way a Four likes it best. The mix is found on page 250.

Mix   2 c. Homemade Biscuit Mix
                 2/3 c. milk

Knead gently for 30 seconds. Grease a cookie sheet and roll the dough on it with a glass or simply pull it to the edges as thin as possible. A child gets less sticky if his hands are oiled first. To prevent a soggy crust

Bake   10 minutes
Cool   10 minutes
Drain   one 16-oz. can tomatoes

With a vegetable peeler

Slice   1 c. mozzarella OR cheddar cheese

Let your child break the tomatoes between his fingers and scatter them on the pizza crust. Cover with the cheese.

Add   1 tsp. olive oil
                 ½ tsp. salt
                 1/8 tsp. pepper
Bake   10 minutes

Boiled Shrimp

In New Orleans, mothers cover the supper table with newspaper and pile spiced shrimp on it. A Three can peel his own; a Four can put everything in the pot but the shrimp and a Five can make the sauce. In a large soup pot

Combine   5 qts. water
                 1 bunch leafy celery, broken
                 1 large onion, quartered
                 4 lemons, quartered
                 12 bay leaves
                 4 cloves garlic
                 4 whole allspice
                 1 sprig thyme
                 5 tbsp. salt
                 1 tsp. cayenne pepper
Boil   10 minutes
Add   5 lbs. fresh OR thawed shrimp

Do this yourself, for the water may splash.

Boil   10 minutes

Cool in the broth to absorb more flavors. Drain in a colander, fish out celery, onions and lemons and serve warm or cold with Mayonnaise Sauce.

Mayonnaise Sauce

Mix   1 c. mayonnaise
                 4 green onions, chopped
                 3 tbsp. chopped parsley
                 1 tsp. lemon juice
                 ¼ tsp. hot sauce
                 salt and pepper

Lentils and Sausage

Serves 8

This is the sort of hearty meal so popular with a father, whose appreciation will encourage a Three to eat some of the beans and all of the sausage, just as a way of saying, "You're welcome."

Lentils, a staple in Europe, are found in the supermarket with other dried beans. This dish needs no rice or potatoes to complement it.

Combine   6 c. water
                 1 lb. lentils
                 ¼ lb. salt pork
                 4 stalks leafy celery, broken
                 4 onions, quartered
                 2 carrots, unpeeled
                 1 bunch parsley, tied
                 2 bayleaves, crumbled
                 ½ tsp. basil
                 1 tbsp. salt
                 ½ tsp. pepper

Simmer covered for 1½ hours.

Add   2 lbs. smoked sausage

Simmer covered a half hour longer and remove the limp celery and parsley before serving. Use leftover lentils as a salad, served in equal parts with chopped tomato and green onion. Mix with a vinegar and oil dressing.

Beef Stew

Serves 6   **Preheat Oven 250°**

This is the perfect stew for children who don't like their flavors mixed. The heat is kept so low each vegetable remains whole and crisp and each taste pure and colorful. The gravy is dark brown. A

Three can make this stew right after nap and not look at it again until dinner. In a Dutch oven

Combine
- 1½ lbs. stew beef
- 1 medium onion, quartered
- 2 whole carrots
- 2 sprigs parsley
- 2 c. hot water
- one 16-oz. can tomatoes
- 1½ tsp. salt
- ½ tsp. peppercorns

Cover.

Bake 2½ hours

In a small saucepan, have your child

Melt 3 tbsp. butter

Add 3 tbsp. flour

Stir and let bubble for 2 minutes. To prevent lumps, add a tablespoon of hot broth to the flour—a job for you—blend well and return all to the casserole. Stir on top of the stove for about 5 minutes, until thickened. For a 2-lb. frozen chunk of chuck

Bake 3½ hours

Now you have a pot roast and with a lot less trouble.

Red Beans (and Rice)

Serves 6

In almost every culture, a native dish has evolved with such balance that it makes a whole protein, whether it has meat in it or not. Red beans and rice are like that. This dish is such a staple to Louisiana that Louis Armstrong signed his letters "Red Beans and Ricedly Yours."

The food value will be less if you use white rice but still much higher than it would be if either the beans or the rice were served alone. A Four can boil the beans and a Five can bake the rice.

Wash 1 lb. kidney beans

In a soup pot

Measure 8 c. water

Add beans. Soak overnight or boil for 2 minutes, turn off heat and soak 1 hour. A child feels a sense of accomplishment just watching his beans soak.

Add
- ham bone OR
- ½ lb. salted pork
- 1 large onion, quartered
- 1 green pepper, quartered
- 1 garlic clove
- 1 tbsp. salt
- ½ tsp. pepper

Simmer 2 hours, covered

Stir occasionally. The water must cover the beans at all times, to soften them. Serve with Baked Rice.

Baked Rice

Serves 6   **Preheat Oven 350°**

Few dishes are as easy to ruin as rice—unless you bake it. In a casserole have your Five

Sauté
- 2 tbsp. butter OR oil
- 2 tbsp. chopped onion
- 1 c. long grain rice

Stir until the grains are clear.

Add
- 2 c. boiling water
- 2 bouillon cubes
- ½ tsp. salt

Stir and cover.

Bake 20 minutes

All water should be absorbed. For some reason if you double the recipe you should cook it 10 minutes longer. With brown rice

Add 3½ c. boiling water

Bake 1 hour

For a mid-Eastern flavor

Sauté
- ¼ c. raisins
- ¼ c. blanched almonds
- 2 tbsp. butter

Add just before serving.

Vegetables

If you want your child to like vegetables you should use fresh ones and he should help you fix them. The tastiest vegetables—and the most nutritious—are the easiest to prepare. A Two can wash and snap green beans (catching about half of them), a Three can shell peas, and a Four can scrub carrots. No vegetables should be peeled before cooking, because most of the vitamins are just below the skin, and all green and yellow vegetables should be steamed, because water dissolves some vitamins.

Steamed Vegetables

You'll need a steamer or a pot big enough to hold a colander. In it have your child

Boil 1" water

Add the colander of vegetables—green beans, beets, carrots, summer squash, spinach or whatever. Cover.

Steam 10-20 minutes

Remove as soon as they're cooked, when the color is still bright, the texture, crisp, the flavor, fresh.

Crisp Baked Potatoes

Serves 4   **Preheat Oven 350°**
    Some baked potatoes are more equal than others. Like these. A late Two can make them.
Halve   4 medium potatoes
Lay flat side down, on a well-buttered cookie sheet.
Bake   30 minutes
Small potatoes take 20.

Zucchini and Tomato Casserole

Serves 4   **Preheat Oven 350°**
    This recipe requires very fresh vegetables to bring out the purity of flavor. An old zucchini tastes bitter and a hothouse tomato doesn't taste at all. A Six can make this handily.
Steam   1 large zucchini, thickly sliced
               1″ water, boiling
Cover and cook for 10 minutes only. Grease a 2″ casserole with olive oil and layer the following ingredients, in this order, saving some of the cheese for an extra layer on top. You'll have to add the zucchini yourself with a slotted spoon if it's still hot.
Layer   steamed zucchini
               2 large tomatoes, sliced
               ¼ lb. Swiss cheese, sliced
               ¼ tsp. basil
               salt and pepper
Pour   1 tbsp. olive oil
Bake   10 minutes
It's ready when the cheese on top is melted.

Salads

    There's nothing quite so rewarding for a child to make as a salad. He plays in water, stirs the ingredients with his hands, tears the lettuce to pieces—and everyone congratulates him for being so good. Even if he eats earlier than his parents he'll enjoy joining them for his specialty, and he may eat it too, just to play grown-up.
    All raw fruits and vegetables are more nutritious, but leafy greens—the darker the better—have vitamins and minerals which are hard to find anywhere else.
    A Two can wash and dry the greens reasonably well, but a Four can do the whole job himself, which he should start after a nap and return to at dinnertime. First the leaves are floated in a pot of cool water about 10 minutes, so dirt sinks to the bottom, then they're shaken in a colander and dried with a paper towel, for the oil coating added later won't stick if they're wet.
    Your child should remove spinach stems and for better flavor, have him tear, but not cut, the

lettuce leaves. Refrigerate with more paper towels to crisp again.

Basic Dressing

    Any vegetable oil can be used. The French use peanut oil, the Italians use olive. In a large measuring cup, have your Four
Pour   1 c. oil
               1/3 c. vinegar OR lemon juice
               2 tsp. salt
               ½ tsp. pepper
Let him transfer the dressing to the cruet with a funnel, or he'll surely lose some of it.
    He also can use four 3-ounce baby food jars instead of a single bottle and put a different flavor in each one. In the jars
Add   1 oz. crumbled blue cheese OR
               1 garlic clove OR
               ¼ tsp. curry OR
               1 tbsp. fresh OR 1 tsp. dried herbs
These dressings keep indefinitely if refrigerated.

Green Salad

Serves 4-6
    Aplomb is a Four mixing salad at dinner, but don't use the word "toss," or no bowl will be big enough.
Peel   1 garlic clove
Cut and rub the inside of a wooden bowl.
Combine   greens
               1 tsp. vegetable oil
The leaves are coated first with oil so the acid in the dressing won't wilt them. Any or all of these additions may be used.
Add   ½ c. croutons
               2 crisp bacon strips, crumbled
               3 raw mushrooms, sliced
               2 tomatoes, quartered
               ½ c. leftover vegetables
               1 hard-boiled egg, grated
Just before serving
Add   2 tbsp. Basic Dressing
After dinner your child should wipe the bowl clean with a paper towel so the residue of oil continues to season the wood.

Tomato Salad

Serves 4

Fresh basil is to tomatoes what ham is to eggs. A third as much of the dried herb will always do, but in this case it doesn't do so well. To make this salad, have your Five

Combine   2 tomatoes, sliced
2 tbsp. chopped fresh basil
2 tbsp. Basic Dressing

Desserts

Raspberry Peaches

Serves 6

We've probably never seen a dessert so pretty or so simple, and though we first found it in our fanciest French cookbook, we discovered a Four could make it. Into a deep saucepan

Stir   6 c. water
2¼ c. sugar
1 vanilla bean OR
2 tbsp. vanilla

Bring to a simmer.

Add   6 peaches

Cook, just below the simmering point, for 8 minutes. Lift the peaches with a slotted spoon—your job—and let them drip onto a cake rack over a plate for 30 minutes. Have your child slip the skins from the peaches when they're still warm—a very easy act which transforms them from sodden, tan blobs into fruit that looks more luscious than they did when they were picked. Refrigerate until dinner. For the sauce

Blend   one 8-oz. pkg. frozen raspberries
¼ c. sugar
½ lime, squeezed

It works just as well to beat this sauce for 2 minutes or even stir it, if the berries are thawed. Just before serving, in the place of the stem

Add   1 pair mint leaves

Pour the sauce over part of each peach so the blush of the peach can show.

Chocolate Mousse

Serves 6

If you like chocolate, this dessert has no rivals. Its elegance is almost overwhelming; its simplicity, disarming, and if you do a few of the steps your-self even your Three can make it. In a heavy saucepan, let him

Combine   6 oz. semisweet chocolate bits
2 tsp. hot water

Cook over a low fire, for chocolate burns easily, and use a rubber spatula to scrape the melted bits into the blender—your job. Let him

Add   ½ c. whipping cream
2 tbsp. confectioners sugar
4 egg yolks

Separate the eggs yourself, but your child can operate the blender.

Blend   3 minutes
Add   4 egg whites
2 tsp. vanilla

Blend 3 minutes longer. Refrigerate in demitasse cups for 2 hours to set the cream. If your child is cooking for adults, you can substitute 2 teaspoon-fuls of strong coffee for the water and a tablespoon of brandy for the vanilla.

Baking

Baker's Box

By the time your child is nine months, he'll lose more and more interest in his toys—in favor of yours. Since each room should have its collection of playthings, we recommend for the kitchen a Baker's Box of unbreakable tools, duplicating many of your own. He still will play with yours, but when he starts cooking at Two, he can assemble most of the equipment he needs from his own assortment. We've found a Baker's Box is one of the cheapest—and to be fair, noisiest—toy investments you can make. In the box, put

plastic measuring pitcher
measuring spoons
wooden spoon
rubber spatula
large metal bowl
cookie sheet
cake pan
pie tin
cake rack

Breads

Breadmaking, like soup, is supposed to be another mysterious art, beyond the powers of most women and all children. Actually bread became the staff of life because even a Cro-Magnon bride couldn't ruin it. Any miscalculation simply became a new kind of bread. Since measurements don't have to be too exact, a modern Three can make it too—with your help.

The process is both a scientific and a physical exercise as well as a civilized way for a child to work out his aggressions. As you have learned by now, if one person in the house is tense at breakfast you can expect chaos by noon. Fortunately, 10 A.M. is a good time to start making bread. It takes five hours, with hardly more than an hour's help altogether from the baker, and you can control the rising time to fit your schedule.

Breadmaking does require a real understanding of the process before you start the recipe itself. You should know—and tell your child—that the whiter the flour the finer the texture, but darker flours have more nutrition and, we think, more flavor. It's the yeast that makes the bread rise and sweetening that makes it rise higher, but the salt you need for flavoring does hinder this a little. Shortening tenderizes bread and keeps it fresh, and milk adds nutrition and freshness and helps it brown better.

Your child will be fascinated with the science of breadmaking from the moment he learns that the yeast in the package is alive but asleep and only warm water will make it wake up and grow (and hot water will kill it).

He watches the fungus bubble and grow, kneads the dough until it builds enough gas to be pliable, hears the "whoof" it makes when he punches down the first rising, watches it double its height again and then discovers the odd smell of fresh yeast has baked itself into an ovenful of glory. He'll admire his bread hugely—almost as much as himself. Following these principles, you and your child can make any yeast bread—including the Swedish Rye (page 133).

Preparations

You'll have much less mess if you cover the part of the floor where you work with newspaper and even the space where you measure the dry ingredients, or they will turn pasty when you wash the counter. Measure wet ingredients in the sink and mix everything together with a long wooden spoon in a 4-quart bowl or a refrigerator crisper to contain them best, because a child is a messy mixer. If you use a pair of 5-cup meat loaf pans to bake the bread, it will rise as high as the bakery's best.

Techniques

Mix—Stir all ingredients with the spoon, adding as much of the extra flour as needed and stopping when the dough sticks to itself and not much else—about 15 minutes.

Knead—Divide the dough for easier handling, keeping half on a floured table top for you and the rest in a floured bowl for your child, which is less messy. Put the bowl on the seat of a kitchen chair, so he can have more leverage. Push your batch forward with the heel of the hand and fold it back on itself—the classic kneading style—but let your child pull, twist and slam it down, then punch it like a boxer. Swap batches to give them an equal work-out and add more flour as needed until the dough loses its stickiness and is smooth and springy—about 10 minutes.

Rise—Let the dough grow in a greased bowl so it can climb up the sides as high as it would like but first roll the dough in the bowl so it won't form a crust, for this also inhibits rising. Cover with a dry dishtowel to prevent evaporation and place it in a warm kitchen (about 72°) or in an oven which was preheated to 200°, then turned off and left open. In about an hour your child can start checking to see if the dough has doubled in bulk by poking it with his finger. The dough will spring back if it's too soon (which does no harm) but will stay indented when finished—usually no more than 2 hours. Refrigerate the dough whenever you want to double the rising time.

Rest—Cover the dough with a cloth and let it sit for 10 minutes before kneading or shaping so the gluten relaxes and the dough won't fight back.

Shape—Divide dough and stretch each batch into a rectangle, 14" X 7" and ½" thick. Roll the short side and pinch the long seam and the ends, tucking the ends underneath as you put the loaves in their pans to rise again—about 1 hour.

Bake—Center pans in a preheated oven and remove when the loaves shrink from the sides, sound hollow when thumped with the wooden spoon, are light brown on the top and smell great—about 45 minutes. After baking, the top of each hot loaf is rubbed with a stick of butter for soft crusts. The bread is then removed from the pans and cooled on a rack to prevent sogginess.

Health Mix

For better nutrition and texture, your Two can make a batch of this mix for you to add to bread and cookie recipes.

Mix   1 c. soy flour
               1 c. powdered milk
               1 c. raw wheat germ

Store in a small canister or a jar with a lid. Use in breads, biscuits, muffins or cookies by removing 2 tablespoons of flour from each cup and replacing it with this mix.

Health Bread

Yield: 2 loaves

This is an easy recipe to double, but don't attempt it the first time. You may be overwhelmed. If you don't read the preceding Bread rules first you surely will be and so will your Three. He can add everything except the boiling water. In a teacup

Dissolve   1 pkg. yeast
               ¼ c. warm water

Into a very large bowl

Add   1 c. water, boiling
               1 c. cold milk
               1 c. Health Mix
               1 c. unbleached flour
               2 tbsp. sugar OR honey
               2 tbsp. vegetable oil
               1 tbsp. salt

Stir this mixture with a wooden spoon and add the dissolved yeast. Since the milk cools the water there's not enough heat to kill the yeast.

Add   4 c. flour

Mix and add as much as 2 more cups of flour until the dough loses most of its stickiness. Rest, covered with a cloth, for 10 minutes. Knead until springy, adding a little more flour to prevent stickiness if necessary, and scatter more on the counter. Roll the dough around in a greased bowl to coat the surface and cover with the cloth.

First rising   1½-2 hours

Punch down, divide, cover and let it rest for 10 minutes before shaping the dough into loaves. Put in greased loaf pans and cover with the towel.

Second rising 1 hour

                         Preheat Oven 350°

Bake   45 minutes

Butter tops, remove loaves from pans and cool on racks. You can make standard white bread by using regular flour in place of the Health Mix.

Short Breads

Homemade Biscuit Mix

This is the basis for biscuits, muffins, dumplings and pizzas.

Stir   8 c. (2 lbs.) flour
              ¼ c. baking powder
              1 tbsp. salt
Add   1 c. shortening

Beat in the shortening, one small lump at a time, at very low speed for 4 minutes, until dough looks like coarse bread crumbs. Store in a 3-quart canister with a tight lid. It will stay fresh for many weeks in the cupboard or for 4-6 months in the refrigerator.

Biscuits

Yield: 1 dozen   **Preheat Oven 450°**

Would you believe, a Two can make these biscuits. Let him

Stir   2 c. Homemade Biscuit Mix
             2/3 c. milk

Knead 10 times to give the biscuits a smoother shape. Spoon onto greased cookie sheet.

Bake   10 minutes

Muffins

Yield: 1 dozen   **Preheat Oven 400°**

Have your Three butter two muffin tins before he combines these ingredients. Then in a bowl he can

Stir   2 c. Homemade Biscuit Mix
             3 tbsp. sugar
             2 eggs
             2/3 c. milk
             2 tbsp. oil OR melted shortening

Fill each cup halfway with the lumpy mixture or spoon ½ teaspoon of preserves, raisins or chopped dates between 2 tablespoons of the batter.

Bake   15-18 minutes

Dumplings

Yield: 1 dozen

A Two can make these dumplings, but you'll

have to drop them into the hot pot. In a bowl

Mix   2 c. Homemade Biscuit Mix
           ¾ c. milk

Knead dough a few times and drop by spoonfuls into a bubbly stew pot, after the gravy has been made, or into soup. Cover and simmer 10 minutes. Remove lid, turn them and cook 10 minutes more.

Cookies

A cookie is to a child what a cigarette might be to you: tasty, soothing—and mighty addictive. If only for your own waistline, you'll have to limit cookies to morning and afternoon snacks. This will be easier to do if you bake just a dozen at a time and use a recipe so nourishing that two cookies will satisfy.

Cookie baking should be a pleasant, half-hour interlude, with little mess, one bowl and no tears. Gathering the utensils from the Baker's Box—a spoon, a spatula, the bowl, a cookie sheet, and a cake rack—have your child dump in the ingredients and beat with the portable mixer. Unless the recipe calls for a great deal of butter, the cookie sheet must be greased.

A child can drop the balls of dough onto the sheet and decorate them with nuts, raisins or the tines of a fork, pressed flat to make a checker board. We don't recommend a cookie press even for a Six and, in fact, except for special occasions, it takes much too long to ice cookies or cut them into shapes. Cookies should be baked in a preheated oven until the edges brown—usually no more than 10 minutes—then removed with a spatula (your job) and left to crisp on the rack.

You can substitute up to ½ cup of sugar with honey in any recipe, but you'll need to use ¼ cup more flour and bake them at a temperature that is 25° lower than required. Refrigerate or freeze leftover dough in cylinders of wax paper.

Aggression Cookies

Yield: 15 dozen   **Preheat Oven 350°**

We don't know where this recipe came from, but we don't know a better one for what they call That Kind of Day. In a huge bowl, let your Two

Combine   6 c. oatmeal
           3 c. brown sugar
           3 c. butter OR
           3 c. half butter/half margarine
           3 c. flour
           1 tbsp. baking soda

Mash, knead and squeeze, it says, "until you feel better"—and until there aren't any lumps of butter. Your child will need some help, but he can form the dough into small balls himself, not as big as a walnut, and put them on an ungreased cookie sheet. Butter the bottom of a small glass and have him dip it into granulated sugar. This is what he uses to flatten each ball of dough, dipping it into sugar each time.

Bake   10-12 minutes

Remove when lightly brown, cool a few minutes and crisp on a rack. Store in a tight container. The dough keeps well in the refrigerator.

Sugar Cookies

Yield: 4 dozen   **Preheat Oven 350°**

The nutmeg makes these so special, they'll win many compliments for your Two.

Beat   1 c. sugar
           ½ c. soft butter
           ½ tsp. nutmeg
           ½ tsp. vanilla
           1 egg
           1 tbsp. milk
Add   2 c. flour
           1 tsp. baking powder
           1 tsp. baking soda
           1/8 tsp. salt

Help him hold the beaters deep into the bowl until mixed and then drop by spoonfuls onto greased cookie sheets. He can decorate each cookie with a nut if he likes.

Bake   10 minutes

Crisp on a rack.

Banana Cookies

Yield: 4 dozen   **Preheat Oven 375°**

Two of these cookies with juice after a nap can carry most energetic children through the 5 o'clock miseries. A Two likes to mash the bananas best of all (and through his fingers, of course) but it takes a

Four to add the rest of the ingredients. In this order

Beat	¾ c. honey
	¾ c. soft butter
	1 egg
	1 tsp. vanilla
	1 c. (2-3) very ripe, mashed bananas
	1½ c. flour
	¼ c. soy flour
	1½ c. rolled oats
	¼ c. wheat germ
	½ tsp. baking soda
	1 tsp. salt
	½ tsp. nutmeg
	¾ tsp. cinnamon
Stir	½ c. chopped nuts
	½ c. raisins

You can substitute a third of the butter with soft peanut butter, but the dough will be sticky either way. Chill for 30 minutes. Drop by teaspoons onto greased cookie sheets.

Bake   12 minutes

Crisp on a rack. Your child can coat them with confectioners sugar on high feast days.

Pies

No matter what kind of pie shell you use—homemade, frozen or lady fingers end to end—a pie guarantees so much praise that your baker will glow with success, and it is the success of a job, and not the doing of it, that grows a child.

There are many complicated skills a pre-Six can master—stitching on a sewing machine, catching crabs, skiing—that have one common point. The child is regularly with an adult to whom that particular task is very easy.

Pie dough is like that. If you can handle dough deftly a Six or even a well-coordinated Five will be able to handle it too, although not so well. However, until you learn to be an adequate pastry chef, don't let him help you or at least one of you may cry.

This is a fast, simple method to learn and then to teach.

Pastry

Yield: Two 8-9" pie crusts

Before we knew any better, we beat our pie dough with an electric mixer—and it worked. It's heat that toughens pastry, but this method is so quick the dough stays cold. Add as little of the water as possible, so the crust will flake, and use the extract for dessert pies only. A Six can do everything but lift the dough. In this order

Beat	2 c. flour
	¼ lb. cold butter
	3 tbsp. cold lard OR oil
	3-5 tbsp. ice water
	¼ tsp. salt
	1/8 tsp. sugar
	1 tsp. almond extract

Use a low speed for 1 minute, quitting when the shortening is cut to the size of peas and the dough sticks together when squeezed. Slap it around several times with the heels of your hands (the palms are too warm) to break down the fat further.

Divide the dough and roll each ball between sheets of wax paper for easier, cooler handling. Your child should roll the dough in quick, short strokes with a rolling pin or a smooth highball glass, making each circle slightly bigger than the pie pan. For the first crust, peel away the top piece of paper in strips—often the only way it can be done—and lay the pie pan over the dough. Invert the pan for him. The dough will sink to the bottom and the second sheet of paper can be pulled away. He can press the torn dough together like modeling clay and fill the pie, slowly but well.

Drop the second crust over the filling, after your child has pulled away its top sheet of paper. Tear away the last sheet of paper and have him cut his initial on top for steam to escape. Press the flat tines of a fork around the rim, which mashes the crusts together to contain the juices. Bake as each individual recipe requires.

Baked pieshell—Prick the bottom of a single crust to prevent puffing and bake at 400° for 15-20 minutes.

Cinnamon Strips—Dip leftover dough in cinnamon sugar and bake at 400° for 15 minutes.

Jam Tarts—Fill scraps with a spoon of jam and fold the dough over itself, sealing them shut with a fork. Bake at 400° for 15 minutes.

Unbaked Blueberry Pie

This is a summer wonder, with or without a baked pie shell. A Three can make the filling.

Clean   1 qt. blueberries

You'll do most of this tedious job yourself. In a saucepan

Combine
- 1 c. sugar
- 1 c. blueberries
- 1 c. water
- 3 tbsp. cornstarch
- 1/8 tsp. salt

Stir over low heat about 10 minutes, until thick. Turn off heat.

Add
- 3 c. blueberries
- 1 tbsp. butter

Stir and mix well. Cool.

Whip
- ½ pt. heavy cream
- 1 tbsp. sugar

Pour berry mixture into a baked pie shell, or simply into a bowl, just before serving. Cover with the cream.

Cherry Pie

Preheat Oven 425°

Fresh cherries are hard to find but canned ones aren't worth your time. A Five is not too young to learn that sometimes you go first class or not at all.

Pit   1 qt. sour cherries

A dreary job, much of which you'll do yourself. Pour them in a pie shell, heaping most in the center. In a bowl, have him

Mix
- 1 c. sugar
- 1 tbsp. flour
- 1/8 tsp. salt

Sprinkle over the cherries, then cover with a crust, seal edges and slit dough.

Bake   40 minutes

Cakes

Once upon an unbelievable time, the cook just added water to a cake mix, but it wasn't very good. Then fresh eggs were required, sometimes milk or juice instead of water, then oil and, finally, pudding or gelatin mixes. We think if you look at the list of ingredients you have to add to a prepackaged mix and the chemicals the company already has added, you'll find a homemade cake is easier, healthier, cheaper and certainly better.

Cakes call for a light touch, which is why old recipes have the butter and sugar whipped to a pale froth, the eggs separated and beaten, the flour sifted and the dry and wet ingredients added alternately. Despite what the cookbooks say, today's flour has been milled so much it needs no sifting and the electric mixer whips such a fast, airy batter, you needn't separate the eggs. You only need to add dry and wet ingredients alternately to avoid spatter.

When mixing, a child must keep the beaters deep in the bowl and scrape the sides often with a rubber spatula. For baking, we find a Bundt or a fluted pan, muffin tins or tin cans give the best results, because cakes will rise more evenly and crack less than they would in regular round pans. All containers should be buttered and floured, filled no more than halfway and positioned slightly off center in the oven, each on a different shelf, so the air can circulate around them.

When the cake has smelled good for at least five minutes, it's probably done. Let your child see if it has pulled away a little from the sides of the pan, if a broom straw comes clean when he pokes it in the middle or the center springs back when he touches it—all true signs of readiness.

Any cake must be cooled on a rack for 10 minutes after taking it from the oven, so the air can circulate, or it may break when you take it out of the pan. When cool, invert it on a plate—a job which you must do—rapping the bottom of the pan with your knuckles if the cake sticks.

Ultimate Chocolate Cake

Preheat Oven 375°

This is the chocolate cake that stops you and your Four from trying any other chocolate cake. There's no need to keep looking. In a cup

Combine
- ½ c. milk
- 1 tsp. vinegar

Canned milk is better; cream is best. The vinegar sours it, to act upon the soda. In a saucepan

Combine
- 1 c. boiling water
- 4 sqs. unsweetened chocolate
- ½ c. chopped butter

Stir until melted, heating if necessary, and add the soured milk. To the saucepan

Add
- 2 c. flour
- 2 c. sugar
- 1½ tsp. baking soda
- 2 eggs
- ½ tsp. vanilla

Beat well with a wooden spoon. Pour into two greased and floured cake pans.

Bake   40 minutes

Cover with Chocolate Icing II, which follows.

Pound Cake

Preheat Oven 350°

This is a good traveling cake—sturdy enough to carry, rich enough to be proud of and big enough for a little girl of Five to give her big brother's Scout troop. Use buttermilk or let her curdle sweet milk so it can combine with the soda for the batter to rise. To do this

Combine   1 c. tepid milk
                 2 tsp. vinegar

Let it curdle—about 10 minutes. Meanwhile, in a large bowl

Beat   2 c. sugar
                 1 c. vegetable shortening
                 4 eggs
                 1 tsp. vanilla
                 1 tsp. almond extract

Beat at high speed for 3 minutes.

Combine   3 c. flour
                 ½ tsp. soda
                 ½ tsp. baking powder
                 ¾ tsp. salt

Add half the flour mix to the sugar mixture, then add half the milk, beating thoroughly each time. Repeat and beat 2 minutes at medium speed. Pour into an ungreased 9″ tube pan.

Bake   60-70 minutes

Lemon Tea Cake

Preheat Oven 325°

If you decide to have a tea party with your daughter this is the cake to make. It deserves a party. Since it's more delicate than our other cakes, all ingredients must be well beaten, which is why it takes a Five to make it. Grease and flour a loaf pan. Into a bowl, let her

Beat   ½ c. butter
                 1 c. sugar

Grate   zest of 1 lemon

Add the zest to the sugar.

Add   2 eggs
                 1½ c. flour
                 1 tsp. baking powder
                 1/8 tsp. salt
                 ½ c. milk

Beat each ingredient into the batter well before adding the next. Once all ingredients are in the bowl, beat 2 minutes, using the medium speed.

Bake   1 hour

Remove the cake from the oven when the sides leave the pan and immediately pour over it:

Lemon Sugar

Mix   juice of 1 lemon
                 ¼ c. sugar

Remove from the pan, right side up and serve cold.

Icings

Icing cakes, like gilding lilies, isn't necessary, but even a Two wants to do it and he can, if you help him follow some basic principles.

- Lay a square border of 4 wax paper strips on the cake plate, to catch the drips of icing, then add the bottom layer.
- Cool any cake before covering it, or the icing will melt and the cake will shed crumbs.
- Mix any additions, like raisins or nuts, at the last minute or the icing might not harden.
- Ice between layers, then the top of the cake and the sides last.
- Spread the icing with a knife, dipping it regularly into a glass of warm water for smooth results.
- Beat a teaspoon of hot water into the bowl of icing if it hardens before you finish.
- Put extra icing in a small plastic bag, cut a tiny corner and let your child squiggle a picture on top.
- Pull away the paper strips before serving.

Chocolate Icing I

This icing is rich, dark, drippy and shiny enough to justify an éclair and it can be mixed beaten or blended. In a pan let your three

Melt   4 sqs. unsweetened chocolate
                 2 tbsp. hot water

Cook over low heat, stirring and watching carefully so it doesn't burn. Remove from the stove for him.

Add   1 c. confectioners sugar
                 2 eggs
                 6 tbsp. chopped butter

When smooth, your child can spoon it over an éclair or dip a cupcake into it.

Chocolate Icing II

This recipe is so simple it can destroy a child's belief in the mumbo-jumbo of the kitchen. We hope it does. In a double boiler have your Five

Heat   one 14-oz. can condensed milk
                 2 sqs. unsweetened chocolate

Stir until the chocolate has melted and then spread on the cake.

Confectioners Dust

This is the easiest one of all. Simply let your child—a pre-Two will do—sift this sugar over a cake. It gussies it up nicely.

Gardening

There's no magic in making plants grow. Any plant hardy enough to survive in a dimestore is magic in itself. If you take it home and give it its quota of light and soil and water it will love you.

Your child will find that a few house plants can satisfy his parental instincts almost as much as a puppy and, besides, they don't throw up on the rug. In fact, there will come a time, we guarantee, when you'll decide a Bird of Paradise looks better than a bassinet.

A child's efforts at gardening will be very clumsy, but this is part of his learning process. These early years should be his time of slow appreciation when he learns from you to draw as much pleasure from the first shoot as he will from the full flower. Gradually he'll learn the principles of botany—probably just a step behind you.

You will teach him that every seed develops into four basic parts—the roots, the stems, the leaves and the flower that in turn fruits with new seed. He learns that plants eat minerals through their roots, that earthworms fertilize the soil and aereate it so the roots can breathe better, and that the leaves inhale carbon dioxide and exhale oxygen, which is why nature needs a balance between its animals and its plants. You'll need to explain that plants are the only living things that make their own food and that this chlorophyll is like blood to them.

Your child will learn that indoor plants enjoy each other's company, growing best when the pots are grouped together, and that cross-pollination is to petunias what making love is to people—productive, if not as jolly.

Whether you live on an Iowa farm or in a New York City apartment, there always should be room in your life to bring the outdoors inside. The smallest infant deserves to smell fresh earth in his room and watch a young plant inch higher, just like himself. When a child feels he is a part of nature he is better able to sort out his place in it.

When you begin the carriage walks—in the first few weeks of life—you stimulate his awareness by brushing his cheeks with mimosa puffs and letting him smell the differences between geraniums, roses and violets. His sense of observation is sharpened every time you show him a new plant or an autumn leaf.

Between six months and a year, a baby is thrilled to crawl through grass and blow away enough dandelion puffs to seed a city block. In the next eight months, he'll start to dig in the dirt while you weed the flower bed and if you aren't watching, he may help you by flowering the weed bed.

Gardening and a Two go best together we think, not because a child does it well (which he doesn't), but because by then a mother's ego is so low she needs to nurture something that won't have a tantrum when watered, fed or taken inside.

Now you'll have him soaking the clay pots (especially the gurgling new ones), finding pebbles for drainage and cracking charcoal in a paper bag for the potting soil. He'll stick his orange seeds in sphagnum moss, plant carrot tops and a whole sweet potato in water and feel as clever as Mendel when anything sprouts. In fact, we suspect a Two can find more beauty in a morning glory than an adult finds in a whole art gallery. This sensitivity either will grow or diminish, depending on the encouragement you give it.

A Three can root his own cuttings, tend his first cactus and help water the plants, which takes a deft touch. This is the time to tell him that some gardeners think plants grow best when people sing to them. This may or may not be true, but the sound of a small child's tune will put equanimity in your day. This also is the time to emphasize the names of different plants, particularly the fifty or more that are named for animals, like the orange tiger lily with its black stripes, the ever-multiplying hens and chickens and the flappy, green elephant ears. We've even seen a Three run off the Latin names of every plant in her garden, simply because it was the normal way to learn about them in her family. As always, whatever comes easily and customarily to parents will be simple for their child to master: a good reason for parents to develop more skills. This is the time to plant bulbs outdoors—the easiest of all flowers to grow—but he'll need the cunning of a Six to fox them into blooming in the house.

A Four should grow some of the food he eats, starting with the sprouts of beans and seeds that he mixes with soups and sandwich spreads. He can grow an herb garden in the kitchen, lettuce in the garden and cast birdseed into a flower bed to see what corn and wheat and sunflowers look like. Since a Four likes to show off so much, let him help you lug the house plants outside in summer. He'll learn for himself how direct sunshine gives a plant enough energy to thrive the rest of the year indoors with filtered light.

The curious Five likes to grow exotic fruit seeds—dates, pomegranates and mangoes—and he wants to hear about the lands they come from and why they need the care they do. You'll need to explain that most house plants are tropical and need warmth and moisture and rich soil,. but cacti need extra sand and sunshine to make them feel at home. Help your Five compare the woody-stemmed plants to succulents, which store water in their fat stems and therefore need it less often, and let him find the spores on the fern and grow pineapples, the best known of all the peculiar bromeliads.

With your guidance, a Six can plant a 3' X 3' outdoor garden or a smaller rock garden—in his own haphazard way—but he needs help to transplant delicate seedlings and make a terrarium. Let him sow a few melon seeds in a tub outdoors, which will come to fruition with its vine creeping along the patio floor. You can move it out of the way when necessary, the way watermelon farmers do in Indiana, before the cultivator goes through.

We've found if you have enough plants growing all the time, your child won't be disappointed at the ratio of success to failure—about 50-50. In fact, we've found the most successful gardeners are the ones who plant so much no one notices their mistakes—especially themselves. That's the attitude your child should have about gardening and everything else.

House Plants

It took a lot of house plants—and a lot of children—for us to learn that a preschool child can't care for a plant all alone any more than he can care for a kitty—or for himself. As always, he needs experience, he needs competence and, above all, he needs to know exactly why he's doing what. The more he knows, the better gardener he'll be. Unless you're quite knowledgeable yourself, you'll probably want to start your indoor garden with plants from the dimestore.

This is where you first begin to see that a green thumb is no more than a sharp eye for the right plants. The inexpensive ones, like the spider plant or the philodendron, are usually the easiest to care for, but all plants should be chosen from a fresh shipment and all should have a few light green leaves—the sign of new growth, and no brown or yellow ones—the sign of disease or poor care. You'll have better luck with a flowering plant if you buy it during the blooming season, and not before—or its adjustment will be difficult—and only if you can baby it with winter sunlight, a cool house by day and a colder one by night—all necessary to force the blooms.

As you learn to gauge the water and light your plants need, you and your child will want to start others from seeds or even from cuttings. Finally you succumb to those luscious beauties at the nursery. They can be as disastrous to the budget as a day at the races, but when you can keep them alive they're a lot better for the morale.

Light

All house plants need light to photosynthesize water and carbon dioxide into food, but the more direct the rays, the less they need. If you're lucky enough to have the triple exposure of a bay window with three hours of sun a day, you have almost as much intense light as a greenhouse. If not, you must gauge the intensity of indoor sunlight by the size and location of the window and how brightly the sun can shine through it. For us, this was enough to make us wash the windows.

Most plants should live no farther than three feet from a window since the sunlight diffuses quickly. The time we give for indoor sunlight is based on this distance, and it's always one to two hours more than a plant needs when placed outdoors.

A bushy plant from a nursery, acclimated as it is to special lights, can't feed so much foliage at home and it rapidly drops all the leaves it can't support. If the bushy plant means so much to you, you might consider a light unit, but every room can have greenery if you rotate the plants and if you choose them carefully.

Any strong plant can live in a dark corner for a few weeks and some, like the Chinese evergreen and the spider plant, need no sunlight, thriving in bright, well-lighted areas, although they grow more slowly. A rubber tree needs only an hour of sun, a flowering plant needs three to five hours, and a citrus tree needs four to five.

All plants are heliotropic and must be turned around a little every few weeks or they will grow crooked: an important assignment for a Two.

Wintering

Group potted plants together, since they are as convivial as children. They enjoy sitting on a radiator, either in a planter on a bed of dampened peat moss or sand or simply with their pots resting on saucers full of stones and water. The heat raises the moisture and envelops their leaves in humidity, which gives them, like English maidens, nifty complexions. However, if you place them near hot or cold air vents, the intermittent blasts will choke the plants.

Summering

If possible, bury pots in the ground outdoors in summer but bring them inside several weeks before you turn on the heat in the fall, so they may adjust. If you forget them outdoors, you may have to treat them for frostbite by showering the pots and then by soaking them in a bucket. Place the pots in a room below 70° until they begin to gain consciousness.

Water

One of the best parts of gardening is the side interests it develops—in food, in beauty, in all the wonders of science. One of the most wonderful must be the story of evaporation, which every child should know. Explain that the soil dries when some of the invisible water molecules become restless (not unlike children) and rush to the top and out into the air. More of them slip out of the leaves. The most obvious facts to you are revelations to a child.

Although water is essential to plants, the soil needs to dry out between waterings so it can fill with oxygen and the tiny root hairs can breathe. It is these root hairs which also draw food and water into the roots themselves.

Some plants need more water than others, depending on their origins, and the smaller the pot the more frequent the watering. All plants need more water when they're flowering, so the blossoms don't fall, and less when they're dormant. Plants, like people, can't eat and sleep at the same time.

A plant needs water when it droops or when the soil feels as dusty as it looks, which a Three can discover if he carefully pokes his finger down near the side of the pot, as deep as it can go. If the soil is loose, you can pour water until it runs out through the bottom. However, the water will race through old, hard soil, without absorption, or puddle on the top, which means the pot needs cultivation, a long soak or new soil.

There are four ways to water plants, but it is best to do it very slowly with lukewarm water (for better absorption) and only as the plants need it. This seldom is every day—a hard lesson for an enthusiastic child to learn.

Method I

Soak the pots—especially new transplants or large plants—in a basin of water, letting them drink as long as they wish. Unlike people, they know when to quit. Remove the pots when the soil is damp on top—an hour to overnight.

Method II

Poke a fork deep into the soil around the sides of the pot, 4-6 times, and drizzle water around and around the plant with the spout of the can close to the earth. The drier the earth, the more it will gurgle.

Method III

Use 6 ice cubes in a hanging pot, instead of water, since they melt so slowly and therefore cause no drips.

Method IV

Water the pineapple and other bromeliads from above, filling the leaves.

Misting

Although the fuzz on some leaves, like the African violets, protects them from dust, the slicker the leaves the more they need bathing. Dust blocks sunlight and without that, the leaves can't photosynthesize. In a job your child will chortle over, let him spray them with a mister filled with lukewarm water. Some overzealous housekeepers wipe the leaves with oil to make them shine, but this just clogs the pores, attracting more dust. It's a great bother, besides.

Soil

We once knew a proper headmistress of a proper school for young ladies whose gardenias were the most splendid in town, but no one knew she got them that way by sending her distinguished husband outdoors every night for a "turn in the garden." However, you don't have to ask your husband to pee in the pots if you use the right soil mixture.

Although it's hard to believe, plants don't grow very well in dirt. They need a combination of sterilized potting soil for food; a humus such as peat moss to hold water and anchor the tiny root hairs; sand, vermiculite or perlite for drainage and grit with charcoal to keep the soil sweet.

Although most house plants will thrive in the balanced Basic Soil we give, some, like delicate woodland plants and the exotic gardenia, need extra peat moss for more acidity, and others, like succulents and cacti, need extra sand for quicker drainage.

We recommend making a big batch of fertilized Basic Soil with your child and using it as needed, adding the extra sand or peat moss if necessary for some plants. As you make it, rub the soil between your fingers so you and your child can learn to judge textures. The quality of soil isn't constant and it's time to change it when the consistency changes—probably about once a year.

Definitions

In this gardening section we use the same technical names you and your child will hear at the garden center. This is what they're talking about:

Potting soil—a prepackaged mix of soil, sterilized to kill bacteria, mold and weed seeds. It's blended with some sand and humus, but not enough to hold water and anchor roots well. We use it in our Basic Soil recipe.

Humus—anything that was once alive and has decomposed, such as rotted sawdust, leafmold from the woods, compost and any of the peat mosses. All humus anchors roots, distributes fertilizer and helps the soil hold water, but they contain no nutrition. Humus is used in Basic Soil.

Peat moss—an assortment of plants which have decayed in water. It's commercially packaged, the easiest humus to find and comes from many parts of the world. Sphagnum and Michigan peat are the most common.

Sphagnum—an especially good medium for sprouting seeds, because it prevents mildew. It must be scalded to make it absorbent—a bother, but it's worth it.

Michigan peat—the most acidic peat moss. It's packaged wet, which accounts for its rich, dark color and its higher cost.

Drainage—an important ingredient of Basic Soil, needed to aereate the roots and anchor them. Sand, vermiculite and perlite are used interchangeably, but none have any nutrients.

Sand—the grittiest of all. The more you add to the soil, the faster the water will drain. Use builder's sand or sandbox sand or the sharp quarry sand sold in garden centers, but never use sea sand, which packs too hard and is salty.

Vermiculite—refined mica, mined in flat brittle sheets and expanded by extreme heat into spongelike bits which absorb water more than the other drainage. It's excellent for cuttings and for germinating seeds.

Perlite—a volcanic mineral also treated under heat to expand, but it absorbs no water.

Charcoal—a freshener used in either soil or water to keep it sweet and sold commercially in chips.

Fertilizer—either organic or chemical. All fertilizers contain nitrogen, phosphorus and potash in varying proportions, all of which are needed by plants.

Nitrogen—causes leafier plants and is found in cow manure, bloodmeal and any organic fertilizer.

Phosphorus—added to make strong roots and promote development of flowers and seeds. It's found in bonemeal, rock phosphate and manure.

Potash—helps improve the quality and size of fruits and vegetables and is found in the ashes of wood, cigars and cigarettes.

Cow manure—now dehydrated, nearly odor free, socially acceptable and prepackaged. It contains nitrogen and some phosphorus and can be added to Basic Soil.

Bone meal—slow-acting fertilizer, ground from animal bones, safe enough for young roots. It's used instead of manure and is excellent for bulbs, but since it takes as much as two years to be absorbed most gardeners use it outdoors. For pots they prefer steamed bone meal, which is fat free, enabling root hairs to absorb it quicker. Too much of either kind will mildew the top of the soil but this is harmless.

Cellated iron—fertilizer to correct the yellow leaves caused by anemia—a special problem for citrus.

Basic Soil

Yield: three 4" pots

Your Three will want to help you mix this batch. In a big roasting pan

Combine	2 c. sphagnum OR peat moss
	2 c. potting soil
	2 c. sand OR vermiculite OR perlite
	1/3 c. cracked charcoal
	1 tbsp. steamed bone meal OR
	2 tbsp. dried cow manure

Any of these drainage materials work well but perlite is the least messy when a child is helping you. If you use peat moss as the humus, we recommend the sphagnum—the least acidic, most available, most compact to store. It's highly absorbent if scalded first, for its fibers remain expanded. This definitely is a job for you. Put it in a colander and over it

Pour	boiling water
Cool	3 hours

Don't touch any sooner for its stays hot much longer than you'd think. Extra sphagnum can be stored in a plastic bag after treatment.

Sandy Soil

Your child can transform Basic Soil to suit cacti by doubling the amount of drainage.

Spongy Soil

To make the spongy soil that ferns need, have your child add twice as much humus as he did in the Basic Soil mix.

Techniques

It's no use pretending. Your child needs to use some tricks to grow happy house plants, but they're not nearly so esoteric as the experts say they are.

Potting

There are three types of containers—the clay pot, which allows plants to breathe better but requires more watering; the plastic pot, which is especially good for the especially forgetful (but holds water so well the roots sometimes rot), and the nonpot, which is any container, like an enamel bowl, that has no drainage holes. Any but the nonpot needs a saucer to catch the water.

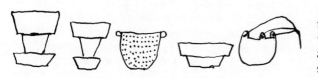

Preparing the Pot

Have your Two soak a clay pot in water before using it, for a soaked pot won't draw moisture from the soil just as soaked brick won't dry out its mortar. In a bucket

Soak	small pot—1 hour
	big pot—overnight

Stop when the pots quit gurgling. Over the drainage holes of a plastic or a clay pot

Prop	large clay shard
Add	1" pebbles OR shards
Fill	Basic Soil, dampened

Line the pot with this soil, pressing it down and against the sides, to prevent mold and to snuggle the roots. Leave a hole as deep and wide as the plant you'll press into place. In a nonpot use 2" of pebbles and the special commercial soil mixture found at the dimestore, which is much airier than other packaged potting soil or our own mix.

Transplanting

Seedlings should be transplanted when they have four leaves, but most house plants should be transplanted every year. The old soil is worn out and often the pot should be bigger. If the pot is too small the roots become bound and push through the drainage hole—a clear sign that the plant needs more room. Plants with thick leaves and stems—succulents, bromeliads and cacti—need larger pots only every two or three years, because they like to feel snug. No plant should be transplanted into a pot that's more than two inches bigger in diameter than the old one. If the pot is too big the soil can sour, like a child whose boundaries are so wide his roots have no stability.

Although moving is traumatic for any plant, the crisis will be less severe if the job is done in the more temperate times of the year. First have your Four water it well and then slide a knife around the sides of the old pot while you hold the stem of the plant between your thumb and index finger as he thumps out the plant. He can knock away the old soil and sink the plant into a prepared pot, tamping the earth firmly around the plant and adding more soil if needed. The soil level on the stem must stay the same: if it's higher it may rot the steam; if lower, it may expose the roots. This is the only trick of transplanting. Water once more and keep it out of direct sunlight for two days.

Fertilizing

Any plant in a pot needs extra vitamins. We find fish emulsion, that smelly stuff, is best. As with any fertilizer, be sure to use only half as much as it says on the label, because the roots are burned so easily. Mix it with lukewarm water—so the root hairs can absorb it in only hours instead of days—and feed the plants in spring and summer. Plants also should be fertilized when you see new buds or shoots, but in any case only once a month.

The Hothouse

A homemade hothouse makes rooting and germination much faster and even waters plants when you're on vacation. To make, have your Four water the pot well, then enclose it in a plastic bag, securing it with a rubber band and place it near an east or west window. Never put this Hothouse in direct sunlight or the plastic will intensify the heat and damage any leaves. The bag should look dewy in the morning and dry in the afternoon. If it doesn't dry remove the rubber band temporarily for evaporation.

Cultivation

Watering packs the soil if there are no bugs or worms to aereate it as there are in the garden. If it doesn't crumble when you press it have your Four ruffle the earth by poking it with a fork to a depth of 2-3". This is necessary every 4-6 weeks—a good job for a so-so child on a bad day.

Pinching

Good-looking plants, like good-looking bottoms, are frequently pinched. To have a bushy plant, instead of a stick, have your Four press off the top pair of leaves. This frustrates the plant into sending side shoots.

Cross-pollination

Without the help of bees, butterflies and southwinds, the flowering tree, like the miniature orange, may need sex on a toothpick to bear fruit indoors. Let your Six use a cotton swab or his soft poster paint brush to dip inside each bloom, which shakes the pollen from the pistils down into the stamen. This fertilizes the seeds in the ovum, which expands to become the fruit—something for your child to remember the next time he sinks his teeth into an apple.

Problems

The leaves of your plant will show the first symptom of trouble, whether it's caused by bugs, disease or the wrong sort of care. Help your child look under the leaves for insects, and if they're there, protect the top of the soil with foil, then hold the plant upside down to dunk the leaves into hot soapy water. Rinse in cold water and isolate it until you're sure all the bugs are gone.

If there were no bugs but the leaves are brown, then the plant is burned, either by too much sunlight or too much fertilizer. If the leaves are yellow the plant needs more light, better drainage or a fertilizer with iron to correct its anemia. If many leaves fall without replacement, most plants need more light or water—and then there are the aralia and the zebra plant, who drop their leaves every time their feet get too wet.

For final proof of a problem, run a knife around the sides of the pot and tip out the plant. You can see any damage from disease, because it strikes roots first, or from too much water, because the roots will smell bad. There's no hope for such a plant; weep and throw it away. If no trouble is obvious your plant needs about the same thing you should give a peaked child—better food, more sunshine, new friends, much love.

The Beginnings

There are three ways to start a plant. The easiest is from seeds and bulbs, but plants can be started from cuttings. It's especially good for that most particular child, the pre-Three, to understand that there are a lot of ways to do anything.

Sowing Seeds

A child's sense of drama swings to the miracle of life as he watches a simple bean unfold almost overnight. Most seeds will sprout in a warm place eventually, planted in either soil, water or wet cotton. The seed contains all the nutrition a plant needs until its second, or true, set of leaves appears. The first set is merely the seed's division of itself.

The seeds in a child's food can be divided into two categories: the ones he eats and the ones he spits. Even to show a child these seeds encourages his curiosity, but a fussy eater often improves enormously when he tries to grow his own food right from the meals he is served.

Let your child study the eating seeds in a tomato, an eggplant, a cucumber, a squash, a strawberry or a lima—a seed that sprouts best if it has another lima for company. Every one of these can be planted even by a Two and some of them will grow, although the smaller the seed, the harder it is to keep it alive after it germinates, for these seedlings are very fragile.

The bigger, spitting seeds have longer pregnancies (like elephants to ants). Their shells are tougher, such as peaches and pecans, but their sprouts have much more endurance. Citrus seeds and pips from grapes and apples and pears are in this category and so is an avocado, a fine handling size for a child.

Some kitchen gardeners dry the seeds first to imitate the life cycle, but this doesn't seem necessary to us. For faster germination, however, you can soak any seed overnight in a cup of water. This softens the shell.

Kitchen Table Pot

The French have their *pot au feu* simmering on the back of the stove, but we prefer our pot germinating on the kitchen table. This is the place to plant the seeds of the day. They need no window light to sprout, but the soil must stay moist. Use a clear plastic pot so your child can see what's going on below. In a 6" pot

Layer	1" pebbles
	3" Basic Soil
	1" scalded sphagnum moss

The layer of moss keeps the seeds from mildewing. Press the tiny seeds into the moss, cover bigger ones with a dusting of it and bury any large seed just below the surface. Transplant when 4 leaves have appeared.

Water	2 times a week

Kitchen pots prefer to sit in a saucer of water to drink through their drainage holes, so the small seeds don't float.

Citrus Tree

We know a little girl named Alix whose mother put a grapefruit seed in a pot when she was born. Both now are Twelve and beautiful, but the tree is much taller and, unlike Alix, very thorny, vibrant green and bushy. Use a Kitchen Table Pot. A Two can start this tree but it takes a Five to care for it.

Germination	15-30 days

When it has 4 leaves, transplant into a small, individual pot.

Soil	Basic
Indoor sunlight	4-5 hours
Outdoor light	partial sun
Water	3 times weekly

This frequent watering is essential in the first six months, when citrus trees often die from dehydration, and in spring and summer, when they bloom. The trees may fruit in seven years if you cross-pollinate them, which your child will do, but if the trees live outdoors year round, the bees will do it for you.

Date Tree

Date pits from the dates you put in your Christmas fruitcakes will sprout into palm trees for your Five, but they need good aereation—helped by bits of leaves and twigs—and a tall pot, because their roots have learned to travel deeply for water. A plastic pot is best, for the roots should never dry completely. Dig up one seed in about three weeks to show your child how the silvery eye in the center begins to form a pearl, the first sign of growth.

Soil	Sandy
	1 tbsp. dried manure (cow or camel)
Germination	8-10 weeks
Indoor sunlight	3 hours
Outdoor light	partial sun
Water	twice weekly, in the saucer

Keep young palms away from drafts. Your child won't have to transplant for a year if there are no more than three pits in a 5" pot.

Mango

Every seed deserves to be tried at least once, especially when it's four inches long, heavy, flat, hairy and has a big eye at one end. Have your Five scrub the seed first. In a bowl

Combine	water
	cracked charcoal
	seed

Soak for a week to soften the tough shell. In a tall 5" pot

Plant	vertically, eye pointed down
Soil	Basic
Water	heavily

Let the pot dry out completely once a month to develop good breathing space for the root hairs.

Germination	4 months
Indoor sunlight	4-5 hours
Outdoor light	partial sun

A mango chills easily. Keep it away from cold windows inside, beware of frosts outside, and use only tepid water. It needn't be transplanted for a year.

261

Avocado

This seed grows into a lush, bushy tree if your Four pinches it. Otherwise, it will be straight as a flagpole and about as handsome. We've found the California fruit you buy in January often has roots when you open them, which makes it easy. If not, have him dry the seed for a couple of days, peel the papery brown skin and warn him that the seed may take up to three months to sprout. Some people start these seeds in a cup of water but we find Basic Soil in a 5" pot is better. Plant base down 2/3 into the soil leaving the tip exposed. For a stronger root system keep well watered in a dark cupboard until the seed germinates.

Germination	30-90 days
Soil	Basic
Indoor sunlight	3-5 hours
Outdoor light	light shade
Water	weekly

Remind your child to pinch off the top leaves every few inches.

Pomegranate

A Five finds a pomegranate such an adventure to eat he'll want to grow his own.

A pomegranate develops into a bushy shrub if pinched and finds the dry heat of a city apartment rather like its native Persia. The flowers are brilliant orange and they can fruit outdoors as far north as Baltimore, but if yours fruits inside, write "Believe It or Not" and make your own grenadine.

To begin, have your child suck the seeds clean before he plants them in the Kitchen Pot.

Germination	6-8 weeks

Transplant several seedlings into a 5" pot and keep them away from the humidity of other plants.

Soil	Sandy
Indoor sunlight	2-3 hours
Outdoor light	partial sun
Water	weekly

Cuttings

It's easier to meet a neighbor over a rose bush than a coffee party and a lot more interesting to a child. The old-fashioned custom of swapping the cuttings of favorite plants is a good way to multiply your friendships and your house plants too.

Swap anything—chrysanthemums, impatiens, begonias—and expect best results in spring to midsummer, when plants are most energetic. Make many cuttings; they like to root around with friends.

Cut	2-4" stems

Slice just below the node, a growth point that looks like a bump. The lower leaves should be removed. Keep the stems turgid in water or refrigerated in a plastic bag with a little water in it, or the cuttings may wilt and lose their rooting power. Otherwise, almost anything seems to root if you wait long enough—but some people help luck along by dipping the cut ends in a commercial root booster before planting in a rooting medium, either water or the sand mixture given below.

Water Method

	In a glass, have your Two
Add	1 tbsp. cracked charcoal
	6 oz. water
	cuttings

Sand Method

	In a pot or a plastic tray, have your Three
Layer	1" pebbles
Add	1 c. vermiculite OR perlite OR sand
	1 c. scalded sphagnum moss
	1/3 c. water
Plant	cuttings or leaves

Imbed them at a slant, so water can't collect at their bases, and about 2" apart, so the roots don't tangle. Press drainage around cuttings and add a little more water so particles can fill the air pockets. If you put the entire pot in the Hothouse, the cuttings will root faster.

Indoor sunlight	1 hour
Rooting	3-6 weeks

Transplant when the roots are 2-3" long and keep out of sunlight for the next two days.

Root Cuttings

Plants store all extra food in their roots, which is why carrots and other tap roots are so good for your child and why they have the energy to send up new stalks when only the tops of the roots are planted. No new roots will grow, but you'll have a few weeks of pretty foliage. Use a cake pan, either nestling the carrot, beet or radish tops in drainage or in a little water with charcoal to keep it smelling fresh. Keep in a well-lighted area.

Pineapple

This air plant only uses its roots to keep it from flying away. Cut the top ½" of the pineapple and let it dry for a day or two. Remove 1" of leaves from the base and you can see the tiny roots; they look like worms. In a pot

Fill	sand OR vermiculite OR perlite
Imbed	pineapple top

Water from above to fill the cupped leaves. It will send out new leaves within 10 days. The old ones will die at about the same rate this new core grows and they should be clipped with scissors as they brown, for good looks. Transplant when the new leaves are 1-2" long and treat like any bromeliad.

If you wait a few years, you may be able to make the pineapple fruit by putting an apple in the pot and putting the entire pot in a sealed plastic bag for 5 days. The apple releases ethylene, a gas that inspires the pineapple to flower in 2-3 months. If cross-pollinated it eventually will bear a baby pineapple, growing at the end of a tall spike in the center of the foliage.

Bulbs

There is magic abroad in the land (as every child knows), but a bulb in bloom is the best example we know of nature at its most miraculous. Before you start a bulb garden, let your child slice down through the center of a bulb—any one from the lowly onion to the exotic amaryllis—to see its tiny woody core. This is the embryo of the plant itself, with the stem, the flower and the leaves in miniature. It will draw all the nutrition it needs to bloom from the layers of skin around it. This is why many bulbs are so easy to grow.

Hyacinths, paper narcissus, crocuses and daffodils will grow in water, soil or rocks, but tulips, prima donnas that they are, must have soil. Nurserymen do sell bulbs recommended for forcing, but we've found almost all bulbs will bloom indoors if they've been cooled. If bulbs are planted outdoors in well-fertilized soil they will rejuvenate themselves in the summer, unless the ground is too hot, and bloom again the next year. None of them should be planted outdoors until the weather gets fairly cold, for bulbs, like bears, need cold weather to hibernate. Bulbs planted inside for winter blooming must be tricked by a spell in the refrigerator, so they will think they've gone through winter. Bulbs have many positive qualities, but they are not very smart.

Indoor Bulb Garden

Bulbs will bloom indoors if your Six lets them pretend to follow the seasons, first with a short winter in the refrigerator, then in a cold, dark place to root—as in early spring, and finally in a bright window for spring. It's easy to force bulbs if you can force yourself to remember when to move them from place to place.

Buy the bulbs in fall, four months before you want them to bloom. Any bulbs will do, although "precooled" or "tender" forcing bulbs often do better. Refrigerate whatever bulbs you buy in a brown paper bag for at least one month, but the longer they winter the better their blooms will be.

Planting

Your child should plant the bulbs when the air on the back porch or the basement is nippy but never freezing. He can put them in water, sand, rocks or, for tulips, in Basic Soil. All bulbs should be planted point up. If your child uses water the bulb should fit snugly in its own container or the flower will topple, but if he uses sand or soil he can crowd many together in a bowl, which makes a better effect. Use a pretty container since the bulbs won't be transplanted and fence the edge of it with 3-4 popsicle sticks and a length of yarn to keep the plants from flopping. Start a new pot every two weeks if you want constant flowering.

Water—Suspend the bulb over its jar with just enough water to tickle its base. Since bulbs rot easily, they mustn't soak. You can buy special glass jars designed for bulb forcing, if you prefer, but they are expensive.

Sand
In a bowl

Pour	3-4″ sand OR peat moss OR pebbles
Add	1½-2½″ water
Imbed	bulbs, half exposed

Soil
Prepare a pot with good drainage.

Soil	Basic
Imbed	bulbs, half exposed
Water	thoroughly

Rooting

No matter what medium you've chosen, the bulbs, once potted, must start to grow in a cold, dark place. Some gardeners who force bulbs in soil like to bury their pots outdoors in the earth and under glass, because here they need no watering. Your child will have the same effect with sand, which is cleaner than dirt and never freezes. Have him sit the pots in a wooden liquor box filled with 4″ of sand and then fill the top of the box with more sand to insulate the bulbs. Unless the pots are buried in soil or sand, they should be checked every two weeks to make sure the medium is moist, but be careful not to soak them.

Temperature	40-55°
Light	none

The longer the bulbs are in darkness, the better they will root.

Germination	6-8 weeks

When the shoots are 2-3″ tall they can be moved indoors. To check the buried pots you must lift them out of the sand. Even if the shoots aren't tall enough, they can live without another burial until they're ready.

Blooming

Move the plants to the coolest room in the house where the leaves and stalks get their color and grow tall enough to bloom.

Temperature	65°
Water	constant moisture
Indoor sunlight	indirect
Budding	2-3 weeks

When the bud is full, have your child move the pot to its place of honor, away from any source of heat, for any flower lasts longer if it isn't too warm.

Temperature	68-72°
Water	twice weekly
Fruition	1 week

The blooms will last two weeks. After they have bloomed, have your child save the bulbs to plant outdoors when the weather permits. Forced bulbs can't get enough sunlight or nutrition in their pot to form a new embryo even if the soil has been fertilized, but they can flower again if planted in the garden.

The Varieties

There are hundreds of kinds of plants and you'll want your child to have as many as possible—a fern and a bromeliad, because they have a story to tell; a vine, because it's the mainstay of the dimestore; a succulent, because it's the most varied of all, and a flowering plant, because it will bring such happiness.

Flowering Plants

Like a lady in a corset, pot-bound plants have bigger blooms.

Soil	Basic

Use Sandy Soil for flowering cactus.

Indoor sunlight	3-5 hours
Outdoor light	partial sun
Fertilize	weekly in budding season
Water	2-3 times weekly
Mist	weekly

Sunlight triggers the blooms and cool temperatures keep them fresh. If you limit the water and sunlight in summer you'll enforce dormancy and have winter flowers instead.

Vines and Foliage Plants

A vine like pothos is the easiest for a child to grow, since it even thrives in water. Other foliage plants such as dumb cane or schefflera or a palm tree are almost as easy if you keep them indoors in winter, for most are tropical.

Soil	Basic
Indoor sunlight	1 hour or less
Outdoor light	shade
Fertilize	monthly in spring and summer

Water when the soil feels dry when you poke into it. Keep the leaves dusted so they can photosynthesize.

Ferns

Ferns, once as tall as dinosaurs (before there were any dinosaurs), are the most primitive plants of all, reproducing not by seeds in fruit but by a two-step operation of spores and eggs. Let your Five see the rows of black spores that dot the back of each frond or hide in their own stalk case—and which people once thought could make them invisible. The fern skips a generation when their spores drop to the ground and sprout a scarcely noticeable little plant that hatches eggs and dies within a few hours. These eggs send up new stems several inches from the fern, which sends up new shoots too. Old stems continually wither and need to be clipped every week so the pot looks pretty. If a child keeps his potted fern on a bed of stones it can have the same humid atmosphere it knew in the forest to produce more spores.

Soil	Spongy
Indoor sunlight	2 hours
Outdoor light	shade
Water	3 times a week

Succulents

A succulent is any plant such as a jade tree or a cactus that stores water in its thick stems and leaves. It usually hates to be pinched, likes to be potbound and, because of its shallow roots, wants only 2-3" of soil, which may mean a few extra inches of gravel in the pot. Flowering succulents, like geraniums, impatiens and begonias, need more earth, two more hours of sunshine a day. and the casual care of a Three.

Soil	Sandy
Water	heavy and infrequent

Water lightly at transplanting, drench it several days after settling and allow the soil to get dry as dust before each watering.

Indoor sunlight	2 hours
Outdoor light	partial sun

After eons in the desert the cactus developed prickles to protect itself against punctures and the loss of water from its leaves. It only needs water every 2 weeks—less often if it is bigger, more often when it's blooming—and enjoys as much as 5 hours of indoor sunlight a day, any time.

Bromeliads

These Latin American plants come in an astonishing variety and often have exotic flowers that take weeks to unfold and last just as long. At home their shallow roots are attached to tall trees so their feet can stay dry and so they can' get near some sunlight. Bromeliad leaves are cupped to catch and ration rainfall and also to trap dead leaves and insects, which feed the plant as they decompose. One gardener we know claims a few dead flies dropped in the cups during budding season improve the blooms as well as delight the children in her kindergarten class. Bromeliads make interesting indoor plants and need little soil and small pots.

Soil	Spongy
Indoor sunlight	3 hours
Outdoor light	partial sun
Water	twice weekly, from above
Mist	weekly

A new plant will grow from the side. Transplant it when the big mother dies.

Terrarium

A terrarium is an excellent present to get and to give and is also a good way to teach a child about the environment, for he sees the terrarium create its own life cycle, turning its little bit of sunshine into food and its dew into rainfall. Growth here is so slow the scene is almost static, so you'll need very small plants and much variety. You can use ones from a dimestore, if they're divided to fit the small space, and rooted cuttings, but there are tiny plants in every back yard if your child looks closely enough. You need at least six plants—tall and short, fat and skinny, and even one with berries—and then you need some ground covering and moss. No clump of earth you collect should be bigger than 2" square. In a glass canister, a goblet, a little jar or a big fish tank

Layer	½" stones
	gravel
	cracked charcoal
	2-3" Basic Soil

The stones are for drainage and the bigger the terrarium, the thicker this layer should be. The gravel fills in the bigger spaces between them and the charcoal keeps the soil sweet. Have your child make a hilly terrain of the soil, to make the garden more interesting. He should poke holes in the earth with a pencil and press the plants into them, firming the soil around the roots with his fingertips. Each plant must include roots, a stem and a leaf. Cover the earth with the moss and add a few stones, sea shells, bits of bark or tiny pine cones for contrast.

Add	water

It should partly cover the first layer of stones. Clean the plants and the inside of the bowl by spraying with a mister. Cover with clear plastic or glass.

Indoor sunlight 1 hour OR
3 hours lamplight

The terrarium should look dewy in the morning and be clear by evening. Add more water if it doesn't cloud, but if it doesn't clear all day, remove the cover so some of the extra moisture can evaporate. If your child has added a flowering plant like a begonia, the terrarium needs 2-3 hours of sunlight a day. A desert terrarium requires Sandy Soil, a top layer of pure sand instead of moss and no cover at all.

If the terrarium is big enough your child can add a chameleon, a small box turtle or even a frog, but you must include a bowl of water. Cover this terrarium with a screen and water it more often.

Outdoor Garden

Perhaps babies recognize beauty because they're so beautiful themselves, but we've never known a child who didn't smile at the sight of a flower or call each one "pretty" almost from the time that he could talk. These are the moments that make your soul sing.

You cultivate your child's love of beauty in many ways, but a little garden patch of his own, no bigger than a window box, does it very well. Your Two likes his own trowel—the only tool he'll need for years—and then he's ready to begin.

We found bedding plants are better than seeds because he'll step on them less than on young sprouts, and flowers are better than vegetables because blooms come long before the fruit, and this satisfies his eagerness. We don't recommend insecticides at all, not only because ladybugs and praying mantises are superior, but because every child eats a certain number of flowers in his time and eating a peck of dirt is a lot healthier than eating a pinch of insecticide.

A Three can plant his first bulbs, and a Four plants both flower and vegetable seeds. The patch he had at Two can grow bigger every year until a Six can handle a rock garden too. No matter what kind of garden he has, this child can care for his land if the area is small, if the plants are easy to tend—and if you're taking care of your own nearby.

Basic Garden

An outdoor garden, either for flowers or vegetables, needs a half day of sunshine and dark,

rich, well-drained soil. If the soil is reddish—a sign of clay—buy some topsoil and pile your old dirt in a corner of the yard, the foundation for a rock garden. If the drainage is bad there will be moss on the ground, puddles after a rain and plants that rot at the roots. In that case, dig up a 6-7' patch of earth—a job for your husband to do and your child to pretend to do. In a 3' X 3' plot

Layer 1" gravel
2 bushels topsoil
Add 2 c. dried cow manure
1 c. bone meal

Crumble the soil and water thoroughly.

Add 100 earthworms

Unless you saw many worms when you dug, this addition is necessary to keep the soil friable. Buy them at a garden center or a bait store, releasing them at sundown so they have time to get into the ground before the birds eat them. The worms will thrive if you don't use a heavy dose of chemical fertilizer.

Vegetable Garden

Help your Four plan an interesting garden, but he should choose which vegetables to plant. He might like squash, with their blossoms that could have come from Mars, and a tomato plant—a delight, for he'll never forget the taste of the warm, red tomatoes eaten right in the garden—and green peas, which are lovely to shell. Add onions and marigolds to keep away the bugs and lettuce to edge the plot. Plant seeds as directed on the package, but for planned gardenhood, don't plant many more than the soil can support. Thin the extra seedlings after the second set of leaves appears and you can tell which plants are the strongest.

Bulb Garden

Bulbs send up shoots in spring, an anticipation almost as joyful to a child as Christmas.

Choose the driest spot in the yard, for bulbs rot easily if drainage is bad. To look their best, bulbs should be planted in clumps about 6" apart. Dig a trench or individual holes, with your child measuring the depth with his ruler, for arithmetic makes more sense when it can be applied. The bigger the bulbs the deeper they're planted. The lowest depth for tulips will let them bloom as long as five years. Into each hole

Sprinkle 1 tbsp. bone meal
Plant crocus, 4″ deep
hyacinths, 6″ deep
daffodils and tulips, 8-10″ deep

Cover and tamp, a job every child enjoys. If the soil is clay, you'll have to dig 6″ deeper to line the bed with stones for drainage and add a layer of top soil—the nutrition for next year's flowers. This is hard enough work to make it a family production.

Rock Garden

This is especially good because it calls for as much creativity as it does energy. A rock garden should look like a rough hillside, with flowers and mosses growing between the rocks. Either arrange it against a corner of the fence or dig out a small slope in the yard to imbed it. It can be any size or height, depending on the strength of your small child's arms. It's his garden, from the collection to the compliments, although he'll need your help to make it and to keep it going. For a low garden

Collect small, angular rocks
Lay 1″ gravel OR cinder drainage bed
Cover 8″ Basic Soil
Arrange rocks

The rocks should be planted rather irregularly but close together, jammed two thirds of the way into the earth and, for harmony, with the grain of the rocks going in the same direction, like wood. Press more soil between the rocks.

Plant sweet alyssum/bulbs/phlox/
candytuft/forget-me-nots/moss

Nestle these or other plants among the rocks and imbed smaller rocks beneath the plants to hold them and to help with drainage. A child will enjoy this garden best if he gradually adds other rocks and plants, rather than planting all at once. Cacti may be substituted if Sandy Soil is used.

Candy Tree

There are some days so full of sameness the mind seems stultified. For this you need a different sort of gardening. Our Kate and Mike, at Seven and Eight, invented the Candy Tree.

They took six pennies to the corner store, selected a crop of candies, ran home, balanced the candy in a camellia bush and called their little sister quickly.

The Candy Tree had bloomed.

The bush gained enormously in prestige and became the wonder of the block, watered by young gardeners when all other plants were ignored. Now the little sister has a little sister who occasionally gets bored and for whom, very occasionally, the Candy Tree blooms again.

Naturally it's never asked for, because no one knows how it happens, and it's never expected, because no one knows when it will happen, but there are always enough blooms to give each child an equal amount.

This is a simple diversion, costing little in time or money, and it will boggle a child's imagination nicely.

Epilogue

Each of us weeps—at least inside—when a child begins first grade, not because of the child we are losing, but because of the chances we've lost. So much is left undone.

Certainly it was that way for us. We hadn't the time or the sense of duty to use every recipe and suggestion in this book for each of our seven children and, besides, we were still learning what to do for the youngest when the oldest were practically grown.

When we disciplined one child with kindness and firmness, it was only because we had learned how at the expense of those who had gone before, and if we helped all to know the joys of play we did have some trouble when it came to teaching the rewards of work.

In the years between first and sixth grades, you may be surprised to find your child change gears so slowly you can't believe he's going through stages any more. His accomplishments are harder to notice; his moods, though not so merry, last much longer. A boy particularly seems to go through agony, for he needs to prove himself—to himself—day after day.

We think you'll find, as we did, that a child's ups and downs during his first six years are repeated during the next twelve, when his disposition falls apart and comes together, again and again. Still you'll want to give as much of yourself as you ever did before, keeping the channels open by talking and especially by listening, but now it's not so easy. This is his period of absorption, when his social and physical and mental development all must learn to mesh again.

You start to notice the change at Seven when you watch him twist his way through the first bout of puberty (now he knows for sure that the world is against him), and by Eight, you see him try harder every day to act like all the other Eights. This fledgling is alert to every sight and sound, but seldom makes a move that's different from the flock: the opinions of his friends are paramount. This has mixed effects. For the first time, your extraordinary child may be just a little bit boring. Where once he was full of bright sayings, now he only repeats those same silly riddles you knew as a child, and when he goes to a movie he has to tell you the whole plot, which takes almost as long as the movie itself. Even his teeth look too big for his face, and besides, he whistles a lot.

At Nine, he may limit himself to one super best friend, each reinforcing the other to be as much alike as possible until you almost think your child has lost his originality. By Ten he will surprise you one more time. Slowly all the ideas he's absorbed in the last few years begin to surface. Now he amazes you with his fresh insights, his new competence and even his wit, a rebirth that continues for the next two years. At the same time he rebels in a dozen small ways to break those molds he made. Feel blessed. Each stage is as right for him as all the ones that have gone before.

Between Thirteen and Sixteen your child will go through the same outrageous rule breaking as he did at Two and Four, and though it may wrench your heart, these should be good years too. If your teenager still can count on you for as much time and praise and affection and respect and trust as he's had at every age, he can grow up to be a strong, happy, self-confident adult—and a good friend for life. You can't ask for anything more.

Recommended Reading

Mother

Pregnancy

Fleming, Alice, *Nine Months*. New York: Harper and Row, 1972. $1.95. Gives a practical picture of pregnancy.

Ingelman-Sundberg, Axel, and Wirsen, Cloes, with pictures by Nilsson, *A Child Is Born*. New York: Dell, 1966. $4.95. No one has ever matched these photographs of fetal development.

Montagu, Ashley, and Matson, F. W., *Touching—the Human Significance of the Skin*. New York: Columbia University Press, 1971. $8.95. Makes a woman aware of the importance of touch and sensitizes her for it in motherhood.

Childbirth

Bean, Constance A., *Methods of Childbirth*. New York: Dolphin, 1974. $1.95. A straightforward book to help a mother decide which delivery is best for her.

Any one of the following will give a persuasive picture of natural childbirth:

Dick-Read, Grantly, M.D., *Childbirth Without Fear*. New York: Harper and Row, 1954. $1.25.

Karmel, Marjorie, *Painless Childbirth—Thank You, Dr. Lamaze*. New York: Dolphin, 1965. $1.45.

Lamaze, Fernand, *Painless Childbirth: The Lamaze Method*. New York: Pocket Books, 1972. $1.25.

Breast feeding

If you contemplate breastfeeding, either of these books will answer your questions:

Carson, Mary, *The Womanly Art of Breastfeeding*. Franklin Park, Ill.: La Leche League International, 1963. $3.95.

Pryor, Karen, *Nursing Your Baby*. New York: Pocket Books, 1973. $1.50.

Working Mother

Schwartz, Felice N., Schiffer, Margaret H., and Gillotti, Susan S., *How To Go to Work When Your Husband Is Against It, Your Children Aren't Old Enough, and There's Nothing You Can Do Anyhow*. New York: Simon and Schuster, 1972. $2.95. The title tells it all; a good book.

Day Care

Steinfels, Margaret O'Brien, *Who's Minding the Children?* New York: Simon and Schuster, 1973. $2.95. The story of day care in America, past and present.

Weaver, Kitty, *Lenin's Grandchildren*. New York: Simon and Schuster, 1971. $7.50. A good account of Russian day care, starting at four months.

Single Parent

Caine, Lynn, *Widow*. New York: William Morrow, 1974. $6.95. A book that should comfort others in this crisis.

Despert, J. Louise, *Children of Divorce*. New York: Dolphin Books, 1962. $1.95. This advice will help a child see that divorce is not the end of the world.

Klein, Carole, *The Single Parent Experience*. New York: Avon, 1973. $1.95. A helpful book.

Krantzler, Mel, *Creative Divorce*. New York: Signet, 1972. $1.95. A comprehensive book and a good one.

Child

Caplan, Frank, editor, *The First Twelve Months of Life*. New York: Grosset and Dunlap, 1973. $4.95. A charming book, with month-by-month photographs.

Fraiberg, Selma H., *The Magic Years*. New York: Lyceum Edition, Scribner's, 1968. $2.45. One of the best books you can find on the total child.

Gesell, Arnold, M.D., *The First Five Years of Life*. New York: Harper and Row, 1940. $8.95. Anything by Gesell is worth reading.

Ginott, Hiam G., *Between Parent and Child*. New York: Avon, 1969. $1.50. Basic techniques to encourage good behavior.

Homan, William E., *Child Sense*. New York: Bantam, 1970. $1.25. A pediatrician's rich, warm advice on rearing a child from infancy to teens; one of the best.

Hymes, James, *Teaching the Child Under Six*. Chicago: Merrill; second edition, 1974. $3.95. Straightforward and informative.

Ilg, Frances L., M.D., and Ames, Louise Bates, Ph.D., of the Gesell Institute, *Child Behavior from Birth to Ten*. New York: Harper and Row, 1955. $1.25. Classic book to help a mother keep her child in perspective.

Salk, Lee, and Kramer, Rita, *How to Raise a Human Being*. New York: Paperback Library, 1973. $1.25. A readable book to help you rear a stable child.

Art

Brittain, W. Lambert, and Lowenfeld, Viktor, *Creative and Mental Growth*. New York: Macmillan, fifth edition, $9.95. The definitive book that explains why every child needs art in his life.

Adoption

Rondell, Florence, *New Dimensions in Adoption*. New York: Crown Publishers, Inc., 1974. $5.95. Latest information on adoptions of interracial or foreign babies and young children.

Books

Arbuthnot, May H., and Sutherland, Zena, *Children and Books*. Glenview, Ill.: Scott, Foresman, fourth edition, 1972. $4.50. A full guide on the books you can offer your child with descriptions of them.

Baker, Augusta, *The Black Experience in Children's Books*. New York Public Library; revised edition, 1971. $.50. A fine bibliography available in most public libraries.

Cooking

Cadwallader, Sharon, *Cooking Adventures for Kids*. Boston: Houghton Mifflin Co., 1974. $4.95. Colorful line drawings and recipes that use natural foods.

Claiborne, Craig, *Kitchen Primer*. New York: Vintage, 1972. $1.95. Excellent book to learn the basics of cooking.

Parents' Nursery School, *Kids are Natural Cooks*. Boston: Houghton Mifflin Co., 1974. $3.95. Wide variety of good, simple recipes.

Coordination

Prudden, Bonnie, *How to Keep Your Child Fit From Birth to Six*. New York: Harper and Row, 1964. $7.95. Describes body development, exercises, play equipment and some psychology; excels in both text and photographs.

———, *Your Baby Can Swim*. New York: Reader's Digest Press, 1974. $6.95. A self-confident book that will make your child a self-confident swimmer.

Crafts

Carico, Nita Cox, and Guynn, Jane Calvert, *The Dried Flower Book*. New York: Doubleday & Co., 1962. $5.95. Everything a novice needs to know on this subject.

Croft, Doreen, and Hess, Robert, *Activities Handbook for Teachers of Young Children*. Boston: Houghton Mifflin Co., 1972. $6.25.

Klimo, Joan Fincher, *What Can I Do Today?* New York: Pantheon, 1971. $1.95. Brightly illustrated selection of imaginative crafts.

O'Neil, Sunny, *Pressing Flowers for Lasting Beauty*. Washington, D.C.: Smithsonian Institution. $1.25. Sixteen pages tells it all.

Dance

Findlay, Elsa, *Rhythm and Movement*. Evanston, Ill.: Summy-Birchard Co., 1971. $6.75. Uses principles of eurhythmics to help a child get the most out of music and dance.

Laban, Rudolf, *Modern Educational Dance*. Boston: Plays, Inc., 1974. $4.00. For those parents serious about dance, Laban is the Piaget of movement.

Death

Grollman, Earl A., *Explaining Death to Children*. Boston: Beacon Press, 1967. $4.95. Common-sense guidance to help a mother explain the harshest reality of all.

Drama

Lease, R., and Siks, G. B., *Creative Dramatics in Home, School and Community*. New York: Harper and Row, 1952. Good, basic book in the field; not in print, but available in most libraries.

Education

Ames, Louise Bates, Ph.D., and Chase, Joan Ames, Ph.D., *Don't Push Your Preschooler*. New York: Harper and Row, 1974. $6.95. Shows the dangers of expecting too much of a child.

Crandall, Joy, *Early to Learn*. New York: Dodd, Mead and Co., 1974. $5.95. A charming book with photographs that describe a good preschool.

Curtis, Jean, *A Parents' Guide to Nursery Schools*. New York: Random House, 1971. $6.95. This tells a mother how to choose a nursery school, as well as how to start one and maintain it.

Furth, Hans G., and Wachs, Harry, *Thinking Goes to School: Piaget's Theory in Practice*. New York: Oxford University Press, 1974. $8.95. Although designed for school children, there are many games here for younger children, all amusing and all designed to prevent or correct learning problems.

LeShan, Eda J., *Conspiracy Against Childhood*. New York: Atheneum, 1973. $3.95. An emotional warning against overemphasis on education.

Neill, A.S., *Summerhill*. New York: Hart, 1960. $3.95. A book that describes this radical, free-wheeling system of education, by its founder.

Orem, R. C., editor, *Montessori, Her Method and the Movement*. New York: G. P. Putnam's Sons, 1974. $7.95. Gives the Montessori philosophy, listing books and materials used.

Steiner, Rudolf F., *A Modern Art of Education*. London: Rudolf Steiner Press, 1972. $3.50. Explains the Waldorf brand of education.

Winn, Marie, and Porcher, Mary Ann, *The Playgroup Book*. New York: Macmillan, 1967. $4.95. The value of a playgroup and how it is organized.

First Aid

Hend, David, *Save Your Child's Life!* New York: Dolphin Books, 1974. $1.45. A concise little book every parent should own.

Gardening

Peters, Ruth Marie, *Bulb Magic in Your Window*. New York: William Morrow, 1975. $2.45. An inspiring book, even for the novice; with photographs.

Pettingill, Amos, *The White Flower Farm Garden Book*. New York: Knopf, 1971. $10. One of the most exquisite, informative garden books.

Rottenberg, Harvey, and Riker, Tom, *Gardener's Catalogue*. New York: William Morrow, 1974. $6.95. Huge paperback compendium of text and photographs.

Skelsey, Alice, and Huckaby, Gloria, *Growing Up Green*. New York: Workman Press. $4.95. A book that makes a child even more curious about nature and teaches a lot about gardening too.

Health

The Concise Home Medical Guide. New York: Grosset and Dunlap, 1972. $9.95. The kind of instructive book a family needs, especially in the country.

Pomeranz, Virginia E., M.D., and Schultz, Dodi, *The Mothers' and Fathers' Medical Encyclopedia*. Boston: Little Brown, 1975. Up-to-the-minute medical advice.

Spock, Benjamin, M.D., *Baby and Child Care*. New York: Pocket Books, 1968. $.95. A trusted guide for mothers and an excellent one if not relied upon more than the baby's own pediatrician.

Learning

Beadle, Muriel, *A Child's Mind*. New York: Anchor, 1971. $2.95. A comprehensible, readable account of the way a child's mind develops.

Copeland, Richard W., *How Children Learn Mathematics*. New York: Macmillan, 1970. $7.95. A book to show how Piaget methods are applied to math.

Isaacs, Susan, *The Nursery Years*. New York: Schocken Paperbacks, 1968. $2.45. A good account of the way children think.

Pulaski, Mary Ann Spencer, *Understanding Piaget*. New York: Harper and Row, 1971. $7.95. Piaget deciphers the way children learn; this book deciphers Piaget.

Music

Aronoff, Frances Webber, *Music and Young Children*. New York: Holt, Rinehart and Winston, 1969. $5.95. If a mother has some knowledge of music this may be of value.

Glazer, Tom, *Eye Winker, Tom Tinker, Chin Chopper*. New York: Doubleday & Co., 1973. $4.95. Fifty musical finger plays with a lot of charm.

Suzuki, Shinichi, *Nurtured by Love*. New York: Exposition Press, 1969. $6.00. An explanation of the world-wide Suzuki violin method for preschool children.

Nutrition

Castle, Sue, *The Complete Guide to Preparing Baby Foods at Home*. New York: Doubleday & Co., 1973. $5.95. The definitive book on the subject.

Jacobson, Michael F., *Eater's Digest*. New York: Anchor, 1972. $1.95. This book represents the encyclopedia of additives in processed food.

——, *Nutrition Scoreboard*. Washington, D.C.: Center for Science in the Public Interest, 1974. $1.75. This rates the value of most foods, and we think it should be in every kitchen.

Outings

Golden Nature Guides. New York: Golden Press. $1.50. A series of inexpensive, informative paperbacks to take on outings.

Peterson Field Guide Series. Boston: Houghton Mifflin Co. $3.95-$4.95. A comprehensive series for an older child with a developed interest in nature.

Rey, H. A., *Stars*. Boston: Houghton Mifflin Co., 1970. $7.95. A splendid book on the heavens.

Shuttlesworth, Dorothy, *Exploring Nature with Your Child*. New York: Hawthorn, 1952. Though out of print, this superlative book is in most libraries, and so full of information it will answer every question your child could have, from humpback whales to bashful snails.

Stix, Hugh, and Stix, Marguerite, *The Shell, 500 Million Years of Inspired Designs*. New York: Ballantine Books, 1972. $4.95. Exquisite photographs that will prompt any child to collect and identify shells.

Pets

Charles, Elizabeth, *How to Keep Your Pet Healthy*. New York: Collier Books, 1974. $1.50. A good, basic book on general pet care.

Play

Fox, Lorene K., Brogan, Peggy, Butler, Annie Louise, and Livingston, Maxine, *All Children Want to Learn*. New York: Grolier Society, Inc., 1965. This book is good for making some simple play equipment. Out of print; check your library.

Marzollo, Jean, and Lloyd, Janice, *Learning Through Play*. New York: Harper and Row, 1972. $7.50. Activities that give a child good times at home.

Sharp, Evelyn, *Thinking Is Child's Play*. New York: E. P. Dutton, 1969. $4.95. Shows that children understand concepts through play.

Sutton-Smith, Brian and Shirley, *How to Play with Your Children*. New York: Hawthorn, 1974. $7.95. General playing and games for a family.

Play Space

Aaron, David, and Winawar, Bonnie, *Child's Play; A Creative Approach to Playspace for Today's Children*. New York: Harper and Row, 1965. $4.95. A book to show the importance of play.

Problems

Clark, Louise, *Can't Read, Can't Write, Can't Talk Too Good Either*. New York: Penguin, 1974. $1.95. A mother's account of her child's dyslexia.

DeVries-Kryut, T. A., *A Special Gift: The Story of Jan*. New York: Peter H. Wyden, 1971. $4.95. How a mongoloid child enriched this family.

Ellingson, Careth, *The Shadow Children*. Chicago: Topaz Books, 1967. $6.50. A book about children's learning disorders.

Feingold, Ben F., M.D., *Why Your Child Is Hyperactive*. New York: Random House, 1975. $7.95. This author believes diet to be the cause of hyperactivity.

Nichtern, Sol, M.D., *Helping the Retarded Child*. New York: Grosset and Dunlap, 1974. $8.95. Shows parents new potentials.

Spock, Benjamin, M.D., Lerrigo, Marion O., Ph.D., *Caring for Your Disabled Child*. New York: Macmillan, 1965. $1.95. General book to help a parent care for a child with a long-term or short-term handicap.

Thomas, Linda, *Cooking and Caring for the Allergic Child*. New York: Drake Publishers, 1974. $7.95. Contains not only hyperallergenic recipes for food but for play dough too.

Wender, Paul H., M.D., *The Hyperactive Child, a Handbook for Parents*. New York: Crown Publishers, 1973. $3.95. Another approach to control hyperactivity.

Second Baby

Samson, Joan, *Watching the New Baby*. New York: Atheneum, 1974. $5.95. An excellent, factual book for parents to tell their firstborn about the new baby's growth from fetus to two years.

Travel

Hardwood, Michael, *Games to Play in the Car*. Des Moines, Iowa: Meredith Press, 1967. $2.95. The games will amuse your child; the book will amuse you.

Workshop

Grotz, George, *The Furniture Doctor*. New York: Doubleday & Co., 1962. $5.95. Gives solid advice to refinish furniture and gives a few laughs too.

Complete Do-It-Yourself Manual. Pleasantville, New York: Reader's Digest Association, 1973. $12.98. The most usable (and expensive) book we've seen in this field.

Acknowledgments

Professionals and friends, parents and children, all contributed to this book. Our warmest thanks to:

Audubon Naturalist Society
Helen Baldwin
Lillian Barrett
Jeanette and
    Robert Bernstein
Barbara Bolling
Sophy Burnham
Constance Burr
Mary Cassidy, Ph.D.
Doris Celarier
Susan Chalker
Shirley Cochrane
Margaret Coughlan,
    Library of Congress
Sheila Cowen, Ph.D.
Kay Crane
Clare Crawford
Sally Crowell
Julia Daniel
Edward F. Dillon. Ph.C.
Tom Donnelly
Patricia Driscoll
Asher Etkes
Eve Eggers
Minor Elson
Lydia Finkelstein
J. Morton Franklin
Amy Gardner
Sue Gartner
Mariana Gasteyer
Jean Getlein
Judy Gleason
Bette Glickert
Judith Goldinger
Bea Hackett
Ann Hanks
Sharon Hanley
Marifrances Hardison

Virginia Haviland,
    Library of Congress
Robin Hirsh
Ann Hochstein
Carl I. Hoffmann, Waldorf School
Jane Horton
Margaret and Susan Howard
Clara Davidson Huus
Faith Jackson,
    Academy of Washington Ballet
Timmie Jensen
Helmut Jaehnigen
Joan Keenan
Leonard Kirsten
Adelaide Krizek
Barbara Kubeck
Louise and Marion Lelong
Virginia Mahoney
Thomas Mann
Amelia Manning
Mary Markley
Rita and Kathy Markley
Gail McCarthy
Nancy McCrae
Judy McKnight
Rita Mendez
Beverly Mischer
Patricia Molumby
Roberta Mora
Betty Moskowitz
Barney Nehring
Dorothy Newman
Nutrition Department,
    Cornell University
Gloria Panton
Edith Parsons
Ida Prosky
Pat Rafuse

Susan Reid
Enid Requé
Judy Reynolds
Arlene Roback
Sallie Ann Robbins
Miris and Richard Sanchez
Mary Scheltema
Lisa Schlossberg
Kathryn Shollenberger
Helen Skinner
Mildred Skinner
Myra Sklarew
Janet Stratton
Martha and Stephen Swaim
Kathy Smith
Nancy Stewart
Robert Thurston
Cora Toliver
James True
Elizabeth Van Kluyve
Kenneth Watkins, Jr., D.V.M.
Kitty Weaver
Kathryn Williams
Lorna Williams
Miriam Wolf, M.D.
Elizabeth Young
Katharine Zadravec
Joanne Zich

Priscilla Burr
Sarah Burr
Eben Burr
Andy Hackett
Alan Keenan
Leah Swaim
Michael Swaim
Suzannah Swaim

Index

The earliest age your child may enjoy an activity, a skill or a toy is listed parenthetically in this index, but this shouldn't be considered either a goal or a limit. Just as a child can't do everything suggested for his age—for no one is equally adept in all areas—neither will he outgrow old pleasures.

For additional information on many of these subjects, see the list of Recommended Reading (page 270).

284